The Failure of
the Centralized State

The Failure of
the Centralized State

Institutions and
Self-Governance in Africa

EDITED BY

James S. Wunsch
and Dele Olowu

Westview Press
BOULDER, SAN FRANCISCO, & OXFORD

tview Special Studies on Africa

Westview softcover edition is printed on acid-free paper and bound in library-ity, coated covers that carry the highest rating of the National Association of State Textbook Administrators, in consultation with the Association of American Publishers and the Book Manufacturers' Institute.

Published in 1990 in the United States of America by Westview Press, Inc., 5500 Central Avenue, Boulder, Colorado 80301, and in the United Kingdom by Westview Press, Inc., 36 Lonsdale Road, Summertown, Oxford OX2 7EW

Library of Congress Cataloging-in-Publication Data
The Failure of the centralized state.
   (Westview special studies on Africa)
   Includes bibliographies and index.
   1. Africa—Politics and government—1945–1960.
2. Africa—Politics and government—1960–
3. Decentralization in government—Africa.   4. Africa—
Economic policy.   I. Wunsch, James S. (James
Stevenson), 1946–   .   II. Olowu, Dele.   III. Series.
JQ1875.A1F35   1990   960'.32   86-32516
ISBN 0-8133-7378-6

Printed and bound in the United States of America

⊗   The paper used in this publication meets the requirements
      of the American National Standard for Permanence of Paper
      for Printed Library Materials Z39.48-1984.

'0   9   8   7   6   5   4   3   2   1

Contents

Preface

This book grew out of the intellectual exchanges in which we participated at the Workshop in Political Theory and Policy Analysis at Indiana University, Bloomington, Indiana, during the 1985/86 academic year. That workshop was (and is still) led jointly by Vincent and Elinor Ostrom and included approximately a dozen other scholars from several disciplines from Western Europe, Asia, Latin America, Eastern Europe (Poland and Yugoslavia), and the United States. In this multi-national and multi-disciplinary environment, we were led to reexamine and reintegrate our previous research and teaching on African politics and public administration. Repeatedly we sought to make sense of the crisis we see currently in Africa. The idea for this book developed in this context and was guided and molded by the analytical frameworks used at the workshop. Particularly important to us has been a principle, we daresay, implicit in all the workshop has done: human beings can govern themselves in peace and dignity, though the pathway to such a world is one requiring care, thought, willingness to trust the people with their own governance, and increased attention to the origin, role, and nature of human institutions.

Colleagues at the workshop contributed immensely to the development of our work. As well as helping to frame our agenda of issues, their criticism helped in its development. While everyone there deserves our appreciation, we are particularly grateful to Roger Parks of the School of Public and Environmental Affairs (SPEA) at Indiana University, Peter Bogason of the Institute of Political Studies in Denmark, Susan Wynne of the workshop at Indiana, and, of course, Vincent and Elinor Ostrom. We are also indebted to others who have helped us with their support and criticisms, including particularly Thomas Mans of Creighton University, Donald Rothchild of the University of California, Davis, and Catherine Newbury at the University of North Carolina. Patrick O'Meara, the director of the African Studies Program at Indiana University, read the first drafts of several chapters of the book and gave very helpful comments. Our contributors to this volume also deserve our deep gratitude: for their excellent chapters, of course, but just as much for their excellent criticism of our chapters. The latter added much of value to the book. John Harbeson of CUNY and Sheldon Gellar of Michigan State University are to be much thanked for their persistent, ever courteous, ever valuable, almost "co-editorial" efforts.

Westview Press encouraged the completion of the book through their editorial personnel's patience and careful attention to technical details. We particularly thank our editor, Barbara Ellington. Our two universities, Creighton University, Omaha, Nebraska, and the Obafemi Awolowo University, Nigeria, assisted the work by releasing us for the academic year of 1985/86 to enable us to spend our sabbatical leave developing the project. In this respect we are grateful to our respective deans (William Cunningham and A. O. Sanda) and presidents (Michael Morrison, S.J., and W. Abimbola) for making this arrangement possible. Dean Michael Lawler of Creighton University's Graduate School, furthermore, helped with several grants which supported the completion of the manuscript.

The typing, corrections, and final reproduction of the manuscript were made possible by the tremendous secretarial assistance we received from the Workshop in Political Theory in Bloomington, as well as from our respective departments at Obafemi Awolowo and Creighton. We especially appreciate the time and talent of Kristin Crose and Patty Zielinski of the Workshop in Political Theory. Sincere thanks also go to Helen Schaefer of the Political Science Department at Creighton for her careful secretarial assistance, as well as to her numerous student assistants. We are also indebted to Kent Day of Omaha for his help in proofreading the manuscript.

Our wives, Mary and Bukky, had to suffer our sometimes lengthy absences from home while we were working on the book. We both feel lucky to be married to such patient women who gave their support to the enterprise from beginning to end.

The work is dedicated to Vincent and Elinor Ostrom. The theory which informs the work is based largely on their work. They have read, re-read, and helped strengthen several chapters of the book. Both of us and several of the contributors to this volume have at one time or another benefited from the strength of their scholarship and the warmth of their friendship. While acknowledging their assistance and that of others not mentioned here, we hasten to add that we are solely responsible for the ideas expressed in the book. Whatever its shortcomings, they are ours.

James S. Wunsch
Dele Olowu

1

The Failure of the
Centralized African State

James S. Wunsch and Dele Olowu

Introduction

Nearly thirty years ago in Accra, Ghana, Africa's march to independence began. With substantial cash reserves, a strong domestic agricultural economy, a skilled and professionalized civil service, a popular leader, and an apparently well-functioning, competitive-party, parliamentary system, hope for the future was bright.

Today, these hopes have faded. The economy is at present only beginning a recovery from collapse and near bankruptcy. Its GNP declined at an average of 1.3 percent *each year* from 1960 to 1982, and its average inflation rate was 34.8 percent annually over the same period (World Bank 1984b). Five military coups have buffeted Ghanaians' political hopes, which had twice risen since the first coup in 1966 on the backs of two now-discarded constitutions. The civil service has been demoralized by political instability and military intervention, and the economy has been devastated by incredible inflation rates. Many of the best trained and skilled personnel have left the country. One wonders, why?

Ghana is not alone. Of Africa's 54 independent states, *only 18* have avoided successful military coups. Of these 18, at least 6 have experienced serious coup attempts, military revolts, or sustained civil conflicts. Coups by generals have given way to coups by colonels, captains, flight lieutenants and, finally, sergeants and corporals. A weary sameness sets in: each regime denounces the previous one and promises an early return to civilian government after it "cleans up" and "reforms" the government. Too often the military regime has indeed "cleaned up," but not in the way it promised. Samuel Decalo, in his book on the military, shows quite graphically how the struggle for power within regimes intensifies once constitutional rules are discarded, and how factionalism, mutual distrust, fear, and countercoup are the most usual consequences (Decalo 1976). Uganda, Congo-Brazaville, and Benin, as well as Ghana, seem exemplary cases of this process. In too many cases, military regimes have turned their guns, or at least their rifle butts, on their own people, stifling dissent and repressing the opposition. In Liberia, Ethiopia, Central African Republic, Uganda, Sudan, and others this has happened. Bloody civil wars have been fought in seven countries (Nigeria, Sudan, Chad, Ethiopia, Angola, Zaire, Uganda), ethnic programs have torn through several (Nigeria, Uganda, Rwanda, Burundi), and corruption is so deep in Zaire that there are, according to David Gould, over eighty different nouns to describe its various distinguishable manifestations (Gould 1977).

Economically, Africa has fared no better. While *all* developing countries grew at a 3.5 percent rate (GNP) from 1960 to 1970 and at a 2.7 percent rate from 1970 to 1979, Africa's record was only 1.3 percent and 0.8 percent over those same time periods. Food sufficiency has generally declined since independence, rural per capita income has on average declined, and few sheltered, infant industries have grown up. In fact, 10 sub-Saharan African countries had average negative growth (GNP) from 1960–1982, 10 were stagnant or near stagnant (0.1 to 1.5 percent), and excluding South African client states and oil exporters, only 8 had rates of growth of more than 1.5 percent during that time period (World Bank 1984b). More disconcerting because it suggests future stagnant growth, is the continuity of pricing and currency exchange systems biased against agriculture which continues to employ the vast majority of Africa's peoples and produces between 30–60 percent of African GNP. Partially as a result of this, an index of per capita food production shows only four sub-Saharan African countries were producing more food per capita in 1982 than they were in 1969 (Rwanda, Central African Republic, Cameroon, Ivory Coast). Fifteen were producing 80–89 percent of their 1969 per capita, three at 70–79 percent, and two at 60–69 percent (Angola, Mauritania, Ghana; Somalia and Mozambique)! As a whole, from 1960–1970, African agriculture increased its per capita production by only .2 percent. From 1970–1980 it declined by an average of 1.1 percent *per year* (World Bank 1984a; 1984b).[1]

These figures are indeed grim, and justify considering much of Africa to be at a point of crisis. Still, some states have fared better.[2] These, however, are most often states with substantial petroleum reserves or states which have had to sacrifice a substantial amount of autonomy to what are commonly regarded as neo-colonial or "dependency" relationships with developed states, and are based on a single, key leader or "strong man." Furthermore, when one looks behind their impressive GNP rates, one finds broader social indicators such as literacy, life-expectancy, caloric intake, and food production are not distinctly better in these countries than in the others (World Bank 1984b). Finally, recent events have suggested that the apparent political stability of these countries may be ephemeral, with coups or violent coup attempts occurring in several of them (Nigeria, Kenya, Cameroon). It has become an accepted hypothesis in contemporary social science that the processes of economic development and social change carry with them forces promoting political instability. However, the performance of many other third world nations and the theory we will discuss below lead us to argue that critical flaws in the fundamental political structures of African states have made this instability far worse and have made economic development far slower than ought to have been expected.

Many factors have contributed to Africa's problems. We have no doubt, for example, that changes in the international economic system would dramatically improve the African situation, particularly changes in pricing structures for agricultural and mineral products (Independent Commission 1980). South African adventurism has severely damaged several African states. Furthermore, the scale of recent natural disasters such as drought and famine will continue to require international assistance. These international and natural problems have contributed to Africa's current problems. Certainly the literature on dependency provides an important, even if controversial, body of theory regarding the international roots of Africa's problems. But these external sources of Africa's crisis can be exaggerated, and may preclude an objective appraisal and analysis of the domestic aspects of the African predicament: what Africans *do* have control over and *can* do something to improve. A preoccupation with external/environmental problems sidesteps something long understood in human affairs: social development has always been premised on a people's ability to effectively manipulate their environment to advantage over a period of time in spite of odds imposed by that environment (Mabogunje 1980; Riggs 1976).

Many would agree with the position of the Independent Commission on International Development headed by Willy Brandt which, even though quite sympathetic to the environmental constraints on countries of the South, submitted that:

> The government and people of the South (Africa, Asia and Latin America) have the *primary* responsibility for many of their own problems; they will have to continue to generate most of their resources by their own efforts, and to plan and manage their own economies. Only they can ensure that the fruits of development are fairly distributed inside their countries and that greater justice and equity in the world are matched by appropriate reforms at home (Independent Commission 1980: 41–42, parenthesis and emphasis added).

Our argument in this book derives from a body of theory implicit in the burgeoning research on domestic African institutions, that suggests there is a vast reservoir of energy and potential untapped at Africa's grass roots. This literature is complemented by other research on national politics that underscores the critical role played by domestic political processes and policies in ethnic conflict, political instability, and economic performance. We will argue in this book that ethnic conflict, political inefficacy, administrative weaknesses, and economic stagnation can be understood in part as caused by attempts over the last two decades to impose a high level of centralization in contemporary African states, and that these explanations argue forcefully for changes in political structure and development strategy.

Centralization in Africa

Measures of centralization pose conceptual and statistical problems given problems already identified in delineating between state and society (Nisbet 1962; 1975), private and public sectors (Hood 1986), and in measuring the public sector or its growth (Ozgediz 1983; Grunow 1986; Grestchmann 1986). The problem is compounded in Africa where reliable cross-national data are hard to find. Nevertheless, the contemporary African state can be characterized as centralized through a variety of measures. The proportion of public revenues expended by national as opposed to local governments, the taxes raised by national vs. local governments, the proportion of GNP expended by government, the juridical weakness of sub-national governments, and the absence of competitive political parties or contested elections are all conventional indicators.

It is easier to demonstrate that the African state is centralized in qualitative rather than in quantitative terms. Some African central governments spend a high percentage of their country's gross national product (Mali 69%, Botswana 45%, Congo 44%), but the average is just under 30%. While this might be high for the level of industrialization and urbanization in these countries, it is relatively comparable to those of several other developing and industrialized countries: Panama 40%, Nicaragua 49%, Mexico 28%, Netherlands 59%, Ireland 58% and Sweden 47%. Still, it is worth noting that while the number of public sector employees in less developed countries is not dramatically higher per capita than in OECD countries, their cost is a far higher proportion of non-agricultural employment (OECD = 24%; LDC = 44%). Thus, governmental function seems to include a rather high portion of the modern sector of the economy (Heller and Tait 1982: 47).

The critical difference between African states and most others across the world, however, lies in the qualitative dimension, specifically in the distribution of authority, responsibility and resources available to central vs. local governments. In virtually no African countries have local governments any independent juridical authority. Even in states where local governments are largely arms of national governments, the percentage of total budgetary resources allocated by them is far greater than in Africa. For example, from France at the lower ranges (17%) to Sweden at the higher (66%), local level institutions are major partners in the delivery of public services. Equivalent African figures are as low as 2%.

The percentage distribution of personnel at the local levels also reflects this pattern. African countries as a whole have the least of their modern sector employees at the local level (2.1%). This figure is low compared with Asia (8.0%), Latin America (4.2%) and the Organization for Economic Cooperation and Development (OECD) states (12%) (Heller and Tait 1982).

Generally in Africa there has been a shift of power from the provinces to the capital. In virtually every African country, local self-governing institutions have been supplemented with or replaced by field administrative agencies (Mawhood 1983; Hyden 1983; Smith 1985). Even within the central government there is a disproportionate share of manpower and financial resources (in quantitative and qualitative terms) located at the headquarters compared with field agencies. The most senior trained and experienced officials live and work at the headquarters. The result is that inexperienced and junior officers located in the more populated countryside have to wait for instructions even on routine matters (Moris 1981), and focus most of their attention on what they must do to gain a posting at the center (Rondinelli 1979).

This pattern, finally, can also be seen in the area of non-governmental and private organizations such as unions, churches, cooperatives, universities, benevolent associations and the like, which have almost everywhere come under close governmental control. In a few cases they have been eradicated. Private bases for collective action have been carefully destroyed. Within the political realm, competing political parties have been legislated out of existence (with the exception of a few countries notably, Gambia, Botswana, Mauritania and Nigeria) while voluntary associations, labor unions, etc., are kept under close surveillance nearly everywhere (Zolberg 1966; Young 1982; Liebenow 1986). Powers have been stripped from the judiciary and the legislature in almost all African countries in favor of concentrating these powers in an executive presidency (Selassie 1974; Tordoff 1984; Jackson and Rosberg 1982). Some commentators refer to this situation as one of personal rule (Hyden 1983; Sandbrook 1985), and such presidents are often leaders of a single-party or of a military regime: in neither situation is opposition institutionalized or tolerated.

It is important, furthermore, to underscore a point made by other scholars: the centralization of the formal institutions of government has been futile as well as destructive. It has been destructive because it has preempted negotiation with and real cooperation by elements of the society whose willing commitment and efforts were needed for development. It has been futile in that the African states did not have enough power to compel key elements of the society to act as the state demanded (Riggs 1964; Hyden 1980; 1983; Bunker 1987; Mawhood and Davey 1980). The result has been characterized as the "disengaged" or "soft" state (Hyden 1983; Rothchild 1985). In trying to do and be too much, it ended up too little.

In general, what might be called "civic capacity" has been reduced, and "constitutional concentration" has been increased. The first refers to the legal capacity of the populace to engage in diverse collective action; and the second refers to the tendency to concentrate constitutional power in the hands of one or very few persons. We will argue in this book that these two tendencies have slowed economic growth and weakened the political capacity of Africa's peoples.

As we shall argue and develop throughout this volume, this multi-faceted centralization process requires an equally multi-faceted process of decentralization. It would include such changes as:

(1) devolution of real·responsibility and authority to choose and provide social services and development projects to local governments (see Chapters 4, 6, 8 and 9);

(2) substantial shrinkage of the role of the central state in the economy, including size of national budget, regulation of the small-scale economic sector, reducing the cost of the civil service, and reducing the entrepreneurial, managerial and production role of the state (see Chapters 5, 7 and 9);

(3) opening up politics to much greater public participation, though not necessarily trying to emulate Westminster or American forms of competitive political parties (see Chapters 3 and 8);

(4) legalizing and protecting extra-state voluntary groups organized for social, communal, community, occupational, professional, religious, labor, etc., purposes, and encouraging their activity in social, economic and political affairs (see Chapters 6, 7, 9 and 11); and

(5) constricting the role and power of public office holders to those tasks necessary to manage the state, rather than offering them the ability to redefine the rules of the state to facilitate their interests (see Chapters 7, 9, 10, and 12).

Centralization, Political Decay and Development

Centralization and Development

A centralized approach to political order was advocated strongly by social scientists when the new states emerged from the breakdown of colonial empires after the Second World War (for a review see Esman 1963; Apter 1965; Huntington 1968).[3] Today, however, virtually no contemporary scholars argue that the "centralized" strategy for overall development has performed well in post-independence Africa. Scholars have noted instead such patterns as the frequency of severe errors in development policy (Hyden 1980); the emergence of autocratic and corrupt governments (Ekpo 1979; Austin 1984; Jackson and Rosberg 1982); the exploitation of the rural masses by minuscule urban elites (Bates 1981; Lofchie 1985); and the wastage of vast amounts of resources on poorly planned development projects (Moris 1981; Rondinelli 1979; Wunsch 1986). Other dysfunctions include the difficulty of administering effectively from the center when problems are poorly understood, resources are short, and management systems are inappropriate (Moris 1976; 1981; Leonard 1986; Leonard and Oyugi 1985; Wunsch 1986); the effective withdrawal in self-defense of the rural masses from the market economy (Hyden 1980; 1983); the erosive effects such policies have had on the entire economy (World Bank 1981);

and the use in a few cases of brutal tyrannies to hold power (Jackson and Rosberg 1982; Austin 1984; Decalo 1985). Indeed, much of this was foretold some twenty years ago by Rene Dumont (Dumont 1966).

The torment of many Africans and their frustration with their highly centralized governments is made poignantly and powerfully clear in their contemporary literature, particularly by such authors as Achebe and Soyinka (Achebe 1966; Soyinka 1965; 1967). A number of African social scientists have also called our attention to the relationship between centralization and regional and ethnic inequalities (Mabogunje 1972; Filani 1981), and abuse of office by public officials (Ekpo 1979; Olowu 1988). Scholars have also explored the implications for political and administrative management. (Kasfir 1976; Adamolekun 1986). The questions we must ask are why has the centrist state strategy failed so dismally? What may now be done about it?

Social Organization and Development

To begin with, let us posit at the start that no single factor or "variable" explains Africa's recent disappointments. As noted above, international economic patterns, climate and weather patterns and changes, the diverse legacies of colonialism, economic distortions and disturbances generated by events in the West and the Middle-East, South African interference, the massive scale of development needed by Africa, all are important contributors to Africa's contemporary political and economic problems. While these are no doubt real problems, the focus of this book is on another problem which, we believe, has worked with these to impede Africa's ability to surmount them: the overcentralized state. The purpose of this book is to describe the origin of that state, review its effects, discuss and analyze efforts made to remedy it, and to begin discussion of alternative strategies which we believe might enhance developmental prospects. In large measure, our argument will be that the unleashing and encouragement of African peoples' "self-organizing" capabilities through what we call "self-governance" is a critical pre-requisite for human development to occur. We will argue that the excessive centralization of institutions of government in Africa since independence has seriously impeded Africans' ability to do this and to engage in the art of self-governance. For our message to be understood, however, we must first pause and discuss what we understand "development" to be.

There are few concepts in the social sciences of which there has been more writing and debate than the concept of "development." Various authors stress its economic, social, and political dimensions to varying degrees, and many paths to it are posited. Cutting across them, however, and subsuming most of the values they posit (economic abundance, social freedom, political capacity) is one human reality: development requires the production of complex economic, social and political goods, ones requiring complex and coordinated behavior by diverse peoples across large areas of time and space. Economists stress its economic aspects (specialization of labor; massive capital investments; international trade; discovery and utilization of new technologies; coordinated production systems; protection of the natural environment; and human conceptual artifacts such as the corporation, the state and law). On the other hand, sociologists have tended to stress its social aspect (developing norms of trust and stable expectations which make possible cooperative behavior beyond face-to-face groups; foregoing immediate advantages for longer-term gains; pursuing social goods and abstractions such as justice, equity and equality); while political scientists have emphasized its political aspect (using the authoritative sanctions of the state in ways which provide both individual freedom of choice and protect complex interdependencies among people as disparate as the entire globe; facilitating generalized collective choice in circumstances of uncertainty, disagreement and incomplete understanding; maintaining cohesion through choice rather than threat; providing public goods; protecting common resources). Common to all these perspectives, however, is the view that development means people must be able to relate with confidence to many more people and in many more roles than are required by smaller, simpler, and less ambitious economies, societies and polities. Once this concept of development is understood, then our stress on humans' "self-organizing" capabilities, and on rules and institutions can be more easily understood.

The relationships among our ideas of "development," "self-organization" and "institutions" grow from several assumptions. We begin by assuming the complex relationships characterizing development are always changing, and develop only over time, in diverse places, and eventually involve nearly all members of society in complex, multiple and changing roles. We also assume that a powerful element of uncertainty is always involved in planning, anticipating, and attempting to deal with the social, political and economic opportunities, discontinuities, disruptions and dangers these processes offer. This is due, at least in part, to the unpredictable and recursive nature of these changes; the diverse political, social, economic, and physical micro-climates in which people live; the varying norms and mutual expectations characteristic of human relations; and our inevitably limited knowledge and understanding of causality in human affairs.

As a result of these problems, there is a premium to be placed on a people's capacity to engage in flexible, innovative, adaptable, experimental, risktaking, entrepreneurial and learning behavior (Barkun et al. 1979). This behavior, to sustain development, must continuously confront emerging problems with creative solutions, have the capacity to weed out error, rebound with new experiments, and learn.

Recent theorizing and writing on hierarchical, monopolistic, bureaucratic mechanisms such as the centralized state suggests this is the very challenge they are weakest at resolving (Landau 1969; 1973; 1979; 1985; Landau et al. 1980). Martin Landau recently characterized hierarchical bureaucracies as ". . . extremely susceptible to displacement of goals . . . not experimental . . . [and entities which] do not learn easily or quickly." He saw them as possessing typically "a severely limited response repertoire" and with "fairly weak coordinating capacities" (Landau 1985: 5–6). Instead of hierarchy, Landau recommends what he calls "loosely coupled" organizations for situations when answers are incomplete, the environment is rapidly changing, and problems are continuously emerging (Landau et al. 1980; Landau 1985). Here, persons and organizations are horizontally linked with one another, possessing the authority and incentive to organize and reorganize in order to respond to and attempt to resolve rapidly emerging and changing problems. Such arrangements, Landau has concluded from research as diverse as Philippine provincial development and San Francisco transit, are powerful problem-solving and learning modes of human organization (Landau et al. 1980; Landau 1985). They are, "pragmatic, goal-searching and problem-oriented; and they detect and correct error more easily then does hierarchy. Their most striking property, however, is that they are self-organizing and self-regulating, the stimulus for which are not the *a proiri* demands of planners, but the information generated by experience" (Landau 1985: 10–11). Similar lines of reasoning have also been developed by Vincent Ostrom (1988) and Michael Crozier (1964).

For such "loosely coupled" organizations to develop and fulfill their role, broad, widely shared and confident "self-organizing" capabilities must exist among a people: the people must at least be able to conceptualize themselves as active, problem-solving, risktaking "entrepreneurs"; be capable of working with others; and believe the state (and other powerful entities such as corporations) will allow them to pursue these activities.

While our understanding of all that is necessary for these conditions to be met is incomplete, we hypothesize in this work that two prerequisites are essential: space and structure.

When we offer "space" as a prerequisite we mean primarily political, social and economic room for such self-organization to occur. At its extremes, the overcentralized state denies this, arrogating all authority to act to itself, preempting the social learning that midwives new norms which help resolve new problems, and soaking up the economic surplus of the periphery to fund the center. Social organization outside the center is often perceived as a threat to the regime, and its dual monopoly of political authority and economic power is used to co-opt, preempt or, at times, to destroy such organizations (Bates 1981). Little space and few resources are left for those outside the state to use in their organization and learning. And even though these cases of extreme overcentralization make up only a minority of states, relative levels of overcentralization still lead to relative levels of social enfeeblement.

When we offer "structure" as a prerequisite, we are noting the importance of rules and institutions to ensure that productive rather than predatory or exploitative relationships occur in the self-organization process; to serve as comprehensible symbolic representation of the social and normative learning loosely coupled organizations generate; to generalize this learning as a common social property; to offer routines to accept and promulgate this learning in comprehensible and legitimate ways; and, to retain it for future generations. To summarize, institutions and rules are important because they are needed to protect and facilitate "self-organization" among humans, and because they are one of the ways in which the knowledge these processes generate is generalized for society as a whole. Political institutions which operate in this way we refer to as regimes of "self-governance." Because of the important role that rules and "institutions" play in our theorizing, we will now discuss them in some detail.

Rules, Institutions and Development

Rules are the "nuts and bolts" which organize the complex behaviors involved in self-organization and development. They are the human-created mechanisms which guide, facilitate and strengthen humans' ability to work together: rules are the midwives of organization. Rules establish understandings with which men and women organize their relationships to deal with the perplexities and limits of the human condition: to cope with fear, vulnerability, human uncertainty and error; to satisfy the need for trust and restraint to produce costly human, social, and political capital; to efficiently allocate limited resources; to make, legitimize and promulgate collective choices; to retain the experience of past and present, and to pass experience on to new generations; to train and induct new role occupants, and so on. Because societies, economies and polities are extraordinarily complex, producing many different goods at different places and under varying and changing circumstances, rules which encourage and facilitate a broad repertoire of organizational forms are essential if development is to be sustained.

In the absence of the ability to formulate rules (because of social, economic or political disabilities), or in the presence of rules which encourage the predation and exploitation of some by others, development stagnation and even decline must be expected. Without the ability to make collective choices (i.e., formulate rules), public goods cannot be provided and common pool resources will face accelerating pressures (V. Ostrom and E. Ostrom 1977; Hardin 1968). When predation and exploitation are encouraged by the working rules, broadly based cooperation and exchange are replaced by withdrawal from economic, political and social relationships. While the "war of all against all" of Hobbes may not be frequently seen, peasant-producer withdrawal from the market economy, flight of local capital, disinvestment in local enterprises, withdrawal of savings from credit markets, and generalized rent-seeking behavior rather than productive investment, are all too frequent (Hyden 1980; 1983; Bates 1981; Brett 1986; Lofchie 1985; E. Ostrom 1985). We believe these experiences clearly demonstrate an important point: sustained development cannot grow from rules which encourage coercion; there are too many ways a people can resist such force. Development is a creative process which, in the long run, can occur only insofar as the people in general choose to sustain it.

The nature of a people's rules then, powerfully affects the behaviors which occur among them, the ways they organize, and their ability to undertake complex social endeavors requiring teamwork, co-operation, trust, forbearance, restraint and the like. The underlying hypotheses of this book are: (1) a paucity of authority to make and implement rules at the sub-national level in both the public and private spheres (i.e., limits on contract, property, market relations) will impede the broad, varied, and adaptable public organization needed for development; and, (2) rules which centralize vast authority in the hands of a very few will facilitate exploitation of others that leads directly to social and economic conflict, fragmentation, and then to developmental decline. Put positively, this book grows from our belief that if societies are to become larger, more diverse, and more complex (with ever more specialized and interdependent roles), the rules which organize political relations must work to sustain broad self-organization, to facilitate complex relations, and to protect persons within the social interdependencies and vulnerabilities which develop. Centralization of nearly all legal authority and effective power in the hands of a few works against this.

In a very real sense this is an issue which reaches all the way from the most local of concerns to such global problems as the arms race, the ecology, and the world economy. At all levels, human beings require institutions which allow them to make choices which deal with their interdependencies. Similarly at all levels, concentration of power in the hands of a few opens the door to self-centered and protectionistic behavior by that few. Because it is the fundamental prerequisite to enhancing human beings' capacity to act, we see rules which facilitate "self-governance" as close to the very essence of "development."

Centralization and Underdevelopment in Africa

The policy of centralization has established institutions which have worked in three specific ways to hinder, stifle, or even at times to erode broadly based human development in Africa.

First, and perhaps most familiar to political analysts, it facilitates exploitation and abuse of the powerless by the powerful. When political power is concentrated in the hands of some and effectively removed from the hands of others, it requires only the mildest assumptions of human fallibility, self-interest, or indeed, paternalism-*cum*-limited knowledge, to expect some to pursue policies at odds with the interests of others. That such situations lead to political conflict, economic disruption, and social deterioration is common knowledge and hardly requires any further discussion at this point. Their examples, though of varying severity, in Africa are many (Bates 1981; Lofchie 1985; Jackson and Rosberg 1982); the problem is elaborated in detail in Chapter 3 of this volume, and discussed throughout the book.

Centralization's *second* erosive effect on a broadly based development process has grown from human (and organizational) cognitive limitations:

it stimulates our propensity to error. In the last 50 years, our understanding of human organizational abilities has moved from the (earlier) overly optimistic views of bureaucracy as an ideal type developed by Weber to an understanding of the many limitations and flaws of hierarchy. Rational-legal bureaucracy, no doubt a vast improvement over charismatic or pa-trimonial orders, has been seen to be highly vulnerable to problems of span-of-control, goal displacement, personal ambition, incomplete control by political leaders, pressures and ambiguities at the delivery level, the difficulty of establishing co-production systems, and what some economists refer to as "moral hazard" and "opportunism" (Williamson 1967; Tullock 1965).

When these well known and documented problems of managing bu-reaucracies are combined with the severe shortage of information in African rural areas, the dearth of skilled personnel and other resources, and the theoretical and technical ambiguity and counter-intuitive effects of current development models, then the reliance on hierarchical, centrally controlled structures for the development task becomes a major obstacle to overall resource development. Such structures, regardless of the training, dedica-tion, and effort of government officials (often quite remarkable in the face of severe constraints), have simply not operated as the adaptable, learning-oriented, far-reaching, and creative institutions that contemporary research on rural development agrees are necessary for there to be any hope of success. There is much evidence of these problems in contemporary Africa (Moris 1981; Rondinelli 1979; 1983; Hyden 1980; 1983; Wunsch 1986). As Crozier suggested, "A bureaucratic organization is an organization that cannot correct its behavior by learning from its errors" (Crozier 1964: 187). Indeed, several scholars have recently noted that the uncertainty and complexity of social reality in developing countries make the Weberian bureaucratic model counter-productive as the major institution for man-aging the development process (Wunsch 1983; 1986; Rondinelli 1983; Hy-den 1983). Bureaucracy thus becomes a part of the problem rather than the solution!

This brings us to the *third* negative impact of centralization: it has attempted to preempt and at times erode the local social "tools" or "technologies" of human action; it has thus weakened the diverse small-scale organizations needed for development. As centralization progressed in the post-independence era, many African states moved to restrict the ability of non-central-state actors to authoritatively allocate values, to en-gage in extra-state social organizations, and to engage in private economic pursuits (Bates 1981; Mawhood 1983; Hyden 1980; 1983). While the severity of the restriction obviously varied, in extreme cases all political roles, virtually all economic roles beyond the most simple enterprises, and most social organizations were preempted or co-opted by the state. Labor unions, cooperative organizations, private enterprises, the market, local govern-ments, traditional political authorities, education, voluntary organizations, even religious organizations were banned, preempted or controlled. Their roles as rule-governed organizations to structure complex human relationships, to sustain "self-organization" were restricted. Their capacity to serve as arenas and structures through which new rules might be developed and new forms of organization might be spawned was similarly hindered. The vital roles played by them in diverse levels of African life (particularly as played in the late de-colonizing and early independence eras) were constrained. This occurred as centralizing authorities eroded their fiscal base (Bates 1981), preempted their juridical authority (Kasfir 1976), and attacked their social and economic autonomy as a fundamental threat to the effectiveness of the state (Leibenow 1986; Hyden 1980; 1983). And, as we have suggested above, the capacity of the centralized state organizations to abstain from abuse of power and to avoid error in their absence is problematic, in Africa as elsewhere. (These processes are discussed in more detail in Chapter 3.)

Stubborn and resilient as most Africans have been, these organizations have survived, but often in a defensive posture which limited their opportunity to contribute to development (see Chapters 5, 6 and 11, this volume). Ironically, as Chapter 12 discusses, the key structuring, supporting and integrating roles which the center could and should have pursued to support these diverse organizations, to take account of their interdependencies, to help them grow beyond exploitative or destructive internal and external patterns of relationships by clarifying and strengthening institutions which sustained self-organization, have rarely been fulfilled. As we shall argue below, it is important that the center fulfill certain key roles; the obliteration of the center is explicitly *not* the argument of this volume. Rather, developing for it a role which allows for and encourages the mobilization of human resources into the complexity of development is what we seek.

Rural Development and Africa

If the logic behind the rural development revolution is sound, and we believe for Africa in particular it is, then development requires a broadly based and far-reaching expansion of people's capacity to live, work and cooperate with one another *throughout* the nation (Owens and Shaw 1972). A developed society, in this paradigm, is one where the agricultural populace, to begin with, has the human skills, resources, and incentives to work together to build better lives. However, because human cooperation at any level is a complex process, requiring restraint by some, teamwork by many, and the creation of opportunities for even more people, it is unlikely to occur without a supportive social infrastructure: without institutions which sustain many and diverse organizations.

The economic erosion which one finds in much of rural Africa can be related to the erosion of these diverse organizations (Moris 1981; Smock 1971; Hyden 1980; 1983). Indeed, studies highlighting successful African development, interestingly enough, have usually pointed away from the centralized state and the organizations it has spawned. Instead, key roles have been played by organizations it has generally attempted to weaken or destroy (Jackson and Rosberg 1982): by community and mutual improvement unions; age-grade associations; co-operatives; labor unions; rural, market, social welfare, and trading voluntary associations; local governments; traditional political institutions; religious associations, and others (Little 1966; Smock 1971; Wunsch 1974; Owusu 1970; Cohen 1969; Barkun and Holmquist 1979; Keller 1974; Berry 1985; Bunker 1987; Olowu 1987). Current research has shown in contemporary Africa how these are key arenas where humans have organized to produce complex goods through complex, coordinated behavior, at times transcending historical social units. In and through these organizations new relationships have developed, and many key social, political, and physical needs have been met. There, people have also learned the need to "give and take" in order to sustain all these crucial functions.

Nowhere is the hostility of the centralized state to non-statist institutions been more evident than to extended kin groupings, or ethnicity. Yet, when the intense zero-sum competition engendered by the centralized state is removed, ethnicity is not clearly a negative force (Owusu 1970; Smock 1971; Cohen 1969). Indeed, as Robert Nisbet has argued the kin grouping can contribute much to micro-organization and to development, but often at the expense of the hegemony of the central state:

> The great contributions of kinship to society are, on the one hand, *the sense of membership in and continuity of the social order, generation after generation; and on the other, the spur to individual achievement, in all areas, that the intimacy of the family alone seems able to effect.* These are the essential psychological functions of family, and may be seen as the sources of the desire for autonomy and freedom of the household and kindred which has for many millennia been the strongest force against the kind of military or political power that atomizes a social order. *Between family and state there has been everywhere, throughout history, an inverse relation so far as the influence of each on society is concerned* (Nisbet 1975: 250) (emphasis added).

Self-Governance and Refounding the African State

Self-Governance

The label we have placed on our alternative to the "centralized state" is "self-governance." By this we mean a polity where the people are able to seek and develop partnerships with *one another* in the development process: where they can fulfill their potential for self-organization at multiple levels on which they hold the legal rights and diverse resources to engage in collective action. Under a regime of self-governance, the state's primary role is to act as a framework of rules which empowers and facilitates the people, encouraging relations of mutual respect and co-operation among them and abating opportunities for predation and exploitation. Under this regime they can organize, learn, and act with one another to construct the more complex social, economic and political relationships which are necessary for development to occur. The state's role is to "set the stage" rather than "write the script."

We have chosen and utilized this term "self-governance" because of its double connotation: "self," emphasizing the grounding of the polity in self-organizing capabilities and rights of the individual citizens and communities which compose it; and "governance," emphasizing governing as an open and open-ended process dealing with the development of institutions which sustain many organizations rather than the single organization, rulership connotation of the term "government." We also have chosen these terms to describe our goal rather than a more conventional term such as "democratic" or "development" because of contemporary theorists, commentators and actors' tendency to equate "democracy" with simple national plebiscitary procedures, and "development" with either material abundance or centralized power.

Their approach ignores, and indeed often justifies destroying, the diverse ways through which human beings have participated in and influenced political decisions under which they live. At best, they inadvertently work to encourage power asymmetries where the centrist-elite is able to exploit the periphery. It also ignores the reality that diverse decisions at multiple levels are made within any state, and that nominal "democratic" control of a center often neither offers little effective control by persons over those decisions and policies which most directly and intimately affect their lives, nor allows them opportunity or incentive to take responsibility for improving their lives and communities. Both we see as necessary for self-organization to occur (see Chapter 4). As Tocqueville wrote of democratic government some 150 years ago:

> It does little good to summon those very citizens who have been made so dependent on the central power to choose the representatives of that power from time to time. However important, this brief and occasional exercise of free will will not prevent them from gradually losing the faculty of thinking, feeling, and acting for themselves, so that they will slowly fall below the level of humanity. . . .
>
> It really is difficult to imagine how people who have entirely given up managing their own affairs could make a wise choice of those who are to do that for them. One should never expect a liberal, energetic, and wise government to originate in the votes of a people of servants.
>
> A constitution republican in its head and ultramonarchial in all its other parts has always struck me as an ephemeral monstrosity. The vices of those who govern and the weakness of the governed will soon bring it to ruin. Then the people, tired of its representatives and of itself, will either create freer institutions or soon fall back at the feet of a single master (Tocqueville 1966: 694–695).

We emphasize the idea of "self-governance" because we see the people of any society (who are in fact members in *several* working societies at any given time, in all of which they can and must fulfill these critical roles), as playing critical roles in the experimental and normative processes that build self-organizing societies. For it is the people who engage in the activities, successes and failures that lead to new organizations and to development. And it is equally the people who undergo the learning which leads to emergence of new rules to resolve new problems.

Refounding the African State

The problem of social development, is, we believe, a universal one, and therefore one that enables lessons to be learned across the diversity of human experience. Indeed, as ethical creatures we are compelled to seek out such lessons wherever possible. One of the most important understandings that emerged from the several centuries of struggle in Europe to bring about a stable and free society, is the tradition that emphasizes society's organic quality apart from the instruments of the state (Bendix 1964; 1978; Nisbet 1975; Tocqueville 1955). Great human disasters such as the Third Reich, the starvation of the Ukraine, the Cultural Revolution, and the Cambodian holocaust are clearly linked to the complete domination of all other social institutions by the state. Where there was resistance to the terror of the state, it came from organizations which had preserved some measure of autonomy: in Germany, for example, the church and the military; in South Africa today, the church and, at times, the universities. The magnitude of degradation in Stalinist Russia may in part grow from the extreme centralization of the Russian State under the Tsars.

However, it is frequently argued and accepted that the magnitude of Africa's developmental challenges *requires* "strong" government. In this we do not disagree; we disagree with what most people understand "strong government" to be. Centralization does not equate with "strong government" nor is its opposite a "weak government." Indeed, we will try to show in this book how centralized African governments have been extremely weak, and that truly effective mechanisms of human self-governance essential for development can only emerge in a political structure which allows for "decentralized" human organization.

We believe the African experience clearly shows that effective governance does not flow from centralizing sovereignty, decision-making, and dominance of political life. African states have met these three criteria and still have been extremely feeble in facilitating the broad and sustained productive social relations generally accepted to be essential for "development" (Zolberg 1966; Lofchie 1985; Jackson and Rosberg 1986; Hyden 1980; 1983). "Strong" governance may well require not "centralized" authority, but instead that a people is able to set and achieve goals through collective action at a variety of levels, and among a diversity of communities. However, this neither presumes nor requires *homogeneous* action; indeed, the attempt to homogenize human behavior may be both operationally impossible and counter-productive given the diversity of conditions and problems which exist in the real world, and our always limited human abilities to know, to understand, and to control (Hyden 1983; Wunsch 1986; Chambers 1974; Moris 1981; Mickelwait 1978).

Instead, a system of strong governance might be conceptualized as composed of many rule-making organizations, nested and linked with one another in rule-governed relationships which both encourage general reciprocity and allow for variations in choice and policy within that general framework (E. Ostrom 1985). Effective performance may require some fairly stringent consistency among them, where rules of due process, equity and civil and criminal liability are clear, predictable, and uniformly applied. It might similarly require clear and agreed-upon rules of conflict management and resolution among them. "Nested" relationships can provide cohesion where national priorities and requirements such as procedures for final adjudication of inter-governmental disputes, a stable currency, reliable weights and measures, unified foreign policy, etc., are spelled out. Alternatively, broad areas of discretion as well as the ability to negotiate lateral linkages among diverse governmental units can exist to facilitate locally oriented programs and shared concerns, complementary skills, and economies of scale. These systems can meet legitimate and unavoidable requirements for cohesion and consistency without seeking centralization of rule, homogenization, or precluding a very broad autonomy for organizations within parameters. The challenge, then, for institutional analysis is to determine which relationships need such consistency and cohesion, and how to structure relationships among the various organizations to maintain their relative authority, autonomy, and independent spheres of action (Madison, Hamilton, and Jay 1966; V. Ostrom 1987).

It is our judgment that the forces behind centralization are immensely powerful in today's world, and require equally powerful measures to blunt and challenge their progress. Centralizing forces include a laudable and humane impatience with human suffering; unrealistically unbounded confidence in both our technical knowledge and our ability to implement that knowledge in human affairs; a limited understanding of the role individuals as citizens and as members of diverse communities must play to bring about development, including in collective action; a limited understanding of the crucial role that social infrastructures, both old and new, must play in facilitating that citizen involvement; and a very poor understanding of the crucial role fundamental constitutional choices play in predetermining the whole direction of political life.

The goal of this book is to articulate an alternative approach to development and institutional analysis which we believe is a key prerequisite for reversing this momentum toward centralization, and for providing a strong foundation for the future of African societies. Its purpose is to *begin* afresh the debate on the design and character of domestic political institutions in Africa: *we do not pretend to have a blueprint,* but instead are articulating one conceptualization of human development in order to help sustain what must be a lengthy and challenging debate and inquiry.

Conclusions and Summary

Contemporary Africa faces great economic and political problems. Performance during the first twenty to thirty years of independence has been dismal according to most key indicators of political, economic or social well-being. While natural disasters and the disadvantages Africa faces in the international markets have much to do with these problems, the centralization of domestic political institutions has also been a critical factor. The highly centralized state establishes rules and institutions which are prone to: serious errors in policy and slow recognition of and recovery from these errors; growth of a parasitical elite class supported by the state apparatus; and rural and urban entropy as local organizing and empowering organizations are displaced, co-opted and compromised by the central state. The centralized system is the last, and perhaps, most serious vestige of Western colonialism. A system of "self-governance" is recommended to ease these problems and to provide a stronger and sounder foundation for the growth of complex human relationships that are the essence of development.

In the next several chapters we shall discuss the impact of colonialism on centralization in Africa; how centralization has led to such problems as elite abuse, the politicization of African economies, political-ethnic conflict and the decline and erosion of political legitimacy and social trust; and contemporary efforts to address the African development crisis.

Notes

1. Obviously drought, civil disturbances and international trading problems contributed to these figures. World Bank econometric analysis indicates that about 50 percent of Africa's economic decline can be attributed to climatic or international factors (World Bank 1981).

2. For example, Ivory Coast (GNP growth rate, 1960–1982, 2.1 percent), Kenya (2.8 percent), Nigeria (3.3 percent), Gabon (4.4 percent), Togo (2.3 percent), Malawi (2.9 percent) (World Bank 1984b).

3. "Centralized" and "powerful" are not necessarily synonymous. The assumption that they are and the belief that "powerful" governments were needed to lead economic development has been a great problem to post-independence Africa. More of this below, this chapter.

References

Achebe, Chinua. *A Man of the People*. London: Heinemann, 1966.

Adamolekun, Ladipo. *Politics and Administration in Nigeria*. Ibadan: Spectrum Books, 1986.

Apter, David. *Politics of Modernization*. Chicago: University of Chicago Press, 1965.

Austin, Dennis. *Politics in Africa*. Hanover, N.H.: University Press of New England, 1984.

Barkun, Joel, Fritz Holmquist, David Gachuki, and Shem Migot-Adholla. "Is Small Beautiful? The Organizational Conditions for Effective Small-Scale Self-Help

Development Projects in Rural Kenya." Paper presented at the 22nd Annual African Studies Association Meeting, Los Angeles, November 2, 1979.

Bates, Robert. *Markets and States in Tropical Africa: The Political Basis of Agricultural Politics.* Berkeley: University of California Press, 1981.

Bendix, Reinhard. *Nationbuilding and Citizenship.* Berkeley: University of California Press, 1964.

_____. *Kings or People: Power and the Mandate to Rule.* Berkeley: University of California Press, 1978.

Berry, Sara. *Fathers Work for Their Sons.* Berkeley: University of California Press, 1985.

Brett, E. A. "State Power and Inefficiency: Explaining Political Failure in Africa." *IDS Bulletin* 17 (1) (1986): 22–29.

Bunker, Stephen. *Peasants Against the State: The Politics of Market Control in Bugisu, Uganda, 1900–1983.* Urbana: University of Illinois Press, 1987.

Chambers, Robert. *Managing Rural Development: Ideas and Experience from East Africa.* Upsala, Sweden: Scandanavian Institute of African Studies, 1974.

Cohen, Abner. *Custom and Politics in Urban Africa.* Berkeley: University of California Press, 1969.

Crozier, Michael. *The Bureaucratic Phenomenon.* Chicago: University of Chicago Press, 1964.

Decalo, Samuel. *Coups and Army Rule in Africa: Studies in Military Rule.* New Haven, Conn.: Yale University Press, 1976.

_____. "African Personal Dictatorships." *Journal of Modern African Studies* 23 (2) (1985): 209–237.

Dumont, Rene. *False Start in Africa.* New York: Praeger, 1966.

Ekpo, M. U., ed. *Bureaucratic Corruption in Sub-Saharan Africa.* Washington, D.C.: University Press, 1979.

Esman, M. J. *The Politics of Development Administration.* Bloomington, Indiana: International Development Research Center, Indiana University, 1963.

Filani, M. O. "Nigeria: The Need to Modify Centre-Down Development." In *Development from Above or Below? The Dialectics of Regional Planning in Developing Countries,* edited by W. B. Stohr and D. R. Fraser-Taylor, 283–304. Chichester: John Wiley, 1981.

Gould, David. "Disorganization Theory and Underdevelopment Administration: Local 'Organization' in the Framework of Zairian National Development." Paper presented at the Joint meeting of the African Studies and Latin American Studies Associations, Houston, Texas, 1977.

Grestchmann, Klaus. "Measuring the Public Sector: A Contestable Issue." In *Guidance, Control, and Evaluation in the Public Sector,* edited by F. X. Kaufmann, G. Majone, and V. Ostrom, 139–158. Berlin and New York: Walter de Gruyter, 1986.

Grunow, Dieter G. "Development of the Public Sector: Trends and Issues." In *Guidance, Control, and Evaluation in the Public Sector,* edited by F. X. Kaufmann, G. Majone, and V. Ostrom, 25–58. Berlin and New York: Walter de Gruyter, 1986.

Hardin, Garrett. "The Tragedy of the Commons." *Science* 162 (December 1968): 1,243–1,248.

Heller, Peter, and Alan Tait. *Government Employment and Pay: Some International Comparisons.* Washington, D.C.: International Monetary Fund, 1982.

Hood, Christopher. "The Hidden Public Sector: The 'Bureaucratization' of the World?" In *Guidance, Control and Evaluation in the Public Sector,* edited by F.

X. Kaufmann, G. Majone, and V. Ostrom, 183–207. Berlin and New York: Walter de Gruyter, 1986.

Huntington, S. P. *Political Order in Changing Societies.* New Haven, Conn.: Yale University Press, 1968.

Hyden, Goran. *Beyond Ujamaa in Tanzania: Underdevelopment and an Uncaptured Peasantry.* Berkeley: University of California Press, 1980.

———. *No Shortcuts to Progress: African Development Management in Perspective.* Berkeley: University of California Press, 1983.

Independent Commission on International Development Issues. *North-South, A Programme for Survival.* London: Pan Books, 1980.

Jackson, Robert, and Carl Rosberg. *Personal Rule in Black Africa: Prince, Autocrat, Prophet, Tyrant.* Berkeley: University of California Press, 1982.

———. "Sovereignty and Underdevelopment: Juridical Statehood in the African Crisis." *The Journal of Modern African Studies* 24 (March 1986): 1–32.

Kasfir, Nelson. *The Shrinking Political Arena.* Berkeley: University of California Press, 1976.

Keller, Edmond. "Harambee!: Educational Policy and the Political Economy of Rural Community Organization in Kenya." Paper presented at the African Studies Association Meeting, Chicago, Illinois, 1974.

Landau, Martin. "Redundancy, Rationality, and the Problems of Duplication and Overlap." *Public Administration Review* 29 (July/August 1969): 346–358.

———. "Federalism, Redundancy and System Stability." *Publius* 3 (2) (Fall 1973): 173–196.

———. *On Multi-Organizational Systems in the Public Administration.* Berkeley: University of California, Committee on Public Organization, Institute of Governmental Studies, 1985.

——— and Russell Stout, Jr. "To Manage is Not to Control: Or the Folly of Type-Two Errors." *Public Administration Review* 39 (2) (March/April 1979): 148–156.

———, Suchitra Bhakdi, Ledivinia Carino, Rolando Tungpalan, and James Wunsch. *Final Report: Provincial Development Assistance Project.* Berkeley: Institute of International Studies, 1980.

Leonard, David K. "The Political Realities of African Management." In *Report of a Workshop on the Management of Agricultural Projects in Africa,* 58–74. Washington, D.C.: USAID Special Evaluation Study No. 33, 1986.

——— and Walter Oyugi. "Procedures for Decentralized Programming, Budgeting and Work Planning: Lessons from Kenyan Mistakes." *Agricultural Administration* 19 (1985): 123–137.

Liebenow, J. Gus. *African Politics: Crises and Challenges.* Bloomington, Ind.: Indiana University Press, 1986.

Little, Kenneth. *West African Urbanization: A Study of Voluntary Association in Social Change.* Cambridge: Cambridge University Press, 1966.

Lofchie, Michael. "Africa's Agrarian Malaise." In *African Independence: The First Twenty-Five Years,* edited by Gwendolen M. Carter and Patrick O'Meara, 160–187. Bloomington, Ind.: Indiana University Press, 1985.

Mabogunje, A. L. *The Development Process: A Spatial Perspective.* London: Hutchinson University Press, 1980.

———. *Regional Mobility and Resource Development in West Africa.* Montreal: Methuen, 1972.

Madison, James, Alexander Hamilton, and John Jay. *The Federalist Papers.* Edited by Roy Fairfield. Garden City, N.Y.: Anchor Books, 1966.

Mawood, Philip, ed. *Local Government for Development: The Experience of Tropical Africa.* Chichester: John Wiley, 1983.

_____ and Ken Davey. "Anglophone Africa." In *International Handbook on Local Government Reorganization,* edited by D. C. Rowat, 404–414. Westport, Connecticut: Greenwood Press, 1980.

Moris, Jon. "The Transferability of the Western Management Tradition to the Non-Western Public Service Sectors." *Philippine Journal of Public Administration* 20 (4) (1976): 401–427.

_____. *Managing Induced Rural Development.* Bloomington, Ind.: Indiana University, International Development Institute, 1981.

Mickelwait, Donald, et al. *The "New Directions" Mandate: Studies in Project Design, Approval and Implementation* (revised). Washington, D.C.: Development Alternatives, Inc., 1978.

Nisbet, Robert. *Community and Power.* New York: Oxford University Press, 1962.

Nisbet, Robert. *The Twilight of Authority.* New York: Oxford University Press, 1975.

Olowu, Dele. *African Local Governments as Instruments of Economic and Social Development.* The Hague: International Union of Local Authorities, 1987.

_____. "Bureaucratic Morality in Africa." *International Political Science Review* 9 (2) (1988): 215–229.

Ostrom, Elinor. "The Rudiments of a Revised Theory of the Origins, Survival, and Performance of Institutions for Collective Action." Bloomington, Ind.: Indiana University, Workshop in Political Theory and Policy Analysis, 1985.

Ostrom, Vincent. *The Political Theory of a Compound Republic: Designing the American Experiment.* Rev. ed. Lincoln, Neb.: University of Nebraska Press, 1987.

_____. *The Intellectual Crisis in American Public Administration.* 2nd rev. ed. Tuscaloosa, Alabama: University of Alabama Press, 1988.

_____ and Elinor Ostrom. "Public Goods and Public Choices." In *Alternatives for Delivering Public Services,* edited by E. S. Savas, 7–49. Boulder, Colorado: Westview Press, 1978.

Owens, Edgar, and Robert Shaw. *Development Reconsidered: Bridging the Gap Between Government and People.* Lexington, Mass.: Lexington Books, 1972.

Owusu, Maxwell. *Uses and Abuses of Political Power.* Chicago: University of Chicago Press, 1970.

Ozgediz, Selcuk. *Managing the Public Service in Developing Countries Issues and Prospects.* World Bank Staff Working Papers, No. 583. Washington, D.C., 1983.

Riggs, Fred W. *Administration in Developing Countries.* Boston: Houghton-Mifflin, 1964.

_____. "Introductory Concepts." *Administrative Studies* 16 (1976): 84–88.

Rondinelli, Dennis. *Administrative Decentralization and Area Development Planning in East Africa: Implications for U.S. Aid Policy.* Washington, D.C.: USAID/ST/RD, 1979. Mimeo.

_____. *Development Projects as Policy Experiments.* London: Methuen, 1983.

Rothchild, D. "State-Ethnic Relations in Middle Africa." In *African Independence: The First Twenty-Five Years,* edited by Gwendolen M. Carter and Patrick O'Meara, 71–96. Bloomington, Ind.: Indiana University Press, 1985.

Sandbrook, Richard. *The Politics of Africa's Economic Stagnation.* Cambridge: Cambridge University Press, 1985.

Selassie, Bereket H. *The Executive in African Governments.* London: Heinemann, 1974.

Smith, Brian C. *Decentralization: The Territorial Dimension of the State.* London: Allen and Unwin, 1985.

Smock, Audrey. *Ibo Politics: The Role of Ethnic Unions in Eastern Nigeria.* Cambridge, Mass.: Harvard University Press, 1971.

Soyinka, Wole. *The Interpreters.* London: Deutsch, 1965.

————. *Kongis' Harvest.* London: Oxford University Press, 1967.

Tocqueville, Alexis de. *The Old Regime and the French Revolution.* Garden City, N.Y.: Anchor Books, 1955.

————. *Democracy in America.* Edited by J. P. Mayer. New York: Anchor Books, 1966.

Tordoff, William. *Government and Politics in Africa.* Bloomington, Ind.: Indiana University Press, 1984.

Tullock, Gordon. *The Politics of Bureaucracy.* Washington, D.C.: Public Affairs Press, 1965.

Williamson, Oliver. "Hierarchical Control and Optimum Firm Size." *Journal of Political Economy* 75 (2) (1967): 123–138.

World Bank. *Accelerated Development in Sub-Saharan Africa.* Washington, D.C.: World Bank, 1981.

————. *World Development Report, 1984.* Washington, D.C.: World Bank, 1984a.

————. *Toward Sustained Development in Sub-Saharan Africa.* Washington, D.C.: World Bank, 1984b.

Wunsch, James. "Voluntary Associations: Determinants of Structure and Activity in Two Ghanaian Secondary Cities." Ph.D. Dissertation. Bloomington, Ind.: Indiana University, 1974.

————. "Strengthening Rural Development Management Through International Assistance Projects." *Public Administration and Development* 3 (1983): 239–263.

————. "Administering Rural Development: Have Goals Outreached Organizational Capacity?" *Public Administration and Development* 6 (1986): 287–308.

Young, Crawford. *Ideology and Development in Africa.* New Haven, Conn.: Yale University Press, 1982.

Zolberg, A. R. *Creating Political Order: The Party-States of West Africa.* Chicago: Rand McNally, 1966.

2

Foundations of Centralization: The Colonial Experience and the African Context

James S. Wunsch

Colonialism and Institutional Development

Colonialism must be seen as an epochal event in Africa's history (Ekeh 1980). In many powerful respects it worked to prepare and incline the path of post-independence politics toward Hobbesian theories of sovereignty (see Chapter 10), to depreciation of the value of indigenous and decentralized social infrastructure, and to reliance on centralized, hierarchical mechanisms to order human relationships. To understand how this worked, one must briefly review key features of the colonial system.[1]

On philosophical grounds, in organizational constitutions, in policy making and policy, colonial regimes were essentially elitist, centrist, and absolutist (Crowder 1968: 165–248; Obichere 1971; Austen 1971; Deschamps 1971). Philosophically, when colonial powers did attempt to justify their rule it was, as is well known, on elitist grounds. Whether this was phrased in terms of the "white-man's burden," the spread of Christianity, the propagation of French civilization, or of British principles of law and government, colonialism was justified on grounds that one civilization was going to remake and impose a better order on a second (Crowder 1968: 3–6, 71–75).

Perhaps its most complete statement in the English language is Lord Lugard's famous "Dual Mandate," which argued that British colonial role was to see that African states were administered to the mutual benefit of African peoples and the world economy (Lugard 1922). This argument moralized elite rule as it simultaneously justified an essentially absolutist system of governance; the ruler-ruled relationship took the form of governor-subject rather than official-citizen. The metropole was the "center" leading the "periphery" (the colony) toward enlightenment and progress, and by definition, subjects were not qualified to evaluate this process. Officials were thus not regulated by citizens who possessed legal rights to define laws and relationships between them. Indeed, in many situations, "subjects" (particularly in the "Indigenant" system) had very limited rights even of due-process in the exercise of the law (Ajayi and Crowder 1974). Government did not exist, therefore, as the agent of the governed to facilitate their action, but as an instrument of an external center reconstructing a periphery in the *periphery's* supposed interest (Crowder 1968: 165–251; Huessler 1971; Deschamps 1971; Austen 1971). As Lugard put it, the Nigerian system of native administration was established to bring about, "the regeneration of Nigeria . . . through its own governing class and its own indigenous institutions" (Sklar 1985). Only under the tutelage of the British administration, however, was it expected that this regeneration might be reached.

Daily administration reflected this. Policy was made either in the metropole or by the governor, and implemented by his administrative cadres, and with little or no participation by the governed (Deschamps 1971; Ajayi and Crowder 1974). In theory, at least, *all* legislative authority in French Africa was centralized in Paris, in the Office of the Minister of Colonies and the President of the Republic (Ajayi and Crowder 1974). Legislative power was similarly centralized at the Governor's level in British Africa (Crowder 1968: 524–526). In either case, rules of action defined few limits on the legislators and concentrated operational control of both constitutional and collective choice decisions on the same persons without any real checks by the colony's population. "Advisory assemblies" were in most instances late in coming, often dominated by ex-officio members, and of course, only advisory (Crowder 1968: 201–206; Ajayi and Crowder 1974).[2] Momentous policies were made without any attempt to consult with the indigenous population: the immigration of large numbers of Lebanese and Asians (in East Africa) to fill craft, clerical, and commercial positions; the alienation of land for white settlers; taxation; the compulsory development of cash cropping; location of infrastructure and administrative units; civil and criminal law (Crowder 1968: 252–344). Bureaucrats, rather few in number, and in the British case drawn from a self-conscious elite, did not perceive themselves as accountable to the people, but to the government (Austen 1971). Guided loosely by the Governor, they made policy on appropriate "technical" grounds, and were often puzzled by the reluctance of the "natives" to do what was so clearly in their interest. The color line (or in French Africa, the line between citizen and subject) tended to divide rather sharply senior bureaucrat from junior subordinate, and even more sharply to divide the senior bureaucrats from the population. The British district officer or his French equivalent, the *commandant de cercle,* had immense discretion in his territory and was accountable only to the colonial governor's office. Disbursement of funds and supplies on the other hand, was highly centralized as were decisions on policy matters (Crowder 1968: 163–238; Ajayi and Crowder 1974).

Much has been made of the different colonial administrative styles pursued in British and French Africa. The centralizing aspects of French policy are easy to see, both in personnel attitudes and administrative procedures. As Governor-General William Ponty wrote in an official circular to his governors in 1914:

> My long experience in West Africa among the black populations has permitted me to conclude in the dearest fashion, and you certainly have made the same observations, that the native intermediaries between the mass of the population and the administrators of the *cercles* or their subordinates are mostly nothing but parasites living on the population and existing without profit to the treasury (Ponty 1914, cited in Deschamps 1971: 498).

Deschamps, himself a former colonial officer, wrote:

> In France, a continental nation threatened by its neighbors, local rule was considered a centrifugal force threatening the unity of the nation. In its history the French people found ample evidence to show that local rights were upheld by feudal or regressive forces, whereas progressive forces were represented by central authority. In France, until recently, centralization has been considered a good, and local rule has been thought of as a perilous system which gave the enemies of the state a base from which to challenge it (Deschamps 1971: 497).

In the field these attitudes were manifested in an absolutist, if benevolent, role for key administrative personnel. As Deschamps wrote:

> The administrator was responsible for his *cercle* vis-a-vis the governor, and the heads of subdivisions were his subordinates. His role was totalitarian: responsible for order, head of the militia, judge, census taker, tax collector, bookkeeper, supervisor of labor, constructor of roads and buildings, organizer of markets, urban planner, nurseryman, in charge of the progress of the economy and of public health, protector of the forests, inspector of education, chief of the Europeans. He had to see all, rule all, conceive all, accomplish all. Besides, theoretically he had to supervise the application of an enormous mass of regulations contained in the official journals, and which constantly varied. He had all the powers. Nothing could be done without his aid or his authorization. Ten days each month at least he was on tour over the roads in order to insure contracts, explain instructions to the villagers, receive their complaints, arbitrate, activate and, if need be, punish. The order and progress of the country depended upon him. As a result, there were sometimes abuses or oversights the governor had to sanction (Deschamps 1971: 547).

While it is a common generalization that the British colonial service embodied more respect for traditional authorities in attitudes and in its "Indirect Rule" structure (where the latter was workable), what is not so clearly seen is how the weak communication between district offices and governor combined with the roles of "civilizing agent" and "overlord," and worked to centralize great power in the district officer (Huessler 1971). As Lugard himself wrote:

The policy of the Government was that these chiefs should govern their people, not as independent, but as dependent rulers. The orders of the government are not conveyed to the people through them, but emanate from them in accordance, where necessary, with instructions received from the Resident. (The resident's) advice on matters of general policy must be followed (Lugard 1919 and 1926, cited in Crowder 1968: 217).

While Crowder and others properly emphasize the diversity of British colonial administration in practice, one thing appears to be consistent: the concentration of authority to establish, revise, and interpret rules in a structure entirely removed from local, popular mechanisms of control. Even where this authority was "shared" because of operating realities with a local traditional figure, most scholars agree that popular input was usually not increased by this: if anything, the "chief" used indirect rule to attenuate his vulnerability to customary controls (Huessler 1971; Crowder 1968: especially 198–221).

The outcome of these characteristics was the absence of a real constitutionally based rule of law or of enduring structures to institutionalize local development efforts. Those with power, the district officers, often did succeed in bringing tangible, material improvements to their districts. But it was through a forum and in a manner particularly ill-suited for long-term, organizational development. It was not based on local political processes, nor even on consistent national procedures, policies, and routines: it was paternalistic, *ad hoc,* and ephemeral. When the particular officer who led certain projects left, he left only the project behind, not a set of working, locally legitimate rules to allocate authority, obligation, initiative, influence, rewards, and the like, on which further local collective action might be based. He left no *institutions* to facilitate or sustain local organization. In an essay fundamentally complementary of such efforts, Huessler inadvertently brings out these features:

> In the absence of any practical lead from headquarters—just as well, as headquarters had little knowledge of the districts—empiricism was the order of the day. Individual officers had the only authority worth talking about in their areas, and the governor was not at pains to deny it. . . . Everyone had his special assignment or pet project: Wyatt's road . . . Baker's schools . . . Longland's field engineering; Malcom's land development scheme . . . Leechman on tsetse control . . . Johnson on markets; Culwick on rice (Huessler 1971: 588).

Such variety is good. But when it came from the top-down, and when local dwellers were neither allowed nor forced to develop institutions to establish and sustain these projects, the projects and their momentum faded with the change in officers.

The "empiricism," flexibility, and personalism of district officers described by Heussler (and noted as still present in East Africa by Moris) further reinforced political centralization, albeit in a "decentralized" structure, because it left the localities paralyzed in terms of formal political structures (Moris 1977). The key point here is this: colonial administration, whether British or French, neglected, distorted and sometimes destroyed local rule systems through which persons were able to take collective action. Even where it was benevolent, such government disabled societies in a fundamental sense, as they removed the *necessity* for persons to discover, and the *opportunity* for them to sustain local collective mechanisms to solve local collective problems. Needless to say, without any primary units of self-governance to "link" or "nest" with others, the art of intergovernmental organization was left underdeveloped. Thus, the contemporary political structure provides only for the central state and its agents to take political action.

In an ironic way, colonies created the worst possible situation as far as developing broad empowerment through multiple institutionally based organizations. Sovereign authority was highly centralized in the hands of the governor or even in the metropole; effective governance was in the hands of the district officer who was highly paternalistic and operated in a personalistic and *ad hoc* manner because of distance from the capital; and logistical support was centralized, slow, and unresponsive. Local residents were therefore neither involved in their formal governance (centralized in the capital or overseas), nor left alone to solve their own problems and to build on their existing institutional infrastructure. Instead, local governance was preempted by a sometimes benevolent, usually foreign, and almost always arbitrary autocrat. Local action of any sort, of course, whether by district officer or anyone else, waited upon clumsy and slow logistical structures.

All this is not to say that all local organizations were eradicated. Africa's rich history of peasant co-operatives, market associations, communal improvement organizations, professional organizations, religious societies, labor unions and the like clearly belies this (Little 1966; Jones 1979). What is being said here is that these organizations were not institutionalized through law, but rather were left out of the mainstream of government. Thus, African associational skills and organizational energy were focused largely *out* of developing local formal political structures which could later serve to receive devolutionary authority and sustain local autonomy in the give-and-take of politics with national institutions. Perhaps a major "exception" helps "prove" the rule here. Evidence from Eastern Nigeria suggests that the structure of Ibo village and status-systems, particularly among the central and Cross-River Ibo, made the "warrant-chief" system particularly amenable to integration into the local political and social systems. This integration of the warrant-chief system into this structure made possible the powerful, essentially pseudo-governmental role played by Ibo communal improvement associations during the mid- and late-colonial era, as well as during the 1960s (Jones 1979; Smock 1971). However, only rarely was the colonial political structure so neatly integrated into a local, participative political system. Even here, of course, the links between the two were informal, and the communal improvement union system remained out of the formal political structure.

To be sure, in the waning years of colonial rule, the major powers began to allow for greater local government. In the Creech-Jones era the British particularly made remarkable progress in devolving authority to elected local councils, and turning back the authority of district officers to override council decisions. Beginning only in 1947, however, the reforms were too short lived and too quickly embroiled in the post-independence political conflict over control at the center to last long (Kasfir 1983; see Chapter 4 for a fuller exposition of these events).

It is unclear how this experience in general affected African governments. It would be simple minded and condescending to suggest that the leaders who struggled for independence simply emulated the colonial "model," and I do not contend that they did. However, institutions and the organizational patterns they spawn have lives of their own, as contemporary organization theory has shown, and the leaders at independence were forced to continue to carry out the day-to-day affairs of the state with essentially the same structure, and many of the same personnel which had governed the colony. Many leaders placed a high priority on rooting out "colonial tendencies" in the civil service, and Africanized it rapidly. However, routines of decision making, mechanisms to disburse funds and resources, routines to appeal decisions and actions, channels through which paper and information flow, gaps between hierarchical levels and among vertical segments, and gaps between populace and administration are harder to change. The press of daily business tends to "squeeze out" reform efforts. As James Thomson notes, the independent state of Niger continued this administrative framework:

> Somewhat larger units, based on either quarters or villages, might have served as appropriate levels at which to devise common resource management efforts when scarcity became apparent toward the end of the period, if state-imposed rules emasculating local organization had been relaxed. As it happened, most villages had lost their power of independent activity as a result of colonial, and then independent regime efforts to establish controls over major forms of organization in rural areas. Villages (or quarters within them) had no authority to enforce sanctions against violators of locally-devised use rules. In practice, few such results appear to have been made (Thomson et al. 1986: 13).

Many analysts find pervasive evidence that these patterns and practices have endured even into the 1970s and 1980s within the bureaucracy and in the population's view of it. Malcolm Odell's analysis of local government in Botswana clearly shows how routine local policing tasks such as keeping cattle out of fields became extraordinarily difficult as the independent government arrogated all police authority to itself, stripped traditional local governments of their ability to regulate local affairs, and failed to place sufficient personnel or resources in the field to take on these tasks. Odell cites direct evidence of social disruption and economic loss growing from this (Odell 1985).

As Kirk-Green found, there is more continuity in the presuppositions and routines of post-independence administration than there appears to be change: "administration procedures and bureaucratic control have too often remained untouched" (Kirk-Green 1975: 97). Rubin and Weinstein observe:

> Statutes governing the civil services have rarely been altered significantly; the same salary scales and codes of behavior continue; administrative law books have not changed. The same elitist attitudes are absorbed, including a generalized disdain for elected officials and technicians, in spite of egalitarian socialist ideology (Rubin and Weinstein 1974: 201).

Insofar as this is accurate, the centralizing, elitist, and (sometimes) absolutist features of the colonialism have survived the post-independence period (Moris 1976; 1981; Wunsch 1983; Leonard 1973; 1977). Furthermore, there is no doubt that many African leaders, when challenged by apparently serious dissent over policies they believed essential for security and economic progress, have responded in much the same way colonial governments responded. Both Nkrumah and Nyerere, for example, acted to ban peasant purchasing cooperatives in key cash crop areas when the cooperatives demanded pricing policies inconsistent with the government's. Similar fates have befallen labor unions and student associations in most African countries. Preventative detention and political imprisonment have been used in several countries as well (Rubin and Weinstein 1974: 201–204; Tordoff 1985: 105–108).

In summary, colonial rule left the instruments of power available to Africa's independent leaders. Furthermore, these leaders had seen the instruments used to solve problems of political controversy. Perhaps what is more important, the colonial regimes had distorted and stifled alternative political organizations, or only allowed them to begin functioning again too late in the colonial era to reestablish themselves. So local governmental organizations which might have been able to resist such centralizing forces were highly underdeveloped. Finally, as we discuss below, insofar as African leaders themselves became another elite with a mission, the institutional structure and the role models were there.

Colonialism predisposed African independent regimes toward centralized constitutions in other ways as well. Its treatment of traditional governance systems is one of the most important. In many situations, they had been co-opted and, in some measure, fundamentally corrupted by the power that the colonial system exercised through them. The structures of law and local participation which had hitherto limited and guided their functions were erased, while new demands were placed on them and through them on the people (Cohen 1974; Deschamps 1971; Crowder 1968: 163–238, 464–466; Ajayi and Crowder 1974).

Their evolution into modern instruments of self-governance was constrained by suspending their constitutional relationship with the people and by colonially based restrictions on their ability to tax, establish rules, and let contracts. These four changes (suspension of traditional constitutions and laws, non-accountability to the people, policy control by the colonial power, and restrictions on authority) effectively froze their evolution. Indeed, the strain between traditional accountability to the populace and unpopular policies set by colonial governments, and the disruption of historical constitutional relations in some cases reduced their legitimacy to function at all (Ajayi and Crowder 1974: 523; see Crowder 1968: 217–235, 464–466).[3] Thus local traditional institutions were simply not a realistic alternative to central government and a hierarchical bureaucracy at the time of independence.

Although some traditional leaders competed with the educated, Westernized elements over control of the state, the latter were better positioned by their experience in the capital, their command of Western, liberal political philosophy, and their cultural Westernization. Reinforcing this was the clarity and simplicity of the universalistic-individualistic argument they made, their relative distance from close ethnic identification, and their advanced knowledge of mass political organization. The organic model of the state that the traditional leaders could point to was at the same time an argument against the same traditional leaders. They reflected several organic nations within one state, and granting them authority stepped into the multi-ethnic paradox (Johnson 1974; Webster 1974; Aluko 1971; and O'Brien 1974).

Weakened by colonial policy, discredited by their role in colonial governments and by the support of some for delayed independence, and disparaged by their identification at times with "backward" ethnic groups relatively distant from coast lines and capital cities, the traditional leaders and their institutions were unlikely to receive much of a role from the nationalist-westernized elites which won independence. Thus, as Azikiwe observed:

> We will retain and respect our institutions of Natural Rulers. Where a legislative assembly is established for them, its function shall be purely advisory and consultative. In establishing our new government we must keep or revise those institutions that make Africa Africa. We are proud of them and we shall cherish them (Azikiwe 1961, cited in Sklar 1985).

However, the nationalists were not about to let them govern, and with few exceptions (most notably in the Northern Region of *federal* Nigeria until 1966, and in Uganda), they did not. As a counterweight to national government, as an alternative to hierarchical solutions to material and organizational problems, and as sets of rules and rule-governed relationships which might evolve to take up new tasks, traditional government was irrevocably damaged by colonialism.

Exemplifying the cost of destroying basic social infrastructure, it has often been noted that the development of institutions to solve problems is always problematic. Among other factors, it is dependent in some measure on the costs of innovation and the institutional "resource stock" at hand. According to James Thomson, et al.,

Whether change will occur depends, however, on the supply of institutional change . . . the willingness and capability of the fundamental institutions of government to provide/permit new arrangements. The capability depends in part on the cost of institutional innovation which in turn depends in part on the stock of existing knowledge of the design and operation of institutions (Thomson et al. 1986: 5).

Not insignificantly, they add, are the interests of relatively more powerful governmental figures:

The willingness to provide new arrangements also importantly depends on the private benefits and cost of providing change to the agents who are in a position to do so, the elite decision-makers of government. Thus the existing set of institutions and initial distribution of power will have a significant impact on the kinds of new institutional arrangements which are supplied (Thomson et al. 1986: 5-6).

As things worked through, one can find few instances where local institutional "stock" and elite interests have combined to restore authority and capacity for collective action to any areas below the national state.

A particularly poignant example of this problem is brought out by Thomson, et al., in their analysis of deforestation in the Sahel:

. . . the French West African imperial forestry code formalized control over the commons. The French code removed, or drastically restricted, what had hitherto been fairly broad local-level discretion in dealing with woodstock management. While little, if anything, had been done along these lines before 1935 because wood was plentiful, the option of developing local management solutions presumably existed before forestry code legislation eliminated the prerogative. As a result of the forestry code, devising new local political solutions to management problems became a much more difficult and expensive process. While most regulations outlined above were sporadically enforced at best, villagers recognized foresters' authority to control woodstock use. Very few if any attempted to establish alternative controls on access and use. The independent state of Niger inherited and maintained the common property framework institutionalized in the forestry code imposed by the French (Thomson et al. 1986: 15).

Colonialism, Material Conditions
and the Environment

Colonial policy reinforced centralism and elitism in the physical and human legacies it left as well. The administrative and supporting infrastructure was generally concentrated in a single city: administrative headquarters, educational facilities, public utilities, consumer goods, and communication facilities. Furthermore, most opportunities in paid employment, commerce, and the professions lay there. Africans fortunate enough to find a place in the primate city had far greater opportunities to advance, and

this began development of a domestic African petty bourgeois and professional elite (Crowder 1968: *en passim*).

The structures of colonial law in the French and Portuguese colonies
reinforced elite development, and they added a cultural dimension as well.
The opportunity for French and Portuguese Africans to escape the "citizen-
subject" distinction through assimilation meant that those wishing to escape
colonial absolutism could do so by absorbing themselves into the colonizer's
culture. Those who did became members of an elite which later inherited
power from the colonial masters (Crowder 1968: 165–172, 372–392, 433–
453, 482–490; Crowder and O'Brien 1974; Cohen 1974). How much understanding and sympathy they would retain for the capacity of their fellow
Africans to function as citizens would remain an open question. If Senghor
is taken as typical, however, the answer would have to be toward the
negative. For although he often stressed the intangible value of African
culture (Negritude), he stressed in practice the tangible utility of French
institutions and laws (Mazrui 1983).

British "cultural" policy was less dramatic than French or Portuguese
policy, but it also worked to draw ambitious Africans into a Westernized
elite. To hold positions in the colonial bureaucracy, in teaching, in the
mission churches, and later on, in the professions and in government, one
had to be educated in the British system. While neither of these arrangements was deterministic, each encouraged development of an elite class
with far greater opportunities to hold and exercise political power than
non-elites (Crowder 1968: 198–216, 372–392, 454–481). Furthermore, insofar as these nascent elites believed the Francophone or Anglophone
systems to be superior, they were well positioned to adopt the same
rationalizations for absolutist and centrist rule the colonial powers had
originally articulated. Finally, these elites were, in most cases, essentially
literary classes with little opportunity outside government and the high
levels of the civil service. The economic and social futures of a majority
of them were tied to some sort of Western-oriented, central, elite-oriented
government (Lofchie 1985).

Colonialism's centralizing impact can also be seen in the economic
conditions these states faced at independence. These policy-derived centralizing conditions were, furthermore, generally reinforced by natural conditions and by the international environments in which African leaders
had to work.

In a recent major report on development in Africa, the World Bank
wrote:

> When the sub-Saharan states won independence some 20 years ago, they faced
> formidable constraints to development. These included underdeveloped human
> resources, political fragility, insecurely rooted and ill-suited institutions, a
> climate and geography hostile to development, and rapid population growth
> (World Bank 1981: 9).

These characteristics, it has become generally accepted, were largely the result of colonial economic policies. In summary, African economies have generally been described as small, open, dependent, and poorly integrated; as facing serious constraints (and some opportunities) in natural resources; and, as complicated by ethnically fragmented societies (World Bank 1981). In general, considering political and economic models dominant at the time of independence, these conditions seemed to call for strong, national efforts to stimulate economic development and solve problems of national unity (Owens and Shaw 1972). Let us consider these questions in more detail.

Most African States were throughout the colonial experience (and are still, today), *small and agricultural* economies. Thus, gross domestic product was small, the size of their internal market was small, they had accumulated little wealth on which to base their own development, the scale of their production systems was small, and they were highly vulnerable to economic trends and cycles well out of their control. Their agriculture, in technological terms, was simple and land-intensive. It is still today, by one estimate, over 50 percent in subsistence production. Furthermore, from 30–60 percent of their GDP is still in agricultural production (World Bank 1981). In general, complex economic institutions such as banking systems, equity markets, and personnel skilled in the management of large, modern corporations were never developed under the mercantile and state-authorized monopoly systems characteristic of colonial rule, and have remained weak to this day (Fieldhouse 1971; Crowder 1968).

As well as their agricultural basis, small size, and low technological and institutional development, most African economies could, in 1960, be characterized as "*dependent*." As a product of colonial policies, they depended on one or two major commodities for most of their export earnings, and depended on the former metropole to purchase the bulk of their production (World Bank 1981). Colonial policy prevented them from adding much value to those products in the production process (Fieldhouse 1971; Crowder 1968: 271–332, 345–355). Furthermore, at independence they competed with other primary producers at world-market prices, to sell the commodity, whether it be agricultural or mineral.

African economies could also be characterized at independence as *poorly integrated*. Colonial policy decisions encouraged most to develop with "enclaves" or with dual sectors, where one urban or rural area was heavily involved in export and cash production, and the rest of the country lagged far behind. The "enclave area" would have far higher incomes, greater access to education and other social services, and consume manufactured items largely imported from overseas. The advanced area and the rest of the country had limited economic relations, and the former did not act to stimulate economic growth in the latter (Crowder 1968: 271–332, 345–355; Mabogunje 1980).

Poor integration could also be seen in limited and export-oriented transportation and communication infrastructure; clear divisions among areas of the country which were largely subsistence as opposed to cash cropping areas; the existence of primate cities which dominated social, political, economic, and intellectual affairs; and a bureaucratic-managerial class tied to government employment which earned many multiples of the average peasant's income, with virtually no "middle class" to bridge the two. Finally, these economies were at independence very dependent on foreign trade, with the latter accounting for some 25 percent of GDP (World Bank 1981; Hyden 1980; 1983).

Africa, while famous for its mineral wealth, faced similar problems in that sector as well. Copper in Zaire and Zambia, gold and diamonds in South Africa and Ghana, bauxite in Ghana, iron ore in Guinea, oil in Angola and Nigeria, uranium in Gabon and Niger, are but some of the known, economically viable resources. Developed largely during the colonial era and in production for several decades, these minerals are crucial exports and sources of exchange currency for African governments. Yet, these have also been points of vulnerability, and grow in part from Africa's economic "openness." At independence, without exception, their continued production depended on expatriate involvement. Neither personnel, technology, nor capital sufficient for their exploration had developed in African hands throughout the colonial experience. Furthermore, their economic value also lay outside African control as prices set by world markets would control the actual benefit African governments received. Expansion of production and the discovery and development of additional resources were similarly out of the control of Africa's leaders (World Bank 1981; Crowder 1968: 273–331, 345–355). Parallel circumstances applied to Africa's vast agricultural sector whose production was priced on a world market and was vulnerable to new competitors in other tropical areas. In part to expand the production of these goods, in part to stabilize markets, and in part to "capture" them for central control by the state, colonial governments established the marketing boards and state monopolies which became so important to the centralized structure of post-colonial rule (Bates 1981). The *openness* of the production of these agricultural and mineral commodities and the institutional legacies of colonialism worked together to reinforce the perceived need for and apparent benefit from centralized, statist economic policies in the post-independence era (World Bank 1981; Crowder 1968: 273–331, 395–355; Bates 1981).

This brief review of the critical circumstances of the African states at independence would be incomplete without mentioning the ethnic complexity which characterized (and characterizes still) African states at independence. Often described as "tribes," a term ethnologists feel more culturally condescending than analytically useful, Africa has hundreds of distinct nations: groups of people who share language, history, cultural values, territory, economic institutions, and usually, political institutions. They range in size from many millions, such as the Hausa, the Buganda, and the Ashanti, to the thousands, such as the Nzima.

As is well known, imperial states carved out the boundaries which eventually became today's states at their convenience, to support other interests, and in competition with other imperial states. In no situation was a border adjusted to make sense for ethnic reasons. Thus, states at independence included multiple nations within one boundary, and often divided self-conscious, ethnic-national groupings among two or more states (Ewe between Ghana and Togo; Ibo between Nigeria and Cameroon; Somali among Ethiopia, Somalia, and Kenya; and many others). Groups with traditional rivalries, or even histories of warfare, were often included within a single state (Ashanti and Brong in Ghana; Yoruba and Hausa in Nigeria) (Crowder 1968: 45–162).

Colonial policy often worked to intensify ethnic awareness and competition; it often stimulated insecurity and conflict. Groups close to original points of settlement or administrative centers advanced more quickly into education, trade, civil service, and the professions. Some groups were regarded as uniquely suited for military service and came to dominate the rank and file of the armies; very often the officers (when Africans were officers at all) were drawn from a different group. Some groups, most clearly the Fulani Emirs of Northern Nigeria, were favored by colonial policy and evolved with a politically dominant position in the national government. Others grew to dominate the civil service; ethnic tensions developed from all these disjunctions of influence, power and status. Unitary constitutions acted rarely to afford backward or minority groups any entrenched security, often trapping smaller groups under the authority of larger and more advanced groups that they feared or at least envied. Several constitutions, for example in Nigeria and Sudan, thus worked to intensify suppression of minority groups. In Nigeria, an inherently unstable system tied to three regions and three major and competing ethnic groups led to minority group suppression, while the three big regions, groups, and parties, played out an unstable balancing act which ended in the riots of 1966 (Melson and Wolpe 1971; Rothchild and Olorunsola 1983).

Colonial policy also frequently drew sub-national administrative boundaries which placed one group in a dominating position over another. As "chiefs" were designated from one ethnic unit and granted unprecedented powers over a second, previously quiescent group, ethnic relations grew rivalrous, and at times hostile (Crowder 1968: 217–235; Rubin and Weinstein 1974: 46–50). Agricultural, labor, and tax policies worked to drive young men into urban areas and into competition for limited opportunities (Crowder 1968: 335–342). Again, ethnic awareness and sometimes conflict grew from this (Smock 1971; Cohen 1969; Epstein 1958).

It is important to note that the vast majority of Africans live at peace and in cooperation with their multi-ethnic neighbors. Ethnicity has only rarely grown into violence, and often when it has, as in Sudan, Nigeria, Rwanda, Uganda, and Burundi, it can be very clearly related to policies and constitutions constructed and left by colonial powers: majorities (and in some cases minorities) were given great advantage over other groups, and then placed in a constitutional structure which either sustained or worsened the situation (Rothchild and Olorunsola 1983).

Needless to say, the newly independent states rarely possessed a single, obvious, ethnic-cultural identity seen in the social science theory of the time as necessary to undergird statehood; when they did, as in Somalia's case, even nationalistic identities were found to be a mixed blessing. It tied the state together but led to destructive wars later on as the Somali people sought reunification with Somalis in Kenya and Ethiopia. A cohesive political culture which grew from a single dominant "core" nationality (along the Karl Deutsch model) was thus only to be wished for in most cases (Deutsch 1961). A real dilemma for African leaders was the weaknesses of any alternative paradigm explaining how multi-ethnic social relations within a single state could lead to a "modern, nation state" in the Western tradition (Gellar 1972). Thus, African leaders were ambivalent about ethnicity: they could not ignore it, but rarely could they see how to build with it and on it to create a stronger constitutional structure. Neither could they see how to use it to build momentum in social and economic development. Most have alternatively criticized, disparaged, bemoaned and attempted to balance it in national policy (Rothchild 1985). At least two states (Ghana and Gabon) have, at one time or another, "abolished" it! Rarely if ever have they tried to build upon the organizational and normative potential such communities offered. Instead they attempted to synthesize what was essentially an artificial, cross-ethnic identity which would deny rather than build upon these existing identities.

These factors added up to a perplexing picture for new leaders. The smallness, openness and dependency of the economy made it terribly vulnerable to international economic patterns. It lacked diverse production capacities, markets, and capital to insulate itself from external patterns. Its poor integration (duality) meant that "growth" was not always "development," and much wealth produced locally did not connect into linkages stimulating further domestic growth. Its fragmentation made it in some ways highly resilient, as its peoples were able to provide basic subsistence needs for themselves. But, it also made it rigid and unresponsive to national policies, as small proprietors could and did simply opt out of the exchange economy. The last itself became another impetus for centralization, as leaders sought greater control in their frustration with recalcitrant small holders (Lofchie 1985; Hyden 1980; 1983).

Its primate cities were centers of political activity which could support or destroy a regime, as well as centers of the "good life" for those wanting more than what was to be found in rural villages. At the same time, the primate cities were expensive, requiring costly utilities and social services to keep lives there decent and politics peaceful. Still it was unclear how investment in the primate cities would spread out to encourage national development (Huntington 1968; Mabogunje 1980). Finally, the disparity in economic opportunity between the rural subsistence sector and the urban, professional, civil service was dramatic, and government employment was a secondary school or university graduate's first choice; indeed, it was often his only choice as the small, weak, private sector could rarely offer salary, perks, or security comparable (Lofchie 1985; Hyden 1983). Even for those with fewer educational qualifications, the choice between rural employment and government employment was no choice at all: the latter won without a doubt, when jobs could be found at all. Thus urban unemployment grew as rural areas remained stagnant.

When African leaders viewed these circumstances they reacted almost as a body, by concluding that a massive, coordinated and nationally led attack on underdevelopment was necessary to bring progress. Socially fragmented; economically backward, weak, and distorted; and internationally vulnerable, something had to be done, and quickly (Kasfir 1983). While this commitment is clearest in the ringing speeches and writings of such socialists and radicals as Nkrumah, Toure, and Nyerere, as John Saul points out even the African capitalists such as Houphouet of the Ivory Coast were clear on their commitment to state-dominated development. And while Sklar argues that African leaders' identification of capitalism with European colonialism led many to espouse socialism, this may only have reinforced a predictable orientation to centralized development, given the array of challenges and problems the leaders faced (Sklar 1985). As Zolberg observed in 1966:

> The assumption of responsibility for the affairs of the new states produced a shocking awareness of the magnitude of the burdens of government in an underdeveloped country. . . . Not only are the new rulers new at their jobs, but in a fundamental sense their jobs are new as well because of the very different conceptions of government that prevail in a colonial dependency and in a new nation (Zolberg 1966: 39).

The wild card in all this, furthermore, was ethnicity which many national leaders lamented but still accepted as an important political force. Most governments quickly evolved into a sort of ethnic group balancing, "hegemonial" style of government that required careful control at the center to keep all forces and shares of the "pie" in balance (Zolberg 1966; Rothchild 1985; Rothchild and Olorunsola 1983). As Jackson and Rosberg noted:

> Leaders of the newly independent states had high expectations of themselves, had promised much to their populations, and knew how large a task lay before them. Indeed, the very process of politicization that occurred before independence made that task even more difficult, as ethnic identifications, regional insecurities, and other internal fissures had usually been intensified during the independence struggle (Jackson and Rosberg 1982: 51).

Finally, the international environment of the newly independent states tended to emphasize again their need to speak with a single voice in national policy. International organizations and donor nations were prepared to offer aid to the new states, but required host governments to enter complex, long-term agreements to be eligible for this assistance. Complex management, disbursement, repayment, and co-financing agreements were the norm to implement donor projects. The "project by project" approach to international assistance itself tended to fragment the impact of development assistance, as it simultaneously called forth ever more centralized managerial effort by the recipient nations and made that very management more difficult given the number and diversity of donors! Donors also generally expected complex planning and project analysis on the part of recipient states, further drawing on and concentrating public sector management resources (Wunsch 1986; Moris 1981; Mickelwait 1978).

Furthermore, if private business corporations were willing to accept less supervision from the new governments, the governments' natural concern over the terms and implementation of international economic ventures would itself incline them to seek some such supervision. Questions of taxation, profit repatriation, personnel status, co-ventureship, security of investment, real and other property rights required answers.

Finally, the international arena was also important in the intellectual biases it carried to the new regimes. The 1960s was an era when capital-intensive, technologically oriented agriculture; urbanization; industrialization; and bureaucratic rationality, were the dominant development models (Owens and Shaw 1972). The American agricultural-technological model and the progressives' faith in impartial management technology (planning, hierarchy, management by objective, PPB, civil service professionalization, concentrated authority, job specialization, and other elements of the Weberian model) were the programmatic and intellectual biases of the donor institutions and nations. Regardless of the problem, it was likely that these would be ingredients of the prescription. Indeed, even alternative models from the Eastern, Marxist nations carried managerial rationality and centralizing assumptions in both political and economic areas. Leninism is, if anything, a rationality and blueprint for political centralization, while Stalinist economic practice pushes economic centralization perhaps as far as is humanly possible (Lindblom 1977; Gellar 1972).

Summary and Conclusions

In this chapter we have explored those characteristics of Africa which I believe were critical in leading to highly centralized national governance. I have emphasized attitudes and assumptions, the institutional features, and the environmental characteristics that we believe worked together to bring forth highly centralized regimes. Colonialism, the international environment, and domestic socioeconomic conditions were the most important sources of these factors. Key factors included the formation of Westernized and Westernizing literary, elite groups which inherited state apparatus at independence; a bureaucracy organized on highly centralized, hierarchical and directive principles; seriously weakened traditional institutions and still young modern structures of local self-government; severe economic problems; potentially serious social fragmentation; an intellectual climate in both Eastern-Marxist and Western states which emphasized bureaucratic rationality and national planning; and international opportunities and dangers which seemed to require centralized national decision making.

These ideal and material factors were soon to be focused on "new" parliamentary and presidential constitutions—ones not rooted in domestic philosophy, experience, or institutions. Leaders, sometimes described as "inheritance elites," believed they had to take charge at the center, and from the center establish their authority to govern, to solve pressing economic problems, and to maintain (or sometimes attain) national unity. Not least of all they had to protect the rather substantial personal or class prize that the state had become (Gellar 1972). Chapter 3 will turn to this process in some detail.

Notes

1. Although my discussion here will dwell mostly on French and British colonial systems, the Belgian and Portuguese systems are generally more extreme cases of the same general tendencies, so the logic still applies.

2. Indeed, Michael Crowder notes that the consolidation of British colonial administration led to the "disinheritance" of educated Africans from significant occupational or political opportunities and roles they had held hitherto (Crowder 1968: 199).

3. This point is particularly well brought out by Michael Crowder in his *West Africa Under Colonial Rule*. He notes that most African pre-colonial societies were organized politically around constitutions which balanced power between ruler and population, much the way we discussed the subject in Chapter 1. However, "Indirect Rule" fundamentally destroyed these constitutional relations. The *Gold Coast Leader* criticized the Native Jurisdiction Ordinance for this in 1927, noting "The time is coming when a chief once installed will sit firmly on the neck of the people, like the old man of the sea, and rule them in his own way without any lawful means of getting rid of him." Crowder emphasized the decentralized political structure of traditional Akan society and notes, "It was thus particularly galling for the educated elite to see the authority of the chiefs strengthened by the colonial authorities to such an extent that even the traditional sanction of destoolment by the people now lost its force, since Government had to uphold it" (Crowder 1968: 465). It is absolutely critical to see how social infrastructure can be destroyed, or at least seriously damaged, just as much by "support" and "strengthening" as it can be by "opposition" and "abolishing" when another political level without popular accountability becomes involved: it loses its legitimacy and therefore the moral force behind its rules.

References

Ajayi, J.F.A., and Michael Crowder. "West Africa 1919–1939: The Colonial Situation." In *History of West Africa,* edited by J.F.A. Ajayi and Michael Crowder, Vol. II, 514–541. London: Longman, 1974.

Aluko, Olajide. "Politics of Decolonisation in British West Africa, 1945–1960." *History of West Africa,* Vol. II (1974): 622–663. London: Longman, 1974.

Austen, Ralph A. "Varieties of Trusteeship: African Territories Under British and French Mandate, 1919–1939." In *France and Britain in Africa: Imperial Rivalry and Colonial Rule,* edited by Prosser Gifford and William R. Lewis, 515–542. New Haven, CN: Yale, 1971.

Bates, Robert H. *Markets and States in Tropical Africa: The Political Basis of Agricultural Policies.* Berkeley: University of California Press, 1981.

Cohen, Abner. *Custom and Politics in Urban Africa: A Study of Hausa Migrants in Yoruba Towns.* Berkeley: University of California Press, 1969.

Cohen, Michael. *Urban Policy and Political Conflict in Africa: A Study of the Ivory Coast.* Chicago: University of Chicago Press, 1971.

Crowder, Michael. *West Africa Under Colonial Rule.* London: Hutchinson, 1968.

Crowder, Michael, and D. Cruise O'Brien. "French West Africa, 1945–1960." In *History of West Africa,* Vol. II, edited by J.F.A. Ajayi and Michael Crowder, 664–699. London: Longman, 1974.

Deschamps, Hubert. "French Colonial Policy in Tropical Africa Between the Two World Wars." In *France and Britain in Africa: Imperial Rivalry and Colonial Rule,* edited by Prosser Gifford and William R. Lewis, 593–570. New Haven, Conn.: Yale, 1971.

Deutsch, Karl W. "Social Mobilization and Political Development." *American Political Science Review* 55 (September 1961): 493–514.

Ekeh, Peter. *Colonialism and Social Structure.* An Inaugural Lecture delivered at the University of Ibadan, June 5, 1980. Ibadan, Nigeria: University of Ibadan, 1980.

Epstein, A.L. *Politics in an Urban African Community.* Manchester: Manchester University Press, 1958.

Fieldhouse, David K. "The Economic Exploitation of Africa: Some British and French Comparisons." In *France and Britain in Africa: Imperial Rivalry and Colonial Rule,* edited by Prosser Gifford and William R. Lewis, 593–662. New Haven, Conn.: Yale, 1971.

Gellar, Sheldon. *State-Building and Nation-Building in West Africa.* Bloomington, Indiana: International Development Research Center, Indiana University, 1972.

Huessler, Robert. "British Rule in Africa." In *France and Britain in Africa: Imperial Rivalry and Colonial Rule,* edited by Prosser Gifford and William R. Lewis, 571–593. New Haven, Conn.: Yale, 1971.

Huntington, S.P. *Political Order in Changing Societies.* New Haven, Conn.: Yale University Press, 1968.

Hyden, Goran. *Beyond Ujamaa in Tanzania.* Berkeley: University of California Press, 1980.

———. *No Shortcuts to Progress: African Development Management in Perspective.* Berkeley: University of California Press, 1983.

Jackson, Robert, and Carl Rosberg. *Personal Rule in Black Africa: Prince, Autocrat, Prophet, Tyrant.* Berkeley: University of California Press, 1982.

Johnson, G. Wesley. "African Political Activity in French West Africa, 1900–1940." In *History of West Africa,* edited by J.F.A. Ajayi and Michael Crowder, 542–567. London: Longman 1974.

Jones, G.I. "Changing Leadership in Eastern Nigeria: Before, During and After the Colonial Period." In *Politics in Leadership: A Comparative Perspective,* edited by W.A. Shack and P.S. Cohen. Oxford: Clarendon Press, 1979.

Kasfir, Nelson. "Designs and Dilemmas: An Overview." In *Local Government in the Third World,* edited by P. Mawhood, 25–48. Chichester: John Wiley, 1983.

Kirk-Green, A.H.M. "The New African Administrator." *Journal of Modern African Studies* X (1) (1972).

Leonard, David. *Rural Administration in Kenya.* Nairobi: East African Literature Bureau, 1973.

———. *Reaching the Peasant Farmer: Organization Theory and Practice in Kenya.* Chicago: University of Chicago Press, 1977.

Lindblom, Charles. *Politics and Markets: The World's Political-Economic Systems.* New York: Basic Books, 1977.

Little, Kenneth. *West African Urbanization: A Study of Voluntary Association in Social Change.* Cambridge: Cambridge University Press, 1966.

Lofchie, Michael F. "The Roots of Economic Crisis in Tanzania." *Current History* 84 (501) (1985): 159–184.

Lugard, Lord Frederick J.D. *The Dual Mandate in British Tropical Africa.* Edinburgh, 1922.

Mabogunje, A.L. *The Development Process: A Spatial Perspective.* London: Hutchinson Press, 1980.

Mazrui, Ali. "Francophone Nations and English-Speaking States: Imperial Ethnicity and African Political Formations." In *State Versus Ethnic Claims: African Policy Dilemmas,* edited by D. Rothchild and V. Olrunsola, 25–43. Boulder, Colorado: Westview Press, 1983.

Melson, Robert, and Howard Wolpe. "Modernization and the Politics of Communalism: A Theoretical Perspective." *American Political Science Review,* LXIV (4) (1970): 1112–1130.

Mickelwait, Donald, et al. *The New Directions Mandate: Studies in Project Design, Approval and Implementation.* (revised). Washington, D.C.: Development Alternatives Incorporated, 1978.

Moris, J. "The Transferability of the Western Management Tradition into the Public Service Sectors: An East African Perspective." In *Education and Training for Public Sector Management in Developing Countries.* New York: The Ford Foundation, 1977.

———. *Managing Induced Rural Development.* Bloomington, Indiana: International Development Institute, Indiana University, 1981.

Obichere, Boniface. "The African Factor in the Establishment of French Authority in West Africa, 1880–1900." In *France and Britain in Africa: Imperial Rivalry and Colonial Rule,* edited by Prosser Gifford and William R. Lewis, 433–490. New Haven, Conn.: Yale, 1971.

Odell, Malcolm J., Jr. "Local Government: Traditional and Modern Roles of the Village Kgotla." In *The Evolution of Modern Botswana,* edited by Louis A. Picard. Lincoln: University of Nebraska Press, 1985.

Owens, E., and R. Shaw. *Development Reconsidered: Bridging the Gap Between Government and the People.* Lexington, Mass.: Lexington Books, 1972.

Rothchild, Donald. "State-Ethnic Relations in Middle Africa." In *African Independence: The First Twenty-Five Years,* edited by G.M. Carter and P. O'Meara, 71–96. Bloomington, Indiana: Indiana University Press, 1985.

——— and V. Olorunsola, eds. *State Versus Ethnic Claims: African Policy Dilemmas.* Boulder, Colorado: Westview Press, 1983.

Rubin, L., and B. Weinstein. *Introduction to African Politics: A Continental Approach.* 2nd Edition. New York: Praeger, 1977.

Sklar, Richard. "The Colonial Imprint on African Political Thought." In *African Independence: The First Twenty-Five Years,* edited by Gwendolen M. Carter and Patrick O'Meara, 1–30. Bloomington, Indiana: Indiana University Press, 1985.

Smock, Audrey. *Ibo Politics: The Role of Ethnic Unions in Eastern Nigeria.* Cambridge, Mass.: Harvard University Press, 1971.

Thomson, James T., David H. Feeny, and Ronald Oakerson. "Institutional Dynamics: Evolution and Dissolution of Common Property." *Proceedings of the Conference on Common Property Resource Management.* Washington, D.C.: National Academy Press, 1986: 391–424.

Tordoff, William, ed. *Government and Politics in Africa.* Bloomington, Ind.: Indiana University Press, 1985.

Webster, J.B. "Political Activity in British West Africa, 1900–1940." In *History of West Africa, Vol. II,* edited by J.F.A. Ajayi and Michael Crowder, 568–595. London: Longman, 1974.

World Bank. *Accelerated Development in Sub-Saharan Africa.* Washington, D.C.: World Bank, 1981.

Wunsch, James. "Strengthening Rural Development Management Through International Assistance Projects." *Public Administration and Development* 3 (1983): 239–263.

———. "Administering Rural Development: Have Goals Outreached Organizational Capacity?" *Public Administration and Development* 6 (1986): 287–308.

Zolberg, A. *Creating Political Order: The Party-States of West Africa.* Chicago: Rand McNally, 1966.

3

Centralization and Development in Post-Independence Africa

James S. Wunsch

Introduction

Chapter 2 discussed the mixed heritage colonialism left for Africa's independence leaders. This chapter will review the paradigm with which they interpreted their goals in the light of this heritage, the strategies they developed to pursue these goals, and how these strategies contributed to the political instability, economic failures, and social disappointments too typical of contemporary Africa.

Statism and Centralization in Africa

Nearly all independent African states have pursued a largely statist and centralized strategy of economic and political development during the past thirty years. While extent of implementation of this strategy obviously varies among them, the general direction of the strategy has been shared. Leaders as diverse as Houphouet-Boigney of the Ivory Coast, Nkrumah of Ghana, Toure of Guinea, Kenyatta of Kenya and Nyerere of Tanzania early on committed themselves to an essentially statist approach to development. For most African states, it is only recently that this strategy has slowed.

Sekou Toure, for example, justified the single-party system of Guinea by its supposed ability to rise above the individualism, regionalism, ethnicity, and class-orientation which had "corrupted" the territorial assemblies from 1945–1955, and stifled economic growth by the mass of people. He wrote:

> These anti-democratic, anti-popular trends of parliamentary life were the direct result of the importation into our countries of the bourgeois regime and of French political customs. . . . The Democratic Party of Guinea was to put a final end to these practices which prejudiced the political and moral evolution of the people and prevented the establishment of sound foundations

for our nation. Instead of electoral mystification and methods which resulted in imposing unpopular representatives, the P.D.G. established the rule of free and judicious choice by the people of their representatives in law-making bodies at all levels (Markovitz 1970: 218–219).

The P.D.G., Toure emphasized, was the mechanism by which the people would rise above sub-national and divisive loyalties, and being thus united would:

> . . . choose their representatives by consciously mobilizing themselves in the rank and file of a national party, which focused their activities on the implementation of one program, aimed at happiness for one and all, wide democratic progress, effective emancipation of our society, and full development of the human person (Markovitz 1970: 218–219).

Julius Nyerere (1970) echoed these words a few years later: "To build and maintain socialism it is essential that all the major means of production and exchange in the nation are controlled and owned by the peasants through the machinery of their Government and their cooperatives. Further, it is essential that the ruling Party should be a Party of peasants and workers." His concern with unity was equally clear:

> TANU is involved in a war against poverty and oppression in our country; this struggle is aimed at moving the People of Tanzania (and the people of Africa as a whole) from a state of poverty to a state of prosperity. . . . We have been oppressed a great deal, we have been exploited a great deal and we have been disregarded a great deal. It is our weakness which has led to our being oppressed, exploited and disregarded. We now intend to bring about a revolution which will ensure that we are never again victims of these things (Markovitz 1970: 267–268).

Union through the single party, TANU, was the necessary prerequisite to ending these weaknesses.

The fundamental presupposition lying beneath this strategic orientation was that a strong central government was regarded as essential to the national unity and modernization of African societies. That this presupposition was made should not be overly surprising: it was consistent with the structure and habits of the colonial-administrative state, it was selected in an era when both Eastern and Western models of development emphasized central direction and planning, it complemented nicely the expectations of international assistance organizations for "rational" planning, management, and negotiation of assistance programs, it emphasized the relatively stronger *juridical* claim to international recognition above the somewhat tenuous *de facto* reality of sovereignty, it was encouraged by the hierarchical and centralist leaning of post-enlightenment rationalism in the West, and it provided an apparently possible solution for the real challenges African leaders faced. As Aristide Zolberg put it in 1966:

Strains arise not only because the new rulers adopt more burdensome goals and perceive problems differently, but also because new problems indeed arise around the time of independence. . . . It may even appear that the country is less united at the time of independence than it was a decade earlier. . . . There is an increased awareness of the importance of the central authorities, and hence more demands are directed at them. . . . The opportunity to participate in politics and administration has opened up the floodgates of claimants. At the same time, with all these new burdens, governments must shoulder the added expenses of sovereignty and accomplish all this with a relatively new and inexperienced civil service. At worst, precisely when they become aware of how much is to be done, the leaders are like an executive who frantically pushes the battery of buttons on his desk only to discover that the wiring is non-existent (Zolberg 1966: 41).

The centralized state was an apparent solution to many of these challenges.

Africa is vast and diverse, composed as it is of over fifty independent states encompassing many different peoples, facing radically varying geographic problems and advantages, drawing from four major colonial heritages, and drawing from a variety of philosophical-ideological schools. Given all this it is all the more remarkable that states as diverse as Kenya (capitalist, market, anglophone, single-ethnic dominant, industrializing, prospering, a settler-territory), Ghana (radical, statist, anglophone, single-ethnic dominant, largely agricultural, poor, non-settler), Ivory Coast (capitalist, market, francophone, ethnically fragmented, industrializing, prospering, non-settler territory), Tanzania (radical, statist, anglophone, fragmented ethnically, agricultural, poor, largely non-settler), Mali (radical, statist, francophone, agricultural, poor, non-settler), and many other states would perceive the world through so similar a paradigm, and pursue so similar a set of strategies. In fact, with remarkable consistency, though varying intensity of implementation, the core presupposition of the "centralized state" has led to five complementary strategies. These are:

- replacement of competitive politics by one or no-party systems ostensibly dedicated to national unity;
- reliance upon unified bureaucratic structures exclusively accountable to the central government to define, organize, and manage the production of public goods and services along lines determined *at all levels* by a "national plan";
- no legitimate significant role to be allowed for local government, including traditional, ethnically related groups as well as modern institutions of true local government;
- executive authority to be maximized at the expense of such other institutions as the legislature, judiciary, regional governments, and press and private organizations;
- and the national budget to be regarded as the primary source of funding for the development agenda, and to be raised out of the largest economic sectors: either agriculture or mineral extraction.

Our purpose in this chapter is to explore the impact of these strategies on African politics, economics, and society in the post-independence era. In the clearest cases where this logic was pushed to extremes, these strategies meant that development was seen as a process of *national* consolidation, where unity of purpose around the clearly paramount goal of economic growth and political cohesion would preempt or displace irrelevant or subversive contention over strategy. Technically based, rational and efficient decision making would replace narrow, uninformed, or selfish contention over tactics. A modernizing, honest (and incorruptible), and able elite would have the technical capacity to conceptualize and manage a developed economy and thereby eliminate the dangers of market error, the excesses of capitalism and the danger of neo-colonialism from hobbling the economy. National identities and loyalties would supplant "parochial" and narrow ones, and marshalling all resources in an already obvious and accepted program of action would be the greatest prerequisite for development. Ends were obvious, tactics were technical questions, and will and discipline were the primary ingredients required for economic development and political capacity to be realized.

What are the implications of these strategies for African political and economic life? Do they help explain Africa's recent disappointments?

Centralist Policies and Their Implications

We do not argue that all events in post-independence Africa can be understood by analyzing the implications of these strategies. Similarly, we explicitly acknowledge that Africa's many states have "walked" varying distances down these paths. Our purpose here is first analytical and theoretical, and second to draw a broad picture into which various states may be differently placed. Nonetheless, we do believe that this analysis can make an important portion of post-independence politics intelligible, particularly among the "outliers" of the empirical world. In this section of the chapter we will therefore review the consequences of acting upon these five corollary presuppositions.

Political Parties

We have suggested that the majority of African leaders began their development tasks at independence with a primary presupposition: that a strong and unified state was necessarily the primary actor in development. As a consequence of this presupposition, African leaders were inclined toward single- or no-party regimes in order to diminish political conflict and enhance support for national unity around the new leadership. In fact, most independent regimes did move rather quickly to *de jure* or *de facto* single-party systems. Today the only functioning multi-party systems to be found in Africa are in Senegal, Gambia, Mauritania, Botswana, Zimbabwe, and Nigeria (with the last currently suspended under military rule, and Zimbabwe's threatened by leadership promises to move to a single-party state). Most liberal, multi-party democracies became at least *de facto* single-party states or fell to military coups before the end of the 1960s.

The implications of this move to single-party systems depends in some measure on one's assumptions about the extent, nature, and significance of social diversity in independent Africa. It also depends on how one understands political legitimacy to be granted to one set of actors by a body of people. Finally, it varies with ones understanding of development as a more or less technical process versus a political process.

If one sees Africa's social diversity as either trivial or ephemeral, a single-party system has less worrisome implications than if such diversity is understood to be a fundamental aspect of African life, one likely to be relevant to public decision making. Similarly, if the public is willing to grant legitimacy to its rulers on grounds of the latter's technical or ideological superiority, then a single-party system has less disconcerting implications than if the public expects a broad public debate and discussion regarding the nature of the commonweal as prerequisites for granting legitimacy. Finally, if development decision making and implementation are essentially technical rather than political processes, then again single-party systems may be expected to work better than if development is a more ambiguous, debated and subjective process. With these assumptions, one would expect single-party systems to operate well; one would be baffled should they not.

If instead, social diversity is a genuine and significant element of the African social reality, then single parties may be expected to be fragmented, factionalized and ineffective tools of government. Also, if indeed legitimacy is not granted to a ruling cadre on ideological or technical grounds, we may expect to find some parties becoming repressive and others turning to distributional exchanges in order to generate support. In neither case will a debate about the common good and collective purposes be likely to develop. Finally, if development policy making and implementation are not merely technical exercises, but tasks in which debatable and incompletely understood strategies are implemented by equally debatable and incompletely understood tactics, then single-party systems may be expected to be ineffective in leading the development process. The absence of institutionalized debate may be expected to lead to slower reporting of error, slower development of alternative approaches to development, and slower change in strategies.

Africa is diverse. Certainly no simple picture appears when considering the last two to three decades. Nonetheless, there are disturbing signs regarding all three of these propositions that single-party systems have been found wanting.

The parties' search for legitimacy and support, and their attempts to deal with national diversity suggests that some of the worrisome implications of centralization have been proven true. Nowhere can one point to a case where the leadership's claims for legitimacy were easily or widely accepted much beyond the early years. Leadership responses have varied, but have included most frequently "wheeling-and-dealing" processes to co-opt dissenters; carrot-stick strategies including personal and regional political isolation, personal persecution, and occasional violence; recourse to ideological claims coupled with political imprisonment; and rare instances of severe and wide-spread oppression and violence. Nowhere did popular legitimacy and national unity develop behind and beneath the single-party system. From Ghana to Kenya, from Ivory Coast to Tanzania, from the single-party dominant regions of the first Nigerian Republic to Zambia, these patterns can be seen (Rothchild 1985a; 1985b; Sklar 1985).

Almost everywhere in post-independence Africa, a combination of distributional and coercive politics was pursued to weaken opposition parties and draw legislators and other leaders "across the aisle" into the majority party. Ghana, Kenya, Ivory Coast, and Nigeria provide particularly clear cases of this (Zolberg 1966; Schwarz 1968; Leys 1975). Junior Ministries with attendant perquisites, appointments to parastatal corporation boards, and liberal servings of benefits for constituencies were used to precipitate and cement these alliances. Various other strategies were also employed to encourage the process, including manipulating the electoral system, intimidating opposition candidates, co-opting members of the opposition, and occasionally detaining, harassing, and exiling stubborn opponents.

Elections, for example, were widely manipulated to strengthen control by the majority party. In Ivory Coast, PDCI election lists were not made public until hours before the filing deadlines. As most candidates preferred to run under party approval than outside it, little time remained for an unsuccessful candidate to explore his chances as an opposition candidate without destroying his PDCI standing (Zolberg 1966: 79–80). Shrinking the number of constituencies and using multi-member slates for each district was another method used to multiply the power of a majority party. Guinea, Senegal, Mali, and Ivory Coast used this approach.

Intimidation of opposition members or candidates was used to varying though uncertain degrees. Clearly, Ghanaian and Nigerian elections were so marred in the early 1960s, while Liberia in recent years has followed suit. In Tanzania, members of the minority party were threatened with loss of jobs and had public meetings banned (Jackson and Rosberg 1982). Similar actions occurred in Cameroon (Johnson 1970). In some cases murder of dissident leaders may have also occurred (Bates 1981).

To keep this in perspective, however, one must bear in mind that co-optation was almost always the preferred strategy to build a single party, and that in almost every African state "members of the opposition" were welcomed into the majority party. Imprisonment, murder, and exile were extreme measures, reserved for the most stubborn and effective opponents. Nonetheless, in many cases, among them Ghana (Ashanti), Nigeria (all regions pre-1966), Sudan (south), Ethiopia, Kenya (non-Kikyu), Uganda (Buganda), Zaire (Shaba), Angola (Ovimbundu), Zimbabwe (Shona), and others, key political divisions occurred nonetheless on regional and/or ethnic grounds, and were suppressed by force, or muted by buying-off and/

or destroying key leaders. The issues that underlay these divisions were never really resolved, and single-party regimes became either arbitrary and authoritarian, or flaccid and impotent. At times, they became sources of subversion and conspiracy. By 1966, Zolberg reports that in West Africa these single parties were largely politically impotent and irrelevant as a result of this process. They were replaced by an administrative state which worked primarily to distribute benefits to the faithful and gather resources from the rural areas (Zolberg 1966; Bates 1981).

The scope of tolerable public debate and discussion tended to narrow with this process. Public roles formerly legitimate for unions, producer associations, regional and religious leaders, the press and other private interests and groupings were closed off. These events were particularly visible in Ghana, Tanzania, Kenya, and Zambia, with the vital and lively late-colonial public lives of these institutions slowly stifled in the interests of "unity" and "harmony" (Sklar 1985). Governmental leaders often pressured these groups and their leaders to close down open political debate on public questions. In most states, once free and active trade unions and agricultural producers' cooperatives were co-opted, stripped of authority, or banned. Most newspapers and all radio and TV stations, furthermore, are government owned and/or managed. Few African newspapers now function as much more than bland digests of routine events. Even those few, in such states as Kenya, Nigeria, and Zimbabwe, function under often unspoken limits, whose violation has led to serious consequences for the media and its personnel (Austin 1983). In Kenya, beneath and surrounding the apparently lively and open public political debate, there have been unspoken but definite limits as to what the government would tolerate, and harsh punishments for those who went too far:

A limited democracy? Perhaps. There was, however, only one party, and those who tried to challenge its decisions were harshly treated. There was always a sinister end to the seesaw of politics. Opponents of the regime felt the heavy hand of a government which barred Odinga from standing for election, threatened with closure papers like *The Nation* when it transgressed some invisible boundary of tolerance, and dealt peremptorily with university teachers, students, doctors, and lawyers when they tried to stand out against the party. The last years of Kenyatta's rule were marred not only by bomb explosions in Nairobi and Mombassa but political murders, including the death in 1975 of J. M. Kariuki, a junior minister and former Mau Mau detainee, who had tried to champion the rights of the ordinary citizen against the political elite. Nor were members of parliament immune from government displeasure: a number were detained under presidential order, among them the Deputy Speaker (Austin 1984: 66).

In the most ideologically radical countries, severe violence was accepted as the price to be paid for single party dominance. For example, in Ethiopia today and in Toure's Guinea in the past there was ruthless suppression of those elite members deviating even slightly from the dominant leader's views (Liebenow 1986). According to one estimate, Toure had several hundred thousand supposed opponents killed, including 35 close associates and cabinet members. Recently, in Ethiopia all but one of the four political movements which participated in the joint civilian front established in 1977 were suppressed by the Ethiopian Dergue. Even in Tanzania, for example, where a more humanistic style of socialism might be expected to have moderated policy, Nyerere became convinced that persuasion and voluntarism would leave his Ujamaa villagization program languishing for an indefinite period of time. He accelerated its implementation radically during the late 1970s with severe consequences (Lofchie 1985a; 1985b; Hyden 1983). In this and other cases, dissent was viewed at best as mistaken and wrong-headed. At worst, and in the most ideological regimes, it has been regarded as verging upon treason or reflecting so defective a view of ideology that it would justify utterly disqualifying the dissenter from legitimate participation in the councils of government (Rothchild 1985b). Diversity, it would seem, did not fade away under single-party leadership; nor was legitimacy as easily given by the people as it was claimed by the leadership.

Single parties have similarly been found largely inadequate to the development task. While the sources of Africa's developmental problems are manifold, including international trading patterns and natural calamities, few African states have demonstrated sufficient flexibility in responding to changing circumstances and the world's changing understanding of development. In the face of the collapsing agricultural sector and the patent failure of the parastatal-urban-industrial development strategy in virtually all African countries by the early 1970s, African governments continued to hold to the same strategy with the same tactics until the crisis situation of the 1980s and international organizations forced choice upon many. The gradual reduction of the parastatal sector in Senegal and Nigeria, the development of the second tier foreign exchange system in Nigeria, the liberalization of agricultural prices in Ghana, are late but positive moves which have marked significant progress in the economies of each of these states. It is notable, however, that these reforms usually came only after pressure by external institutions, and thus did not reflect local interests, perspectives, or knowledge, and probably were likely to be more disruptive to local economies than they would have been were they a product of a domestic political process (Lofchie 1985a).

As African governments centralized by reducing and sometimes even eliminating the pluralism of groups, organizations and interests which had developed during the nationalist, anti-colonial era, they succeeded in removing actual and potential competitors from their political space. Criticism, organizational bases for opponents, passive and active resistance to policies and programs, strikes, and the like were accordingly reduced. Regimes felt more secure and for the time being were probably more likely to see their rule unchallenged.

However, due to the paucity of debate concerning objectives and strategies, in many states ill-founded or badly implemented policies, programs, and projects happened with increasing frequency. In extreme cases, monistic regimes found themselves without alternative structures to communicate information on problems, to reinterpret events, to develop alternatives, or to act as allies when the regime came under pressure. In a pluralistic but integrated system, even opponents of the day, the person, the policy, the program, etc., develop an interest in sustaining regimes into which they are integrated, if only to replace the governing cadre. When organizational pluralism is eradicated, differing understandings of the common good, needs, and interests remain. What *has* been destroyed is a cybernetic and negotiating structure through which public debate on leadership and policy could occur, criticism could be articulated, policy and program alternatives could be aired and developed, and diversity could be recognized, accorded a legitimate role, and integrated into the regime without bribery or suppression. Furthermore, when independent but parallel institutional structures are eliminated, regimes become terribly vulnerable to the breakdown of what "monocultural" institutions are left. Like a forest of one species, once breakdown occurs in the face of unexpected stress, there are no backup systems or resources to carry on the functions (Hyden n.d.). Ghana, Guinea, Liberia, Sudan, and Tanzania seem to be diverse examples of this process. Political decisions thus led to economic stagnation.

Bureaucracy and Planning

Bureaucracy is an attempt to routinize the application of already-determined solutions to already-established and readily perceived categories of problems. Such an organizational recipe presumes that several characteristics are met by the task at hand. First, known solutions must exist for the problems. A body of theory pertinent to the task must exist, be understood, and be applicable to various forms in which the problems may appear in order for reliable solutions to be determined and prescribed. Second, the facts which describe given cases must be ascertainable if the responsible official is to be able to adopt the appropriate organizational response. Third, given that most problems require sustained attention and coordinated action, reliable communication and management systems must exist to support and sustain complex organizational responses.

National planning, as it has been generally understood in Africa, has been the process by which the many bureaucracies have ostensibly been linked with one another to produce a coordinated, synergetic development program. It presumes the prerequisites of bureaucratic operation have been met, that parallel understandings of national development exist, and that comparable national analytical and managerial capacities also exist.

Virtually all public business in Africa is carried out through the instrument of the hierarchical, centralized bureaucracy. Local governments are essentially local administrative authorities, hired, paid, evaluated and directed by superiors in the central government. What true local government actually exists has extremely limited powers to set and collect revenues, hire personnel, let contracts and pass ordinances (Mawhood 1983). Furthermore, in most African states, all bureaucratic decisions and programs are to emerge from the "national plan." However, the prerequisites discussed above for bureaucratic and development planning work in Africa rarely exist. Instead, there is broad disagreement as to the very nature of the problem of underdevelopment; disagreement as to the key characteristics of the clients whom administrators are attempting to reach; highly uncertain reliability, validity, and meaning in what little data there are to describe and analyze the "target" groups; and weak communication and management systems (Moris 1981). Paradigms and facts are in severe dispute, and as Robert Chambers persuasively argues, centralized bureaucracies have been even more likely to err as analytical actors than they have been as operational actors, given their deep cultural, climatic, class, urban, and other biases (Chambers 1983). Finally, nationally planning authorities generally have great nominal authority but limited resources, operational responsibilities or power (Hyden 1983).

When Africa's high level of bureaucratic centralization is considered along with the apparent absence of the prerequisites for effective bureaucracy, serious questions of performance must be raised. Whether administrative structures will be able to coherently manage themselves, follow through on tasks and responsibilities, adapt to varying and changing environments, question and modify working hypotheses and theories, avoid excessive coercion, and avoid premature programming and policy rigidity, are real issues in this environment (Landau 1969; 1979).

Research which I conducted on third world development projects confirms this. In an analysis of fifteen centrally managed rural development projects, including major development projects in Ghana, Upper Volta and Sudan, this research found serious disfunction between the models utilized to design, interpret and direct projects by their centrally based managers and apparent operational realities in the field; goal conflict among the various bureaucracies and other parties active and involved in the project; and serious problems of technical complexity. These overwhelmed all but one project, and that project was organized along decentralized and non-blueprint lines (Wunsch 1986). Problems of passing detailed and often idiosyncratic information up tall hierarchies, assuring that agreements among diverse participants made at one level actually "stick" at subordinate levels, and bargaining through working arrangements among key actors at several layers are always severe (Pressman and Wildavsky 1973). When these perhaps chronic problems of complex and "tall" administrative systems were confounded by harsh and spartan environments, and by complex and poorly understood tasks, project and plan failure were the norm.

When the African administrator's work has gone beyond service delivery and has been aimed at modifying public behavior in support of development, hierarchy and central direction have again been real liabilities to effective performance (Thomson 1981; Odell 1985). In cases where innovation and risktaking were to be encouraged, where local effort to provide public goods was needed, or common pool resource regulation was required,

African bureaucracies have been generally ineffective (Wunsch 1986; Moris 1981). Detailed knowledge of local conditions is necessary to control common pool resource problems. Credible enforcement agencies are also required (Thomson 1981). Similar problems are related to the provision of public goods (Wunsch 1986). Instead, however, detailed knowledge and effective enforcement are both often lacking in Africa; the first because of the hierarchical and centralized nature of the bureaucracy; the second because the cost of reaching far enough into the rural areas to provide such enforcement is so high (Thomson 1981; BOSAT 1987). Unreliable performance has turned many innovation-risk involved programs into "markets of lemons" for rural Africa (Popkin 1981; Hyden 1980). The dependence of service delivery bureaucracies upon other administrative agencies for release of funds, import permits, delivery of goods, etc., has meant that critical inputs needed at critical times (i.e., the crop cycle) have not arrived. Crops have failed or rotted in the countryside for lack of fertilizer or transport, and draft animals have died for lack of medicine, ruining small-holder agriculturalists who took loans as part of comprehensive development programs (Moris 1981; Wunsch 1986; Hyden 1980).

Bureaucratic and plan inflexibility has often been the cause of program failure because of the inappropriateness of regional or even national common schedules of assistance, instructions on input usage, repayment rates, etc., at the local level (Hyden 1980; 1983). To surmount this, programs have at times been "adapted" in the field by creative and energetic program officers. However, when those personnel are eventually transferred, what they laboriously constructed is found to be ephemeral in practice (Moris 1981). Once again, farmers find the central bureaucracy to be an unreliable and sometimes dangerous partner in their struggle for survival. Since the most energetic bureaucrats seem to be at or near retirement age, and they have found it impossible to institutionalize such adaptations, the tendency to try such schemes seems gradually to be fading out of the civil service (Moris 1981).

Finally, because centralized planners needed to develop broad, single, organizationally acceptable solutions to problems, dictated in reality as much or more by the imperatives of organizational coherence than technical considerations, programs and projects have all too frequently developed which are bland, broad, blueprinted, and critically flawed from inception (Mickelwait 1978). Because their operation has depended on the consent and support of numerous officials whose personal goals are frequently only loosely related to the purposive rationality of the organization, vast resources have been spent and much technical effectiveness is blurred building and rebuilding coalitions necessary to carry forth with any project at all (Leonard 1986). Additionally, because of the political weakness of clients (never "constituents") and field personnel, programs are rarely designed to fit local needs, wants, experiences or conditions (Leonard 1977). Furthermore, program and project managerial personnel have generally dumped a plethora of miscellaneous administrative tasks and problems on the lowest personnel without regard for their ability to perform these tasks and do their service delivery functions (Moris 1981). Neither do the superiors pay much attention to the impact of these responsibilities upon the relationship among field personnel and between field personnel and client. A typical solution to program criticism from domestic or external sources is to lay educative, regulative, coercive, and information gathering responsibilities and tasks upon the same field personnel, usually leading to failure in all areas (Moris 1981; Wunsch 1984). Since their superiors are also their only constituents, and the recipients of programs have little but a passive role to fill, it cannot be surprising that the political economy of the center squeezes out virtually all input from the field (Wunsch 1988).

Long-range problems have developed from these situations, particularly in implementing plans made distant in time and space from rural realities.

Where national leaders were dogmatic on implementing comprehensive programs, as Tanzanian leaders were during the late 1970s regarding Uja-maa villagization, bureaucrats have been reduced to authoritarian and coercive methods of getting compliance (Hyden 1983; Lofchie 1985a; 1985b). Lacking any positive relationship with the bulk of citizens with which they might bargain, like power-wielders elsewhere they find they are relatively "powerless" short of coercion (Muir 1977). Coercion itself, however, is a counter-productive tool, as it damages or destroys any trust and forbearance which might have existed between people and government, can seriously undermine social order, and leads to economic decline and popular political withdrawal. In fact, Lofchie illustrates how all these consequences nearly led to the economic collapse of Tanzania in recent years (Lofchie 1985b).

Even where national leaders have been more flexible in programming development or reluctant to engage in coercion, but still insist on a monopoly of public authority through the centralized bureaucracy, the developmental public service has drifted into near irrelevancy as far as the citizenry is concerned. Moris and Leonard have noted this in Tanzania (pre-Ujaama) and Kenya, as has the author of this chapter found in parts of Ghana (Moris 1981; Leonard 1977; Wunsch 1983). Finally, as the national government long before eliminated the capacity of sub-national institutions to raise taxes, to hire personnel, to develop programs or projects, to pass ordinances (beyond the most trivial of matters) and to let contracts, an organizational entropy settles over the nation that stifles nearly all public, collective endeavors (Mawhood 1983). Much vaunted "decentralization" efforts such as Kenya's District Planning effort have been found to be long on rhetoric, but rather disappointing in impact (Cohen and Hook 1985; Wunsch 1988). Indeed, local passivity and dependency are encouraged just as national structures prove increasingly ineffective (Hyden 1983; Moris 1981; Thomson 1981).

Goran Hyden recently captured a fundamental contradiction between the bureaucratic paradigm and the operational reality of Africa when he noted:

The predominant orientation in modern management, as articulated in western countries, can be summarized as follows: rational is better than non-rational; objective is closer to rational than subjective; quantitative is more objective than qualitative, thus quantitative analysis is preferred over judgement based on wisdom, experience and insight. The results of this orientation are generalizations, conceptual hierarchies, categorizations, and formation of syllogisms and comparison processes, all with a view to finding the answer or the solution to a problem (Hyden 1983: 158).

It is extremely problematic whether this approach is appropriate to the African reality. When tasks are broad and interdisciplinary in their implications, when answers are uncertain, and when resources available to a given task are both limited and unpredictable, a more subtle and subjective management mode is appropriate (Leavitt 1975). Since, as Hyden argues, "deductive rationality and analysis are only examples of one mode of thought," one least useful in an uncertain and unpredictable environment, other modes of perception and judgement ought to be utilized. The application of the former to Africa is likely to lead to serious problems of "premature programming" (Landau 1979).

An open-systems strategy, where broad parameters of action and decision are drawn (basic human and property rights, rights of appeal, rights of suit, etc.), and within which trial and error, inductive generation of solutions, open-ended responses to flow of demands, information and resources, is one such approach. Here what has been called the "intuitive-synthetic" thought process may develop (Hyden 1983). However, bureaucratic centralization generally allows little if any room for such methodologies of perception, analysis and choice.

Executive Centralization

A third strategy generally coupled with the presupposition that a strong, centralized, united state was necessary for development, was the concentration of legitimate authority in the hands of the executive. This process began early in the post-independence era, and was supported by the development of the single-party state, the preemption of regional and local politics by central planning and bureaucracy, the powerful discretionary economic resources controlled by government, the parallel rise of a spoils-distributional political system, and the erosion of constitutional limits on executive power. The last occurred in a process followed by nearly all African states, where autonomous legislative authority was eroded in law or in fact, and usually in both. Powerful single-party majorities gave parliamentary leaders virtually unchecked powers; strong executive presidencies tended to displace all independent legislative authority, reducing legislative bodies to debating and formalizing roles (Jackson and Rosberg 1982). As Rothchild observed, "Anxious to remove any constraints placed on their institutions by the departing colonial power, the new African governments frequently sought to consolidate the political power by redefining or abolishing what they considered to be needless or undesirable limitations on their freedom of maneuver" (Rothchild et al. 1978: 69).

By the early 1980s most observers acknowledged that the majority of African governments were executive instruments, and constitutional provisions were essentially what an enduring strongman (Ivory Coast, Kenya, Tanzania, Zaire, Zambia, Malawi, Cameroon) or the ruling circle of the moment said they were (Jackson and Rosberg 1982). In some instances the potential excesses of such arrangements have been moderated by the tendency of some African governments to leave the judicial system less compromised (Rothchild et al. 1978). Certainly there have been instances of judicial pressuring, and some particularly explosive political cases have been simply removed from normal judicial processes. Nonetheless, on balance, African governments have largely left criminal and civil proceedings alone, and have respected the autonomy of the courts, even while restricting their scope of action through constitutional modifications. What the courts have not been allowed to do is make decisions which limit the permissible range of action by African governments. Of course, what this does mean is that constitutional protections and limitations on governmental action have been rendered largely ineffective. The most serious challenges to judicial institutions have come in some military regimes, where the process of executive centralization has reached an extreme, or in the few cases where arbitrary tyrannies have displaced entirely the rule of law (Guinea under Toure, Uganda under Amin, etc.). Typical of military rule is Nigeria, where military governments have ruled by decree, and denied the courts any authority to question actions taken under the decrees (Obasanjo and Shyllar 1980).

There are several potential outcomes of this concentration of authority. First, one might expect that the propensity for error which was discussed as a consequence of single-partyism (which is equally applicable to military regimes) would be reinforced by the restriction on independent decision making attendant to this institutional consolidation. Second, one might expect the value of the unconstrained political offices to inflate greatly for current and potential office holders. Third, and finally, the eradication of constitutional and institutional checks upon executive leaders suggests that there might develop a serious deinstitutionalization and rise of personalism in African politics. As we have already discussed the propensity for error in our section on single-partyism, we will focus here on the tendency for inflation in the value of public office and the linked problems of deinstitutionalization and personalism.

The Value of Political Office. It does not require a revelation to note that as the stakes of political victory and defeat grow higher, the tenacity with which people hold onto office and the violence with which others seek to control offices grows apace. As constitutional limitations eroded in Africa, political victory came to mean control over virtually the entire modern, urban economy, including the civil service, higher education, major domestic corporations, allocation of national development investments, access to hard currency, and control of virtually all tax revenues. Defeat meant relegation to the rural economy which fed the centralized state. Not surprisingly, who could accept defeat? In some cases, for example in Ghana, Nigeria, Ivory Coast, Uganda, and Kenya during the early post-independence era, and in Sudan and Zimbabwe in recent years, these dynamics can be clearly seen. This led to intense political conflict and even civil violence as leaders consciously and intentionally intensified and inflamed ethnic and/or regional fears to solidify their political support. In many cases African leaders settled this by co-opting opposition figures into the ruling circle (Liebenow 1986; Rothchild and Olorunsola 1983; Zolberg 1966). However, three problems remained.

First, even if key leaders have been visibly co-opted into the elite circle, their regional and/or ethnic bases remained as serious latent fractures in the body politic, ever sensitive to the possibility of exclusion (Rothchild 1985a). As we will discuss below regarding what some have called "factional" and "hegemonial" ruling systems, such arrangements are in fact tenuous and once unraveled, have led to severe political violence. Second, the power and flexibility sought and used by leaders in order to pursue a co-optation-purge strategy have contributed to the deinstitutionalization and personalization of government. This, in turn, raises the value of office yet again, as impersonal rules are weak and position is key (Jackson and Rosberg 1982; Kasfir 1976). Third, who guards the regimes from the guardians? As several scholars have noted, many coups have been the result of the corporate interest of the army as a whole, or are caused by the decision of one or another military faction that *their* "turn" is overdue (Price 1971; Decalo 1976).

Thus the paramount value of controlling public office has led at times to such problems as: intense political competition and ethnic conflict; precarious balancing acts where getting the ethnic-regional-interest coalition partners properly sorted and satisfied is critical; purges and rehabilitations which enhance yet again the value of holding office at the top; and military interventionism. Military intervention can be well interpreted as the last stage in executive centralization, as their tendency to suspend the constitution and rule by decree preempts whatever role might still have been filled by legislative bodies, and sharply circumscribes the authority of the judiciary. Furthermore, their hierarchical approach to administration has tended to further limit the role of extra-governmental and extra-bureaucratic institutions (see Chapter 9 of this volume). Finally, when the military itself has begun to fragment into competing corporate groups or factions, political instability and even violence have sharply escalated. Ghana, Congo-Brazaville, Uganda, and Nigeria after the 1966 coup can be seen as examples of this last danger (Schwarz 1969; Decalo 1976).

Personalism and Deinstitutionalization. Institutions have been defined elsewhere as "rule sets" which instruct, guide and help pattern human behavior around particular problems or tasks (Commons 1959; E. Ostrom 1986). The rules which form an institution answer such questions as: who may participate in a particular activity; what they must do or who they must satisfy before they may take a particular action; what effects they may and may not have upon "the world"; who they may, may not, and must communicate with; what costs and benefits they may receive for certain actions under certain conditions; and other such instructions. Rule sets may be "open" where little is specifically prescribed or proscribed. Or, they may be rather dense, and highly detailed, specifying quite clearly many requirements to be met before an action may be taken.

As rule sets are more fully filled by explicit delineations of required and prohibited behavior, and are more widely observed and accepted, then generally predictable and stable expectations, actions, and related consequences can develop among both participants and observers of the institution concerned. Or, as sociologists tend to define "institutions," patterns of human behavior regarding a particular task, problem or function, emerge and become "institutionalized."

Institutionalization in the realm of public or civic life is particularly important because of the state's control of coercive power and the potential for abuse this monopoly has always brought. Developing complex and detailed rules to map, guide, and stabilize government and the related political processes is necessary to avoid the dangers associated with unsure, manipulable, incomplete, and arbitrarily changeable rules. These dangers would include:

- fragility and instability in transfer of authority from one figure or generation to the next;
- large gaps between public and official behavior, and privately held norms of behavior;
- low capacity to legitimately change the procedural and constitutional rules of the regime; and
- an ever-present and open-ended fear that unlimited advantage taking by "winners" will critically hurt or destroy those outside the regime.[1]

A major aspect of institutionalization is differentiating between the various levels of rules which are used to fashion a polity, and using such differentiation to limit the amount of power available to any single office-holder. "Rules of daily life" are defined and promulgated to guide people in the economic and social relationships they develop and pursue. They are passed according to "rules of collective choice" which delineate how political institutions are to operate: who might pass a law, under what circumstances, etc. These rules, in turn, are established according to "rules of constitutional choice," which determine who must agree and under what procedure the basic structure of institutions are established, and over time, revised (E. Ostrom and Kiser 1982).

By differentiating among these levels of rules, a people is able both to guide and encourage routine operations of government and to retain control over how that business is transacted. Different levels of consent can be delineated which are appropriate to the varying tasks at hand, and those authorized to perform tasks can be prevented from serving as "judges of their own cases and causes" by allocating elsewhere both adjudicatory authority and the authority to revise rules of constitutional choice.

The constitutional consolidation brought by political centralization destroyed most of the differentiation among levels of rules established in the first constitutions. Furthermore, differentiation of function or authority among more than one institution at any *single* level of choice was also weakened. In effect, constitutional and collective levels of choice have tended to collapse into a single person, the leader and chief executive of the government. Similarly, most executive, legislative, and judicial political functions have also tended to collapse (Zolberg 1966; Rothchild et al. 1978; 1985a; Jackson and Rosberg 1982; Bates 1981).

Insofar, then, as constitutional provisions might have provided some of the "rule sets" to institutionalize politics along predictable and stable lines and some fixed structure upon which other rule sets might be built, they were neutralized by the concentration of power toward the hands of a small group or even a single person. In that way, it helped set the stage for radical personalization of polities. Military intervention generally has worked to further these processes. By the early 1980s, most major observers of African politics acknowledged that the political leaders ruled essentially by decree (Jackson and Rosberg 1982).

The key role of the leader in the bargaining relationships characteristic of one-party systems worked to further the "deinstitutionalization" of African politics. Single-party regimes largely survive by balancing the apportionment of political and economic plums among key groups, leaders, regions, and interests. This bargaining and subsequent arrangements occur behind closed doors, and in a largely informal process. Both these features are reinforced by the constitutional erosion we have discussed. As long as all links in long chains of patron-client relationships are satisfied, then the regime can continue for an indefinite period of time in relative stability. Donald Rothchild, in his analysis of what he labels "hegemony," suggests that in fact such regimes can survive because they do develop *some* rules:

> . . . hegemonial exchange [is] described as offering a framework for coordinating and facilitating political exchange under conditions of frail institutions, heady expectations, and severe economic scarcity. Hegemonial exchange channels conflict along negotiable lines, making amicable agreement over conflicting issues more likely. In doing so, the hegemonial exchange process primarily follows informal but known rules, in particular the principle of proportionality (Rothchild 1985a: 82).

In some measure, this norm reflects at least the beginning of a national-level ethical order defining relations among diverse persons. However, it is fragile and vulnerable. There are several reasons for this. First, while the "rules" are critical to stabilize hegemonial rule, the policies which undergird them face real world obstacles. For example, ethnic proportionality may threaten to disrupt a professionalized civl service when some groups are well in advance of others. Kenya's go-slow policy on the civil service reflects this tension. Similar tension has occurred in Sierra Leone, Ethiopia, Uganda, Rwanda, Burundi, Guinea, Zambia, Ghana, and post-coup Liberia.

Secondly, regimes which have traveled furthest down this path are vulnerable to conflict because in the absence of a constitutional order they are usually dependent on a *single* key integrating leader. These regimes depend heavily on the judgement of a single man, one sophisticated in the art of statecraft in the fluidity characteristic of deinstitutionalized regimes. As Jackson and Rosberg have noted, the skills of Machiavelli's *Prince* are needed here, but are not always available (Jackson and Rosberg 1982). Similarly, succession is usually a crisis, and many regimes have not outlived the first leader who established and operated the system. The rules are almost never written, and rarely specified other than as informal agreements. During succession, misunderstanding or misjudgment have often occurred, and the concentration of power in the hands of one or of a few has meant that there have been few "checks" to allow for reconsideration before conflict erupts. Thirdly, economic stress can bring on the same result by upsetting the economic balance which sustains the patron-client systems undergirding the hegemonial leader: ". . . a system based largely on informal linkages necessarily remains precarious and can disintegrate, especially under severe strain" (Rothchild 1985: 92). It is instructive for example, that both Kenya and Cameroon, each often cited as African success stories, experienced serious and violent coup attempts shortly after their first leadership successions. The evidence suggests that in the Kenyan case this can be directly traced to Moi's disruption of the factional constellation managed by Kenyatta. How Senegal, Tanzania, Guinea and, soon, Ivory Coast will fare as time passes under their new leaders is worthy of close attention. Zaire, Gabon, Malawi, and Zambia must also eventually face this transition.

When "hegemonial" leadership has been unable to sustain such a "balancing act," disintegration into what has been labeled "factional" politics has occasionally resulted. In factionalism, leadership turnover is rapid, and unstable coalitions of bureaucratic-military leaders with varying ethnoregional groups govern, until the next coup deposes them for another clique. Allies and arrangements can change almost overnight. Stable rules of proportionality do not exist, and the stakes and tools of politics take on an explosive "anything goes" tendency. The unstable dynamics of zero-sum and, finally, negative-sum game relationships begin to drive the political process. Ghana since Nkrumah, Congo-Brazaville, Benin, Sudan, Uganda since the mid-1960s, and Nigeria from the early 1960s until the Civil War, have been examples of this pattern.

Hegemonial and factional regimes have much in common. In each system, extreme executive centralization and the erosion of formal institutions go hand in hand, and facilitate the rise of personalistic bargaining political patterns. These systems, because of their delicate balancing acts, have encouraged regional and ethnic isecurity, and conflict over the spoils of state.[2] Administrative suboptimization has been rampant because of their politicized economic decision-making and the costs of central administrative control and hierarchy. The erosion of the rural economy is accelerated in each by the decision to fund an expensive urban-state apparatus and the extensive patron-client systems which undergird the regimes at the expense of rural agriculture (Lofchie 1985a; Bates 1981; World Bank 1981; Jackson and Rosberg 1982; Hyden 1983; Picard and Morgan 1985).

Extreme executive centralization tends then to lead to deinstitutionalization, and in turn to personalization of political rule. This personalization, in turn, has led to serious loss in legitimacy by some African national governments. "Hegemonial" regimes are well known to be primarily mechanisms of distributing the "booty" of the state. While citizens might respect the power of those who distribute the wealth and envy those who receive it, the governing clique's lack of concern over justice is open to anyone: resources are generally distributed according to clout rather than to publicly chosen purposes, and even the noblest of rhetoric is frequently belied by elite privilege and occasional brutality (Gellar 1972; Rothchild 1978; Jackson and Rosberg 1982). The type of legitimacy which grows from serious debate and search for public purposes is perforce absent. Government has little moral standing because it does not act on nor seek to define moral grounds of action.[3] Finally, regimes have led to cycles of severe instability and conflict that threaten the very fabric of the polity.

Regional and Local Government

Quick to feel the impatience of independence era leaders were the "bargaining encumbrances" left behind by colonial authorities as democratic-constitutional legacies. Federalism, electoral systems, bicameralism, multi-partyism, entrenched protections of the constitution on such issues as amendments, ethnic representation and the status and authority of regional units of government, were quickly eliminated or neutralized as counter-poses to centralized authority (Rothchild et al. 1978: 70). These were seen by independence era leaders to impose unacceptable costs on decision making and to reflect unacceptable distrust for African governments. Federal clauses were quickly removed from constitutional law in Ghana, Cameroon, Kenya, and Uganda. Only in Nigeria, where ethnic competition reinforced federal divisions, were they maintained. (The impact of the diversity and complexity of Nigerian society on its constitutional experience is discussed below, in Chapter 9.)

Once the assumption was made in the post-independence era that development and unity required a highly centralized, strong state, the role of local governing institutions became problematic. Institutions which had the capacity to organize people for collective action, to raise resources, and to resolve conflict outside the direction of the central state were also its competitors. At best they would occupy political space that the state wished to monopolize; at worst they might become overt obstacles to the state in policy and program.

A corollary, then, to the statist strategy was removing or preempting these potential competitors from political life. This has led to the use of law to abolish their authority, of state largess to purchase the support of role occupants, and the use of force when the first two strategies failed. These strategies in turn have their own disconcerting consequences, including rural organizational decay and development stagnation should state bureaucracies fail to carry the local organizational burden.

Almost without exception, the first years after independence marked the general elimination of genuine local government. During the latter colonial era, particularly during the tenure of Creech-Jones as British Colonial Secretary, substantial devolution of authority to local governments had occurred. Local elections, authority over revenues, policy-making and implementation responsibilities were the norm, particularly in Ghana, Nigeria, and Uganda. In fact, "decentralization well served the purposes of building an effective nationalist movement," and nationalist leaders often used local elections to help stimulate political mobilization in the countryside (Kasfir 1983: 29).

However, the largely middle-class and urban-based leaders who took power after independence soon found the activated countryside to be a base for political opposition to them. Furthermore, the centralist paradigm and urban-industrial development model adopted by most independence-era leaders meant that genuine local governments' days were numbered. The continuing influence of traditional leaders in rural areas, and the tendency of rural leaders to agitate for rural interests were a challenge to the control by the leaders at the center over rural resource needed for urban-industrial development (Bates 1981; Kasfir 1983). Nkrumah's struggles with Ashanti over the flow of resources from agriculture to urban-industrial projects reflect this conflict.

Within a very few years, local government had become local "administration," and the pre-independence, colonial prefectoral model was re-established nearly everywhere. This was accomplished through largely peaceful means, as the national authorities simply redefined the authority of local governments, and reestablished the familiar colonial era administrative models. As Chapter 4 discusses in some detail, most of the vaunted "decentralization" reforms since that time have been only superficial attempts at administrative deconcentration (for example, Tanzania's 1972 program or Kenya's efforts since independence); potentially more serious attempts have been swept away by military intervention or political opposition at the top (Sudan).

Paralleling these events was the fate of what remained of traditional government in the independence era. In regards to this question, it must be understood that "traditional authority" meant more than "chiefs" and "councils of elders." The latter are often seen as the sum and substance of these institutions, ignoring the complex bodies of common law, jurisprudence, and checks and balances, which srrounded and guided their actions (Mair 1977). Had they been but petty despots, as colonial propaganda often advertised them to be, Africa would have existed in an anarchy which no responsible scholars today suggest existed.

Instead, traditional institutions must be understood as the diverse mechanisms by which Africans regulated social and economic affairs, and exercised and controlled political power. They included, for example, village councils which promulgated and enforced access rules that regulated the balance between livestock, water, and forage, assuring that overgrazing was minimized (Thomson 1981); local councils which required livestock owners to regulate their animals to protect crops (Odell 1987); complex rules of access and use that assured young men over most of Africa access to fallow land; rules of organization, financial obligation and authority which were used to organize vast markets and which sustained trade over thousands of miles; and complex rules of bridewealth, familial involvement and spousal obligation that provided stable environments and personal rights for children and aged adults alike. While these systems did not operate perfectly, it is not at all clear that their failings were any greater than comparable systems in the more "developed" countries have been.

In all fairness to the independence era leaders, it must be understood that colonial rule had a devastating affect upon these traditional institutions. In much of Africa, particularly the French and Portuguese territories, colonial authorities sought systematically to destroy the relationships among Africans which sustained and evolved these rule systems. Legitimate authority was denied traditional bodies; civil law was abrogated; formerly self-governing territories were torn apart and administered with pieces of other formerly self-governing territories; and traditional role occupants were, variously, removed, exiled or co-opted into the colonial service. British colonial rule, which varied across the territories it governed, often nullified the local laws that traditional role occupants were to administer, removed indigenous checks and balances, and made those role occupants sometimes into local despots (Crowder 1968). As noted in Chapter 2, traditional institutions were seriously damaged by these policies, as well as their related inability to adapt themselves to the multiple economic and social changes brought on by colonial rule. As illustrated in Chapter 11, however, they are by no means dead, particularly as norms of behavior in the countryside. Still, their effectiveness has been greatly diminished, as illustrated in some detail in Chapter 7 on Liberia.

In the post-independence era, nearly every state has abolished what legal authority remained to traditional institutions with the exception of some authority in civil law (Jackson and Rosberg 1982). Even civil law, however, has largely been enforceable only in official state courts. Traditional leaders have, as during the colonial era, frequently been co-opted by recruitment into the civil service or by pensioning them off. In some cases, however resistance to state policies has developed along regional or ethnic lines and these strategies have not succeeded (Rothchild et al. 1978). Here traditional leaders and institutions have at times become involved in conflict with the state. When this has occurred, serious violence and force has been employed by the state to end the conflict, often with tragic results. These situations have included the bloody civil war in Southern Sudan, one raging off and on some fifteen years; the conflict between Milton Obote of Uganda and the Kabaka of Buganda, a conflict which helped establish Amin as a major political actor and erode civil liberties in Uganda; the conflict between Nkrumah and Ashanti region during the early 1960s, a conflict which heralded both the rise of authoritarian government in Ghana and the eventual decline of the cocoa industry; the two-front civil war in Ethiopia; current conflict in Zimbabwe between the Matabele and the Shona; the civil war in Angola; and less severe conflicts in Ivory Coast, Zambia and elsewhere.

Even where the co-optation and erosion of local governments in general and of traditional institutions in particular occurred peacefully, there have nonetheless been costs. Recently, several researchers have noted the paralyzing effects of institutional weakness on rural development, and the difficulty of adapting general social norms to changed conditions or new problems when there exist no formal institutions to adopt and articulate such changes. The absence of local institutions able to regulate tree use and livestock foraging has been traced directly to the deforestation and desertification process in the Sahel (Thomson 1981). In Botswana, the abolition of local authorities has meant local dwellers found it far more difficult to solve such local problems as regulating individuals whose livestock ravage crops (Odell 1985). In Ghana, local powerlessness has meant roads, bridges, and buildings await repair, and local improvement projects stand idle for months, awaiting national authorizations and funds which come too late or not at all as the section, above, on bureaucracy has explained (Wunsch 1974). The absence of this social "infrastructure" thus threatens common resources, private resources, and community endeavors.

When local dwellers have been able to discover and develop legal, collective mechanisms to take such actions, the results have been remarkable (Smock 1971; Bunker 1987). These, sadly, have been in the minority, and the absence of systems of general local autonomy or of effective systems to integrate these efforts into regional government have meant even these efforts have at times been for naught, as in the "Harambee" movement in Kenya. The latter has been troubled by the problem of coordinating local efforts with available teachers and supplies, and the disfunction between spontaneous local efforts and the national educational authority has meant both local labor and national resources have been irrationally applied (Wallis 1982; Keller 1974). In a variety of ways, then, political centralization has slowed and/or disrupted economic development.

Financial Centralization

A key link in the statist development model is the role played by the national budget. Assuming little competency by local political institutions, and committed to the assumed efficiency and effectiveness of the centrally planned and bureaucratically directed development methodology, central mobilization and management of development resources was usually deemed necessary. Furthermore, as the development task was a massive one, the scale of resources required was proportionately massive. The result was movement toward extreme financial centralization.

Such an approach to development has had serious consequences for African development. First is the overhead cost of such a strategy: how much money would be spent "administering" and "coordinating" development, and how much would actually reach the people in productive ways? Second is the danger of corrupting those benefitting from and implementing this strategy: would they be able to differentiate between their interests and the interests of the populace as a whole, and how might the opportunities to use these resources affect their behavior? Third is the impact of this system on those who would generate the wealth to pay for it.

The problem of "overhead cost" and benefit flow was first noted as long ago as 1966, when Rene Dumont observed that a great paradox was developing on the African continent: those producing the bulk of national wealth, the small-holder farmers throughout Africa, were reaping few benefits from their labors. Instead, a prosperous bourgeoisie-administrative class was rapidly taking over the civil service posts and perks previously occupied by the British, French, and Belgians. Enormous income gaps between civil servants and the public characteristic of the colonial era continued into the era of independent government: average civil service salaries were many multiples of the average farmer or workers' income. In contrast to developed societies, where such incomes might typically exist in a ratio of 1:1 or 2:1, in Africa the ratios of even 20:1 or 30:1, were typical (Dumont 1966). Unfortunately, virtually no scholar has argued that the benefits brought to the vast majority of Africans who live in the rural areas are anywhere near proportionate to these costs (Moris 1981; Leonard 1977; Hyden 1983). This pattern, whose burden on the economy was worsened by the rapid expansion of the public sector, was to affect severely African politics and economics.

As we have noted, one aspect of African leaders' pursuit of centralization was the tendency to deinstitutionalize national regimes and then replace them with systems of personalistic rule (Jackson and Rosberg 1982). Personalistic rule, however, as noted long ago by Machiavelli in *The Prince,* survives by developing networks of rewards (and threats of termination of rewards) dispensed along patron-clientship lines. Such systems require large amounts of resources to fuel them. These resources include positions in a large civil service, employment in parastatal enterprises, positions in public social services, public works, scholarships, etc. Furthermore, efficiency in job performance and economic rationality in capital investment are often displaced as criteria of evaluation by the implications of these appointments or allocations for the patron-clientship system (Gellar 1972).

Several destructive consequences have frequently flowed from this. First, since the only sector earning sufficient wealth to pay what became often severe costs was small-farmer agriculture, that sector became the tax source of first, best, and last resort. Vast amounts of resources held by already poor people were systematically bled from them. Typically, this was done by manipulating substantial price variations between the world price of a given commodity and the fixed, domestic price paid producers for that commodity. Potential capital for agricultural development was systematically taken from the rural areas, and spent on salaries and capital developments concentrated virtually entirely in the urban area. Rural production stagnated and at times nearly collapsed from this (Bates 1981).

Even in mineral-rich states, instabilities in world mineral prices meant agriculture eventually was pressured.

To be sure, long-run economic development requires certain facilities with national benefits to be located at central points. Economic rationality strongly suggests that many of these central points will be in urban areas: ports, warehouses, technical training facilities, utilities to serve these investments, and the like. However, these facts cannot justify the extraction of any level of resources from the rural areas, and the monopoly of nearly all capital investment in a few urban centers. Such an extreme strategy undermines the productivity of agriculture needed to feed the urban dwellers and to serve as markets to sustain industrial investment over the long run.

Second, and not surprisingly, rural-to-urban migration has grown rapidly throughout this era. Well paying jobs, amenities, services, and consumer goods were to be found in the cities rather than in the rural areas: people gravitated to the cities. Few young people saw a career in agriculture as likely to lead to prosperity. Of course, as urban populations grew because the opportunity structure of the urban areas so vastly exceeded the rural areas, the number of urban un- and under-employed also grew. This put pressure on the governments to engage in differential pricing for food products in order to keep explosive (and nearby!) urban populations pacified. This, in turn, drained further wealth from the rural areas, reducing its production and opportunities still more (World Bank 1981).

Third, the same pressures which brought masses to the cities, have often led governments to pad payrolls to absorb as much of the idle labor force as possible. The civil service burden, of course, grew and weighed yet more on the farmer. Meanwhile, urban consumption tastes were, at least among the elites, heavily oriented to the West and to consumer goods. While the urban elites had the cash and clout to import these goods, nearly every unit of hard currency so spent had been earned by the impoverished rural producers. Not only were their earnings going to urban consumers, those consumers spent the earnings on imported goods, which thus did not favor the growth of domestic industries whose production and employment rural persons might have been able to enjoy. Instead, as markets for domestic industries remained static or shrank, tariff barriers were erected to protect the jobs of the urban dwellers employed there. This, in turn, raised the cost of what *few* consumer and capital goods the farmer had hitherto been able to purchase.

Fourth, because of the gradual decline of the entire rural economy, and because of the absence or at best the grave weakness of the private sector throughout Africa, governmental and parastatal employees often perceived that there were virtually no options for their economic survival other than continuation of their parasitical relationship to the rural producers. In this respect, the urban and industrial strategy and need to "fuel" the patron-client system can be seen to have been fundamentally *corrupting* for the African political economy. Urban leaders perforce came often to consider not national development nor justice nor equity in policy (nor alternative organizational approaches), but instead their survival as an economic class and as members of the ruling regime. The irony here, of course, is that since they perceived the state as the only entity which could provide development, and they were in fact "the state," this all could be seen as a perhaps regrettable but necessary situation. The ethical issues were easily skirted and, because of the erosion of popular politics and the constitutional consolidation of the centralized state, the rural dwellers who largely paid these costs had no mechanism with which they could turn the policies around (World Bank 1981; Bates 1981; Hyden 1980).

A number of parallel policies intensified this picture. For example, parastatal performance usually worsened this situation. Lacking the discipline of domestic or international competition, holding in effect the governing coalition members hostage to the parastatal sector's ability to provide jobs to both urban dwellers generally and to elite coalition claimants in particular, parastatals at times became nearly a "black hole" in the economy (World Bank 1981). Overvalued currencies in almost every African state have as well worked to finance the costs of centralization and to encourage those holding central authority to tenaciously continue their control. An overvalued currency cheapens the price paid for imports by those influential enough to win an import permit and/or access to hard currency, privileges controlled by government. There is thus a great advantage to be derived from membership in (or support of) the ruling clique; it is reciprocally a powerful patronage tool held by the ruling group to consolidate and lubricate its control. Once grown dependent upon it, a political coalition may find it terribly difficult to see how it might stay in power without it. On the other hand, those actually earning the foreign currency, generally the small-holder farmer or wage-laborer in extractive industries, find the benefits earned by their industry largely flowing to urban dwellers as consumer goods (World Bank 1981). As noted above, economic shrinkage occurs; the way out is uncertain if the premises of centralization are not challenged.

Were there no benefits for the rural dwellers from the government budget? Indeed, there were some, but the evidence leaves no doubt those benefits were grossly overwhelmed by the costs rural dwellers paid. First, the bulk of services were, with only a very few exceptions, concentrated in urban areas. Secondly, the preponderance of budgets were paid for salaries, which were inexcusably higher than the incomes earned by the vast majority in the societies concerned, and mostly paid to a managerial elite in the capital city whose effectiveness has been questioned (Moris 1981). Third, such services as were directed to the rural areas have generally been evaluated as extremely inadequate, severely hampered by the paucity of personnel and resources assigned to rural areas, made inefficient by the politicization of personnel decisions, and choked by constipated and ineffective procedures to support them with supplies and program funds (Leonard 1977; 1986; Moris 1981; Wunsch 1983). Thus, what benefits reached the rural areas seem, on the basis of a variety of criteria, too little and too late, particularly given the costs paid by these same dwellers.

As a result, much of the small-farmer work force in extreme cases such as Tanzania and Ghana simply "opted out" of the cash economy (Lofchie 1985). The outcome of all this could be conceptualized as a sort of "shrinking political economy," where the decline in goods to distribute intensifies political competition and conflict. This, in turn, tends to intensify the need for those goods even more for political "consumption." Economic decline obviously results.

Conclusions

Chapter 1 opened this book with a review of many dismal statistics measuring Africa's political and economic experience over the past 25 years. We have argued in this chapter that African leaders' understanding of the role of the state in development led to the decision to centralize. It led in turn to five complementary policies which had problematic consequences for political order and economic development. This review of post-independence Africa has attempted to draw together in an analytical and theoretical discussion the consequences of these strategies. While individual African states vary in the extent to which they implemented these strategies, the overall "direction" of travel has been shared. We have tried to explain how these policies worked to damage the economic, social, and political health of many African countries.

For example, a choice of single-party systems confined, eroded, and sometimes seriously damaged the diversity of institutions necessary to sustain public debate about the purposes and strategies of development, legitimize and assist implementation of decisions, and provide feedback on performance. A decision to concentrate control in the hands of the executive branch led to similar consequences in regards to policy-making and implementation, while it also directly eroded national-level constitutional provisions which might have prevented the rise of personalistic government. Erosion of these national institutions intensified a regime's dependence on the decisions of a single person or a small group, thereby increasing the vulnerability of the regime to error. While many leaders carefully sought, for example, to balance distribution of benefits evenly among regions and groups, the frequently personalistic nature of their regimes meant that there were no institutionalized mechanisms to check mistakes or to justify with publicly-chosen broader national purposes, redistribution of resources from one area to another. Centralization can be seen, therefore, ironically to lead to more unstable and less effective governance. Military governments, because of their tendency to ride roughshod over existing law, to circumscribe even more the moderating influence of the judiciary, and to intensify further the use of executive-centered hierarchy, can be seen as largely accelerating these tendencies.

Centralizing decision making in the hands of a hierarchical, centrally directed bureaucracy also damaged institutions which might have contributed to development. While the vulnerabilities and weaknesses of bureaucracy anywhere are intensified by the conditions in which they worked in Africa, their greatest virtue (coordinated implementation of known technologies to solve agreed upon tasks) was vitiated by the ambiguous and complex nature of underdevelopment, and the uncertainty of development technologies. This misfit between organization and task dissipated resources which might have been better spent applying bureaucracy to more appropriate tasks, while a productive role for traditional norms and procedures of governance, and the genuine beginnings of local governmental institutions which were emerging in the late-colonial era were largely preempted by the dominance of central bureaucracy. To be sure, important political, social, and economic functions have continued to be performed by extra-governmental institutions such as voluntary associations, market unions, co-operative communal associations and the like. However, these have had to work with minimal or without the benefit of government support. At times they have had to face overt governmental interference and opposition. The financial dependence of the centralist strategy on the rural areas and the amount of capital withdrawn by it has undoubtedly made the continued health of these institutions still more problematic.

African leaders and scholars have increasingly come to question the viability of these strategies in recent years. Still, coherent alternative paradigms to make sense of the debate among the elites, or to suggest alternative strategies have not emerged. Chapters 4 and 5 will discuss the attempts made by African leaders to address these problems through administrative decentralization and through various national economic reforms. Each, we will argue, has had and will continue to have only limited successes because of their failure to address the key questions of institutional diversity, energy and design needed to obtain self-governance and development.

Notes

1. Clearly rule systems could exist which were "fully mapped" and where these consequences would occur. We do not dispute that. What we are contending here is that without developed rule sets, such undesirable patterns are always a danger. Rule sets are a necessary but not sufficient requirement to avoid these problems.

A fine development of the implications of deinstitutionalization is presented by Jackson and Rosberg (1982).

2. Is such a system one with rules? Yes, in the most open definition of "rules," in the sense that there is no rule except "take what you can." However, in the sense (which we feel is much more analytically useful) that rules are mechanisms which discriminate among behaviors by delineating "may, must, and must not actions," they reflect what one might call a situation of "minimal discrimination." Of course, this discussion must be understood as drawing an "ideal type," and regimes fall at various points on a continuum of these characteristics. Uganda under Amin, Central African Republic under Bokassa, probably reflect extremes; Ghana since 1972 is in a more intermediate position. Perhaps more to the point, it is difficult to find any principles implied by them or guiding them which might be regarded as adding to an overall conception of a moral order. Thus whether one looks for consistent operating rules or moral principles as an indicator of national institutions, one finds neither.

3. Much in the same way, Theodore Lowi argues that the American liberal state cannot achieve justice because it rewards power and indemnifies wrongs when the victims are too visible, active, or numerous to ignore: it has turned from seeking justice to co-opting those with resources it needs as criteria of empowerment. Such criteria can keep a regime in office, but is unable to earn it the moral obligation of obedience and support. One supports such a regime because it is expedient to do so (Lowi 1979).

References

Austin, Dennis. *Politics in Africa.* Hanover: University Press of New England, 1984.

Bates, Robert H. *Markets and States in Tropical Africa: The Political Basis of Agricultural Policies.* Berkeley: University of California Press, 1981.

Board on Science and Technology, National Research Council. *Proceedings of the Conference on Common Property Resource Management.* Washington, DC: National Academy Press, 1987.

Bunker, Stephen. *Peasants Against the State: The Politics of Market Control in Bugisu, Uganda, 1900–1983.* Urbana: University of Illinois Press, 1987.

Chambers, Robert. *Rural Development: Putting the Last First.* London: Longman Inc., 1983.

Cohen, John M., and Richard M. Hook. "District Development Planning in Kenya." Development Discussion Paper No. 229, April, 1985. Cambridge, Mass.: Harvard Institute for International Development.

Commons, John R. *Legal Foundations of Capitalism.* Madison: The University of Wisconsin Press, 1959.

Crowder, Michael. *West Africa Under Colonial Rule.* London: Hutchinson, 1968.

Decalo, Samuel. *Coups and Army Rule in Africa: Studies in Military Style.* New Haven, Conn.: Yale University Press, 1976.

Dumont, Rene. *False Start in Africa.* New York: Praeger Publishers, 1966.

Gellar, Sheldon. *State-Building and Nation-Building in West Africa.* Bloomington, Indiana: International Development Research Center, Indiana University, 1972.

Hyden, Goran. *Beyond Ujamaa in Tanzania: Underdevelopment and an Uncaptured Peasantry.* Berkeley: University of California Press, 1980.

———. *No Shortcuts to Progress: African Development Management in Perspective.* Berkeley: University of California, 1983.

Jackson, Robert H., and Carl G. Rosberg. *Personal Rule in Black Africa: Prince, Autocrat, Prophet, Tyrant*. Berkeley: University of California Press, 1982.

Johnson, Willard R. *The Cameroon Federation: Political Integration in a Fragmentary Society*. Princeton, N.J.: Princeton University Press, 1970.

Kasfir, Nelson. *The Shrinking Political Arena*. Berkeley: University of California Press, 1976.

_____. "Designs and Dilemmas: An Overview." In *Local Government in the Third World*, edited by P. Mawhood, 25–48. Chichester: John Wiley, 1983.

Keller, Edmond. "Harambee!: Educational Policy and the Political Economy in Rural Community Organization in Kenya." A paper presented at the Africa Studies Association, Chicago, Illinois, 1974.

Landau, Martin. "Redundancy, Rationality and the Problem of Duplication and Overlap." *Public Administration Review* 29 (4) (July/August 1969): 346–358.

Landau, Martin, and Russell Stout, Jr. "To Manage is Not to Control: Or the Folly of Type-Two Errors." *Public Administration Review* 39 (2) (March/April 1979): 148–156.

Leavitt, Harold. "Beyond the Analytical Manager." *California Management Review* 18 (3) (Spring 1975).

Leonard, David K. *Reaching the Peasant: Organization Theory and Practice in Kenya*. Chicago: University of Chicago Press, 1977.

_____. "The Political Realities of African Management." Report of a Workshop on the Management of Agricultural Projects in Africa. Washington D.C.: USAID Special Evaluation Study No. 33, 1986, pp. 58–74.

Leys, Colin. *Underdevelopment in Kenya: The Political Economy of Neo-Colonialism*. Berkeley: University of California Press, 1975.

Liebenow, J. Gus. *African Politics: Crises and Challenges*. Bloomington, Indiana: Indiana University Press, 1986.

Lofchie, Michael F. "Africa's Agrarian Malaise." In *African Independence: The First Twenty-Five Years*, edited by Gwendolen M. Carter and Patrick O'Meara, 160–187. Bloomington: Indiana University Press, 1985a.

_____. "The Roots of Economic Crisis in Tanzania." *Current History* 84 (April 1985b): 159–163.

Lowi, Theodore. *The End of Liberalism: Ideology, Policy, and the Crisis of Public Authority*. New York: W.W. Norton and Company, 1979.

Mair, Lucy. *Primitive Government*. Bloomington, Indiana: Indiana University Press, 1977.

Markovitz, I.L. *African Politics and Society*. New York: Free Press, 1970.

Mawhood, Philip, ed. *Local Government for Development: The Experience of Tropical Africa*. Chichester: John Wiley, 1983.

Mickelwait, Donald, et al. *The "New Directions" Mandate: Studies in Project Design, Approval, and Implementation* (revised). Washington D.C.: Development Alternatives, Inc., 1978.

Moris, Jon R. *Managing Induced Rural Development*. Bloomington, Indiana: International Development Institute, 1981.

Muir, William K., Jr. *Police: Streetcorner Politicians*. Chicago: University of Chicago, 1977.

Nyerere, Julius K. "The Arusha Declaration and TANU's Policy of Socialism and Self-Reliance." In *African Politics and Society*, edited by Irving Leonard Markovitz, 266–276. New York: The Free Press, 1970.

Obasanjo, O., and F. Shyllar. *The Demise of the Rule of Law in Nigeria Under the Military: Two Points of View*. Ibadan: Institute of African Studies, University of Ibadan, Occasional Publication, No. 33, 1980.

Odell, Malcom. "Local Government: Traditional and Modern Roles of the Village Kgotla." In *The Evolution of Modern Botswana: Politics and Rural Development in Southern Africa,* edited by Louis A. Picard, 61–83. Lincoln: University of Nebraska Press, 1985.

Ostrom, Elinor. "A Method of Institutional Analysis." In *Guidance, Control and Evaluation in the Public Sector,* edited by F. X. Kaufmann, G. Majone, and V. Ostrom, 459–475. New York: Walter de Gruyter, 1986.

Ostrom, Elinor, and Larry Kiser. "The Three Worlds of Action: A Metatheoretical Synthesis of Institutional Approaches." In *Strategies of Political Inquiry,* edited by Elinor Ostrom, 179–222. Beverly Hills, Calif.: Sage Publications, 1982.

Picard, Louis, and E. Philip Morgan. "Policy, Implementation and the Local Institutions in Botswana." In *The Evolution of Modern Botswana,* edited by Louis A. Picard, 125–156. Lincoln, Neb.: University of Nebraska Press, 1985.

Popkin, Samuel L. "Public Choice and Rural Development: Free Riders, Lemons, and Institutional Design." In *Public Choice and Rural Development,* edited by Clifford S. Russell and Norman K. Nicholson, 43–80. Washington DC: Resources for the Future, Inc., 1981.

Pressman, Jeffrey L., and Aaron B. Wildavsky. *Implementation.* Berkeley: University of California Press, 1973.

Price, Robert. "Military Officers and Political Leadership: The Ghanaian Case." *Comparative Politics* III, 3 (April 1971): 361–380.

Rothchild, Donald. "State-Ethnic Relations in Middle Africa." In *African Independence: The First Twenty-Five Years,* edited by Gwendolen M. Carter and Patrick O'Meara. Bloomington, Indiana: Indiana University Press, 1985a: 71–96.

———. "Hegemony and State Softness: Some Variations in Elite Responses." A paper prepared for the Symposium on "African State in Transition: Fluctuat Nec Mergitur?" Georgetown University, Washington DC, February 22—23, 1985b.

Rothchild, Donald, and Robert L. Curry, Jr. *Scarcity, Choice, and Public Policy in Middle Africa.* Berkeley: University of California Press, 1978.

——— and Victor Olorunsola. *State Versus Ethnic Claims: African Policy Dilemmas.* Boulder: Westview Press, 1983.

Schwarz, Walter. *Nigeria.* New York: Praeger Publishers, 1968.

Sklar, Richard. "Democracy in Africa." *African Studies Review* 26 (3 and 4) (1985): 11–24.

Smock, Audrey C. *Ibo Politics: The Role of Ethnic Unions in Eastern Nigeria.* Cambridge, Mass.: Harvard University Press, 1971.

Thompson, James T., David H. Feeney, and Ronald J. Oakerson. "Institutional Dynamics: The Evolution and Dissolution of Common Property Resource Management." In *Proceedings of the Conference on Common Property Resource Management,* edited by The Panel on Common Property Resource Management, 391–424. Washington DC: National Academy Press, 1987.

Thomson, James T. "Public Choice Analysis of Institutional Constraints on Firewood Production Strategies in the West African Sahel." In *Public Choice and Rural Development,* edited by Clifford S. Russell and Norman K. Nicholson, 119–152. Washington DC: Resources for the Future, Inc., 1981.

Toure, Sekou. "African Democracy and the Western Parliamentary System." In *African Politics and Society,* edited by Irving Leonard Markovitz, 218–225. New York: The Free Press, 1970.

Wallis, M.A.H. *Bureaucrats, Politicians and Rural Committees in Kenya.* Manchester: Manchester University Papers on Development, Nov. 6, 1982.

World Bank. *Accelerated Development in Sub-Saharan Africa.* Washington, DC: World Bank, 1981.

Wunsch, James S. "Voluntary Associations: Determinants of Associational Structure and Activity in Two Ghanaian Cities." Unpublished PhD Dissertation, Indiana University, 1974.

_____. "Strengthening Rural Development Management Through International Assistance Projects." *Public Administration and Development* 3 (1983): 239–263.

_____. "Rural Development, Public Choice Theory and Local Government." A Paper Presented at the International Studies Association Meeting, Atlanta, Ga., Spring 1984.

_____. "Administering Rural Development: Have Goals Outreached Organizational Capacity?" *Public Administration and Development* 6 (1986): 287–308.

_____. *Rural Development, Decentralization and Administrative Reform: Toward a New Analytical Framework.* Washington, D.C.: National Association of Schools of Public Affairs and Administration, 1988. Working Paper No. 18.

Zolberg, Aristide R. *Creating Political Order: The Party-States of West Africa.* Chicago: Rand McNally and Company, 1966.

4

The Failure of Current
Decentralization Programs in Africa

Dele Olowu

Introduction

Thus far, we have reviewed a progressive centralization of political and administrative power in several African countries. We have also examined the historical, political, and economic foundations of these centralization processes and indicated how these forces erode national programs of economic and social development. Partly as a result of growing awareness about the costs of overcentralization and partly as a result of internal and external political pressure, several African countries made a commitment toward decentralization from the late 1960s on. Evaluations of these decentralization programs show that in virtually every case they were failures whether measured by impact on developmental activities or as programs (Mawhood and Davey 1980; Cheema and Rondinelli 1983; Mawhood 1983; Olowu 1987a). These negative evaluations of African decentralization efforts are corroborated by policy statements from African governments and from their leaders as well. In a number of cases, the failure of decentralization has provided added justification for even more centralized governmental structures. It is therefore important and appropriate to examine in this chapter why African governments' decentralization policies have failed, and to consider measures for future change.

This chapter will argue that the failure of current or past decentralization programs in Africa does not invalidate the case for decentralization. Rather, it strengthens it by challenging us to make a closer examination of the nature and assumptions of what currently passes for decentralization on the continent.

One of the most important objections raised to genuine decentralization in developing countries (which includes all of sub-Saharan Africa) is the argument regarding the preconditions for decentralization. Simply stated in its application to African conditions, the argument is that certain social, economic and geopolitical conditions are prerequisites for successful decentralization. In the absence of these pre-conditions, the ultimate goals of governments in new states—rapid socio-economic development directed by the state and its central organs, the drive towards unifying a diversity of culture groups brought together only by the accident of colonial adventure which lasted for less than a century, the desire for a stable political order within which socio-economic development must take place—all lead to the necessity of centralization (Subramaniam 1980; Mawhood 1984). Furthermore, it posits that since one of the primary goals of the national government is unity, egalitarian policies which require the minimization of regional or community inequalities imply that centrally sponsored programs take the pride of place both in economic and political development considerations (Bennett 1980: 281–283; Benz 1987: 468–469).

While conceding the force of such arguments, I intend to argue in this chapter that whereas *some* measure and aspects of centralization are not only desirable but inevitable in the process of socio-economic modernization, African countries at present suffer from a state of premature centralization. Because of this "prematurity," few of the benefits of centralization accrue while its costs increasingly damage the fledgling states. The African "soft" state is no more efficient, integrated or technically superior than the local institutions it seeks to control. It is therefore unclear how the central governmental apparatus as presently constituted is a more efficient organization for the realization of the economic and political objectives it has sought. Moreover, state projects with egalitarian goals have generated their own inequalities often more powerful than earlier ones because they allow economic and political power to be concentrated in the same hands. Finally, even where implementation is not a problem, it is unclear where the resources to "share" among the component units are to be found. Quite clearly, the decade of the 1990s will be one in which African countries will have to be at least as concerned with productive questions as they are with the problems of equity.

Some centralization of the governmental process thus may indeed be necessary, but this should facilitate rather than be at the expense of diverse and vigorous self-governing activity. The controversy on centralization versus decentralization is a broad one. In this chapter I intend to limit my discussion to programs and policy initiatives aimed at strengthening local governments vis-a-vis the state organs, and the publics which they have been expected to serve. To achieve this objective, I shall first review case studies of decentralization on the continent, examine the conventional explanations for failure, and suggest fresh insights for understanding the failure of decentralization programs in virtually all African countries.

Case Studies of Decentralization

The subject of decentralization has attracted substantial academic and policy interest (Conyers 1983; 1986; Olowu 1987c). Hence a broad array of good evaluative studies exists upon which we draw for our purposes in this chapter.

African decentralization reforms usually follow the same prototype. First, the inherited structures of local government are abolished and development administration units absorb the responsibilities and finances of these institutions. Second, a law or decree is passed directing all government activities in a region or district to be coordinated by a very senior political or administrative official, exclusively responsible to the center. Thirdly, popular committees are created (either elected or selected) which advise the regional/district coordinator. Generally, all these units relate to one another hierarchically. District projects must be approved at the regional level and beyond that at the center. Usually these reform efforts are linked to some form of socialist or populist ideology. Not all African countries have adopted this model, but most have. A few country-cases are reviewed below on a regional basis.

Zambia

Zambia (former Northern Rhodesia) became independent in October, 1964. Decentralization measures began with the Local Government Act of 1965, which consolidated and re-enacted the various local government laws. Guided by a pseudo-socialist policy of "humanism," President Kaunda announced in 1969 his new initiative on "Decentralization in Centralism." He defined it as: "a measure whereby through the party and government machinery, we will decentralize most of the party and government activities while retaining effective control of the party and government machinery at the centre in the interest of unity" (Zambia 1986: 13).

Village and ward development committees were set up on the basis of the Village Registration and Development Act of 1971. The essence of this experiment was to decentralize government activities to the localities. These activities were to be run by local officials under the supervision of centrally approved administrative officials. As in other African countries, the coordination of these ministerial activities at the local level by this central corps of officials proved impossible. Personnel, management, accounting, and policy remained centralized in Lusaka (the capital city). Disappointed with the results of this 1971 act, another act was passed in 1980, the Local Administration Act of 1980. It became effective in 1981.

The new law abolished the tripartite local government structure of city/municipal, township, and rural councils. In their place was now established a single structure of fifty-five districts which was to form the focus of all government and party activities. Each district was headed by a party official, the district governor, assisted by a district secretary. Above this level was the province, in which all government activities were carried out by a provincial cabinet minister with the assistance of a provincial permanent secretary. Consultative assemblies were appointed/elected to consider government proposals at each level.

In spite of these arrangements, central government sectoral ministries have been reluctant to decentralize resources and responsibilities to regional departments. Also, even though local representation had been strengthened by the 1980 reform, central administrators posted to the district still dominated the local assemblies because they controlled the budget.

The Minister for Decentralization was widely quoted in 1986 (six years after the second reform) to the effect that decentralization "had not started functioning" (Times of Zambia 1986). The essence of the Zambian reforms seems to have strengthened the central government's control over a wide range of affairs. Decentralization seems to have been designed to enable the country's single party to gain a stronger foothold in the districts (Chikulo 1985; Conyers 1985). Some of these veiled attempts at centralization have been resisted successfully by trade unions in collaboration with the church (Sklar 1983) and by the Zambian Association of Local Governments on some specific issues (Olowu 1987a).

Sudan

Sudanese local governments as elsewhere in Africa acquired increasing participative status, responsibilities, and tax powers from the early 1950s. A 1960 reform had sought to concentrate more of these powers and responsibilities of local governments at the provincial level. The objective of the 1971 People's Local Government (PLG) Act was "to achieve maximum participation of citizens in the administration of their local affairs and thus reduce centralization." The reform was meant to give meaning to the socialist May revolution which had been launched at the national level by the Nimeiri government shortly after it came to power in 1969. The act was followed up in 1977 and 1979 by presidential orders which transferred several executive responsibilities to local governments and made the president of the republic the patron of all the newly created local government units (running up to 5,000) in the country. Seven national ministries were abolished in view of these changes. They included Interior, Religious Affairs, Social Affairs, Youth and Sports, Cooperation, Commerce and Supply. Education, Agriculture, Health and Public Works were all reduced in scale, and the powers of others such as the Ministry of Finance were redefined in favor of the local authorities. Several central officials were seconded to the provincial councils. The realignment of central ministries was undertaken because it was perceived as the major threat to the success of decentralization. Traditional rulers were excluded from the newly created councils in which government representatives constituted about a third except in a few councils where a quarter of the council positions were expected to be filled by women.

At the apex of this decentralization plan was the provincial commissioner, a political appointee who presided over the provincial executive council (PEC), the public service, the police, and security matters in the province. The commissioner also had the power to veto decisions of the provincial council adjudged not to be in the "public interest." Below the PEC were town and rural councils and at the base were the village and "furgan" (nomad) councils. Each council comprised both elected and government officials. The provincial commissioners worked directly under the president's office. Responsibilities were decentralized on paper, but the powers of taxation for a wide range of local activities were retained by government. Moreover, the provincial executive councils were the only bodies with budgetary powers. They budgeted for all other local governments in the province—villages, towns, and camps. These lower level councils had no staff of their own and were heavily dependent on government grants.

A wider array of services were performed by local governments in the Sudan as a result of these reforms. Local government budgeted expenditure increased about a hundred-fold between 1955 and 1980, but over a third (36 percent) of the revenue resources came from the national government as grants. In the southern provinces the proportion was as high as 77 percent. Even these revenue transfers enabled the councils to undertake only a minimal portion of their newly acquired responsibilities. Moreover, the lowest councils had no independent budgets of their own. These councils were generally understaffed and underfunded as staff and finances were generally concentrated at the provincial level in the north and at the regional level in the south. In 1981, the provincial executive councils were abolished and replaced by regional councils with powers similar to the old provincial councils, but with the regional governor appointed by the president rather than by the regional assembly as in the South.

One close student of Sudanese politics suggests that the decentralization of responsibilities to local institutions was actually interpreted more as an "evasion of responsibility by the centre than a genuine program to promote local initiatives" (Norris 1983: 67). Another study of decentralization reforms in the country saw "decentralization" as an article of faith whose tangible benefits were yet to appear (Rondinelli 1983a: 94).

The key to understanding the failure of what appeared to have been a bold decentralization program in the Sudan is the desire to "decentralize" from the center and at the same time concentrate power at another level, either at the provincial or regional level. Either of these levels was still far too distant from the people and disconnected from any representative processes to be considered a true decentralization: deconcentration continued. Finally, as one study concluded in 1980, key fiscal powers were tenaciously held at the center by the Treasury (Leonard and Wunsch 1982).

Tanzania

Few countries' decentralization efforts have been subjected to as much study and analysis as the Tanzania decentralization reforms. Perhaps this was due to its widely publicized ideology of self-reliance, or the fact that decentralization was tied to rural development and a basic needs (BN) strategy nine years before the International Labour Office formally adopted BN as policy.

Tanzania's decentralization programs of the 1970s were premised on that country's leadership ideology of socialist self-reliance as articulated in the Arusha Declaration of 1967. That declaration entailed the abolition of private enterprise, the nationalization of private agricultural and industrial enterprises, the reduction of the country's dependence on external finance, and the redistribution of wealth across social classes and between the urban and rural areas. The national civil service and parastatal agencies were to be relied upon to manage nationalized enterprises. But the decentralization of decision-making and development were also considered necessary for success. The cornerstone of the decentralization program was the promotion of communal farming within "Ujamaa" or "familyhood" villages.

The Decentralization of Government Act of 1972 abolished the country's local government system. Its functions and responsibilities were transferred to the newly created planning and implementation committees. The new framework displaced the system of local government which had performed a range of creditable services in urban and rural areas with a restructured central government field administrative system in each of the 20 regions and 80 districts. Development authorities were established at regional, district, and village levels to coordinate central government activities, planning, and local initiatives at their respective levels. Each of these institutional levels were related directly to equivalent hierarchies of the sole political party. Deliberative assemblies were created at all levels, involving both elected representatives and relevant government function-aries at the district and regional levels. Development secretariats were headed by centrally appointed directors both at the district and regional levels. These coordinated both central and local government activities in their respective jurisdictions. These development directors were senior central "generalist" officials and were assisted by a team of professional officers (for finance, planning, personnel), all seconded from the central government. Above this cadre of administrators were the regional and district commissioners who were accorded ministerial status. District budgets were approved at the regional level and all the plan proposals had to be submitted to the prime ministers' office for final approval before any could be implemented.

The lowest or village level was headed by the local branch secretary of the country's single party. In 1973, this national system of deconcentration was extended to the 8,000 villages into which the government had grouped the country's farmers. To be registered, each village settlement was required to meet stringent conditions set by the government. Machinery for popular participation was provided in each Ujamaa village, but this was under the general supervision of the village manager, appointed by the central government.

The consensus among those who have studied Tanzanian decentralization is that it was a failure from the points of view of agricultural productivity, infrastructure allocation, and administrative management. One can deduce from a number of facts that there was no shortage of commitment on the part of the national political leadership to "decentralization" in at least this form in Tanzania. About 40 percent of the country's development budget was allocated to the regions and districts, and opportunities for participation existed. Yet, participation by the local people in these newly created institutions actually declined (Kasfir 1983: 39). Public sector employment grew and recurrent expenditure increased by more than five times compared to agriculture, and three times compared to industry without improving the overall national productivity or even the coordination of management of public sector programs. Neither the center nor the local electorate could effectively coordinate development activities. Local revenues fell in relative and absolute amounts. "Participation was seen mainly as an affair of the party, and public works as a function of the central government" (Mawhood 1983: 96).

The villagization program succeeded to the extent that it brought together scattered families into village settlements and enabled the government infrastructure to reach the largest possible number of peasants. However, the heavy cost of "inducing" farmers into the new villages—estimated at some 30 million pounds sterling—has been considered prohibitive. Moreover, the socialist objectives of communal production within the village program was a disastrous failure, particularly in the richer and more fertile upland areas. The array of consultative committees designed to encourage citizen participation was largely dominated by administrators and technicians (Samoff 1981: 303). Even ex-President Julius Nyerere conceded the failure of his decentralization strategy with respect to the local governments and cooperatives recently:

> There are certain things I would not do if I were to start again. One of them is the abolition of local government and the other is the disbanding of the cooperatives. We were impatient and ignorant. . . . The real price we paid was in the acquisition of a top-heavy bureaucracy. We replaced local governments and cooperatives by parastatal organizations. We thought these organizations run by the state would contribute to progress because they would be under parliamentary control. We ended up with a huge machine which we cannot operate efficiently (Nyerere 1984: 828, 830).

This appraisal is in agreement with the reports of most of the studies conducted into the Tanzanian decentralization program (Boesen et al. 1977; Hyden 1980; Picard 1980; McHenry 1979; 1981; Rondinelli 1983a; Mawhood 1983). Since 1982, the Tanzanian government has embarked on the revival of old structures of local governments which it had earlier abolished.

Kenya

Decentralization programs in Kenya have concentrated on developing new field administrative units that could assist the process of development planning and implementation throughout the country. Aside from the elimination of regional level governments in 1964 and the assumption of direct control over local government (in contrast to the federal independence constitution which placed this responsibility on regional level governments), government decentralization programs have left the inherited local government system intact. One indirect impact of these policies has been to enervate this country's local government system and bring the country more and more under deconcentrated administration (Oyugi 1983; see also Chapter 8).

The government's decentralization of 1970 was tied very closely to the country's rural development goals and the encouragement of small scale farms and industries. Provincial development committees (PDC) were created to review proposals from district development committees (DDC) and coordinate provincial plans and implementation with respect to rural development.

Both committees were composed of the most senior departmental officers of the central government who were located in the province and district and who were connected with the development projects. They were headed by the provincial and district commissioners respectively. In addition, provincial and district advisory committees were established which included both heads of departmental units as well as parliamentary members and the chairmen, clerks and treasurers of the county or rural councils. These committees possessed neither statutory nor executive powers, they controlled no funds, nor could they enforce their decisions. Department loyalty remained stronger than regional or district vision. The government attempted a change in 1974 by appointing development officers and district planning officers to assist the DDCs and PPCs. But this made the generalist commissioners feel threatened. They found sympathy in the key Ministries of Finance and Planning. As a result, "rural development planning and administration in Kenya remain centralized, and PPCs and DDCs continue to play relatively weak roles. The central ministries retain control over sectoral plans and budgets, and recommendations from the districts rarely influence national policy" (Rondinelli 1983a: 83).

Increasing centralism regarding local affairs also led to a considerable weakening of the county (rural) councils. In a few short years after independence, provincial level administration was strengthened at their expense. While the municipal governments continued to enjoy a number of the tax powers and responsibilities given to them at independence as well as generous grants from the central government, rural councils had their responsibilities and fiscal powers withdrawn in the early 1970s. Education, health and roads were taken over by the central government in January 1970 in the face of increasing financial difficulties by local governments. These accounted for about 80 percent of local government expenditures. The other major service, water, was taken over by the central government in some rural councils in 1974.

West Africa

In 1982, an international conference was convened in Ile-Ife, Nigeria, to review the progress of local government in West Africa since independence. It found that similar problems confronted local governments in both French-speaking and English-speaking countries in spite of the spate of reforms which each country had sponsored since independence. These problems hinged on the denial of resources necessary for local governments to exist as independent institutions by their respective central governments. It was discovered that "even though the thrust of most reform efforts has been towards a participatory model of local government (devolution), they effectively utilized a deconcentrated administrative strategy" (Adamolekun et al. 1986). The fact that the existence of democratic and participatory local governments were written into the constitutions (in Ghana and Nigeria), or were given special legal protections (as in Francophone West Africa) did not seem to have helped matters either.

Nigeria's reform of its local governments in 1976 was aimed at breaking away from this tradition of deconcentrated/administrative decentralization towards a genuine allocation of broad responsibilities and resources to local government. The country's newly created 301 (now 304) local governments were expected to have their own councils, budgets, and secretariats. Old revenue sources were revived and new ones were added from the national treasury. A new niche was given to local governments as a third-tier level of government in a federation in which federal and state units had been dominant. According to the spokesman of the military government which launched the reform, the reform had to: "entail the decentralization of some significant functions of state governments to local levels in order to harness local resources for rapid development." Furthermore, the new "local governments should do precisely what the word government implies, i.e., governing at the grassroots or local level" (Nigeria 1976: 1). The experiment had limited successes up to 1979, but some of the contradictions in the reform model already made themselves evident by 1978. Local governments were heavily dependent on grants. Since these grants passed through state governments, considerable opportunity existed for the latter to ensure that the new local governments operated as local administrations, the very model of decentralization reform that was rejected by the 1976 policy package.

Today, the local governments are effectively subordinated to state governments rather than to the public. They operate more as extensions of the state bureaucracy rather than as local self-governing institutions, and four major weaknesses of the local government system have been identified. First is their increasing dependence on federal statutory allocations which are passed through the state governments. Second is the failure to hold local elections since 1979 when fresh elections were due. The councils have been run since 1979 either by selected management committees or senior officials referred to as "sole administrators." Third, the local governments are very large (ranging from 150,000 to over a million population) and as such are not perceived by very many local communities as local institutions with which they can identify. Finally, even though councils have powers to appoint their officials, senior and middle level local government personnel are recruited and deployed by a local government service commission which is responsible to state rather than to the local governments (Gboyega 1983; Adamolekun 1984; Olowu 1986).

Ghana has recently committed itself to implementing a prototype of the failed Tanzanian model in spite of the lessons that the Tanzanian political leadership seems to be learning from the failure of its "decentralization" experiment (Harris 1983; Akuoko-Frimpong 1987).

Dr. Nkrumah's Convention Peoples Party had replaced the inherited local government structures with regional and district committees based on the one-party "mobilization model." This meant the domination of local councils at district and regional levels by party activists under the general direction of district and regional commissioners. Nevertheless, local field administrative structures were still distinct from local government (Wraith 1972).

After the 1966 coup which toppled Kwame Nkrumah, three administrative commissions were established in 1968 to recommend changes in Ghana's administrative system. Their recommendation made a strong case for a "fused" administrative model which integrated local government and field administration structures at four levels: regional, district, local, and town/village development committees. This was felt to be the only model which, in the view of one of the three commissions mentioned above (the Commission on the Structure and Remuneration of the Public Service or Mills-Odoi Report), could rectify the "excessive centralization of authority and of financial and staff resources in Accra" and the fragmentation of decision making at the center. To improve these problems, ran the report, greater emphasis must be given to professional management of the councils. That is, greater attention ought to be paid to administration and coordination in the system. Ironically, in view of the concern with "overcentralization," this meant the abolition of the local government system and its displacement by central government's field administration.

This system has remained largely unchanged until today. Since 1983 the Rawlings Administration has been pursuing a decentralization proposal which will decentralize virtually all ministerial activities through the regions to the localities. Progress has, however, been very slow because of powerful forces within the administration against this plan; the distrust of elected councilors by the military and civil servants alike; and the opinion of many that decentralization is a diversion from the country's current policy of economic recovery (Harris 1983; Akuoko-Frimpong 1987). In the meantime, the old structures have continued with selected management committees presiding over deconcentrated administration at regional, district and local levels.

Several countries in *Francophone West Africa* have experimented with decentralization reforms. In the Benin Republic, the "Marxist" government which seized power in 1972 launched a "decentralization" reform in February 1974. The objective was to transform inherited structures of local government into popular, socialist-oriented structures that not only afforded people an opportunity for mass participation but also led to the adoption of communal and cooperative agricultural production by the farmers. *Departments* were broken down into urban/rural *districts, communes, and villages,* each with its own legislative and executive machinery. The turnouts at the two local elections in 1982 and 1986 were impressive, but this might have been due to the government's intensive campaign and mobilization efforts rather than to the success of the decentralization program. As elsewhere in Africa, decentralization increased the powers of the government to control the localities, as the local institutions still lacked financial resources and autonomy even though their powers were enshrined in the constitution (Adamolekun et al. 1986; Ayo 1984).

Mali, Niger, Burkina Faso, and Guinea have also attempted varying reforms of their local government systems. The attempt in each country is to decentralize the inherited structures such that more local units are created. Elections, usually based on single party nominations, have generally followed such initiatives. In many of these Francophone countries, however, local governments nonetheless play a limited role. In the Cote d'Ivoire, for instance, total municipal revenue accounted for only 2.7 percent of the current revenue of the central government in 1969 and only 1.7 percent of total public revenue in 1975, most of which (70 percent) is accounted for by Abidjan (den Tuinder 1978; see also Cohen 1974). Twenty-four prefectures and 107 underprefectures were created out of six departments in 1969. Communes were created in 1978 when the first elections were held after two decades. Another reform was introduced in 1980 which created more communes and prefectures. Elections for these councils were in 1985. Abidjan currently has a federated city council as a result of this reform.

Decentralization reforms in Francophone West Africa take the *prefect* as well as central controls as given and concentrate on structural reorganization and democratization (Mawhood and Davey 1980; Laleye and Ayo 1987; Olowu 1987a). In the Cameroon, for instance, a spate of local government reforms have been undertaken, but the president still appoints all the municipal administrators to the country's 170 municipal councils. The four key cities of Yaounde, Douala, Bamenda, and Nkongsamba are in addition headed by government delegates. In July 1987, the government delegates for Yaounde and Douala were replaced by mayors popularly elected through the country's sole party. The Senegalese case is different in important respects, and that experience is reviewed in Chapter 6.

Explanations of Decentralization Failure

Explanations of the failure of decentralization in Africa are interesting more because of the insights they offer as to the assumptions of their exponents than to the real problems of decentralization. As their exponents have also been influential in designing decentralization reforms, a review of the major explanations is worthwhile. We will discuss three here.

The first approach is one generally held by multi-lateral development institutions such as the World Bank, other United Nations agencies, and to some extent the Commonwealth Secretariat. They blame decentralization's failures on poor implementation of decentralization programs by the central government and its agencies. To them, implementation problems have included lack of clear objectives, ambiguous legislation, poor planning of decentralization process, inadequate resources, shortage of skilled personnel to service the reform as well as poor overall management (Cheema and Rondinelli 1983; Conyers 1985; 1986). The prescription for this is better planning of the decentralization process, the commitment of more resources to decentralization, and the improvement of personnel skills (Cochrane 1983). Decentralization has failed for *technical* reasons.

Running through the arguments of this school is a clear tendency to overlook or underplay the political aspects of decentralization, and to emphasize the administrative/technical aspects. As is evident from a passage in a recent review of local government in developing countries:

> The reluctance of politicians in central government to share power with local authorities is not the real problem—on the contrary, one of the greatest threats to the successful reform of local government in developing countries is the politically motivated and, too often, poorly planned decentralization exercises that fail to provide sufficient resources to enable local governments to fulfill their aspirations (Cochrane 1983: 6).

While not denying that there are indeed problems of implementation in every policy field, it is simplistic and superficial to gloss over the critical political questions implied by decentralization reforms, particularly when they were made in expectation of dramatic changes in public participation and official performance. We shall return to this problem later, but we shall for now go on to examine the second school.

For want of a better phrase, we may call this second group the "mobilization" or "modernization" school. Among its adherents are a large number of development economists and political scientists. Development, as they use this concept, borrows heavily from Parsonian social theory. It is seen as a process of moving from a traditional to a "modern" industrialized state. The acquisition of capital and technology necessary for this type of industrialization requires an initial centralization of powers to destroy "old structures" which slow down the mobilization process. Any attempts to grant autonomy to local institutions are bound to be counterproductive. Scholars such as David Apter, Samuel Huntington, Arthur Lewis, and W. W. Rostow take this perspective, often without fully elaborating the position. We owe the full elaboration of the school's thought on this issue to Fred W. Riggs. In a chapter titled, "Local Government and Circular Causation" of his now famous book, *Administration in Developing Countries,* Riggs argues that local government weakness is a consequence of underdevelopment. In turn, local underdevelopment is caused by local government weakness. According to him "the strength of local administration tends to vary directly with the degree of economic development of a region" (Riggs 1964: 374). Local autonomy under conditions of underdevelopment leads to stagnation rather than development. A "breakout" can only come from external forces. One finds a similar line of reasoning in Nellis when he contends that there is a contradiction between local autonomy and economic development (Nellis 1984). The overall underdeveloped economic, social, and political environment constitutes a veritable impossible obstacle to decentralization for an illiterate, poor, and underdeveloped people in this perspective. Under these assumptions only a program of deconcentration makes any sense.

Central to this position is the assumption that the most progressive portions of a country (with respect to modernization) are the capital and major industrial cities, while the least development-conscious people are in the countryside. Indeed, the actual experiences of several developing countries contradicts this assumption as we shall show below. Often the reverse situation exists: rural people show willingness to engage in innovative activities, take risks and make new investments, whereas the urban elites manifest the opposite behaviors (Hill 1970; Berry 1985; Smock 1971). For example, one might consider the massive unethical and wasteful practices in the public and private sectors perpetrated by so-called elites to the detriment of their nations' welfare. A stagnating pattern of rent-seeking behavior growing from the political power derived from centralization seems more characteristic of these classes than are innovation, investment and change (Bates 1981).

While Riggs contends that the urban centers make the greatest contribution to government revenues in the Philippines (Riggs 1964), the African experience depicts the exact reverse. In Africa, most evidence suggests that urban centers exist parasitically on their rural areas (Mabogunje 1968; Lipton 1977; Bates 1981). Once we compare the presumptions concerning the concept of "development" according to this school with the realities of rural peoples' record of innovation and competence, a crucial aspect of the mobilization model seems rather uncertain. We shall return to this issue shortly. To this school, decentralization fails from its own inability to deal with the pressing need for "modernization."

The third school draws on elite/class analysis to interpret the failure of decentralization in Third World countries. In this view, in developing countries, public office is the major institution which the dominant classes use to buttress their rule (Jackson and Rosberg 1982; Bates 1981). It is therefore unlikely that such individuals, clothed with power, will surrender this source of their dominance to local level institutions. In order to appease the lower classes it might be necessary to offer an appearance of local democracy without its substance (Lamb 1979; Smith 1985). In fact, there seems to be some insight in this approach, for the great resistance to decentralization in Africa has not come from the political officials or their allies outside government. It has come instead from senior administrators who occupy strategic positions within the bureaucracy and society (Cheema and Rondinelli 1983; Wunsch 1983; Olowu 1987a). Decentralization is perceived as a loss by those whose positions depend on the closed structures of the government bureaucracy. It is thus paradoxical that decentralization reforms presumed that this same group would promote the dispersal of powers and resources which used to be their exclusive preserves. This illuminates one of the major obstacles on the continent to decentralization (Nti 1975; Subramaniam 1980).

All the three perspectives reviewed above lend important insights into the failure of decentralization reforms in Africa. We draw on each of these perspectives in the attempt to analyze what was actually attempted in Africa and why it failed.

Common Assumptions of Current Decentralization Programs

At the heart of the decentralization programs reviewed above are certain usually implicit assumptions with respect to the goal and strategy of the decentralization effort. These have worked repeatedly to limit the extent of decentralization. Behind the assumptions themselves are models of social transformation underpinned by the political mobilization and development administration models.

The first assumption is in respect of the *goal* of decentralization. Decentralization in fact usually has been intended as a technique (or means) of achieving *central government programs* of economic and social development, especially in the countryside. As a result, it is viewed as a technical rather than a political issue, and as a question of ensuring *better* control by the center rather than opening the door for true local initiative. The premise for such a position has earlier been discussed under the mobilization model. Its consequences are usually central administrative overload.

On the basis of the first assumption with respect to the goal of decentralization is the second implicit assumption, occasionally made explicit as in the Tanzanian reform drawn up by an American management consulting firm. This is that the *central government bureaucracy* constitutes the major *instrument* for ensuring "successful decentralization." This has often led to an expansion of the ministerial department charged with decentralization, or as in several Francophone African countries, and lately in Nigeria, with the creation of special parastatal agencies to stimulate rural development. In addition, central government officials are seen as essential to oversee the process of decentralization, adopting a posture of tutelage to local institutions. This explains, for instance, why the emphasis on training for decentralization is focused more on local officials rather than central officials and part of why national officials feel more burdened after "decentralization" than before. This usually leads to local popular passivity. (See Chapter 6 for a full discussion of the Senegalese experience.)

A third assumption flowing from the first two and reinforced by African leaders' experience with the limited local revenue payoffs of decentralization, is that only when ample *resources* exist at the *central level* can a program of decentralization succeed. This reasoning grows from the belief that decentralization involves giving away central government resources. Given this, when resources, especially revenues, are lacking, decentralization programs are not likely to succeed. This is a common thread running through virtually all of the official reports on decentralization (Cheema and Rondinelli 1983; Rondinelli et al. 1984; Conyers 1986). Only governments such as Libya (Nellis 1983) or Nigeria (Kasfir 1983; Mawhood 1987), fortunate to have wind-falls of oil or mineral revenues, are regarded as having the possibility of making a success of their decentralization reform. Since most African countries are poor, their reluctance to part with tax resources (which they took from the grassroots level in the first place) is thus understandable given the assumptions behind the type of decentralization programs we have examined.

What is important to underscore here is that what has failed in Africa (and many other developing countries for that matter) is not decentralization *per se* but a particular form of decentralization consistent with these assumptions, one which should have simply been labeled "deconcentration." This has taken many forms: a pure prefectoral system, a mixture of native authority rule with prefectoral administration (indirect rule), or the mixture of advisory committees and the prefectoral system. The advisory committees (Tanzania, Tunisia, Zambia) or "people's executive councils" (Sudan, Libya) or management committees (Nigeria, Ghana) are examples of this last form. Either way, the principle is that the central government manages local services through its representatives.

Three complementary schools of thought suggest how the models undergirding deconcentration were in error. Together, they help point the way to a new theory of decentralization. The first argues that the understanding of "development" as "mobilization" is simply mistaken, and the emphasis on limited deconcentration that flows from that is, not surprisingly, a nonstarter. It argues that development based on the mobilization model together with its associated concept of development administration has brought Africa to a point where it is engulfed in an unprecedented economic and fiscal crisis. Sources of failure have included poor economic management, political and bureaucratic corruption, and the problems of dealing with adverse political, physical, and economic environments. It believes that most of these problems are either caused or aggravated by the management strategies dictated by this model of development. As a result, new models of "development" have emerged which rely less on the central government bureaucracy and centralized planning, and more on mobilizing a wide diversity of actors (see next chapter). In other words, the very premise of the mobilization development model, the special group of elites designated as "modernizers" (Apter 1965), has given way to one in which it is increasingly being realized that innovation and change are a broad experimental and learning process that could benefit tremendously from local peoples' knowledge and creativity, as well as that of the educated elites (Fuglesang 1984; Richards 1985; Uphoff 1985a; 1985b). The mobilization-centralist model works no better in the periphery than it does at the center, and deconcentration fails because it does not decentralize enough.

The second school notes that the twentieth century's unquestioning *belief* in the superiority of the bureaucracy is giving way today to an appreciation of the several weaknesses and excesses of bureaucracy. Whereas it was once contended that African states were under bureaucratized, it is beginning to emerge that the poor performance of central government bureaucracies might be due to the fact that they have over-reached their capacities (World Bank 1981; Hyden 1983; Wunsch 1986). This is particularly dramatic in the field of decentralization. The model of decentralization expounded in Africa, in fact, expects the central bureaucracy to shoulder the task of coordinating, initiating, and directing "development" throughout the country. Reliance is put on bureaucratic skills and hierarchy for success. Unfortunately, these skills are usually lacking leading to a breakdown of this "decentralization" model.

Two examples will suffice. Centralized planning has been such a disastrous failure in Africa that several African countries have essentially abandoned it. A recent report argues that no difference in development performance is attributable to greater or lesser commitment to planning (Agarwala 1983). Yet this has been one of the central, major justifications to refrain from genuine decentralization efforts: how to ensure that local institutions complied with central plans? Even if such a model might make sense in theory, African states clearly lack the quantity and quality of public officials that can mobilize development from the top at this time (Rondinelli 1983b; Tordoff 1984). The other example is from Nigeria where a recent assessment of top level political and administrative leadership in Nigeria concludes that it is futile to talk about an "imbalance thesis" between these groups because the two groups are each "fundamentally" weak (Adamolekun 1986). In contrast, several studies have demonstrated the strength of local institutions developed by the local people themselves in Africa and in other developing countries, and which have successfully served local peoples' needs (Owens and Shaw 1972; Jones 1979; Esman and Uphoff 1984). The success contrasts markedly with the failure of several "deconcentrated" institutions and the poor reputation of formal local government institutions as the hot-bed of corruption, ineffectiveness, and inefficiencies (Wraith and Simpkins 1963; Olowu 1987b). Once again we see that deconcentration fails because it is too timid.

This brings us to the third interpretation of deconcentration's failure, one stressing the need to understand development as a political process which must be open to a nation's political forces and needs (individuals, group interests) in order to succeed. This interpretation is in part a reaction to those who viewed government and administration as mechanisms to contain potentially explosive social forces, and the tendency to limit "decentralization" reforms under such regimes. This school accepts that the development process sets forth a number of changes which may be regarded as threatening to any prevailing regime. Such developments might include the possible emergence of a plurality of interests: ethnic, economic, cultural, and political. Accommodating these plural interests does pose a challenge to regimes. The response to this problem in most African nations has been to suppress such forces by the imposition of a single-party system, or draconian legislation which turns any opposition opinions or sentiments into treason (Zolberg 1966; Kasfir 1971; Sklar 1983). Within such a framework only deconcentrated decentralization makes sense. However, the result of three decades of repression has been continuing instability rather than peace (Rothchild and Olorunsola 1983; Luckham 1985). As this school looks skeptically at the capacity of the state to suppress and contain social forces, it looks instead to developing many arenas and institutions through which diverse people can structure their interactions and relationships.

In this respect it is important to note that African leaders failed here to build on relevant past experience. Many of them had accused colonial leaders of failing to involve them and their people in the management of their communities. As a result, self-governing institutions were introduced in several African countries. Impressive results ensued which created opportunities for some of today's leaders to achieve popularity and political power, and independence was achieved shortly afterwards (Hicks 1961). Rather than build and improve on these institutions, they replaced them with expanded state structures, often with disastrous results. Furthermore, historical and anthropological studies indicate that local self-governing structures are more compatible with several traditional African political systems than the nominally "decentralized" structures created by African states. These traditional self-governing structures (ethnic, town and community unions) have continued to coexist with the newly created structures in several African countries with very little interaction between the two structures (Fortes and Evans-Pritchard 1940; Middleton and Tait 1958; Smock 1971; Owusu 1970; Jones 1979; Olaniyan 1985; Olowu 1987a).

Toward an Alternative Model of Decentralization

As discussed above, most of Africa's "decentralization" initiatives have been judged failures. Typically, such failures have led academics, donors and officials to turn away from local governments and refocus their attention to the central state.

However, such a judgement and such a policy conclusion may be premature and mistaken. To fairly and usefully evaluate the decentralization experience, one must consider the criteria being used to judge the efforts, and evaluate whether these goals lay within the reach of the reforms as conceptualized and implemented.

Most analysts judge decentralization a failure because one or more of the following conditions apply to those countries which pursued it once the reforms were completed:

1. local institutions are unable to raise sufficient revenue to fulfill their responsibilities;
2. local institutions increase rather than reduce the workload of central coordinating agencies leading to a need for increased bureaucratization and control by central agencies; or,

3. local peoples appear apathetic toward the decentralized local institutions.

Our argument is that decentralization, as understood and implemented in contemporary Africa, had these outcomes designed into it from the start. These "designs" grew from the contradictions and misconceptions that their designers held. Specifically "decentralization" reforms were advocated and lauded at their inception as mechanisms to increase local participation, raise far greater local revenue, and ease the burden on central bureaucracies. However, once one closely reviews those efforts, it can be seen how the decentralized institutions were consciously subjected to close bureaucratic supervision. That supervision worked, indeed, to increase the administrative load, squeeze out any room for initiative by the "decentralized" units, and finally deny local dwellers any incentive to invest themselves in these institutions.

This approach was consistent with the primary objective of field administrative systems which has been to manage central government programs at the local level. To maximize efficiency under this system, the control capabilities of the central government must be expanded to ensure effective coordination. There is a strict limit to the discretion that field units can be allowed: discretion could be allowed only on routine activities, but certainly not for substantial independent powers such as discretionary tax authority. Also, participation from citizens is limited to a confirmation (or rejection) of central government's initiatives rather than developing or refining their own. Lacking "ownership" of programs, authority to raise and spend money on their own priorities, and an opportunity to learn from and implement the lessons of their experience, not surprisingly, revenues are not raised and the people are passive. Indeed, all the indicators of decentralization's "failure," looked at in this light, can be seen as the *normal outcomes* of the deconcentration that African governments have actually pursued.

We shall now present an alternative model of decentralization based on our criticism of the deconcentrated model above. This is one which we believe can contribute substantially to Africa's economic and social development.

This alternative model posits a different approach to development. African people are regarded as no different from other human beings. As such, they are seen as interested in their own self-improvement. Like all other human beings, they would do all that is in their power to improve their lot. When this cannot be achieved alone, individuals associate with others or with groups in order to produce what they consider as essential goods and services. This is the driving force behind self-governance (E. Ostrom 1982), and many cases of its operation have been documented in Africa (Cohen 1969; Smock 1971; Jones 1979; Williams 1980; Kolawole 1982; Wallis 1982; Richards 1985; Olowu 1987c).

In this context and with these assumptions in view, the issue of all political organization including decentralization becomes clearly a fundamental economic and political rather than administrative problem. It is an economic problem in that it deals with enabling people to join with one another to solve common problems related to the production of goods and services. It is political in that it involves sharing power between the citizen and the official in such a way as to ensure order and facilitate collective action, while simultaneously protecting the citizens from predation by their rulers. The issue of local government is thus fundamentally a constitutional issue. It is one to approach as an issue of organizing and channeling popular collective choice and collective action, rather than imposing policy or solutions from the center to solve technical problems of administration. In this regard, local self-governing units constitute one of the fundamental components of the polity.

The essential characteristics of local self-governing institutions under this context would include the following. The first is appropriate size which, in the African context, generally means smaller than has hitherto been attempted. As much as possible, basic local institutions must encompass the basic local community, since this is the most natural community in which working understandings about human relationships may already be expected to exist or to develop. Opportunities should exist for federation among these communities, but they must be regarded as primary since the opportunities for individual identification and participation and awareness of relationship between personal effort and outcome are highest at this level.

This contrasts with the current attempts on the continent to create the largest possible institution to "manage services." Such reform efforts are based on attempts to imitate local government modernization efforts in the industrialized countries, and approaches "development" as a technical rather than social and organizational process. Even in developed countries, serious misgivings have been expressed recently about this notion of local government modernization through essentially technocratic and consolidation strategies. The evidence that they always lead to the improvement in service delivery is feeble. If anything they may lead under certain circumstances to depreciation in the quality of services delivered (Sharpe 1981; Bish and Ostrom 1973; V. Ostrom et al. 1988; E. Ostrom 1976). Their effects in African conditions have even been more disappointing.

Nigeria provides a very good example of the failure of local government modernization premised on increased size of local governments to improve technical sophistication and economies of scale. By the reform of 1976, local government areas were enlarged to a minimum of 150,000 people. As a result, a total of 301 local government units were created. In a country of approximately 100 million people that meant an average population of 322,580 per local government unit, the second largest in Africa after Mali (373,000). The fact, of course, is that some local governments especially in the big cities have passed the 1 million mark. In many cases, "local governments" have lumped several antagonistic communities together leading to paralysis in such areas. In at least one case in Oyo State, (Oranmiyan local government) it led to serious violence. A government commission which appraised the reformed local government system in 1984 noted its amazement that the claim was made that:

> people would prefer to pay a levy of N200.00 per capita for a community project, the impact and actualization of which were readily visible, they would be reluctant to pay a rate of N10.00 to the coffers of a local government whose impact, in terms of services they hardly felt (Nigeria 1984: 10).

Many other African countries also currently have local government units that are "neither local nor government" (Olowu 1979; 1987b; Oyugi 1983: 137).

A second principle of self-governing decentralization is that self-governing units must have wide latitudes of autonomy to undertake a significant amount and variety of economic and social services which affect the people. As much as possible, the people themselves should be allowed to choose and produce as many of their own goods and services as they can through their local organizations. The central government should thus concern itself with only those services which it can best deliver. That is, it should focus on those that are beyond local scale capacities, are non-excludable and indivisible, or are essential services to sustain more general local action. Appropriate matters for local autonomy must include the power to raise tax resources to finance their activities. Without the requisite autonomy to be relevant, the institution cannot attract the most crucial resources: local public interest and local political leadership. This local energy and local leadership creates most other key resources for local development. It therefore misses the point to argue as Nellis does with respect to Morocco:

> It is true that the formal conditions for decentralization are not yet being met; that is, the local governments, with rare exceptions, do not raise their own funds and disperse them as they see fit. Again, one must acknowledge the harsh realities. The rural countryside is so poor that there is simply no tax base for local self-reliance. The rural local councilors are inexperienced and uneducated (Nellis 1983: 169).

There is some circular causation here, to borrow Riggs's term. The poor vestment of responsibility by the center in local governments leads responsible people to shy away from local governance. Alexis de Tocqueville makes a reference to this point in his *Democracy in America:*

> The New England township combines two advantages which wherever they are found, keenly excite men's interests; they are *independence* and *power*. It acts, it is true, within a sphere beyond which it cannot pass, but within that domain its movements are free. This independence alone would give a real importance not warranted by size or population.
>
> It is important that, in general, men's affections are drawn only in directions where power exists. . . . The New Englander is attached to his township not so much because he was born there as because he sees the township as a

free, strong corporation of which he is a part and which is worth the trouble of trying to direct (Tocqueville 1966: 68). (Emphasis added.)

The point is underscored again from the Nigerian experience. At the elections for local governments shortly after the 1976 reform, several individuals came forward to represent their local communities. They subsequently served as governors and parliamentarians at the state and federal levels. The period of their initial election coincided with the time when the councils had the greatest opportunities to utilize their newly given powers (Adamolekun and Rowland 1977; Adamolekun 1984).

Hence, a refusal to grant local autonomy leads to poverty in local public interest and in local political leadership. Such local authorities are thus unable to generate resources locally as well as organize economic and social services to bring social returns. It is, of course, true that circumstances in some local areas might dictate greater involvement by central officials at the initial stages. To create flexibility for the system, it may be helpful to grant increasing autonomy to local governments on the basis of performance. Those which generate substantial local resources and take a role in delivering local services may be usefully granted more autonomy than those that are dependent on government grants and are largely passive. However, a key point needs to be reiterated: without a basic floor of autonomy to begin with, the dynamic which will lead to growing resources will likely never start (Oakerson 1985).

 A third principle of self-governing decentralization is that self-governance must be approached as a political activity involving the fundamental allocation of governmental powers in society. As a result it should be given a formal legal expression which is not subject to unilateral revision by the central government. Rather the fundamental law or local government acts must be vested with the protections normally granted to changes of a constitutional order. Changes must be made only after broad consultation with the people and local governments, a consultation in which they play a significant role. This is a difficult though important principle. Decentralization as we conceive it here is not an administrative matter which can be continuously tinkered with by the government. As a piece of social engineering, time is required not only for the new institution to stabilize and legitimize itself but also for people to learn from their own mistakes and modify practices accordingly.

Very often, the experience in many African states is that local government councils are suspended for the flimsiest excuse or misdemeanor. At other times, their key responsibilities (as in Kenya with respect to the rural councils) are taken over by central government. In many other cases their tax powers have been suspended or abolished without consultation (as in Nigeria and a number of other countries; see Olowu 1987b). This produces extreme instability at the local level and an attitude of apathy and resignation among the people. Furthermore, the repeated suspension of local governments contributes to the popular image of local government inefficiency and pervasive corruption. The fact is, of course, that local governments are not necessarily less efficient nor more corrupt, solely by virtue of their type, than other governmental levels (Wraith and Simpkins 1963; Olowu 1988).

A final and most important principle is that of accountability. Local governments must be *primarily* accountable to the local people. This contrasts sharply with the present system across Africa in which local officials are primarily responsible to the central government (directly or indirectly). This principle of accountability can help ensure that local institutions are not also captured by a small local oligarchy in the long run, particularly when the people are mobilized into local affairs because local institutions deal with real issues and matters. It rejects the principle of indirect rule by central government officials through local dignitaries. In the long run, even disenfranchised people have learned how to organize to dislodge local oligarchies, a prospect that is foreclosed if local officials represent a national oligarchy or ruling class. This self-learning process is itself at the heart of development through self-governance. Central to the principle is the access of the local people to cheap and effective adjudicatory systems, which can serve as non-bureaucratic mechanisms capable of enforcing universal rules of access, fair play, due process and public responsibility (Tocqueville 1966).

Perhaps the most fundamental implication of our model is that it erases the so-called tension between decentralization and development. Rather what emerges is development through decentralization. Local organizations will then be able to perform critical roles within the law which they have performed to a limited extent through voluntary means outside the framework of government policy. In that regard, local governance should be seen not as nascent anarchy, but as the mechanism through which the collective power of the people is both unleashed and well structured to speed and widen development throughout the countryside.

References

Adamolekun, L. "The Idea of Local Government as a Third Tier of Government Revisited." *Quarterly Journal of Administration* 18 (3 & 4) (1984): 113–138.

———. *Politics and Administration in Nigeria.* London: Hutchinson, 1986.

———, Dele Olowu, and M. Laleye, eds. *Local Government in West Africa Since Independence.* Lagos: Lagos University Press, 1986.

———, and L. Rowland. *The New Local Government System in Nigeria: Problems and Prospects for Implementation.* Ibadan: Heinemann, 1977.

Agarwala, R. *Planning in Developing Countries: Lessons of Experience.* Washington, D.C.: World Bank Staff Working Papers No. 576, 1983.

Akuoko-Frimpong, H. "Decentralized Administration: The Ghanaian Experience." In *Decentralized Administration in West Africa: Cases, Issues, and Training Implications,* edited by Dele Olowu. London: Commonwealth Secretariat, 1987.

Apter, D. *The Politics of Modernization.* Chicago: University of Chicago Press, 1965.

Ayo, S. Bamidele. "Ideology, Local Administration and Problems of Rural Development in the Republic of Benin." *Public Administration and Development* 4 (1984): 361–372.

Bates, R. H. *Markets and States in Tropical Africa: The Political Basis of Agricultural Politics.* Berkeley: University of California Press, 1981.

Bennett, R. J. *The Geography of Public Finance.* London: Methuen, 1980.

Benz, Arthur. "Decentralization in the Federal Republic of Germany: A Case of Pragmatic Adaptation." *International Review of Administrative Sciences* 53 (4) (1987): 467–482.

Berry, S. *Fathers Work for Their Sons.* Berkeley: University of California Press, 1985.

Bish, Robert L., and Vincent Ostrom. *Understanding Urban Government: Metropolitan Reform Reconsidered.* Washington, D.C.: American Enterprise Institute for Public Policy Research, 1973.

Boesen, J., B.S. Madsen, and T. Moody. *Ujamaa-Socialism from Above.* Uppsala: Scandinavian Institute of African Studies, 1977.

Cheema, G.S., and D.A. Rondinelli. *Decentralization and Development.* Beverly Hills: Sage Publications, 1983.

Chikulo, B.C. "Reorganization for Local Administration in Zambia: An Analysis of the Local Administration Act, 1980." *Public Administration and Development* 5 (1985): 73–81.

Cochrane, G. *Policies for Strengthening Local Government in Developing Countries.* Washington, D.C.: World Bank Staff Working Papers No. 582, 1983.

Cohen, Abner. *Custom and Politics in Urban Africa: A Study of Hausa Migrants in Yoruba Towns.* Berkeley: University of California Press, 1969.

Cohen, M.A. *Urban Policy and Political Conflict in Africa: A Study of The Ivory Coast.* Chicago: University of Chicago Press, 1974.

Conyers, D. *Decentralization for Development: Select Annotated Bibliography.* London: Commonwealth Secretariat, 1983.

––––––. "Decentralization: A Framework for Discussion." In *Decentralization, Local Government Institutions and Resources Mobilization,* edited by H. A. Hye, 23–42. Comilla, Bangladesh: Academy for Rural Development, 1985.

––––––. *Decentralization for Development: Supplement to a Select Annotated Bibliography.* London: Commonwealth Secretariat, 1986.

den Tuinder, B.A. *Ivory Coast: The Challenge of Success.* Baltimore: Johns Hopkins University Press, 1978.

Esman, M.J., and N.T. Uphoff. *Local Organizations: Intermediaries in Rural Development.* Ithaca, New York: Cornell University Press, 1984.

Fortes, M., and E.E. Evans-Pritchard, eds. *African Political Systems.* London: International African Institute, 1940.

Fuglesang, A. "The Myth of People's Ignorance." *Development Dialogue* 1 & 2 (1984): 42–63.

Gboyega, A. "Local Government Reform in Nigeria." In *Local Government in the Third World,* edited by P. Mawhood. Chichester: John Wiley, 1983.

Harris, D. "Central Power and Local Reform: Ghana During the 1970s." In *Local Government in the Third World,* edited by P. Mawhood, 201–224. Chichester: John Wiley, 1983.

Hicks, U.K. *Development from Below: Local Government and Finance in Developing Countries of the Commonwealth.* Oxford: Clarendon Press, 1961.

Hill, P. *Studies in Rural Capitalism in West Africa.* London: Cambridge University Press, 1970.

Hyden, Goran. *Beyond Ujamaa in Tanzania: Underdevelopment and an Uncaptured Peasantry.* Berkeley: University of California Press, 1980.

_____. *No Shortcuts to Progress: African Development Management in Perspective.* Berkeley: University of California Press, 1983.

Jackson, R., and C. Rosberg. *Personal Rule in Black Africa.* Los Angeles: University of California Press, 1982.

Jones, G.I. "Changing Leadership in Eastern Nigeria: Before, During and After the Colonial Period." In *Politics and Leadership: A Comparative Perspective,* edited by W. A. Shack and P.S. Cohen. Oxford: Clarendon Press, 1979.

Kasfir, N. *The Shrinking Political Arena.* Berkeley: University of California Press, 1971.

_____. "Designs and Dilemmas: An Overview." In *Local Government in the Third World,* edited by P. Mawhood, 25–48. Chichester: John Wiley, 1983.

Kolawole, A. "The Role of Grassroots Participation in National Development: Lessons in Kwara State." *Community Development Journal* 17 (2) (1982): 121–133.

Laleye, O.M., and S.B. Ayo. "An Overview of Recent Trends in Anglophone and Francophone West Africa." *Planning and Administration* 14 (1) (1987): 61–67.

Lamb, G. "Local Administration: Points about Accumulation, Politics and Development." In *A Revival of Local Government and Administration,* edited by W.H. Morris-Jones and S.K. Pamter-Brick, 77–79. London: Institute of Commonwealth Studies, Collected Seminar Papers No. 23, 1979.

Leonard, David, and James Wunsch. *Recent Decentralization Initiatives in the Sudan: A Preliminary Assessment of Their Implications.* Berkeley, California: Institute of International Studies, 1980.

Lipton, M. *Why Poor People Stay Poor: Urban Bias in World Development.* London: Temple Smith, 1977.

Luckham, R. "Political and Social Problems of Development." In *Africa South of the Sahara.* 15th ed. London: Europa Publications, 1985.

Mabogunje, A.L. *Urbanization in Nigeria.* London: Oxford University Press, 1968.

Mawhood, P. *Local Government for Development: The Experience of Tropical Africa.* Chichester: John Wiley, 1983.

_____. "The Politics of Survival: Federal States in the Third World." *International Political Science Review* 5 (4) (1984): 521–531.

_____. "Decentralization and the Third World in the 1980s." *Planning and Administration* 14 (1) (1987): 10–22.

_____ and K.H. Dawey. "Anglophone Africa." In *International Handbook on Local Government Reorganization,* edited by D. C. Rowat, 404–414. Westport: Greenwood Press, 1980.

McHenry, D.E., Jr. *Tanzania's Ujamaa Villages.* Berkeley: University of California, Institute of International Studies, 1979.

_____. *Ujamaa Villages in Tanzania: A Bibliography.* Upsalla: Scandinavian Institute of African Studies, 1981.

Middleton, J., and D. Tait, eds. *Tribes Without Rulers: Studies in African Segmentary Systems.* London: Routledge & Kegan Paul, 1958.

Nellis, J.R. "Decentralization in North Africa: Problems of Policy Implementation." In *Decentralization and Development,* edited by G. S. Cheema and D. A. Rondinelli, 127–182. Beverly Hills: Sage, 1983.

_____. *Decentralization, Regional Development and Local Public Finance in Tunisia.* Occasional Paper No. 79. New York: Syracuse University, 1984.

Nigeria, Federal Military Government. "Local Government." *Report by the Committee on the Review of Local Government Administration in Nigeria.* Lagos: Supreme Headquarters, 1984.

Nigeria, Federal Republic. *Guidelines for Local Government Reform*. Kaduna: Government Printer, 1976.

Norris, M.W. "Sudan Administrative Versus Political Priorities." In *Local Government in the Third World,* edited by P. Mawhood, 49–73. Chichester: John Wiley, 1983.

Nti, J. "Ghana's Experience in Administrative Reform of the Central Bureaucracy." In *A Decade of Public Administration in Africa,* edited by A.H. Rweyemamu and Goran Hyden, 167–176. Nairobi: East African Literature Bureau, 1975.

Nyerere, J. Interview with *Third World Quarterly* 6 (4) (1984): 815–838.

Oakerson, Ronald J. "The Meaning and Purpose of Local Government: A Tocquevillist Perspective." Washington, D.C.: American Council on Inter-Governmental Relations Working Paper, 1985.

Olaniyan, R. *African History and Culture*. Ibadan: Longman, 1985.

Olowu, D. "Local Government and Urban Administration in Lagos State, Nigeria, 1968–78." Ph.D. Dissertation. Ile-Ife: University of Ife, 1979.

———. "A Decade of Local Government Reform in Nigeria, 1976–1986." *International Review of Administrative Sciences* 52 (3) (1986): 287–299.

———. *African Local Governments as Instruments of Economic and Social Development*. The Hague: International Union of Local Authorities, 1987a.

———. "Local Institutions and Development: The African Experience." Paper presented at a conference on "Advances in Comparative Institutional Analysis," Dubrovnik, Yugoslavia, October 19–23, 1987b.

———. "The Study of African Local Government Since 1960." *Planning and Administration* 14 (1) (1987c): 48–59.

———. "Bureaucratic Morality in Africa." *International Review of Administrative Sciences* 9 (1) (1988).

Ostrom, Elinor. "Size and Performance in a Federal System." *Publius* 6 (2) (Spring 1976): 33–73.

———, and Larry Kiser. "The Three Worlds of Action: A Metatheoretical Synthesis of Institutional Approaches." In *Strategies of Political Inquiry,* edited by Elinor Ostrom, 179–222. Beverly Hills, CA: Sage, 1982.

Ostrom, Vincent, Robert Bish, and Elinor Ostrom. *Local Government in the United States*. San Francisco: Institute for Contemporary Studies Press, 1988. (English version of *Il governo locale negli Stati Uniti*. Milano, Italy: Centro Studi della Fondazione Adriano Olivetti, Edizioni di Communita, 1984.)

Owens, E., and R. Shaw. *Development Reconsidered: Bridging the Gap Between Government and People*. Lexington, Mass.: Lexington Books, 1972.

Owusu, Maxwell. *Uses and Abuses of Political Power*. Chicago: University of Chicago Press, 1970.

Oyugi, W.O. "Local Government in Kenya: A Case of Institutional Decline." In *Local Government in the Third World,* edited by P. Mawhood, 107–140. Chichester: John Wiley, 1983.

Picard, L. "Socialism and the Field Administrator: Decentralization in Tanzania." *Comparative Politics* 12 (4) (1980): 439–457.

Richards, P. *Indigenous Agricultural Revolution: Ecology and Food Production in West Africa*. London: Hutchinson, 1985.

Riggs, F.W. *Administration in Developing Countries: The Theory of Prismatic Society*. Boston: Houghton, Mifflin, Coy, 1964.

Rondinelli, D.A. "Decentralization of Development Administration in East Africa." In *Decentralization and Government,* edited by G. S. Cheema and D. A. Rondinelli, 77–126. Beverly Hills, CA: Sage, 1983a.

_____. *Development Projects as Policy Experiments: An Adaptive Approach to Development Administration.* London: Methuen, 1983b.

_____, J.R. Nellis and F.S. Cheema. *Decentralization in Developing Countries: A Review of Recent Experiences.* Washington, D.C.: World Bank Staff Working Papers, No. 581, 1984.

Rothchild, D., and V. Olorunsola, eds. *States Versus Ethnic Claims: African Policy Dilemmas.* Boulder, Colorado: Westview Press, 1983.

Samoff, J. "Crises and Socialism in Tanzania." *Journal of Modern African Studies* 19 (2) (1981): 279–306.

Sharpe, L.J. "The Failure of Local Government Modernization in Britain: A Critique of Functionalism." *Canadian Public Administration* 24 (1) (1981): 321–357.

Sklar, R.L. "Democracy in Africa." *African Studies Review* 26 (3 & 4) (1983): 11–24.

Smith, B. C. *Decentralization: The Territorial Dimension of the State.* London: Allen and Unwin, 1985.

Smock, A. *Ibo Politics: The Role of Ethnic Unions in Eastern Nigeria.* Cambridge, Massachusetts: Harvard University Press, 1971.

Subramaniam, V. "Developing Countries." In *International Handbook on Local Government Reorganization,* edited by D. C. Rowat, 582–593. Westport, Conn: Greenwood Press, 1980.

Times of Zambia. September 22, 1986.

Tocqueville, Alexis de. *Democracy in America.* Translated by G. Lawrence, edited by J. P. Mayer. New York: Anchor Books, 1966.

Tordoff, W. *Government and Politics in Africa.* Bloomington, Indiana: Indiana University Press, 1984.

Uphoff, Norman T. "Management Traditions: The Role of Village Institutions in Local Development." *Regional Development Dialogue* 16 (1) (1985a): ix–xxix.

_____. "Local Institutions and Decentralization for Development." In *Decentralization, Local Government Institutions and Resource Mobilization,* edited by H. A. Hye, 43–78. Comilla: Bangladesh Academy for Rural Development, 1985b.

Wallis, M.A.H. *Bureaucrats, Politicians and Rural Communities in Kenya.* Manchester: Manchester University Papers on Development, No. 6, 1982.

Williams, G. "Political Consciousness Among the Ibadan Poor." In *State and Society in Nigeria,* edited by G. Williams. Idanre: Afrografika Publishers, 1980.

World Bank. *Accelerated Development in Sub-Saharan Africa.* Washington, D.C.: World Bank, 1981.

Araith, R.E. *Local Administration in West Africa.* London: Allen & Unwin, 1972.

_____, and Edgar Simpkins. *Corruption in Developing Countries.* London: Allen and Unwin, 1963.

Wunsch, James S. "Strengthening Rural Development Management Through International Assistance Projects." *Public Administration Development* 3 (1983): 239–263.

_____. "Administering Rural Development: Have Goals Outreached Organizational Capacity?" *Public Administration and Development* 6 (3) (1986): 287–308.

Zambia, Country Paper. *Training for Decentralized Administration in Eastern and Southern Africa.* London: Commonwealth Secretariat, 1986.

Zolberg, A. *Creating Political Order: The Party States of West Africa.* Chicago: Rand McNally, 1966.

5

African Economic Performance: Current Programs and Future Failures

Dele Olowu

Introduction: The African Economic Crisis

A general consensus exists today that African countries are confronted with an economic crisis. The evidence for such an assessment and the background to it have been discussed in chapters one through three. While the impact of Africa's economic downturn has varied among different African countries, the overall trend is that of a crisis situation. African countries' declining agricultural productivity for both food and export crops up to 1980, stagnant or declining GDP figures, growing balance of payments deficits, etc., have constituted the major features of this crisis. This deplorable economic situation has been compounded by environmental problems (such as drought, deforestation, erosion) and social problems (wars, mass repatriation, high population growth, civil unrest, military intervention, etc.). It is necessary, however, to add two points. First, that several African countries' economies have begun to show signs of recovery; and second, to reiterate the point that sharp variation exists among African countries. Those with white settler communities such as Zimbabwe and Kenya have generally more prosperous agricultural and industrial sectors. Others like the Cote d'Ivoire, which has encouraged large scale foreign investment and personnel, and countries with a large mineral base such as Zaire, Congo, Gabon, Nigeria, Zambia, etc., have fared better compared to others whose economies are based largely on peasant agricultural production. Table 5.1 sums up the trend of African aggregate economic performance on a sub-regional basis. Table 5.1 indicates that the West Africa sub-region was the worst hit by the economic decline described above with a GDP annual growth rate of -6.0% in 1983. The table also shows, however, that, overall, Africa's GDP growth rate has risen from -0.2% (all member states of the United Nations Economic Commission for Africa) in 1983 to 2.8% in 1986.

TABLE 5.1 Gross Domestic Product Growth Rates by African Sub-Regional and Analytical Groups, 1983–1986 (percentages)

	1983	1984	1985	1986
Central Africa	2.8	4.1	2.3	3.9
Eastern and Southern Africa	1.7	0.1	1.8	3.0
North Africa	3.3	3.8	3.1	2.7
South Africa	1.8	1.3	2.8	1.6
West Africa	−6.0	−2.6	2.9	2.7
Sub-Saharan Countries	−2.8	−0.7	2.1	3.0
Sahelian Countries	3.5	−5.7	7.6	4.5
Oil-Exporting Countries	−0.7	1.7	3.1	2.1
OPEC Countries	−3.1	0.7	2.8	2.9
Non-Oil Exporting Countries	0.8	0.2	2.2	3.0
Drought-Affected Countries	1.4	−0.6	2.1	3.3
All ECA Member States	−0.2	1.2	2.8	2.8

Source: United Nations, *Report on the World Economy* (New York: International Economic and Social Development Division, 1986).

Some scholars have warned against a facile comparison of gross national product between developed and developing economies (Karmack 1969; Dalton 1972) because of the poor level of statistical information, the relatively large size of the non-monetized sector, and the tendency to underprice the value of the subsistence sector in the latter countries. Nevertheless it is still worthwhile to note that only five African countries (including those outside sub-Saharan Africa) have a per capita GNP that is higher than US$1,000, only 6 between US$500 and $1,000; the majority (22) are under $300. In terms of the structure of production, recent World Bank studies suggest there is an increasing but expected shift away from agriculture to the "service" sector while the industrial sector (especially the manufacturing sub-sector) remains narrow (World Bank 1986; 1987). Only 11 countries (for which figures are available) derive as much as 10% and above of their gross domestic product from manufacturing activities (Zimbabwe 29%, South Africa 23%, Zambia 22%, Mauritius 20%, Morocco and Cote d'Ivoire 17% each, Senegal 18%, Rwanda 16%, Kenya 13%, Cameroun 12%, Ghana 11%). Other indicators of Africa's economic problems are the increasing dependency on imported cereals and the growing need for food aid (World Bank 1986). The largest cereal importers are Egypt, Algeria, Morocco and Nigeria. Poor overall economic performance together with increasing import dependency have led to rapidly increasing external debts which totalled about US$200 billion in 1986. Recent studies, however, also show one important redeeming feature: life expectancy at birth has increased from an average figure of 45 years in 1965 to 51 years in 1985 (World Bank 1986). It is, however, another issue whether or not a different economic growth strategy would have yielded higher or lower values (see, for instance, Stewart 1985).

While few scholars will contend that the problems confronting African countries today are not extremely serious, substantial disagreement is expressed as to the causes of the problems as well as the best corrective policies. While there have been no lack of opinions as to the best development strategy for Africa (and other developing countries) in the past, views have polarized in recent years around two major diagnoses and prescriptions.

One of these, led initially by the International Monetary Fund (IMF) and later followed by the World Bank, argues that the African economic crisis has largely been brought about by the domestic structures and policies for managing the respective national economies of African countries. For those who hold this opinion, only a drastic redrawing of the boundaries between public and private sectors in favor of the latter can produce improved outcomes for African economies, at least in the short run. On the other hand, the African nations themselves, as represented in their major policy propositions on the issue, the Lagos Plan of Action and related documents, have argued that following the market approach will only exacerbate their already miserable conditions, given the hostile international economic environment in which they operate. Instead, they call for a continuation of the socially inspired actions which African governments have followed since independence as well as proposals for regional cooperation toward greater self-reliance, especially in the field of industrial development.

These two positions may be labelled as "market" and "statist" approaches. Each represents the perception of a powerful lobby in African politics. The first is Africa's creditors and aid donors, the second is Africa's urban industrial elites. I intend to argue that the fundamental weakness of the statist approach is that a number of its central assumptions led to the adoption of a centralized development strategy whose predictable outcome was poor economic performance. The answer to this has been further centralization of the formal structures of the state and of controls over the formal sectors of the economy. Since most of these countries are however not so amenable to such centralist direction, the result has been a further worsening of the economic situation. While the "market" school represents a respectable and credible effort to redress one of the three dimensions of centralization recognized in Chapter 1, it too, perhaps paradoxically, can lead to overcentralization (in areas where the opposite is required) and also leads to generalized state weakness which reduces its likelihood of success. Common to both approaches is the false presumption that actions taken at the national level on the basis of macro-economic considerations are likely to have appropriate micro-economic implications irrespective of what institutions are in place to bring about such changes.

The next section will state the position and premise of each school in some detail and criticize each of these proposals along the lines stated above. Then the chapter will suggest how the economic reform proposals of the market school, as currently being implemented by several African countries, might be reformulated and recast to lead to more viable long-run outcomes.

The Statist Strategy:
Background to the Present Scenario

Using prevailing measures of inter-regional country comparison, Africa is the least developed among the world's regions. Although some scholars still believe that the African bio-physical environment constitutes the critical constraints on the continent's development (Gorou 1969; Karmack 1976), African underdevelopment can hardly be explained in terms of an absolute poverty of resources. Rather, we must turn to such factors as her late incorporation into the global economic system in modern times, the structure of international economic relations, as well as the economic policies of African leaders, before and after independence. With the exception of a few countries in which successful commercial agriculture has taken hold, Africa's economy is based largely on peasant agricultural production. Moreover, a substantial portion of production activities is carried on outside the market through reciprocity and redistribution (Dalton 1972; see also Chapter 11 in this volume). These circumstances continue in an age in which modern technological change and the changes brought about by industrialization epitomize and constitute the basis of economic growth and prosperity. There is, then, a basic tension between economic underdevelopment and the strong desire of Africa's ruling elites to escape from the poverty with which underdevelopment is associated. This circumstance is fundamental to understanding the prevailing economic prescriptions for Africa today.

The origins of the policy programs associated with the statist approach can be traced to the period between the World Wars. This period witnessed the adoption of comprehensive development plans in most African countries and the establishment of corporations charged with economic responsibilities (agricultural marketing, finance, investment, etc.) which derived from pragmatic and Keynesian prescriptions for avoiding cyclical unemployment. The Great Depression, the Second World War, and political independence all served to enlarge the entrepreneurial role of government in the economy. The rationale for increasing governmental activism particularly after independence was based on the following key considerations.

Nature and Pace of Development

Rapid socio-economic development was regarded as one of the major benefits of political independence. Nkrumah's slogan that political independence was the key to economic and social development gained widespread acceptance in post-independence Africa. Economic development was defined generally to mean raising Africa's low per capita output to the level of productivity already attained in the industrial countries. "Encouraged by economic development experts on all sides, the economic transformation program in African countries was defined roughly as requiring the *doubling* of agricultural output and a *twenty-five* fold increase in industrial output for the whole population" (United Nations Economic Commission for

Africa 1963:32, emphases added). To attain this feat meant that African countries, armed with technology and economic aid from the already industrialized world, would have to proceed at a fast pace to achieve within 40–50 years what it had taken at least one century for Western European countries to achieve. A rapid industrialization strategy (starting with import substitution), financed largely from external aid and, most importantly, from agricultural exports, was regarded as the cornerstone of economic development policy. According to the highly influential United Nation's document cited earlier:

> A very rapid industrial expansion would have to form the core of any program for raising the income level in Africa to that in industrial Europe. . . . More than doubling per capita agricultural outputs without a simultaneous expansion of industries, (by a five-fold growth), would create problems of marketing for which solutions are not easily predictable (UNECA 1963: 32; see also Rostow 1961).

In any case, economic development theorists such as Arthur Lewis had reasoned persuasively that economic modernization involved the transfer of resources from subsistence agriculture where marginal productivity is near zero to industry where marginal productivity is higher (Lewis 1955; see also Illchman and Bhargava 1970).

Such an urban industry-biased development program was accepted as the norm by all but a few African countries. The emphasis everywhere was an import-substitution industrialization strategy. This strategy is seen today by all sides as having contributed to the present malaise (World Bank 1981; Mabogunje 1980: 159–216).

Environmental Constraints on Development

The African environment represents special difficulties for economic development. High population growth rates, the predominance of peasant agriculture, small markets, poor intra- and inter-national communication links, and scarcity of capital and trained personnel all seem to dictate the need for state action to augment the market. None of these environmental constraints is, however, as severe as the institutional ones—the absence of market independence and the persistence of traditional social institutions and attitudes in economic and social activities. Even though the forces of modernization have monetized a substantial range of production activities, key factors of production are yet to enter market exchange. Such factors include land, capital, and labor. According to George Dalton, market-place exchange as distinct from market exchange is found widely in Africa as a peripheral pattern while some important output and factor flows are carried on via reciprocity and redistribution (Dalton 1972). As a result, African economies were subject to what economists referred to as an inversely elastic or "backward rising supply curve"—a situation in which higher prices do "not offer a dependable incentive to greater effort or to more regular work" (Boeke 1942: 30; Neumark 1972: 55). Money, it is reasoned, is yet to attain the position it has attained in market economies in these societies which have only an "embryonic exchange economy." The structural rigidities to price incentives, occasioned by such a circumstance, can only be overcome through state action, controls, command and negative incentives such as taxation.

Another factor frequently mentioned as one promoting state action is a combination of circumstances in which both local entrepreneurial spirit and capital are lacking in most African countries. Capital is short because of low savings and the general hostility to expatriate capital. While there is an abundance of petty traders and transporters, there is also a severe shortage of entrepreneurs who are willing and able to try new lines especially in the field of manufacturing. This is due, in part, to the reluctance to try new ways, but much more to the difficulty of surmounting such problems as capital and technological shortages, and the poor infrastructure base. According to Edward Marcus, once we accept that these serious economic disabilities exist—the lack of an industrial entrepreneurial class, inadequate capital, the poor development of basic infrastructure—the implication is quite clear:

> The state must assume the role normally allocated to private enterprise in Western economies such as the United States, the British Commonwealth or the advanced countries of the common market. Two functions must be undertaken: the direction of new enterprise and the active support of most new projects. This later would mean government ownership and operation, perhaps utilizing hired foreign technicians to fill in the skill gaps (Marcus 1965: 310).

Fascination with Socialist Ideology

Virtually all African statesmen shortly after independence espoused socialism as the most appropriate ideology for development. The enthusiasm for "socialist construction" was no lower (indeed higher) among intellectuals, university students and trade unionists—three powerful voices on the African political scene. Even though the socialism espoused by African statesmen has been described as "heretical" because they reject some of the central concepts of doctrinaire socialism such as class struggle or the prerequisite of reaching a capitalist stage, this has in no way bothered its adherents. The reasons for the preference for socialism among African leaders have been well explained by Elliot Berg:

> the identification of capitalism with "exploitation" and colonialism; the ideological tendencies absorbed by African students in metropolitan capitals, particularly in Paris; the belief expressed by President Nkrumah for one that capitalism is "too complicated" for Africa; the view that socialism is more compatible with the communal traditions of African society (Berg 1972: 8; see also Berg 1964).

Most of the criticisms of capitalism are derived from the mainstream of European socialism, and there is often a wide gap between socialist theory and practice. Thus African socialism has its peculiar characteristics in the area of economic policy:

> First, with respect to agricultural development, interest tends to be placed on large scale state-run efforts such as the state farms (of Ghana; or the rural enterprises in Guinea). Second, and more importantly, there is an inclination to give the state a much greater role in internal and external commerce through the creation of state trading corporations (Berg 1972: 18).

A statist road was not confined to those with a socialist program. Even non-socialist states were committed to the basic features of a statist program: emphasis on central planning, the preference for industrialization over and above agriculture or distribution, the state as the sole driving force in development, and expansion of the areas of state action as well as an intensification of existing controls, which had led ultimately to nationalization or semi-nationalization in some countries (den Tuinder 1978; Adedeji 1981; Aboyade 1983; Hyden 1983).

There are three major presumptions of this statist view to economic development. First, only state action (compared to those of private and locally organized interests) is capable of promoting the public interest. Second, there is the belief in the efficacy of controls imposed by the state on the economy. Finally, there is belief that the path to African development lies in large-scale agricultural programs and import substituting industrialization. Each of these presumptions has come under close scrutiny and criticism in recent years. Inevitably, those who hold this statist world view perceive Africa's economic crisis as rooted in the unequal exchange between Africa and the Western nations with which African economies are so closely interlocked. Borrowing heavily from Lenin's theory of imperialism, this core-periphery or dependency theory argues that African economic crisis is rooted in past colonial exploitation. This is seen as continuing to the present as neo-colonialism in that it now involves compliant political elites in the Third World. Using the labor theory of value as its chief explanatory tool, this school sees the unequal exchange between the manufactured goods of the core and the primary products (such as those exported by most African nations), as ensuring the continuing underdevelopment of Third World nations, Africa inclusive. In the words of Gunder Frank, the development of the core and the underdevelopment of the periphery are two sides of the same coin (Frank 1966; Baran 1968; Todaro 1981: 79–85; Leys 1975; Lofchie 1985: 169–176).

Besides the problem of the international environment, other factors listed by African states and their apologists as leading to their economic and social crises include: external conditions beyond the control of the state such as drought, soaring oil prices etc.; insufficient government resources; inadequate public sector performance; poor management; corruption and resistance to state programs; sabotage by backward and ignorant peasants, unscrupulous merchants; and political opposition (Economic Commission for Africa 1982; Gellar 1985).

Both the presuppositions and activities of African governments underpinned by these considerations have been hotly contested, and this argument forms the basis of programs termed the "market approach" which several African nations have reluctantly begun to implement since the early 1980s.

The Market Strategy: Critique of Statism

The simmering critique of what we have referred to as the "statist" view came to a head with the World Bank publication, *Accelerated Development in Sub-Saharan African: An Agenda for Action* (1981), otherwise referred to as the "Berg Report," after the name of its lead writer.

While conceding that the African economic crises is a real one and that external and climatic constraints have contributed in some way to the crisis, it makes a strong case for the argument that the economic development strategy adopted by virtually all African countries has in many cases been decisive in bringing about slow economic growth. The policies include negative trade and exchange rate policies as they affect agriculture compared to industry; government pricing policies for agricultural commodities—both export and food crops; allocation of investments in large scale government-run agricultural projects away from the mass of the peasant producers; and inadequate attention to administrative constraints to development performance. Several of these positions will be briefly reviewed.

First, the critique argues that the potential contribution of small-scale agricultural producers to African economic development has been grossly underestimated. This explains why government policies have been biased against rural producers in favor of protected import-substituting industries and large-scale agricultural projects run by the central government. The fact that these systematic disincentives have now led to an agricultural "malaise" is proof of the sensitivity of African peasant producers to appropriate incentives or disincentives. While it is true that African agricultural production is largely peasant based and is as yet not completely monetized, African peasant producers appear to be rational, self-interested actors who seek to maximize their profits. The Berg Report waxes eloquent on the incontrovertible evidence that African small-holders are outstanding managers of their resources. "All the evidence points to the fact that African small-holder farmers are excellent managers of their resources— their land and capital, fertilizer and water" (World Bank 1981:35).

Some of the studies referred to above include those of agricultural economists such as Theodore Schultz and Robert Bates. Schultz had argued that given appropriate incentives, African farmers will surmount all physical and biological factors confronting production; "they can turn sand into gold" (Schultz 1976: 5). Contrary to the argument of the statists that the lack of full monetization of African production dictated state action, Robert

Bates argues in fact that it is precisely excessive and biased state action which has made agriculture an unprofitable venture for farmers (Bates 1981). Given the appropriate incentives, African agriculture, the market school contends, is still capable of generating much needed resources for development and providing a stronger basis for modernization and industrialization than the present failed policies.

Second, the organizational limits of the state in African circumstances are overlooked by a socialist development strategy which overburdens young and fledgling African states. Besides the conventional responsibilities of governance, states which have adopted this strategy must take on a host of entrepreneurial, planning, managing, evaluating, etc. responsibilities in the industrial, agricultural and service sectors. The poor performance of the state with respect to development planning and a large number of African parastatals, constitutes a waste of resources, ones with particularly high opportunity costs. Absence of a large corps of trained manpower for data collection, project appraisal, plan articulation, coordination and implementation limits the success of horizontal or comprehensive development planning in Africa. In spite of the penchant for development planning, such exercises seem to have only a minimal impact on actual policy-making and investment programming (World Bank 1981: 32; Agarwala 1983).

The performance of public parastatals has been particularly disappointing. According to one study (also prepared under the auspices of the World Bank), the average number of parastatal enterprises (PE) per African country is 300, ranging from 400 in Tanzania (1981) to 7 in Lesotho (1978). The share of these PEs in their nations' GDPs is often substantial: as much as 40% and 37.8% respectively in Sudan and Zambia (against a world average of 10%). PEs are responsible for 75% of modern sector employment in Guinea (1981), and dominate that country's capital and credit markets. Their performance however has been very disappointing:

> The general view is that they have yielded a very low rate of return on the large amount of resources invested in them. While no aggregate figures on PE performance are available for the region as a whole, limited data from individual countries and sub-regional groupings reveal reason for concern. Of the PEs in a sample drawn from twelve West African countries, 62 percent showed net losses, while 36 percent had negative growth (Nellis 1986:17).

Documented losses sustained by African countries through public enterprise operations include Kenya, US$183.4 million (1977–1984) Niger ($90 million 1985; or 4% of Niger's 1982 GDP), Mali (6% of GDP 1978–1979), Togo (4% of GDP, 1980). Similar losses were sustained by public enterprises operating in other African countries including: Ghana, Malagasy, Nigeria, Sudan, Mauritania, Zaire, Sierra Leone and Senegal. The study concludes:

> Across the continent public enterprises have either performed poorly, as measured by standard financial/economic criteria, or not as well as it seems

reasonable to think that they should have. Moreover, there is little evidence to show that they have produced the anticipated levels of non-financial benefits in such areas as employment generation, income distribution, technology transfer and contributions to regional equity (Nellis 1986: 18).

While not denying the existence of a few cases of documented public enterprise success in Africa, this study suggests that they tend to be exceptions rather than the norm, given the difficult political environment in which they function. Even African leaders and policy-makers have expressed concern that public enterprises have performed poorly (Mkulo 1985: 189; Ndiaye 1986).

Third, the market school contends that it is these huge public sector losses combined with the disincentives to agriculture which have resulted in Africa's present problems. Dependency theory and the labor value theories on which it is based are dismissed as non-factual in the case of Africa, in spite of their wide appeal. While conceding that there are problems in respect to pricing levels of agricultural products in the world market, the Berg Report argues, for instance, that on balance developed countries' restrictive trade policies cannot account for Africa's overall poor export performance in the 1970s. During this period, overall Third World access to foreign markets actually increased. When considering non-fuel trade by developing countries, Africa's share fell by half in the 1970s. During this same period, other developing regions were able to surmount trade obstacles and expand their exports (World Bank 1981: 20–21). Other scholars have offered additional evidence to support this position (see for instance, Lofchie 1985: 175–176). Many scholars, while conceding that there are problems raised by the export-led agricultural strategy espoused by the Berg Report, now dismiss dependency theory as non-factual and oversimplified (Karmack 1976: xiii; Ridler 1985; Lofchie 1985).

The alternative development strategy proposed by the market school includes policies which will reverse those pursued since independence:

(1) Pricing policies more in line with the "real market" conditions: to stimulate production and, in particular, exports in agriculture.
(2) Sharp reduction in governmental activities especially in economic matters, and reliance on market incentives to stimulate private sector activity rather than bureaucracy. Need to reduce governmental bureaucracy through privatization, reduction of payrolls and strengthening of cooperatives.
(3) Better management of remaining central government activities through the strengthening of planning, finance, project generation and policy-making functions.
(4) Inward-looking, import-substitution industrialization strategy to give way to outward-looking, export orientation. Devaluation is regarded as an important policy tool in this respect.
(5) In agriculture, focus on small-holder agriculture rather than large-scale government-managed farms; in industry focus on the informal

sector and the encouragement of foreign capital; reduce tariffs. (World Bank 1981; 1987; Hyden 1983; Nellis 1986; Marsdeen and Belot 1987).

Hyden best sums up the critique of African development strategy up to the late 1970s and the essence of the market view:

> The political mood in post-independence Africa has favored things socialist: comprehensive planning; state control; equity; people's power and participation. . . . (Yet), capitalism, in spite of its short-comings, is for several reasons more likely than socialism to hold the key to development in Africa over the decades to come. . . . A centrally planned economy is a virtual impossibility at the present level of development of the productive forces. . . . This suggests that African countries, irrespective of current political ideology, cannot expect to jump the capitalist phase. By studying the phases of transition to socialism in other societies, it will be possible to understand better what kind of issues are likely to be at stake in Africa and what strategies may be possible to pursue in the years to come (Hyden 1983: 1, 25, 29).

The above represents a broadly held position, and one that has been exhaustively debated in the literature (Helleiner 1983; Dell 1983; *African Studies Review* 1984; Berry 1984; United States 1984; Browne and Cummings 1984).

Even though the proposals of the market school outlined in the last section have drawn a welter of criticism, over 20 African countries have begun to implement the most critical aspects of the reform strategy. These include the elimination of subsidies, reduction of the size of the civil service, the privatization of public enterprises, the devaluation of national currencies and liberalization of imports (World Bank 1983; 1984; Rende 1988). A check list of the public sector management improvement measures sponsored by the World Bank in African countries is shown on Table 5.2. Thirty two African countries have started or were planning public service or economic management reforms by April 1987. The countries that have adopted the most extensive reforms were the Central African Republic, Ghana, Uganda, Benin, Guinea, Senegal, Zambia and Ethiopia. The credits supplied by the World Bank for such administrative reforms ranged from US$2.5 million (Malawi) to US$35 million (Uganda) (Adamolekun 1987; see also West Africa 1987a, b).

This however, should not suggest that the earlier "statist" strategies have been altogether abandoned. Both strategies still constitute critical reference points for government policies in several African countries, and the domestic debate on policy continues.

Criticism of the market proposals up to now have focused on:

(1) the implications of the erratic behaviour of the world market prices (which led to a loss of US$19 billion from Africa's commodity exports in 1986) for an export-led development strategy; the world

TABLE 5.2 Checklist of Bank-Supported Public Service Management Improvement Measures

A. Civil Service Management
- Staff reduction and growth control
- Salary and compensation policies review
- Job classification and evaluation
- Documentation and records management (statistics/management information system)
- Strengthening and reorganization of selected ministries and agencies, e.g., Office of the Head of Civil Service, ministries of public service, local government/interior
- Promoting public service training through strengthening of national training institutions
- Administrative decentralization

B. Economic and Financial Management
- Strengthening and reorganization of economic planning and economic financial management institutions, notably ministries of planning and finance
- Improving formulation of economic policy, planning and management
- Public investment and expenditure planning
- Reform of the budgetary system
- Improving government accounting and auditing
- Reform of tax administration and revenue mobilization
- External financial management (aid, debt management)
- Training for staff of economic institutions

Source: L. Adamolekun, "Public Sector Management in Sub-Saharan Africa: The World Bank Experience." Washington, D.C.: Economic Development Institute, 1987. Reprinted with permission.

market price for Ghana's cocoa has fallen by more than a half within the last three years—and greater production tends to depress prices further;

(2) the absence of much needed external resources to help Africa over the initial deflation and economic depression arising from the adoption of the strategy (World Bank 1986);

(3) new forms of protectionism from industrialized countries against industrial exports from Third World nations;

(4) high interest rates on borrowable capital;

(5) the demand and supply elasticities of agricultural commodities in the world market;

(6) the double-edged effect of devaluation increasing the cost of agricultural inputs while raising the prices paid to farmers; also putting more resources into export crops than to food crops, etc.);

(7) the social welfare (nutrition levels, etc.) and political effects of the program (i.e., the active and well organized urban groups polarized against the rural and unorganized farmers);

(8) the high debt service ratios which swallow up the gain of economic reforms particularly in the face of low credit supply; the debt service ratio for Ghana is at present 60% of its export economy; in Nigeria, a high debt service of 44% was regarded as unacceptable by a succeeding military regime.

While many of these criticisms are valid, they tend to underplay the fact that these "market" reform proposals are a necessity (however unpalatable) given the present economic conditions of most African countries. Significant gains have been made by several countries which have introduced these reforms. In Ghana, regarded by some as the IMF/World Bank model case in Africa, the economy is reported to have experienced a turnaround. An economic growth rate of 6% per annum is reported, inflation is down from over 100% to 35%, and the country's major infrastructure— roads, railways, ports and hospitals, as well as her industrial plants which had fallen into neglect, are beginning to function again. Devaluation has brought a big boost to the cocoa industry as farmers are being paid higher producer prices (Rende 1988: 28). There are similar glowing reports for several other African countries (West Africa 1987c). Devaluation is also forcing several African countries to genuinely seek to be self-reliant. Most importantly, significant gains have been made in public service reforms. For instance, the Central African Republic reduced its wage bill from 89.3% of its national budget in 1981 to 58% in 1985 by reducing its public service staff strength from 25,600 (1981) to 22,037 (1985) by following a reorganization sponsored by the World Bank. Other countries such as Gambia, Mali, Senegal, Zambia and Malawi have also succeeded at reorganizations of civil service and parastatal organizations (Adamolekun 1987: 112–115).

Critique of the Market Strategy: The Importance of Micro-Level (Economic and Political) Institutions and Operators

In spite of these obvious gains and initial successes, the market strategy alone is bound to have only a limited impact on economic performance in Africa. First, it has been preoccupied with macro-economic policies and institutions while critical micro-economic issues and institutions have been largely ignored. Second, implicit in it is an attempt to divorce economic reform strategy from the political process. Third, the reform proposals are ambivalent on the role of the state in the economic development process. Specifically, the proposals demand for less state intervention in general, but paradoxically and indirectly require stronger central governmental authority in key areas for success. The sum total of these flaws is to lead to expansion further of state power, but to stultify critical, locally based productive forces and institutions.

Before we elaborate on these points, it is important to point out here that the flaws of the market approach arise from a tendency to assume that the "state" and the "market" operate as they do in the industrialized countries where the market approach originated. The fact, of course, is that neither the "state" nor the "market" operates in Africa according to such theoretical expectations. Both are legacies of the colonial order which are yet to be truly rooted in the people's indigenous experience and psyche. Instead, the African state is similar to contemporary Latin American states or the European states of the 15th to 19th centuries, ones characterized as mercantilist states. The attributes of mercantilism are: the centralization of economic and political decision-making in a small elite; special interest legislating; absence of, or very weak public accountability; and the non-involvement of basic local institutions such as local communities or smaller business groups in the political or economic processes. Its characteristics also include the promotion of monopoly economic and political power; favoritism rather than efficiency; and the repression of genuine entrepreneurship. The mercantilist state tends to exclude the most critical indigenous resources (grassroots level operators and organizations) from the formal political and economic organizations. The latter are usually highly centralized whereas the former are widely decentralized. This interpretation would suggest that the central problem of economic development in a mercantilist state is "the closed system of economic and political decision-making" which characterize such systems (de Soto 1987: 19). This dimension of the problem is lost to proponents of the market school. We shall now elaborate on each of the issues raised above.

Concern with Macro-Economic Policies and Institutions

The debt problem and other symptoms of economic decline are correctly perceived as arising from the pursuit of ill-advised economic policies, which are labeled as "socialist" but are in reality mercantilist and statist. As a result, the market school attempts to counter these with "capitalist" policies and institutions. The problem, however, is that the formal "market" system in Africa is a direct legacy of the colonial experience and remains both highly dependent on state protection and favors and is far from competitive. The "market" as used here refers to the largest categories of private sector operators comprising both foreign and indigenous elements. These are usually few in number and are highly dependent on foreign or state acquired capital and technology. They have remained the focus of public policy before and after independence. This formal "market system" is marked by a structure which is either monopolistic or oligopolistic (Aboyade 1983). Superficial reforms in this area (i.e., marketization) will not significantly alter the mercantilistic forces. They will reappear in a new guise.

In contrast, there is a large number of highly competitive but poorly capitalized small-scale operators who constitute the informal economic system. These produce the mass of the goods and services both in the agricultural and non-agricultural sectors. Yet they have been consistently discriminated against since the colonial times and independence has not changed their lot. They do not have access to capital or legal protection and often even exist on the fringes of the law. They rely on informal structures and contacts with the formal system to survive. Moreover, in the African context they are poorly researched. Enough, however, is known to characterize their major features: they are ubiquitous, they employ a large proportion of the productive labor force (especially women), and they rely on indigenous technology and innovations (Hill 1970; Akeredolu-Ale 1975; Illife 1983; O'Connor 1983; Richards 1985). In the contemporary economic development literature, the marginal productivity of this category of businesses is equated to zero; political scientists regard operators in the sector as a proletariat rather than the vigorously entrepreneurial class which they are (Lewis 1955; Leys 1975).

The market reform proposals seem likely to reinforce these conditions (concerning the formal and informal economic sectors) by focusing policy advocacy on the critical needs of the formal private sector (often in reality only an extension of the state) rather than on the mass of small-scale producers which require critical resources from the state but which are presently denied them. Macro-economic policies that promote large-scale private investment do not necessarily promote small-scale entrepreneurial activities. Vital institutional reform at the micro-economic level which would support them is largely ignored. Appropriate micro-economic policies and institutions are required to bring small operators into the mainstream of the economic development process. This would include legislation which would provide small operators secure property rights, allow them to make contracts, use legal processes, and broaden and improve their scale and quality of commercial operations. This would involve extensive deregulation of limits which work more to raise entry (and exit) costs and reinforce economic rigidity than to encourage important national objective (Bates 1981). The high cost of incorporating businesses (a presidential or ministerial approval is often required to open small businesses in many African countries) and of existing legitimately must be substantially reduced if not eliminated if they are to be able to grow to their potential.

Moreover, access of small-scale businesses to capital, credit, educational improvement and training facilities must be encouraged. Active discrimination against small operators and institutions (e.g., against small-scale manufacturing, etc.) must also now be reversed if their growth potential is to be met (see Akeredolu-Ale 1975; Illife 1983). They require energetic governmental activity at the local level, deregulation of banking legislation, and access to credit and judicial systems. For example, the absence of basic municipal infrastructure—roads, water, electricity, schools, health clinics—constitute additional costs for small operators. All of these require energetic action at the local level. They are important elements of a genuinely indigenous economic development strategy in all African countries. For these changes to occur, the rules which establish and govern organizations responsible for these services and activities must be scrutinized and modified to "institutionalize" these new roles. Given the inefficiencies of the mercantilist bias and the favoritism for large, centralized enterprises shown by the national bureaucracies, rules which encourage alternative organizations and structures seem necessary. Many of the problems of the earlier strategies grew from the fundamental power asymmetries which lay between the "modern" and central sector, and the indigenous, grassroots sector. If these new organizations are to be expected to operate well and last long, the fundamental allocations of political power in African countries must be addressed.

Ironically, even though the reform strategy is quite critical of African state bureaucracies, much faith is placed on them to lead economic reform. Hence, administrative reform premised on a centralist and "blue-print" approach constitutes a crucial aspect of the reform proposals! According to this strategy, central government bureaucracies are in need of urgent reforms (as listed in Table 5.2). However, they are to remain a primary organization utilized to carry forth development. Indeed, these bureaucracies are expected not only to reform themselves, but simultaneously to carry through a number of other fundamental reforms within the economy and the society at large. This strategy labors under the old delusion that officials will act rationally and always in the public interest, and that such organizations are likely to serve as effective agents of development. Yet, much research has demonstrated that neither the state nor its bureaucracies operate rationally in African countries. Let us review some of this research.

In the first instance, the African state is characterized by several key analysts as a "soft" state. It lacks adequate, properly motivated and ethically conscious personnel who can insure the efficient implementation of state policies. The expected values of a Weberian bureaucracy are generally viewed with contempt given widespread poverty, rapidly changing social values, and sharp inequalities in the larger society (Ekeh 1975; Barkan 1979; Okoli 1980; Brett 1986). Bureaucratically focused strategies thus underestimate the ability of officials to implement reform in such a way that it maximizes their own interests while minimizing their losses. Hence, in some states, profit-making public enterprises *have* been "privatized," but many of the beneficiaries are still those close to the corridors of power. The real loss-making enterprises have been slow to receive the axe (West Africa 1988). In some other states, public officials have ensured that those aspects of the reform (such as staff reduction and mass retirement, etc.) which are not in their own best interests are effectively sabotaged from within (Olowu 1987). Moreover, the reform strategy presumes that the additional resources which the reform makes available will be used to bring basic infrastructure to disadvantaged groups such as those in the rural areas. It is not at all clear why this should be assumed, nor that it has happened in the field.

This is the case because the market school focuses its attention on only one of the three aspects of African state centralization which were discussed in Chapters 1 and 3. We advanced the position that the centralization of African government is a three-dimensional phenomena (from the judiciary and legislature to the executive; from the private to the public sector; and from the local/regional authorities to the central government). The market program addresses only one of these dimensions directly (the private-public sector centralization). It deals with another only marginally and indirectly (center-subnational institutional centralization), but it does not confront the last one at all. African countries inherited a highly centralized governmental system. Unless this inheritance is modified, no fundamental change should be expected. This point requires elaboration.

The roots of African centralized government lie in the colonial governments' dislike of accountability and their resistance to involvement by the indigenous peoples in the governmental process. Government was expected to be a benevolent dictatorship of officials (Chapter 2). Lord Lugard, easily the most famous of African colonial officials, is credited with the opinion that "representative institutions, legislative councils are unsuited to African people" (Kirk-Greene 1985: 172). Even though an attempt has been made since independence (earlier in some countries such as Ghana and Nigeria and later in Francophone states like Cote d'Ivoire) to "Africanize" African bureaucracies, their authoritarian and highly centralized character have been retained and strengthened in most cases. As shown in Chapter 3, public services' salaries and perquisites have continued to reflect the colonial tradition rather than the reality of the African socio-economic condition. In the same vein, African bureaucracies remain centralized, remote (physically and psychologically) from the masses of the citizens, and are largely unaccountable to the public.

Heller and Tait provide some evidence to substantiate this claim. Whereas in the industrial (OECD) countries non-agriculture public sector employment (compared to private sector) is 24.2% on the average, for developing countries it is 43.9% with the African countries having the highest average figure of 54.4%. They show that African countries make the most use of public enterprises of any region whether among the "developed" or developing countries. But the most striking fact is that Africa has the highest concentration of its non-agricultural public sector employment at the central government level. Assuming that public enterprises are usually responsible to the central or general-level government rather than sub-national governments, Africa has the least of its officials at the state and local government levels (2.1%) compared to OECD (11.6%), and all developing countries (4.0%).

These figures are more pronounced in terms of the percentage of total employment by the different units of government (Heller and Tait 1982: 9; Ozgediz 1983) and in terms of wage structure: African central governments expended more wages compared to their counterparts in the industrialized and other developing nations; their sub-national level governments expended the lowest share of the total wages among these economies. These patterns also apply to the proportion of government expenditure and GNP disposed of by central compared to local level governments (Heller and Tait 1982).

African public sector bureaucracies are also remote from the mass of the rest of the citizens in terms of their income levels and also in terms of their physical location. Average government pay is 4.5 times the per capita income in developing countries compared to 1.8 in industrialized (OECD) countries (Heller and Tait 1982). Besides, since few countries have basic infrastructures in the rural countryside, African officials prefer to work and live in the major urban centers rather than in the rural countryside where the majority of the people live. This serves to reinforce the urban bias in development policy and implementation, an issue which has been fully discussed in the literature (Lipton 1977; Rondinelli 1979; Bates 1981).

Thus, while the tendency in most developed countries is for central government officials to live scattered among the rest of the population, in Africa the reverse is the case. Approximately only 10% of United States federal officials work in Washington, 25% of the British government's non-industrial civil servants work within Greater London, while only 2 1/2% of French public servants live and work in Paris. This represents the trend in most West European countries (Smith 1967). This contrasts sharply with the arrangement in Africa and several other developing countries. Even in Nigeria, with her relatively decentralized political and administrative structure, 40% of the federal public servants live and work in Lagos, the national capital. The proportion for other African countries is much higher (Smith 1985).

Finally, accountability within African public institutions is weak. Institutions for ensuring accountable performance in African countries—both internal (such as disciplinary boards, audits, monitoring machineries, etc.) and external (legislature, judiciary, the press, etc.) are weak: they are in various levels of rupture and decay (Olowu 1988). This is due in part to the nature of the African state, which as we have shown throughout the book is both authoritarian and increasingly centralized around a personality cult or a small power elite (Ake 1985; Gana 1985; Decalo 1985; Iyayi 1986).

Close students of African bureaucracies have shown that given the absence of the Parsonian characteristics of a modernized society—universalism, industrialism, etc.—and the non-compliance with Weberian values within the bureaucracy, what is required is not the strengthening of centralist structures for planning and command: they are the problem, not the solution. Rather, what is needed is building local capacity within and outside the public sector. This involves the creation and nurturing of organizations within and outside the public bureaucracy. These must be accountable, ones which can learn from their errors, and ones that are sensitive to the realities of their environment. These include informal sector organizations and a host of non-governmental organizations, which can be held accountable through other, non-hierarchical and non-centralist mechanisms. These would include competition in the market, election of local officials responsible for local services, the ability to establish new, special units of governance/collective action, an opening to true private enterprises, and the like (Hyden 1980; 1983: 137–164; Moris 1976; Onyemelukwe 1973; Okoli 1980). These constitute a core of institutional reforms and policies necessary for the dynamic economic growth desired by proponents of the market school. They need to be the focus of economic reform. Instead, they receive only casual attention by exponents of the market school. They are a way of dismantling the power asymmetries which allow current organizations to ignore, exploit and destroy their environments.

The Apolitical Conception of Economic Reforms

A second major weakness of the market strategy is the apolitical conception of its economic reforms. The problem of African economic performance is treated as a purely economic issue with few implications for the political structure. This has three important effects which serve to promote further centralization within the mercantilist state. First, economic reforms proposed by the market school are perceived by entrenched elites in African countries, at least in the short-run, as a threat to their interests. Secondly, the strategy fails to take into consideration the peculiar nature of the African socio-political environment. Third, its limited scope (i.e., leaving political structure outside the analysis) means the elites are generally able effectively to defend their system.

The market strategy proposals strike at the heart of the economic interests of those currently ruling most African countries. Yet it simultaneously ignores the *political* structure which gave them the power they currently hold. The proposals take on all the entrenched political and economic elites who have benefitted from the past statist strategy. Within this group are the urban unionized working classes, and politicians and administrators whose incomes are several times those of the rural peasant producers. This group also includes industrialists and commercial entrepreneurs whose activities have been largely protected from foreign competition, and who have enjoyed high subsidies at the expense of the rural people. Opposition from these various groups is often highly visible and has turned out to be the most vocal and real for national governments. Such opposition is expressed in work stoppages, urban food riots, military coup d'etat etc. On the other hand, the potential beneficiaries—the peasant farmers and other small-scale operators, are not effectively mobilized, are largely unorganized and, given the absence of a democratic regime, do not have the means to articulate their support for these programs or protect their benefits from reform. As a result, several African governments soon took actions which cancelled the gains of economic reform. For instance, the Central African Republic hired an additional 1,500 graduates in 1985 in order to accommodate domestic social pressures. Zambia suspended its IMF Liberalization program in 1987 as a result of urban food riots. Similar experiences have been encountered by Egypt, Algeria and Sudan. Also, Nigeria after a successful devaluation program, began to "reinflate" its economy with a deficit budget of US$2 billion in 1988. In brief, the political structure which allowed the "few" to control the economic levers of the state to their advantage remain intact, and tend to be utilized (Bates 1981).

The alternative to a fundamental political reorganization by Africa's leaders is political repression. Given the severity of the measures and the absence of strong legitimating structures which can communicate with and mobilize the masses of the people who might benefit from the program over the long-run, governments are pressed to impose various forms of repressive measures on what diverse organizations exist: on trade unions, student organizations, churches, manufacturers associations, chambers of commerce, etc. Those governments most successful at economic reform given the current political structure are thus likely to be those which are also the most repressive. In a number of cases, the need for economic reform constituted a sufficient rationalization of military intervention and assumption of political leadership. Some scholars have argued, on the basis of Latin American experiments at economic liberalization, that this is the political price that must be paid to have economic reform (Sheahan 1980). Such scholars tend to argue that implementation of economic reform of this nature has always and everywhere been accompanied by significant negative political consequences (Cooper 1971).

Finally, the market strategy promotes centralization because it requires domestic governments to abide strictly by conditions dictated by foreign governments or multilateral institutions. Reforms are administered in a top-down fashion with most foreign resources loans and additional credits being passed to national-level governments. Some of these resources are used to create additional top-down bureaucracies ostensibly to stimulate employment, exports or economic growth. New "directorates" are launched with fanfare all under the direction of the "president" and his lieutenants. Critical resources are thus poured into the same type of centrally directed institutions that failed to perform under the statist strategy. Since the reforms ignore the social-political forces, the image given to economic reform is that of a foreign imposition, an image which does not often go well in a continent in which nationalist wars are still being fought: further centralized control is needed to sustain the reforms.

To be fair, multilateral agencies and foreign governments which have been the key proponents of economic reform have strict limitations on how far they can go in reforming political institutions. The point here, however, is that without substantial reform of political institutions both at the national and subnational levels, the economic reform programs are likely to be infeasible and ineffective.

The Role of the State in the
Economic Development Process

The market approach, as already pointed out above, demands a strong state which can repress all opposition groups and closely direct many *micro*-economic functions by certain bureaucracies. But at the same time, it demands a retreat by government from overall involvement in the macro-economy. We would argue instead that African states require the exact reverse of the position counseled: a greater opportunity for institutional diversity reaching to localities in the *micro*-economy, and a more active government in certain key *macro*-economic areas. Let us review the argument.

African governments adopting the market strategy are usually required to take on important micro-level responsibilities directly which would stimulate a quick supply response to price incentives—agricultural research, delivery of inputs, marketing system reforms and transport improvement (Schatz 1987: 133). These requirements are questionable. First the market critique itself grows from the literature on the "softness" of the African state generally and in particular from the fundamental weaknesses of state bureaucracies in managing programs of rural change. It is unclear how further or continued centralization in this area should solve these problems. Secondly, several studies have demonstrated the severe limitations of agricultural research sponsored and administered by African governments and their collaborators because of the peculiar characteristics of the tropical environment (Gorou 1969; Karmack 1976; Allaby 1977). One study on major food crop revolutions in West Africa showed that governments and their collaborators have a bias for exotic technology and prefer to address peculiar problems of the African environment with the time-tested technologies of the temperate world. These have repeatedly proven unsuccessful. As a result, innovation and adaptation to the environment are most vigorous where external agencies have interfered *least*. It then went on to demonstrate several cases of successful innovations in food production technology by peasant farmers (Richards 1985; see also Ruttan and Hayami 1984; Esman and Uphoff 1984).

On the other hand, the market strategy also calls for a reduced role of the state in the general or "macro" management of African economies. While there surely is need for vigorous cost-effectiveness in the public sector, a demand for less state intervention in Africa in general at the present time seems inconsistent with the experience of today's industrialized nations, and the contemporary experience of today's rapidly industrializing economies (Aitken 1959; World Bank 1987: 57–77). The critical role of the state in stimulating economic growth—providing a favorable climate for private-economic activities, assumption of critical and marginal risks, land grants, transportation construction, capital borrowing, etc., has tended to be coupled with economic growth. The role and scope of state activities has of course varied from one country to another. In the United States, for instance, critical developmental roles were played by state agencies from the 16th through to the middle of the 20th century. While most of these activities were born by the sub-national level governments (state and local governments), important roles were performed by the national government at critical times (Broude 1959; Fine 1956; Haven 1941). A close student of the subject notes as follows:

Analysis of (economic) growth in the United States before 1800 reveals that decisions having to do with the formation and employment of capital were significantly affected by political agencies. More generally, economic functions performed by government at its several levels exceeded what might be considered minimal. Governments afforded protection and stimulus to capital formation and participated in a wide range of activities, although always in an economy that was predominantly laissez-faire in ideology and in practice, and that became more autonomous (laissez-faire) about the middle of the century (Spengler 1959: 355–356).

The role of the state was more significant in Canada and Australia while such states as Russia, Germany, Turkey, Japan, France and of course the Eastern European countries have tended to create an even more dominant role for the state. The only exception to this general rule was Switzerland. Since the Great Depression, the roles played by government have expanded, and particularly so in the newly industrializing countries. This is particularly so in the oft-cited success cases—Japan, Israel, Taiwan, Singapore and Korea. As World Bank data shows (see also Sandbrook 1985: 152–153), there is nothing unusual about the weight of public expenditure in sub-Saharan Africa (World Bank 1986; 1987).

Thus what is problematic in Africa is not the extent of state intervention but the nature and quality of such intervention. As an illustration, Peter Kilby has demonstrated how governmental participation and protective enactments of the regional and central governments in Nigeria contributed directly and indirectly to the success of the emergence of a strong, indigenous, African bread-baking industry in Nigeria in the 1950s (Kilby 1965: 105–107). The critical question if such general role is to be performed well is therefore how to get the state to direct its energies to essential tasks and to seek the public interest genuinely and spiritedly. Once again, we would suggest the question demanding a response is not one of economics but of politics: how is political power to be distributed to prevent these policy tools from being perverted yet again?

An Alternative Economic Improvement Strategy

Neither the state nor the market institutions function in Africa as expected by theory. The superstructures of both already exist, but the complementary structures to make them functional are grossly underdeveloped. As a result, interactions between the two lead to perverse consequences for citizens.

As we have suggested, one important explanation for this pattern of behavior is that the African state system is basically mercantilist. As a result both governmental and the formal private sector institutions are highly centralized and tend to benefit a minority elite in government and business. A transfer of responsibilities from the governmental to the business sector does not mean that the quality of services will increase appreciably. Taken from this viewpoint, no African country can therefore be characterized as pursuing a "socialist" or "capitalist" strategy. Rather they have all unabatingly pursued a centralized political and economic strategy which is far ahead of their level of social mobilization and economic diversity. This has been characterized as mercantilist.

A mercantilist state whether in Europe, Latin America or Africa is deliberately centralized in order to promote and protect the interests of a few elites. As has been argued elsewhere, the mercantilist state in Europe was finally resolved in favor of modern democracy and competitive markets through progressive economic and political reform in Western Europe. In Eastern Europe it was overthrown by revolution and replaced with socialist dictatorship and command economies (de Soto 1987). The critical question in Africa is how the perverse consequences of a mercantilist and centralized state system are to be resolved.

Some scholars have argued that some amount of centralization represents inevitable correlates of modernization. The forces of commercialization, industrialization, population mobility, the emergence of the mass media, pressures for egalitarian concerns and nation-building are all associated with the process of modernization and propel a country towards greater roles for government and centralization (Wagner 1958; Sharpe 1979; Krane 1986). While there is some truth in this reasoning, it must be pointed out that the African experience has some peculiar characteristics.

First, the process of centralization was not mitigated or compensated by effective decentralizing or non-centralizing forces as happened in other countries (Conford 1975; Sharpe 1979; Smith 1985; Elazar 1987). L. J. Sharpe has shown, for instance, that in Europe the same centralizing socio-economic forces also generated "a political reaction among the putatively integrated" in a decentralizing direction—to communities, localities, regions and the periphery. His argument is that decentralist trends in the politics of the West are paradoxically "also a product of the centralization of the society and the state machine" (Sharpe 1979: 20; see also Sharpe 1986). This dialectical process ensured in Europe and other countries that centralization did not negatively affect economic growth for long. There is substantial support for the position that high levels of central control prove dysfunctional for a country's economic growth because of "large administrative overhead costs" (exceeding economies of scale) which act as a drag on economic growth (Krane 1986: 46; see also Holt and Turner 1966; and Hollingsworth 1982).

In African countries, however, the dominant elites are in most cases urban based. The centralization of governmental machinery is approved and supported on both sides of the political spectrum, especially since centralization is regarded as necessary to break the power of traditional elements in the countryside (Smith 1985: 194–197). Even when a country has a substantial agricultural or rural-based elite, this has made no difference for the outcome as Robert Bates has shown (Bates 1981). The high level of power already concentrated at the center has overwhelmed these interests, often through systems of patron-client relationships that help centralist elites hold power but are economically wasteful and stagnating: they induce no real economic change, but rather "freeze" current patterns in response for support for the center. As a result the centralization of the state machine has continued virtually unabated in Africa since the colonial period in spite of its high costs on the economic and political growth process.

The centralization of African states is actively promoted not only by powerful political forces but also by the prevailing paradigms of political and economic organization. The prevailing paradigm (see especially Chapters 10 and 12) is one of monocentricity and hierarchy. All human and developmental problems are presumed to be resolvable through monocentric control and coordination. I have attempted to show in this chapter how this major flaw of the statist strategy is largely continued in the contemporary "market" approach. Even though the latter calls for decentralization from public to private institutions, it leaves intact or even intensifies the hierarchical structure which created these problems in the first place.

An alternative economic strategy will accept the market critique of the statist strategy, but will address the shortcomings of the market approach highlighted in this chapter. It will address both macro- and micro-economic policies and institutions, giving special emphasis to the latter. It will recognize that economic reform is basically a political and indeed constitutional issue. In particular, it will recommend a polycentric institutional order comprising a diversity of people-based political and economic organizations. Such organizations will be granted broad latitudes of autonomy to enable them to compete or collaborate with one another and to be self-regulating and accountable. Within such a framework, a central government with limited but significant functions for promoting appropriate legislation, research and common services will be required.

There are several reasons why this model should work better than the monocentric model in Africa. First, this is because it confronts the economic problem on the appropriate front: at the political level by breaking the power of the mercantilist state on *both* political and economic fronts. Second, the focus of the strategy is the proven African indigenous resources and organizational capacity, one area in which an impressive literature exists. (See for instance Smock 1971; Wallis 1982; and other citations in Chapters 4 and 12.)

Third, the model stimulates and reinforces Africans' capability for self-governance rather than the prevailing messianic expectations of the dominant state. More importantly, it has the potential of stimulating competitive and collaborative ventures among Africa's self-contained communities for community improvement, a strategy that has worked well under different regimes in Africa when encouraged and stimulated: when given "space" as argued in Chapter 1. Perhaps the most recent illustration of the pertinence of this observation is the critical role played by farmer organizations in boosting production in Zimbabwe at a time when that country as well as others were ravaged by drought (Bratton 1986). Such a model holds a greater promise for Africa's transformation into modern democracies and competitive market systems than the current experiments either of single-party or military dictatorships, or of mercantile "market" systems. Most importantly, this model, by breaking the monopoly of the African state and its bureaucracies, will foster the creation of alternative organizations which provide goods and services that are at present wholly provided by the state or monopoly private sector operations. Such a generally decentralized institutional structure will have a greater potential of fostering "co-production" in such diverse areas as agricultural research and extension, and the delivery of health, educational and other economic and social infrastructures. Co-production means the collaborative production of goods and services by producers and users. Some key goods can be produced only this way.

Some of the details of the reform strategy are advanced in Chapters 12 and 13, but I sketch below some of its general directions. First, there is a need to open up economic participation by ensuring that small operators have access to critical resources that are generally provided only by the state—appropriate legislation, credits, municipal services, power to make contracts, secure land, etc. This will help make the market competitive and thereby increase overall economic productivity. The reason the informal sector (either in the agricultural or non-agricultural sectors) has a low productivity is that it has to operate in spite of, rather than with the support of the state.

Secondly, therefore, there will be a need to seek political reforms in at least four important directions. First, there is a need for a new institutional order which stresses non-centralization or substantial decentralization. This might entail the creation of new decentralized units or the fostering of old local institutions. The hallmark of these organizations will be their empowerment to tackle basic issues relating to the physical and economic infrastructures essential for the successful performance of small-scale businesses. It was only in 1987, for instance, that the Cameroon government began to examine the possibility of decentralizing the licensing of pharmacies. Until then a presidential approval was required. Such organizations must be capable of performing a variety of social and economic responsibilities. More importantly they must be controlled by the local people. The organizations should not be single units but a dense agglomeration of organizations which are capable of contracting with one another, with other public institutions and with the private sector (Friedman 1981). These diverse organizations should be given legal authorization to provide essential services which are at present being provided by monopolies within either the public or private sectors. The results of such experiments are likely to be more rewarding than the current attempts at public-private sector transfers. As important at their economic role, perhaps, will be their political: these organizations, building local supporters as they perform functions, can be expected to resist recentralization, as centripetal forces at the center seek to reestablish old advantages at the expense of this sector.

A second direction of future reforms must be to ensure that the central government is capable of performing selected strategic tasks effectively and responsibly. This will involve the focus of central government responsibilities on essential tasks—policy-making, legislation, provision of highly technical facilities which cut across regions and the assistance of localities in tackling specialized tasks or disasters, etc. To ensure that power is used responsibly, there will be the need to strengthen institutions which promote accountable use of power at all levels—to prevent the monopolistic exercise of government power.

A third direction is public education that mobilizes support for change. Both formal and informal modes of instruction can form the means of disseminating information in respect of required change among the young and the old respectively. There is also a need to encourage further research into the activities and problems of small-scale operators in the agricultural and non-agricultural sectors. This alone will help to draw attention to their contribution to development as well as urgently needed policy reforms.

Fourth and finally is the need to assure that the center never again has the power to exploit the vast majority of Africa's productive peoples. While a strong center is needed, it must grow strong through a political process that ensures the mass of Africans a voice in the policies that determine so much of their fate. The power asymmetries which allowed the urban few to grow rich on the toil of the rural masses are not merely economically insane, they are unjust. To accomplish this, the basic rules which allocate power and constitute and organize the African polity must be considered. To this we will turn in Chapters 10, 11, and 12.

References

Aboyade, O. *Integrated Economics: A Study of Developing Economies.* London: Wesley, 1983.

Adamolekun, L. "Public Sector Management in Sub-Saharan Africa: The World Bank Experience." Washington D.C.: Economic Development Institute, 1987. Mimeo.

Adedeji, A., ed. *Indigenisation of African Economies.* London: Hutchinson, 1981.

African Studies Review. Symposium on "The World Bank's Accelerated Development in Sub-Saharan Africa." 27 (4) (1984).

Agarwala, R. "Planning In Developing Countries: Lessons of Experience." Washington, D.C.: World Bank Staff Working Papers No. 576, 1983.

Aitken, Hugh G.J., ed. *The State and Economic Growth.* New York: Social Sciences Research Council, 1959.

Ake, Claude. "Why is Africa Not Developing?" *West Africa.* London (June 1985): 1211–1214.

Akeredolu-Ale, O. *The Underdevelopment of Indigenous Entrepreneurship in Nigeria.* Ibadan: Ibadan University Press, 1975.

Allaby, Michael. *World Food Resources: Actual and Potential.* London: Applied Science Publishers, 1977.

Baran, Paul. *The Political Economy of Growth.* Second Edition. New York: Monthly Review Press, 1968.

Barkan, J.D. "Comparing Politics and Public Policy in Kenya and Tanzania." In *Politics and Public Policy in Kenya and Tanzania,* edited by J.D. Barkan and J.J. Okumu, 3–40. New York: Praeger Publishers, 1979.

Bates, Robert H. *Markets and States in Tropical Africa: The Political Basis of Agricultural Politics.* Berkeley: University of California Press, 1981.

Berg, Elliot J. "Socialism and Economic Development in Tropical Africa." *Quarterly Journal of Economics* 78 (4) (1964): 549–573.

————. "The Character and the Prospects of African Economies." In *Africa: Problems in Economic Development,* edited by J.S. Uppal and R. Salkever, 5–26. New York: The Free Press, 1972.

Berry, Sarah. "The Food Crisis and Agrarian Change in Africa: A Review Essay." *African Studies Review* 27 (2) (1984): 59–112.

Boeke, J.H. *The Structure of Netherlands India Economy.* New York: Institute of Pacific Relations, 29–30, 1942.

Bratton, M. "Farmer Organizations and Food Production in Zimbabwe." *World Development* 14 (3) (1986): 367–384.

Brett, E.A. "State Power and Economic Inefficiency: Explaining Political Failure in Africa." *IDS Bulletin* 17 (1) (1986): 22–29.

Broude, Henry W. "The Role of the State in American Economic Development 1820–1890." In *The State and Economic Growth,* edited by Aitken, 4–25. New York: Social Sciences Research Council, 1959.

Browne, R.G.S., and R.J. Cummings. *The Lagos Plan of Action vs. The Berg Report: Contemporary Issues in African Economic Development.* Lawrenceville, Virginia: Brunswick, 1984.

Conac, Gerard, ed. *Les Institutions Administratives des Etats Francophones d'Afrique Noire.* Paris: Economica, 1979.

Conford, B. *The Failure of the State: On the Distribution of Political and Economic Power in Europe.* London: Croom Helm, 1975.

Cooper, R.N. "Currency Devaluation in Developing Countries." In *Government and Economic Development,* edited by G. Ranis, 472–512. New Haven, Conn.: Yale University Press, 1971.

Dalton, George. "Traditional Production in Primitive African Economies." In *Africa: Problems of Economic Development,* edited by J.S. Uppal and R. Salever, 45–56. New York: United Nations Economic Commission for Africa, 1972.

Decalo, S. "African Personal Dictatorships." *Journal of Modern African Studies* 23 (2) (1985): 209–237.

Dell, Sydney. "Stabilization: The Political Economy of Overkill." In *IMF Conditionality,* edited by John Williamson, 32–33. Washington, D.C.: Institute of International Economics, 1983.

Den Tuinder, A.B. *Ivory Coast: The Challenge of Success.* Baltimore: Johns Hopkins University Press, 1978.

de Soto, Bernando. "Constraints on People: The Origins of Underground Economies and Limits to the Growth." Mimeo. Bloomington, Ind.: Workshop in Political Theory and Policy Analysis, 1987.

Economic Commission for Africa. *Accelerated Development in Sub-Saharan Africa: An Assessment by the OAU, ECA and ADB Secretaries.* Tripoli: United Nations, 1982.

Ekeh, P. "Colonialism and the Two Publics in Africa: A Theoretical Statement." *Comparative Studies in Society and History* 17 (1) (1975): 91–112.

Elazar, Daniel. *Exploring Federalism.* Alabama: University of Alabama, 1987.

Esman, M.J., and N.T. Uphoff. *Local Organizations: Intermediaries in Rural Development.* Ithaca, New York: Cornell University Press, 1984.

Fine, Sydney. *Laissez-Faire and the General-Welfare State.* Ann Arbor: University of Michigan Press, 1956.

Frank, Andre Gunder. "The Development of Underdevelopment in Latin America." *New Left Review* 18 (4) (1966).

Friedman, John. "The Active Community: Toward A Political Territorial Framework for Rural Development in Asia." *Economic Development and Cultural Change* 20 (2) (1981): 235–261.

Gana, Aaron T. "The State in Africa: Yesterday, Today and Tomorrow." *International Political Science Review* 6 (1) (1985): 129.

Gellar, Sheldon. "Pitfalls of Top-Down Development Planning and Macro-Economic Analyses: Senegalese Grain Pricing Policies in the Post-Berg Era." Paper presented at the Conference on Institutional Analysis and Development, Washington, D.C., May 21–22, 1985.

Gorou, Pierre. *The Tropical World: Principles of Human and Economic Geography.* Paris: University of France Press, 1969.

Havens, R.M. "Laissez-Faire Theory in Presidential Messages during the Nineteenth Century." *Journal of Economic History* 1 (1941): 86–95.

Helleiner, G.K. "The IMF and Africa in the 1980s." *Canadian Journal of African Studies* 17 (1) (1983): 17–34.

Heller, Peter, and Allan Tait. *Government Employment and Pay: Some International Comparisons.* Washington, D.C.: International Monetary Fund, 1982.

Hill, Polly. *Studies in Rural Capitalism in West Africa.* London: Cambridge University Press, 1970.

Hollingsworth, J.R. "The Political-Structural Basis for Economic Performance." *Annals of the American Academy of Politics and Social Science* 459 (1982): 28–45.

Holt, R.T., and J.E. Turner. *The Political Basis of Economic Development.* New York: Van Nostrand, 1966.

Hyden, Goran. *Beyond Ujamma in Tanzania: Underdevelopment and an Uncaptured Peasantry.* Berkeley, Calif.: University of California Press, 1980.

————. *No Shortcuts to Progress: African Development Management in Perspective.* Berkeley, Calif.: University of California Press, 1983.

————. "Urban Growth and Rural Development." In *African Independence: The First Twenty-Five Years,* edited by G.M. Carter and P. O'Meara, 188–217. Bloomington: Indiana University Press, 1986.

Illife, John. *The Emergence of African Capitalism.* Minneapolis: University of Minnesota Press, 1983.

Illchman, Warren, and R.C. Bhargava. "Balanced Thought and Economic Growth." In *Frontiers of Development Administration,* edited by Fred W. Riggs, 247–273. Durham, NC: Duke University Press, 1970.

Iyayi, Festus. "Primitive Capital Accumulation in a Neo-Colony: Nigeria." *Review of African Political Economy* 35 (May, 1986): 27–39.

Kamarck, Andrew M. "African Economic Development: Problems and Prospects." *Africa Report Magazine* 14 (1) (1969): 16–20.

————. *The Tropics and Economic Development.* Baltimore: Johns Hopkins University Press, 1976.

Kirk-Greene, A.H.M., ed. *The Principles of Native Administration in Nigeria: Selected Documents 1900–1947.* London: Oxford University Press, 1985.

Kilby, Peter. *African Enterprise: The Nigerian Bread Industry.* Stanford, Calif.: Hoover Institution Studies No. 8, 1965.

Krane, Dale. "The Effects on Public Policy of Center-Local Relocation: A Cross-National Study." *International Political Science Review* 7 (1) (1986): 39–55.

Lewis, A. *The Theory of Economic Growth.* Winchester, Mass.: Unwyn Hyman, 1955.

Leys, Colin. *Underdevelopment in Kenya: The Political Economy of Neocolonialism.* London: Heinemann, 1975.

Lipton, M. *Why Poor People Stay Poor: Urban Bias in World Development.* London: Temple Smith, 1977.

Lofchie, Michael. "Africa's Agrarian Maliase." In *African Independence: The First Twenty-Five Years,* edited by G.M. Carter and P. O'Meara, 160–187. Bloomington, Ind.: Indiana University Press, 1985.

Mabogunje, Akin. *The Development Process: A Spatial Perspective.* London: Hutchinson University Press, 1980.

Marcus, Edward. "The Economic Role of Government in Independent Tropical Africa." *American Journal of Economics and Sociology* 24 (3) (1965): 307–315.

Marsden, K., and T. Belot. *Private Enterprise in Africa Creating A Better Environment.* Washington, D.C.: World Bank Discussion Papers, No. 17, 1987.

Mkulo, M.A.M. "Interview." *Public Enterprises* (February 1985).

Moris, J.R. "The Transferability of the Western Management Tradition to the Non-Western Public Service Sectors." *Philippine Journal of Public Administration* 20 (4) (1976): 401–427.

N'diaye, B. "African Economies and Governmental Performance." Statement read at the International Conferences on Privatization, February 17, 1986.

Nellis, J.R. *Public Enterprises in Sub-Saharan Africa.* Washington, D.C.: World Bank Discussion Papers, 1986.

Neumark, S. Daniel. "Economic Development and Economic Incentives." Washington, D.C.: World Bank Discussion Papers, 1972, 57–67.

O'Connor, A. *The African City.* London: Hutchinson, 1983.

Okoli, F.C. "The Dilemma of Premature Bureaucratization in New States of Africa: The Case of Nigeria." *African Studies Review* 23 (2) (1980): 1–16.

Onyemelukwe, Clement. *Men and Management in Contemporary Africa.* London: Longman, 1973.

Olowu, Dele. "Bureaucratic Morality in Africa." *International Political Science Review* 9 (3) (1988): 215–229.

―――. "Economic Liberalization and the Nigerian Public Service" *Administration* 21 (3 and 4) (1987).

Ozgediz, Selcuk. *Managing the Public Service in Developing Countries: Issues and Prospects.* Washington, D.C.: World Bank Staff Working Papers, No. 583, 1983.

Rende, Achim. "The IMF in Africa—Model Case Ghana." *Development and Cooperation* 13 (1) (1988): 28–29.

Richards, Paul. *Indigenous Agricultural Revolution: Ecology and Food Production in West Africa.* London: Hutchinson, 1985.

Ridler, N.L. "Comparative Advantages as a Development Model: The Ivory Coast." *Journal of Modern African Studies* 23 (3) (1985): 407–417.

Ruttan, V.W., and Y. Hayami. "Towards a Theory of Induced Institutional Innovation." *The Journal of Development Studies* 20 (1984): 203–223.

Sandbrook, Richard. *The Politics of Africa's Economic Stagnation.* Cambridge: Cambridge University Press, 1985.

Schatz, Sayre P. "Laissez-Faireism for Africa?" *Journal of Modern African Studies* 25 (1) (1987): 129–138.

Schultz, T.W. *Transforming Traditional Agriculture.* New York: Anno Press, 1976.

Selassie, B.H. *The Executive in African Governments.* London: Heinemann, 1974.

Sheahan, John. "Market-Oriented Policies and Political Repression in Latin America." *Economic Development and Cultural Change* 28 (2) (1980): 267–292.

Sharpe, L.J. "Decentralist Systems in Western Democracies: A First Appraisal." In *Decentralist Systems in Western Democracies,* edited by L.J. Sharpe, 9–80. London: Sage, 1979.

―――. "Inter-governmental Policy Making: The Limits of Sub-National Autonomy." In *Guidance, Control, and Evaluation in the Public Sector,* edited by F.X. Kaufmann, G. Majone, V. Ostrom, 159–182. Berlin: Walter de Gruyter, 1986.

Smith, Brian C. *Field Administration: An Aspect of Decentralisation.* London: Routledge and Kegan Paul, 1967.

Smith, B. *Decentralisation: The Territorial Dimension of the State.* London: Allen and Unwin, 1985.

Smock, Audrey. *Ibo Politics: The Role of Ethnic Unions in Eastern Nigeria.* Cambridge, Mass.: Harvard University Press, 1971.

Spengler, Joseph J. "The State and Economic Growth: Summary and Interpretation." In *The State and Economic Growth,* edited by Hugh Aitken, 353–382. New York: Social Science Research Council, 1959.

Stewart, France. *Basic Needs in Developing Countries.* Baltimore: Johns Hopkins University Press, 1985.

Todaro, M.P. *Economic Development in the Third World.* Second Edition. London: Longman Press, 1981.

United States of America. "House of Representatives Committee on Foreign Affairs, Africa." *The World Bank and the IMF: An Appraisal.* Hearing before the Sub-Committee on Africa, 98th Congress, Second Session. Washington, D.C., 1984.

Wallis, M.A.H. "Bureaucrats, Politicians, and Rural Committees in Kenya." Manchester Papers in Development, No. 6 (1982).

West Africa. London, March 30, 1987a.

———. London, June 29, No. 584, Special Issue on "Africa's Stormclouds," 1987b.

———. London, October 5, 1987c.

———. London. "Privatization in Ghana." June 27, 1988.

World Bank. *Accelerated Development in Sub-Saharan Africa: An Agenda for Action.* Washington, D.C., 1981.

———. *Sub-Saharan Africa: Progress Report on Development Prospects and Programs.* Washington, D.C., 1983.

———. *Toward Sustained Development in Sub-Saharan Africa.* Washington, D.C., 1984.

———. *World Development Report.* New York: Oxford University Press, 1987.

———. *Financing Adjustment with Growth in Sub-Saharan Africa 1986–1990.* Washington, D.C., 1986.

Wagner, A. "Three Classics on Public Finance." In *Classics in the Theory of Public Finance,* edited by R.A. Musgrave and A. T. Peacock, 1–16. New York: Macmillan, 1958.

6

State Tutelage vs. Self-Governance: The Rhetoric and Reality of Decentralization in Senegal

Sheldon Gellar

Introduction

In this chapter I shall be primarily concerned with the following: first, the root causes of overcentralization in the African context; second, the ways in which overcentralization—i.e., the concentration of too much political and economic power within a single political authority—can stifle the development of viable institutions providing citizens with the means to govern their own affairs; and third, alternative institutional arrangements to facilitate greater citizen participation and control over local affairs.

The difficulty of moving beyond overcentralization is evident even in African countries like Senegal and Tanzania where national leaders have called for greater local participation and devolution of political authority. In this chapter we shall use Senegal as a case study to explore some of the causes and consequences of overcentralization and the obstacles to transforming the rhetoric of decentralization and participation in Africa into reality.

Defining the Problem: State Tutelage vs. Self-Governance

The state in Africa has come under heavy attack from all shades of the political spectrum. Proponents of the free market accuse the state of stifling agriculture and instigating economic crisis through its heavy handed economic policies and inefficient state enterprises.[1] They are concerned primarily with economic overcentralization and call for less state regulation of the economy. Other critics bemoan the state's reluctance to allow more political competition and promote greater participation.[2] They are concerned primarily with political overcentralization and call for more western-style political democracy. Others complain that the state in most African countries has been captured by a political/bureaucratic elite or class that uses the state to amass wealth and power while exploiting the urban and rural masses.[3] These critics are less concerned with overcentralization than they are with the fact that too much power is concentrated in the hands of the wrong people or class. They propose resistance to the state and call for its takeover by the right people—i.e., those who represent the rural and urban masses. Finally, still others insist that rather than being all powerful, African states are weak—soft states—and lack the authority and resources to implement their development programs despite the great concentration of formal power within the central state.[4]

While all of the above approaches are critical of the state, they define the problem of the state quite differently and stress solutions that meet their particular concerns—e.g., letting the market operate unencumbered to foster economic growth; promoting democratic institutions; checking the power of an illegitimate ruling class; and creating the conditions for the modernization of African society. The "villain," so to speak, is not centralization per se, but central planning, authoritarianism, unrepresentative ruling classes, and underdeveloped economies and class structures.

Centralization is a somewhat static term that simply refers to the concentration of formal power within a single political authority. While the term tells us something about the structure of formal power, it does not tell us much about the relationship between the centralized state and the rest of society. The centralized state functions in one way in France which is a political democracy and another way in the Soviet Union which is not. In Africa, the centralized state is not all powerful. In most instances, it functions as a patrimonial administrative state[5] which greatly resembles its predecessor, the colonial state, in its approach toward dealing with its citizens. Many African rulers use the centralized state to impose their tutelage over the people. They perceive themselves as the guardians of the people. They watch over the people and are reluctant to surrender the power of the central state inherited from the colonial era to other political entities within the nation. They justify their commitment to centralization in the name of national unity since centralization allegedly serves as a bulwark against tribalism and regionalism and other potentially irredentist forces.

While some form of decentralization may be necessary to promote self-governance and local autonomy, decentralization is not synonomous with self-governance. Decentralization does not necessarily foster self-governance if it simply creates smaller scale "central authorities" dominated by local elites or places more state agents with greater decision-making powers at the local level. Self-governance requires a more complex configuration of institutional arrangements which include, among other things: (1) the participation of the citizens in determining the constitutional rules governing their political relationships with the central state and other political entities, (2) the acountability of political and administrative authorities to the citizenry and the rule of law, (3) a considerable degree of autonomy for voluntary associations and other mediating structures between the state and the individual citizen, and (4) periodic elections to provide the people with the opportunity to change leaders.

To govern means to control, to steer, to direct (*American Heritage Dictionary*, p. 570). From this definition, it follows that self-governance refers to the act of controlling, steering, and directing one's own affairs. Tutelage, on the other hand, refers to guardianship. In legal parlance, a tutor is the guardian of a minor (*American Heritage Dictionary*, p. 1,355). The term tutelage thus implies that the guardian (the ruler) is dealing with a minor (the ruled) and that their unequal relationships are based on the greater wisdom of the ruler as contrasted with the relative ignorance of the ruled. As we know, guardians are often slow to admit that their wards have matured and become capable of running their own affairs. Hence, it is not surprising to see African central governments hesitate to end their tutelage by surrendering political power to local and regional political entities and permitting periodic, freely competitive elections.

The Colonial Heritage and
the Centralized State in Senegal

As an overseas extension of the metropolitan state, the French colonial state reflected the French preference for centralization and the central power's distaste for sharing authority with local political structures. French colonialism was ideologically justified by France's "civilizing mission." France thus imposed its tutelage over the indigenous populations under its jurisdiction in order to guide them along the road to civilization. In the process of extending its rule over French West Africa, France destroyed existing political entities and put into place an autocratic administrative state which resisted granting political and civil rights and representative institutions to the subject populations (Cowan 1958; Crowder 1968; Gellar 1976).

Senegal enjoyed a privileged position within French West Africa. Because of a quirk of history, a small minority of Senegal's African and metis populations residing in coastal urban centers enjoyed the status of French citizens and political and civil rights while the localities in which they lived—Dakar, Goree, Rufisque, and Saint-Louis—were granted the status of communes and the right to have municipal institutions patterned on those in France. The so-called "four communes" became schools of democracy for the African and Afro-European "citizens" (Johnson 1971).

As the African populations of the communes grew, and therefore, the number of African citizens grew, the French colonial administration tried to change the rules of the game to make it more difficult for Africans to become citizens. When that did not work, they attempted to reduce the powers of the diverse representative institutions in the colony—the territorial assembly *(Conseil General)* and the municipal governments of the "four communes." The French colonial authorities also thwarted efforts by

Senegalese political leaders to extend the rights of citizenship and communal institutions to the subject populations of the interior.

The relative dynamism of political life in the four communes contrasted dramatically with the absence of political activity and representative political institutions in the interior where the people were administered directly by representatives of the colonial state. Senegalese citizens seeking to champion the prerogatives of local government bodies under African control were constantly locked in battle with the colonial administration.

During the post-World War II decolonization era (1945-1960) when France extended the rights of citizenship and voting powers to the subject populations in Francophone Africa, the power of the colonial administration waned as colonial officials became more subject to pressures exerted by Senegalese political leaders aligned with French political parties in the metropole. Because power was centralized in France, this meant that Senegalese leaders had to go to Paris to effect changes in Senegal. The Senegalese deputy who went to Paris was, in effect, a lobbyist for his territory. For their part, the Senegalese masses were left largely outside the political process, except during election time when they were mobilized to vote for the deputy. The extension of the suffrage to the rural populations, the fierce electoral competition between Senegal's two main political parties, and the organization of local party units by party leaders residing in the interior, were, on the other hand, important indicators of the democratization of the political system.

While extending political rights to large numbers of Africans, the French did little to promote local government or even to decentralize colonial administrative structures. On the contrary, the French pushed centralization even further, especially in the realm of economics where French planners in Paris formulated economic development plans for France's overseas territories. When independence came, Senegal's political leaders inherited the colonial state's centralized adminstrative structures.

In addition to a centralized bureaucracy, Senegal's political leaders also embraced French political traditions and preferences for a unitary state. Thus, it was not surprising that Senegal adopted a unitary state based on the centralizing Jacobin model which regarded the state as the incarnation of the popular will. The unitary state also prevailed in Senegal and throughout much of Africa for other reasons: (a) African leaders wished to preserve national unity and argued that other forms of government—e.g., federal forms which recognized regional differences—might encourage secessionist movements and lead to the disintegration of the nation; (b) little had been done by the colonial authorities to promote local and regional political institutions and attachments based on locality; and (c) African leaders felt the need to build a strong state to promote economic development.

The commitment of Senegal's political elite to a unitary state was never in doubt. From the implemention of the Loi-Cadre in 1957 which granted some measure of internal self-government in the form of an elected African executive which shared power with a colonial governor to independence in

1960, Senegalese intellectuals were more concerned with the future of Senegal's relationships with France and other French West African territories than they were with defining the rules of the game determining the future of political relationships *within* Senegal. The heated discussion over federalism during the period referred primarily to political relationships between Senegal, the French Sudan, and other French West African territories as constituent units of a multi-national federal republic (Dugue 1960; Foltz 1965; Senghor 1964). Senegalese leaders like Leopold Senghor and, to a lesser extent, Mamadou Dia were willing to abandon some of the traditional prerogatives of national sovereignty in favor of a supranational federation. Senegalese and many other Francophone African leaders thus supported federalism as an instrument to promote African unity among Francophone territories while insisting that a unitary state was the best means of building national unity within the country.

Early Administrative Reforms:
Decentralization or Deconcentration?

The official ideology of Senegal's governing party during the early years of independence—African Socialism (Senghor 1964; Dia 1962; Gellar 1980)—called for the creation of self-governing cooperatives and rural communes in the countryside. During the transition period, the cooperatives would remain under the tutelage of state agents who would teach them the skills needed to govern their own affairs. The administrative state would eventually wither away in the rural areas. The new agrarian based ideology of African Socialism coexisted with the longstanding Senegalese concern for promoting democracy through the expansion of municipal government in urban areas.

In 1960, the Senegalese government initiated several sweeping reforms which purported to decentralize and democratize the political and administrative structures inherited from the colonial era.[6]

First, the government redrew administrative districts to bring the postcolonial state closer to the rural populations. As a result the country was divided into seven regions, twenty-five departments, and fifty-five arrondissements, administered by governors, prefects, and sub-prefects. As in the past, these officials served as agents of the central government and were directly accountable to their superiors in the administrative hierarchy rather than to the local government bodies in the areas where they worked. Although the government referred to these changes as administrative decentralization, they were, in fact, examples of administrative deconcentration—i.e., the conferring of more decision-making powers to agents of the central authority working at the local level.

Second, the government extended the scope of local government by establishing a regional assembly in each region and transforming all of the urban centers of the interior which served as departmental seats into full communes with their own elected mayors and municipal councils. While a step toward political decentralization, the evolution of self-governance in the interior was limited by the fact that the urban communes were placed under the tutelage (*tutelle*) of the Ministry of the Interior.

Unlike the urban communes which had roots in Senegalese political traditions, the regional assemblies were embyronic institutions created by the government to represent the populations of the interior who did not live in the urban communes. The regional assemblies had few powers, a very meager budget and no autonomy since they too functioned under the tutelage of the state. The region itself had no legal status. The central government regarded the region primarily as an administrative district and unit for decentralized economic planning rather than a political entity in its own right. The Senegalese constitution which established a unitary state discouraged manifestations of regionalism by formally prohibiting the creation of regional political parties.

Third, the government launched a vast network of rural cooperatives throughout the country as the first step in moving toward an agrarian-based communitarian socialism.[7] The cooperative statutes resembled those of Western cooperatives with their democratic rules of governance based on one man, one vote. But Senegalese cooperatives had little in common with their Western counterparts. Whereas, Western cooperatives had been initiated by groups of individual farmers banding together to pool their resources to improve their bargaining position in the marketplace, Senegalese cooperatives were largely creatures of the state and imposed from above. The co-ops had little autonomy since they too were placed under the supervision of state agents who were supposed to provide them with technical assistance. Moreover, the rules and regulations governing the co-op and the bookkeeping system required by the state were all in French, thereby excluding most of the co-op membership from understanding the formal working rules governing the functioning of the co-op.

Fourth, the central government attempted to make the state bureaucracy more development oriented and set up new development agencies like *Animation Rurale,* rural expansion centers (CERs), and regional development assistance centers (CRADs) to mobilize and provide technical assistance to the rural populations in the countryside (Schumacher 1975; Gellar 1980). The CERs and CRADs had their headquarters at the arrondissement and regional level where local government was non-existent or weak. Moreover, as agents of the central state, their officals were not accountable to local authorities. While the *Animation Rurale* services attempted to encourage the rural populations to organize themselves and to voice their dissatisfaction when state officials, rural notables, or local politicians did them wrong, it remained a marginal agency within the state bureaucracy and one whose influence diminished over the years. With the exception of *Animation Rurale,* the diverse rural development agencies established by the state were more concerned with carrying out the central government's economic policies and enforcing state regulations than in promoting self-governance.

The government's avowed commitment to promote development, democracy, and administrative decentralization were, more often than not, incompatible with the institutional arrangements set up to implement these goals. The emphasis on central planning and the myth of national development[8] led to institutional arrangements which overrode other efforts to promote self-governance and political and administrative decentralization. To insure more uniformity and coherence in implementing national development policy, planners preferred to rely upon a deconcentrated field administration whose officials were directly accountable to the central government through the administrative hierarchy than a decentralized administration accountable to local authorities. It also made more sense to limit the autonomy of local and regional assemblies and place them under the tutelage of the state in order to constrain them from adopting policies and spending patterns that were incompatible with national planning goals. In the name of development, the government thus maintained much the same kind of centralized and hierarchical administrative structures inherited from the colonial era despite the rhetoric of administrative reform.

The unitary-state structures and the perception of those in power as guardians of the nation also restrained the central government from sharing power and economic resources with decentralized governmental units under the control of local party leaders. During the early years of independence, the communes remained the main centers of political activity and the arena where party leaders could build a solid political base. Control over municipal budgets provided elected officials with sources of patronage. During this period, local party leaders and elites frequently clashed with the national leadership of the governing party over local prerogatives and economic issues concerning the allocation of resources. Many deputies in the National Assembly openly criticized Prime Minister Mamadou Dia for imposing his economic policies on the country without adequately taking into consideration the views of the elected representatives of the people.

While espousing democracy, Senegal's national leaders also insisted upon maintaining a strong state that would preserve order in the face of provocation by "disloyal elements." Thus, they did not hesitate to use the power of the state to crush and domesticate a hostile trade union movement, ban opposition political parties, and generally weaken the opposition.

The Reinforcement of State Tutelage:
Overcentralization as an Obstacle to Self-Governance

The tentative movement towards political and administrative decentralization came to an abrupt end following the fall of Mamadou Dia from power in December 1962. During the mid-1960s, President Senghor instituted several major institutional changes which consolidated his own personal power and increased the state's tutelage over local government, the cooperative movement, and the economy.

The 1963 constitution promoted by Senghor created a strong presidential regime by concentrating all executive power in the hands of the president and reducing the initiative of the National Assembly. At the same time, Senghor consolidated his authority within the governing party by purging his political opponents and strengthening the powers of the central organs of the party vis-a-vis regional and local party organizations. Senghor sought to stifle the development of powerful regional party organizations that might serve as a base from which others could challenge his position as national party leader. During the mid-1960s, Senghor also successfully eliminated opposition parties in the country through repression or co-optation. By 1966, there were no longer any legal opposition political parties in Senegal which had been transformed into a de facto one-party state.

Instead of promoting the evolution of local government bodies, Senghor increased the tutelage of the state over these institutions. The prerogatives of local government vis-a-vis the central government had never been firmly established. For example, although a basic unit of local government, the communes are not even mentioned in the Senegalese constitution. Moreover, their legal status is subject to the whims of the state which has the power to create or dissolve communes. Furthermore, the mayor, even when elected, is still legally an agent of the state and therefore accountable to the administrative hierarchy.

During the mid-1960s, Senghor reduced the autonomy of communal institutions in the interior by giving the prefect a more direct role in supervising municipal financial affairs. This measure was taken in the name of efficiency and was designed to depoliticize the administration of communal affairs. The state's direct intervention in communal affairs took much of the luster from the office of mayor. It also dampened the development of local civic pride and responsibility. Tocqueville's remarks concerning the consequences of weak municipal bodies were particularly *a propos* to the situation in Senegal:

> The absence of local public spirit is a frequent subject of regret to those in power; everyone agrees that there is no surer guaranty of order and tranquility, and yet nothing is more difficult to create. If the municipal bodies were made powerful and independent, it is feared that they would become too strong, and expose the state to anarchy. Yet, without power and independence, a town may contain good subjects but it can have no active citizens (Tocqueville 1955: 60).

Senghor's centralizing tendencies also led him to transfer some of the administrative and financial powers of Dakar's municipal council to the governor of the Cap Vert Region. Since Dakar was the capital city, Senghor did not wish to have too much power over the city's affairs fall into the hands of local politicians. Three decades earlier, the Governor-General of French West Africa had taken similar measures to insure that the colonial state would exercise more direct control over Dakar's communal affairs by changing Dakar's status to that of an "Imperial City" under the direction of the French West African colonial administration.

In 1964, the powers of the governors were strengthened to make them into superprefects directly responsible to the president while the regional assemblies as elective bodies for all practical purposes ceased to function. Senghor also delayed the implementation of plans to establish the "rural communities" and elected rural councils envisaged in the 1960 administrative reforms. The country had to wait until 1972 before implementation legislation was passed. Even then, the "rural communities" were implanted very slowly in the countryside.

While reaffirming the regime's commitment to agrarian socialism, Senghor downgraded the cooperarative movement as the main economic development motor in the countryside. Rather than evolving into the democratic, self-governing institutions envisaged by Mamadou Dia, the cooperative movement was under the heavy-handed tutelage of agents from the National Cooperative and Development Assistance Office (ONCAD), and was transformed into an appendage of the state's peanut marketing board. While the state gave some limited, rudimentary training to cooperative officers like the president and the treasurer, little was done to simplify accounting procedures, to translate co-op regulations from French into the local languages, or to provide functional literacy courses in the local languages built around co-op regulations and procedures. The failure to provide adequate training and literacy perpetuated the tutelage of state agents over the cooperatives. State economic regulations also limited the range of economic activities in which the cooperatives could become engaged. Hence, it was not surprising that many peasants regarded the cooperatives as belonging to the state rather than to themselves.

Rather than relying on the cooperatives and the private sector to promote economic development in the countryside, the state created diverse regional development agencies (RDAs) during the late 1960s and early 1970s to organize (*encadrer*) the rural populations and provide technical assistance for developmental activities. Tocqueville's comments about the efforts of the *ancien regime* to foster agricultural development in France could also apply to Senegal:

> However, the central government did not limit itself to coming to the rescue of the peasantry when times were hard; it aspired to teach them how to become rich and to help them make their land pay, even if this meant using what was little short of compulsion. Pamphlets on agricultural science were issued periodically by the Intendants and their sub-delegates, farmers' associations were founded and prizes awarded; moreover, nurseries, whose seed grains were available to all, were maintained at considerable expense. In short, the central power had taken to playing the part of an indefatigable mentor and keeping the nation in quasi-paternal tutelage (Tocqueville 1955: 40–41).

The RDAs worked with farmer producer groups in a tutelary capacity. The rhetoric of participation contrasted with the paternalism of these state agencies and the assymetry of their relationships with the farmer producer groups under their jurisdiction. Thus, in the Senegal River Region, the contractual relationships were one sided. Member farmer groups had to comply with the regulations set by SAED, a state water irrigation agency, in order to receive credit and other support. Sanctions could be taken against farmer groups not fully complying with regulations. On the other hand, there was no legal recourse for farmers to sue the state or get compensation for losses incurred when the RDA did not fulfill its contractual obligations.

Still another indicator of centralization that persisted under Senghor was the state's regulation of voluntary associations. Although Senegal's constitution guaranteed the right of free association, most voluntary associations had to receive the official approval of the state in order to function. Youth associations, for example, needed to be sanctioned by the Youth Ministry while most of the other groups had to be approved by the Ministry of the Interior. Groups not having the official sanction of the state had no legal status.

The May-June 1968 urban unrest in Dakar which shook the regime, the so-called *malaise paysanne* in the countryside, economic stagnation, and the shriveling of Senegalese democracy led to growing demands for political, administrative, social, and economic reform and changes in the presidential monarchy that Senghor had built since the demise of Mamadou Dia.

The reforms initiated during the early and mid-1970s had little to do with decentralization. They were largely responses to the demands of a younger generation of Senegalese intellectuals for: (a) a greater role in governing the country, (b) acceleration of the slow pace of Africanization, and (c) nationalization of the modern sectors of the Senegalese economy. The Senegalese constitution was revised in 1970 and reestablished the office of prime minister while retaining a strong presidential regime. Abdou Diouf, President Senghor's hand-picked choice for prime minister was a young technocrat who had been trained as an *administrateur civil* in France's School for Overseas Administrators. Diouf shared the centralizing perspectives of his French mentors. The nationalization measures taken during the early 1970s contributed to more rather than less concentration of economic power in the hands of the central government.[9]

In 1974, the government introduced legislation to liberalize Senegalese politics and move the country towards a multiparty democracy.[10] These reforms allowed opposition political parties to organize; eased state censorship of the press; and permitted the creation of trade unions not affiliated with the government-backed National Trade Union Confederation (CNTS). The debate over the liberalization of Senegal's political system among Senegalese intellectuals revolved around the powers of the presidency and the degree of openness Senegal's emerging multiparty system should have.

By the end of the 1970s, Senegalese political leaders were rethinking their committment to political and economic centralization. The old ideology of communitarian agrarian socialism based on decentralized rural political and economic institutions began to come back in vogue.[11] State officials spoke about the need to revive the moribund cooperative movement and to reduce the heavy-handed tutelage of the unpopular ONCAD. The RDAs also came under fire for their paternalism and inefficiency. They responded by holding their own auto-critique sessions. The "rural communities" created by the 1972 Administrative Reform were extolled as the centerpiece of rural democracy in Senegal. However, despite all the calls for more decentralization and participation, few people challenged the structure of the unitary state as a primary obstacle to self-governance.

The Limits of Decentralization in a Unitary State

The thrust towards decentralization accelerated during the 1980s when the government pursued policies which transferred more responsibility to local rural institutions and organizations. The failure of past economic policies, the inefficiencies of the regional development agencies, donor pressure to privatize the rural economy, and rural discontent were all factors behind the government's change of direction. The movement towards greater decentralization took several forms: (1) the establishment of "rural communities" and rural councils in every Senegalese region, (2) the 1983 cooperative reform which created village sections with broad decisionmaking powers, (3) greater state acceptance of non-governmental voluntary organizations as development agents, and (4) major cuts in the size of the state rural development bureaucracy.

The rural councils of the "rural communities" created by the 1972 administrative reform were, in theory, granted broad powers to regulate local markets, fairs, cattle walks, and residential zoning patterns, allocate uncultivated land and revise existing land tenure regimes in the areas under their jurisdiction, and finance local community development projects through the rural council budget. In practice, however, the central government maintained its tutelage over the rural council through the subprefect whose presence made it difficult to approve policies and projects not endorsed by the government.[12] Moreover, the power of tutelage gave the central government the right to veto the deliberations of the rural council, to suspend or dissolve individual rural councils, and to remove their presidents and other officers. Tutelage was particularly pronounced in financial matters and justified in the name of protecting the national interest.

Now autonomy can't be total without the risk of undermining national unity; the management of local affairs must be assured in an equitable manner vis-a-vis all the citizens in the national territory; it must not be opposed to the interests of the nation. That is why local financial initiative can be exercized only within the framework defined by national legislation and must be subordinated to the initiative of the central power. Thus, local assemblies can levy taxes only if that principle is first accepted by the National Assembly. And, in order that the local communities present a certain unity, it is again the law that determines the tax rates, kinds of tax categories, and the methods of tax collection (Bouart and Fouilland 1983: 17).

As long as this kind of centralized state tutelage prevails, the rural councils cannot become truly self-governing bodies.

The 1983 cooperative reforms provide still another example of the limits of decentralization and the proclivity of centralized states to impose homogeneous institutional arrangements which do not take into account the great diversity of local conditions. One of the complaints against the existing cooperatives had been that they were too large, dominated by local notables, and not sufficiently accountable to the membership, particularly those living in villages outside the village that housed the coop headquarters. The 1983 cooperative statutes sought to remedy this by establishing smaller village sections which had their own legal status and financial autonomy. This provided smaller population units with far more control over their own affairs than previously. The reforms also explicitly called for more participation by women and youth who had been excluded from cooperative governance (Gellar 1987).

However, the cooperative reforms of 1983, like those of 1960, were imposed from above. Once the central government made its decision, it moved rapidly to organize the entire country into village sections. Thus, within a two month period, the Cooperative Service set up more than 4,200 village sections which had to meet standard criteria laid down by the government concerning size and mode of activity. It is questionable as to whether villages had the option of not joining a village section. While the establishment of the village sections marked some progress towards decentralization and greater self-governance within the cooperative movement, this advance remained problematic for several reasons: (1) the rules of the game were established by the central government and not the local populations, (2) the initiative for organizing the village sections came from the state cooperative service rather than the local populations, and (3) the village sections were organized without taking into consideration local differences.

The Senegalese government's approach towards cooperatives and cooperative reform, of course, reflected the penchant of centralized states like Senegal for nice, neat uniform rules and structures. As Toqueville put it:

> It may be said that every central government worships uniformity; uniformity relieves it of inquiry into an infinite variety of details, which must be attended to if rules have to be adapted to different men, instead of indiscriminately subjecting all men to the same rule (Tocqueville, 1956: 295).

The decision to establish one development cooperative which encompassed all the village sections in every "rural community" seat provided still another example of the passion for uniformity displayed by the Senegalese government.

One of the most promising developments in Senegal in terms of self-governance has been the growing willingness of the central government to accept a greater role for voluntary associations as development agents. During the 1970s and early 1980s, a number of independent peasant-based organizations emerged throughout Senegal that wished to organize their own development programs without submitting to the tutelage of the RDAs or affiliating with the cooperative movements.[13] The independent peasant associations had much more in common with the self-governing, multi-functional cooperatives envisaged by Senegal's communitarian socialists than either the farmer groups organized by the RDAs or the rural coop-eratives. These groups emerged as a result of grassroots rather than state initiatives, established their own rules of governance, and taxed themselves to finance their activities. Some were formally approved by the state while others were not. Even those groups not having official approval were allowed to function freely with little interference by state agents.

The rise of independent peasant-based associations as a dynamic force in the countryside coincided with the decline of the large-scale state agen-cies. The unpopular National Cooperative and Development Assistance Office (ONCAD) was abolished in 1980. During the mid-1980s, several RDAs were disbanded or saw their roles vastly reduced while those that survived loosened their tutelage over the local populations.

Alternative Institutional Arrangements
for Self-Governance: Federalism vs. the Unitary State

Despite its shortcomings, the Senegalese political system is still one of the most democratic in Africa. Its citizens have expressed a strong com-mitment to democratic values—free speech, freedom of the press, freedom of association, and competitive electoral politics. The one-party regime (1966–74) did not endure very long in Senegal because of strong opposition from the Senegalese elite to authoritarian rule. Moreover, the proliferation of non-governmental voluntary associations in Senegal after independence has created a citizenry that has demonstrated that it knows how to build viable organizations and run its own affairs. Their presence and dynamism indicates that the government does not have a monopoly over the social, economic, and cultural life of the nation. The central government has to take their views into consideration. These groups use their organizational clout and skills to extract resources from the state.

Despite these positive aspects of Senegalese society which bode well for the future of democracy, Senegal's potential for a greater degree of self-governance has been held back by the the structure of the unitary state, the concentration of power in the presidency and executive branch, state tutelage over local government, and the hierarchical organization of the state bureaucracy.

One alternative to the unitary state is some form of federal government which would limit national government, preserve the integrity of local government units, and take into account local and regional differences (Ostrom 1986). This issue is discussed at some length in Chapters 10 and 12 of this volume. A federal system would promote self-governance by establishing constitutional rules giving each unit of government the authority to take collective decisions to provide public goods and services for its political community and to take decisions binding all persons in its jursidiction (Ostrom 1987). While the central government has regional policies there is no regional political authority to define its own policies. For example, in recent years, the Casamance has been an area of major unrest, largely because its people resent the tutelage of Dakar. The governor is named by and accountable to the president. He has to call Dakar for his orders. If Senegal had a federal system, the governor would be an elected official accountable to the people of the Casamance and the region would have a regional assembly with extensive powers. While opponents of such a solution worry that a federal system permiting a certain degree of autonomy would encourage secesssionism, it might be argued that such a federal system would defuse a tense situation and leave the people of the Casamance more willing to remain part of Senegal. In a similar manner, regional planning logically should be conducted by local regional political authorities representing the interests of their populations rather than be imposed by the central government. Again the local populations would be more apt to work to implement a regional plan elaborated by their elected representatives than one elaborated by planners which Dakar and officials of the central state posted in the region.[14]

The excessive concentration of political power in the office of the presidency serves as another obstacle to self-governance.[15] The overcentralization of decision-making authority in the hands of the presidency without sufficient checks and balances from the legislative and judicial branches of government can lead to abuses of power and personalization of the office; place an impossibly heavy burden on the shoulders of the president who is called to make rational decisions on an incredible number of issues without adequate information or the time to process the information; and stifle the initiative of other government officials who cannot or will not act until they get the president's approval.

Institutional arrangements to check the tendency towards a highly centralized presidential monarchy would reduce the role of the General Secretariat of the Presidency in initiating legislation, restore more initiative to the National Assembly whose members represent local constituencies, and make the judicial branch of government more independent.

The tutelage of the central state over local government, the cooperative movement, and voluntary associations involved in development activities constitute still another major obstacle to self-governance by stifling local initiative. The reduction or elimination of the state's administrative tutelage over local government and strengthening of the taxing powers of local government would foster more accountability of local government officials to their constituents and make local government less dependent upon the central government to provide public services.

Notes

1. The best known example of this approach is the Berg Report (World Bank 1981). For a thorough review of the literature on the agrarian crisis in Africa, see Berry (1984).

2. The question of democracy in Africa has again emerged as an important issue for Africanists. See, for example, two recent edited volumes on this theme (Ronen 1986 and Chabal 1986).

3. The Marxists are, of course, the leading but not the only proponents of this critique of the state. See, for example, Arrighi and Saul (1973), Gutkind and Wallerstein (1976). Also see Levy (1981) for a general theory of the predatory nature of rulers.

4. The most lucid exposition of this approach is Hyden (1980; 1983). The state's weakness precludes it from being the agent of radical economic transformation. At the same time, the state's economic intervention slows down the development of capitalist economic structures which are necessary for modernization. Hyden thus calls for more encouragement of the private sector and the development of capitalist structures as a precondition for socialism.

5. For a discussion of the concept of the inheritance situation, see Nettl and Robertson (1968: 63–127). For a effort to apply the concept of inheritance and patrimonialism to West Africa in general and Senegal in particular, see Gellar (1973). For a discussion of the patrimonial administrative state, see Callaghy (1986: 30–51).

6. For detailed discussions of these reforms, see Gellar (1980) and Schumacher (1975). For the legal framework see Gautron and Rougevin (1970).

7. Mamadou Dia was the architect of this policy. One of the ironies of Dia's approach is that he attempted to create by state fiat a movement that would eventually lead to the withering away of the state. After being released from prison, Dia reiterated his committment to communitarian socialism but this time using the language of autogestion (Dia 1975). For a detailed analysis of the legal structure of Senegal's cooperative movement during the 1960s, see Camboulives (1967).

8. Senegal's national planners did not see any contradiction between promoting central planning and the national plan, on the one hand, and calling for decentralization. The desire to preserve the coherence of the plan pitted the central planners against the local politicians. The government deliberately placed the major units of decentralized planning at the regional and arrondissement levels where local government institutions were either weak or non-existent to by-pass the "politicians." The Senegalese leadership gave Senegal's First Plan (1961–64) almost sacred qualities. It was elaborated primarily by Mamadou Dia and a small circle of Senegalese technicians and French expatriate advisors.

9. These measures included nationalizing Senegal's peanut processing plants, the phosphate mines, and utilities, all leading sectors of the Senegalese economy previously owned by the French. For analyses of the logic of central control over local politics, see Barker (1971) and Cottingham (1970).

10. Constitutional reform and the future of Senegalese pluralism is now being seriously debated in Senegal. For recent discussions by both supporters and opponents of the government, see Diagne (1984; 1984a), Fall (1977), and Nzouankeu (1984).

11. Peasant discontent with the government's rural policies and the realization by the government that it could not afford to continue to support the regional development agencies without massive foreign assistance which was no longer flowing

so freely made decentralization more attractive. For some, decentralization became a way of cutting state losses in the countryside rather than an affirmation of communitarian socialism. For more details, see Gellar (1987).

12. Wags in Senegal have said that the subprefects did not want to be promoted to prefect because they would lose access to the gravy train facilitated by their control over the rural community's budgets.

13. See, for example, Diop (1982) and Aprin (1980) for an account of the rise of two such independent peasant-based associations.

14. The Senegalese government tended to shift governors rather frequently. The governor was usually a stranger to the region in which he worked and as a representative of the central government not accountable to the local populations.

15. In May 1983, a constitutional revision eliminated the office of prime minister and once again concentrated more power in the presidency. During this same period, the General Secretariat of the Presidency became relatively more powerful vis-a-vis the different ministries.

References

Aprin, Robert. *Developpement et Resistance Paysanne: Le Cas des Soninkes de Bakel.* Paris: 1980.

Arrighi, Giovanni, and John S. Saul. *Essays on the Political Economy of Africa.* New York: Monthly Review Press, 1973.

Barker, Jonathan S. "The Paradox of Development: Reflections on a Study of Local-Central Relations in Senegal." In *The State of the Nations,* edited by Michael F. Lofchie, 47–63. Berkeley: University of California Press, 1971.

Berry, Sara. "Agrarian Crisis in Africa? A Review and Interpretation." *African Studies Review* 27 (2) (June 1984): 59–112.

Bouat, Marie-Claire, and Jean-Louis Fouilland. *Les Finances pubigues des communes et des Communautes Rurales au Senegal.* Dakar: Editions Clairafrique, 1983.

Callaghy, Thomas. "Politics and Vision in Africa: The Interplay of Domination, Equality and Liberty." In *Reflections on the Limits of Power,* edited by Patrick Chabal, 30–41. Cambridge: Cambridge University Press, 1986.

Camboulives, Marguerite. *L'Organisation Cooperative au Senegal.* Paris: A. Pedone, 1967.

Chabal, Patrick, ed. *Political Domination in Africa: Reflections on the Limits of Power.* Cambridge: Cambridge University Press, 1986.

Cottingham, Clement. "Political Consolidation and Centre-Local Relations in Senegal." *Canadian Journal of African Studies* 4 (1) (Winter 1970): 101–120.

Cowan, L. Gray. *Local Government in West Africa.* New York: Columbia University Press, 1958.

Dia, Mamadou. "Pour une Nouvelle Strategie Interafricaine du Developpement a Partir de la Base." In *Internationale Africaine des Forces Pour Le Developpement,* Dakar: Grande Imprimerie Africaine, 1975.

Diagne, Pathe, ed. *Quelle Democratie Pour Le Senegal?* Dakar: Editions PFD Sankore, 1984a.

_____. *Senegal: Crise Economique et Social et Devenir de la Democratie.* Dakar: Editions Sankore, 1984b.

Diop, Abdoulaye. "Jeunesses en Developpement, Memento d'une Peripherie: Une Experience Associative du Foyer des Jeunes de Ronkh a l'Amicale Economique du Walo." *Archives de Sciences Sociales de la Cooperation et du Developpement* (62) (October–December 1982): 105–127.

Dugue, Gil. *Vers les Etats-Unis d'Afrique.* Dakar: Lettres Africaines, 1960.

Fall, Ibrahima. *Sous-Developpement et Democratie Multipartisane: L'Experience Senegalaise.* Dakar: Nouvelles Editions Africaines, 1977.

Foltz, William J. *From French West Africa to the Mali Federation.* New Haven, Conn.: Yale University Press, 1965.

Gautron, Jean-Claude, and Michel Rougevin-Baville. *Droit Public du Senegal.* Paris: Editions A. Pedone, 1970.

Gellar, Sheldon. "State-Building and Nation-Building in West Africa." In *Building States and Nations: Models, Analyses, and Data Across Three Worlds,* edited by S. N. Eisenstadt and Stein Rokkan, 384–426. Beverly Hills: Sage Publications, 1973.

――――. *Structural Changes and Colonial Dependency: Senegal 1555–1945.* Beverly Hills: Sage Publications, 1976.

――――. *Senegal: An African Nation Between Islam and the West.* Boulder, Colorado: Westview Press, 1982.

――――. "Circulaire 32 Revisited: Prospects for Revitalizing the Senegalese Cooperative Movement in the 1950s." In *The Political Economy of Risk and Uncertainty in Senegalese Agriculture,* edited by Mark Gersovitz and John Waterbury, 123–159. London: Frank Cass, 1987.

――――, Robert B. Charlick, and Yvonne Jones. *Animation Rurale and Rural Development: The Experience of Senegal.* Ithaca, NY: Cornell University Rural Development Committee, 1980.

Gutkind, Peter C.W., and Immanuel Wallerstein, eds. *The Political Economy of Contemporary Africa.* Beverly Hills: Sage Publications, 1976.

Hyden, Goran. *Beyond Ujaama in Tanzania: Underdevelopment and an Uncaptured Peasantry.* Berkeley: University of California Press, 1980.

――――. *No Shortcuts to Progress: African Development Management in Perspective.* Berkeley: University of California Press, 1983.

Johnson, G. Wesley, Jr. *The Emergence of Black Politics in Senegal: The Struggle for Power in the Four Communes, 1900–1920.* Stanford: Stanford University Press, 1971.

Levy, Margaret. "The Predatory Theory of Rule." *Politics and Society* 10 (4) (1981): 431–465.

Nettl, J. P., and Roland Robertson. *International Systems and the Modernization of Society.* London: Faber and Faber, 1968.

Nzouankeu, Jacques Mariel. *Les Partis Politiques Senegalais.* Dakar: Editions Clairafrique, 1984.

Ostrom, Vincent. "Constitutional Considerations with Particular Reference to Federal Systems." In *Guidance, Control, and Evaluation in the Public Sector,* edited by F. X. Kaufmann, G. Majone, and V. Ostrom, 111–125. Berlin and New York: Walter de Gruyter, 1986.

――――. *The Political Theory of a Compound Republic: Designing the American Experiment.* Rev. ed. Lincoln, Neb.: University of Nebraska Press, 1987.

Ronen, Dov, ed. *Democracy and Pluralism in Africa.* Boulder, Colorado: Lynne Rienner Publishers, 1986.

Schumacher, Edward J. *Politics, Bureaucracy and Rural Development in Senegal.* Berkeley: University of California Press, 1975.

Senghor, Leopold Sedar. *On African Socialism.* New York: Praeger, 1964.

Tocqueville, Alexis de. *The Old Regime and the French Revolution.* Garden City, NY: Doubleday, 1955.

———. *Democracy in America.* New York: New American Library, 1956.

World Bank. *Accelerated Development in Sub-Saharan Africa: An Agenda For Action.* Washington, D.C.: World Bank, 1981.

7

Proprietary Authority and Local Administration in Liberia

Amos Sawyer

Introduction

A significant factor which has been identified as a contributor to the failure of the African state is the latter's tendency to co-opt or destroy the capacity for self-governance in African societies (Hyden 1980; Kasfir 1983). Usually, the colonial foundations upon which national structures were built are perceived to contribute significantly to such failure. Unfortunately, such analysis is more often concerned with opportunities for making broad generalizations than with clarifying problems about the constitution of order in African societies. These broad generalizations too often overlook experiences such as that of Liberia which was never incorporated as a colony and so did not conform to the standard model of the post-colonial state.[1] Even though Liberia was never formally incorporated as a colony, its political evolution and present day situation manifest features of a post-colonial state. The purpose of this essay is to show how proprietary authority evolved in Liberia and developed a structure of local administration as an instrument of control.[2] It will show how, in the process of developing local administration, the self-governing potentials of the constituent elements of Liberian society were co-opted or destroyed while dependency relationships were encouraged. Finally, it will also show how these patterns led to political and economic stagnation in contemporary Liberia.

In proceeding, I will first discuss the concept of proprietary authority. I will then show how this conception has dominated the constitution of order in Liberian society and has contributed to the development of local administration as an instrument of proprietary control which stifled or destroyed self-organizing capabilities where those existed within the society. I will conclude with some speculations regarding the potential for reversing these institutionalized trends.

Neo-Patrimonialism and Constitutional Choice

The capacity of people in a society to develop institutions which enhance their self-organizing capabilities is crucial to its perpetuation and development. Such capabilities may manifest themselves in a variety of interacting institutions in which individuals as citizens take principal responsibility for their own well-being. Such arrangements can be defined as a self-governing constitutional order and can be articulated in a specific theory of constitutional choice (V. Ostrom 1987; V. Ostrom, Tiebout, and Warren 1961). Patrimonial rule, by contrast, is an antithesis of a self-governing constitutional order. Far from promoting self-organizing capabilities, patrimonial rule is based on principles associated with traditional forms of patron-client relationships.[3] Contemporary manifestations of patrimonial rules are often discussed as neo-patrimonialism (Zolberg 1966; Gellar 1973), personal rule (Roth 1968; Jackson and Rosberg 1982) and political clientelism (Schmidt, Gausti, Lande and Scott 1977; Eisenstadt and Lemarchand 1981). Most of these forms of patrimonial rule are usually characterized by presumptions of a "common patrimony" in which relations between patron and clients are legitimized by tradition, expectations of mutual benefit or perceptions of reciprocity (Lemarchand, in Eisenstadt and Lemarchand 1981).

African Neo-Patrimonial Rule as Proprietary Rule

For about two decades now, students of African political development have been observing the emergence of authority relations based on principles which apply to control of a private or personal domain. In such orders, authority is exercised as if it were a personal bequest or acquisition. Whether justified by a revolutionary ideology or by a perception of divine ordination, authority is personalized and exercised through a patron-client network. Most frequently, repressive measures and unequal exchange replace reciprocity in the maintenance of authority relationships (Hall, in Schmidt et al. 1977). Rules become synonymous with the desires of the proprietor (Jackson and Rosberg 1982). The major puzzle of such orders is how to cope with the stresses and innovations which disrupt patron-client relationships. In such orders, change is often accompanied by violent eruptions and results in a substitution of one set of proprietors and proprietary relationships for another.[4]

African proprietary orders have been derived first from the transformation of indigenous social orders into colonial possessions, and the transfer of the latter to a group of "inheritance elites" at independence (Nettl and Robertson 1968; Gellar 1973; Clapham 1982). In efforts to create "national units" out of diverse societies and to ensure "social progress," these elites have relied on an array of strategies including the establishment of single party political processes, and, in a few cases, the declaration of life presidencies by the leader. In most cases, these efforts have resulted in the establishment of a proprietary relationship in which a dominant leader surrounds himself with a coterie of influentials who in turn function as patrons for various sectors of the population. The public sector becomes the major instrument for the dispensing of largesse which lubricates proprietary relationships (Zolberg 1966; Roth 1968).

As experience has shown in Africa, these proprietary relationships are hardly ever institutionalized or rooted in traditions or customs even though traditional symbols or revolutionary rhetoric may be used to justify or sustain them. Their penetration of society facilitates the development of severely asymmetrical relationships which require personal loyalty instead of an observance of the law, and dependency and submission instead of social autonomy. Local initiatives are constrained and local institutions are ultimately diverted to serving proprietary interests. The challenge to African societies is to develop theories of constitutional choice which can secure the replacement of processes producing proprietary rule with self-governing constitutional orders. An essential first step is to gain a deep understanding of how proprietorships in the public domain and other forms of constitutional order are constituted in Africa. I will now turn to a discussion of the development of proprietary rule in Liberia.

Foundations of Proprietary Rule and Local Administration in 19th Century Liberia

The idea of Liberia was rooted in the debate about slavery in the United States during the 18th and 19th centuries. While the key issue in the debate centered around the question of slavery or abolition, a third option of repatriating free blacks was introduced as a compromise or, perhaps, an expedient measure.[5]

In 1816, repatriation enthusiasts organized the American Colonization Society (ACS).[6] The objectives of the ACS included the removal of free blacks from the United States, the spread of Christianity and western civilization in Africa, and the creation of a society with better opportunities for blacks (Stebbins 1853; Shick 1977; Harris 1982).[7] Most influential blacks were opposed to the plan and, in association with their white abolitionist counterparts, vigorously opposed the ACS (Garrison 1968; Douglass 1857; Stebbins 1853).[8]

Between 1820 and 1847, more than 10,000 free blacks, manumitted slaves and African recaptives had been settled in three clusters of settlements along the Atlantic coast at the mouths of rivers.[9] These clusters were known as the colonies of Montserrado, Grand Bassa, and Sinoe.[10] Each cluster of settlements contained a principal coastal settlement or town and a number of others known as "up-river" settlements established along the banks of the rivers.

Free-born settlers dominated the emerging Liberian society. They constituted the ruling core of the coastal towns. Possessing seed capital (usually brought from the United States), they engaged in trade and were the heirs to the authority of the ACS and the prime propagators of the "civilizing and Christianizing" mission. Up-river settlements, in contrast, were agricultural settlements. Their inhabitants were largely unskilled or semi-skilled manumitted slaves and recaptives. Surrounding the ACS settlements were the indigenous African societies which were eventually incorporated into the settler polity.

In the governance of the new society, the ACS was the sole authority. It appointed the colonial agent who was empowered to appoint a number of subordinate officers such as clerk of court, store keeper, and colonial secretary. Buttressing ACS's authority were the goals which purportedly drove the establishment of the Liberian settlements—the propagation of Christianity and western civilization. Central to the Christian teachings of the ACS was the belief that repatriation was the unfolding of God's plan for Africa. Settlers believed that they were the instruments designed by God for the purpose of redeeming Africa and that adversities were "dispensations" from God which were to be humbly accepted by man (Gurley, 1839; Alexander 1846). A second dimension of the mission was to instruct Africa in the "art of civilized living" (Gurley 1839). This involved efforts to transmit western values and symbols (Blamo 1971), within the framework of Jeffersonian agrarianism (Miller 1975). Christianity was a necessary complement of civilization. Thus, with repatriation construed as a "Christianizing and civilizing" mission, the ACS became owners of the land, custodian of Christian values and propagator of the civilizing mission. The adaptation of certain Christian precepts pertaining to the protection of Providence over earthly souls legitimized the tutelage of the ACS over early settler society (Beyan 1985). Therein lies the core principles of emergent proprietary rule in Liberia.

While the colonial agent and other officers operated from Monrovia, each of the three clusters of settlements was administered by an agent appointed by its sponsoring agency. Although the colonial agent was considered *primus inter pares* and attempted to maintain close supervision over activities within the coastal settlements of Grand Bassa and Sinoe, communication and transportation difficulties prevented him from doing so. In a way, each cluster of settlements was developed as a semi-autonomous enclave dedicated to the same mission of which the Monrovia establishment was the chief patron. This arrangement constituted the foundations for the deconcentration of power in the hands of local political leaders in nineteenth century Liberia.

Merchant Proprietorship and Deconcentration of Authority

Led by free-born blacks, settler pressure to participate in the administration of the affairs of the colonies became more effective as ACS' subsidies declined.[11] Mercantile trade in which free-born blacks engaged became both the source of economic prosperity and the mechanism around which networks of patron-client relationships developed. Each network involved an array of couriers, apprentices and trading agents organized in a socio-economic relationship around a prominent merchant. These relationships were usually reinforced by kinship ties. Thus, merchant proprietorships emerged and eventually replaced ACS colonial control by the mid-1800s. Similarly, the clientel network which developed around dominant local merchants constituted the foundations of local administration.

Despite provisions of the written constitution which called for a unitary state structure, the *de facto* constitutional arrangements which emerged by the mid-nineteenth century recognized the semi-autonomous status of the counties under the leadership of local merchant proprietorships.[12] The *de facto* deconcentration of authority produced two types of tension which plagued authority relations in 19th century Liberia. The first source of tension could be found in the relationship between the central government in Monrovia and local leadership at the level of the counties. The second had to do with relations between coastal settlement and up-river settlements. Both types of relationships involved attempts to exercise control from above, thereby stifling local potentials.

The crucial issues in the relationship between Monrovia and the counties involved the appointment of officials of local administration and control over the collection and use of taxes—especially customs intake. Although the constitution reposed in the president the powers to appoint all county superintendents, judges, customs officers and other officials of local administration, certain adaptations were made so that these officials were usually nominated by the local leadership and then formally appointed by the president. It became customary that the leader of each *de facto* local proprietorship assumed the position of senior senator in the national legislature. This arrangement afforded the best opportunity for contacts with colleagues in other counties and coordination with the Monrovia establishment (Liberty 1977).

Regarding revenue matters, customs duties were the main source of government revenues. The enactment of legislation and the collection and utilization of revenue were issues that required delicate handling. Decisions to impose taxes required the consent of the national legislature and, as such, ensured the approval of county bosses. Tax collection fell under the jurisdiction of local officials. These included the superintendent, county treasurer (known as the national sub-treasurer), a collector of customs, and a number of tax collectors. All tax monies were deposited in the county treasury by the county treasurer who reported to the superintendent and the department of the treasury in Monrovia. A portion of the taxes was to be used locally by the superintendent and his officials for local purposes.[13] In practice, however, given the problems of transportation and communications, the sub-treasurer was usually under the control of the local sub-proprietor through the office of the superintendent. Quite often, the Monrovia government struggled to take steps to exert its authority over local affairs. In the absence of a machinery to enforce its authority, there was very little control that could be exercised from the center.[14]

However, the deconcentration of control in the hands of local leaders did not result in the promotion of self-organizing capabilities; instead, it only reinforced boss rule and subjugated the various interests of local communities to the interest of the local merchant-dominated proprietorships. For example, the crucial economic concerns of local leaderships centered around the pursuit of in-land as well as coast-wide trade in items such as camwood and palm products which were part of the natural vegetation. As these items were exhausted in the regions of the coast, more and more men were recruited from agricultural and other activities to engage in long distance trade (Brown 1941; Syfert 1977). The productive energies of local communities were mobilized in pursuit of the mercantile activities directed by local bosses. These activities included actions to preclude or regulate trade between Europeans and indigenous societies.[15]

These policies, associated with other factors, frequently led to armed conflicts with surrounding indigenous societies and in doing so, did not only detract from agriculture and other productive work, but also required the involvement of the Monrovia-based government in armed conflict.[16] As a result, local communities could hardly rise above subsistence and were constantly forced to mobilize for defense and rely upon government subsidies which, in turn, led to deeper control of local bosses and the central government over the affairs of such communities.[17] Only a few communities up-river from Monrovia enjoyed, for a period, conditions which facilitated the development of self-organizing capabilities. Even these were to falter after a while.

Merchant Proprietorship vs. Self-Governance

While the influence of the Liberian government was strongest in Monrovia, several up-river communities struggled to develop and sustain their self-organizing capabilities. Many of these were relatively poor and inhabited by small holders engaged in agriculture. Inadequate infrastructure put many of these communities out of the easy reach of proprietary relationships from Monrovia political leaders.

Many of these communities were governed under ordinances enacted by the colonial council and approved by the ACS in the 1830s and 1840s. The town meeting was the major decision making body. A major town meeting was held on the first Tuesday of October each year to elect community officers. Officers elected included a commissioner, members of a common council, and members of special committees on agriculture, public works and sanitation, and education, among others.

By mid-nineteenth century (between 1848 and 1865) several groups of immigrants arrived from the United States and the West Indies. The majority of them was interested in agriculture and preferred to live out of the reach of the coastal establishments. Settlements such as Clay-Ashland and Arthington became prosperous agricultural communities. Numerous community associations such as mutual aid societies, literary clubs, and planters associations were active in community life during the third quarter of the nineteenth century (Shick 1977). The vigorous organizational life and agricultural prosperity brought national recognition to these communities. Many coffee farmers earned considerable income during this time. The planters association, as the farmers organization was called, became very influential. A cooperative of planter associations was organized to break the monopoly of the coastal merchants over the export of produce and to ensure higher prices (*The Observer,* February, 1880).

It was not long before the collective efforts of the up-river settlements in the Monrovia area constituted a countervailing political influence in Liberia. By the late 1860s, Clay-Ashland and other up-river communities had become the hot bed of opposition politics. Up-river settlements forged an alliance with a rival faction among the coastal merchants and organized a political opposition which won the elections of 1868. Crippled by scandals and inability to reach an accomodation with the Monrovia establishment, the new government was violently removed in 1871 and Joseph J. Roberts, patriarch of the Monrovia merchants was reinstalled as president.[18]

Elinor Ostrom (1985) has argued that the survival and performance of institutions of collective action depend upon, among other things, the extent to which they are nested in larger institutional frameworks which are conducive for their survival and success. This was obviously not the case with the up-river communities. The violent political situation coupled with the decline of coffee prices in the 1880s had a profound effect on the self-organizing capabilities of these settlements. The decline of coffee prices weakened the economic base of these communities. In the meantime, Monrovia-based merchants who were fast being reduced to agents of European and American trading firms, granted export monopolies to those firms and, thereby, forced up-river planters into submission and destroyed the self-organizing tendencies of their communities (Schmokel 1976). By the turn of the century, with rubber fast becoming the mainstay of the economy, the flow of commerce was diverted away from the up-river settlements to new roadways through the new rubber plantations. This development speeded up the decline of up-river communities such as Millsburg, Arthington and Caldwell which had been prosperous, and rendered them poor and desolate by the first half of the twentieth century.

What we have seen thus far is that due to historical circumstances, political control in nineteenth century Liberia was concentrated in the hands of local political leaders who exercised proprietary control over the counties. This situation obtained despite the existence of formal constitutional structures which were meant to create a unitary state. These structures underwent adaptations so as to facilitate *de facto* local proprietary control. The dominance of mercantile interests of local bosses and the pursuit of those interests at the expense of other productive activities including, ironically, those which in the long run, would have rejuvenated trade, contributed to increasing economic difficulties and conditions of conflict with indigenous communities. Moreover, the desire of settler authorities to establish hegemonic control over indigenous communities also contributed to armed conflicts with those communities. Exacerbated by external pressures, these developments stifled the social processes and retarded the self-organizing capabilities of most settler communities.[19]

A combination of factors, notably among which were the continuing colonial pressures and the introduction of Firestone, stimulated the development of new forms of authority relations which completely transformed the nature of proprietary control in Liberia at the turn of the twentieth century by bringing an end to local boss rule and concentrating authority in the hands of the president. Presidential authority would now be sustained by the exploitation of the hinterland through the instrumentality of a newly organized interior administration. In order to fully appreciate this transformation, a brief discussion of indigenous social processes which were subsumed by the interior administration is appropriate.

Indigenous Political Institutions

Two types of political orders were discernible among indigenous political communities in Liberia. One type of constitutional order was founded on hierarchical principles of political organization. The other type was an acephalous form of organization. The former could be found mainly in western and northwestern Liberia among many of the Mel and Mande-speaking groups and the latter among the Kwa-speaking peoples of south-eastern and coastal Liberia (d'Azevedo 1962).[20] Additionally, in Mande and Mel societies, the existence of Poro, a "secret society," provided a deeper basis for order. The Poro legitimized the political order, guarded the belief system, set rules of conduct and brought sanctions to bear. Moreover, due to its pan-ethnic scope, it ensured a common socializing experience for all members of the numerous micro-political communities of western and northern Liberia and in adjoining societies in Sierra Leone and Guinea (Little 1965, 1966). Prior to the penetration of Liberian government authority, the Poro was the final authority in inter-ethnic and inter-community disputes (d'Azevedo 1969). Within Mande and Mel societies, the Poro also exercised a supervisory and restraining role *vis-a-vis* the hierarchical authority structure headed by the chief.

The widespread existence of Poro societies among the Mel and Mande of western and northern Liberia accentuated the difference in the organization of political authority between these areas and the southern and eastern regions of Liberia where the Kwa live and where there was no Poro or any equivalent institution.

Up to the period of settler intervention, the area now known as Liberia contained numerous indigenous political communities. What I refer to as a political community was largely a lineage social formation held together by a chief whose legitimacy was supported by a myth or the reality of lineage connections, and by a capacity to ensure mutual security and economic well-being among its members. Many political communities were multi-ethnic in their composition. Vigorous inland and coastal trade was the force driving interaction among them and underlay their fusion, transformation, and disintegration. The political environment was usually unstable as these communities worked out an accomodation among themselves.

By the turn of the nineteenth century, political interaction among the political communities of the area had evolved into the formation of two confederations and an assortment of other types of political arrangements.[21]

The existence of a large number of autonomous poltical communities of varying sizes and levels of social development sometimes preying upon each other and at other times collaborating presented an unpredictable picture for settler society. The persistent atmosphere of warfare and intensive trade competition seemed to suggest to the new Liberian society that its survival and the propagation of its civilizing and Christianizing mission demanded the establishment of a hegemony. In time, hierarchical principles of organization which were familiar to the Mande and Mel-speaking groups would be adapted by the Liberian government in the constitution of order in the Liberian hinterland. The novelty of such organizational arrangements for the Kwa, among other developments, would become a source of considerable upheaval in Kwa societies.

Needless to say, the imposition of an hierarchical system of control over numerous autonomous indigenous communities which were also diverse in social organization was bound to disrupt the socio-economic processes and trigger resistance from many of those communities. The government's response to their resistance was to further strengthen centralized administrative control through the instrumentality of a military force and an administrative machinery which were available exclusively to the president. The process through which local administration was established as an instrument of exclusive control by the president and the consequences of this development will now be discussed.

Local Administration, Indirect Rule and Presidential Authority

Unable to compete with their European counterparts, Liberian merchants were reduced to commissioned agents and itinerant employees of European and American firms which controlled trade, including the export of contract labor, shipping and communications in Liberia as of the 1870s.[22] With a faltering economy, Liberian officials also turned to European firms to arrange loans through European banks. At least three such loans were obtained in 1871, 1906 and 1911. These loans proved to be disastrous for Liberia because of the incredible conditions attached to them and the mismanagement and misappropriation of the funds.[23]

New threats were posed by the British and French who by now were intensely involved in the "scramble" for territory. Although these powers had recognized Liberia's independence, they were not prepared to accept

Liberia's claims over territory not under the control of the government. Both powers demanded that Liberia demonstrate effective occupation and control over her territory or claim only such territory as was occupied and controled by the clusters of settler communities on or near the coast (Foley 1965).

In response to these economic and colonial pressures, the Liberian government began to establish a system of interior administration in 1904. The Barclay Plan, as the new administrative design was called, was a blueprint for indirect rule over the interior.[24] It contained two main features. First, it provided for the organization of indigenous political communities into clans, chiefdoms and districts. Several clans would constitute a chiefdom and several chiefdoms would make up a district. Clans and chiefdoms were to be governed by indigenous chiefs. Such chiefs would report to the district commissioner who would be appointed by and responsible to the secretary of the interior. At each level, executive and judicial functions were to be performed by the same officials. Thus, there was to be the courts of the clan and paramount chiefs and of the district commissioner. The second aspect of the plan was the establishment of the Liberian Frontier Force.[25] The Frontier Force was to engage in pacification actions and assist in local administration, especially in the collection of hut and poll taxes and in the recruitment of labor for public works and later, for the growing plantation economy.[26]

Consequences of the New Interior Administration

Although it has been subjected to numerous modifications, the Barclay Plan remains the basic framework for local administration in Liberia today.[27] What the plan had done was to impose an hierarchical authority structure on all indigenous political communities irrespective of what their organizing and operational principles were. While hierarchical authority relations were known to the Mel and Mande peoples, they were very disruptive of Kwa organizational patterns. Kwa resistance to such impositions and other forms of national government domination continued for several decades.[28] The Kru, for example, went to such lengths as seeking alliance with the British and launching an international campaign in their efforts to secede from Liberia (Davis 1975; Sullivan 1978).

Additionally, the government exerted considerable influence in the selection of chiefs. Frequently, the government would intervene and "handpick" a candidate who seemed favorably disposed toward its control irrespective of questions regarding the legitimacy of his claim to authority in his society. The fact that the government had to approve the "elections" of chiefs and reserved the right to dismiss a chief without reference to his people transformed chiefs into representatives of the government among the people rather than representatives of the people in the government. As a result, many chiefs were unable to maintain order within their jurisdictions and had to rely heavily on the Frontier Force to maintain their

authority. In some instances, lineages which presumed to have had legitimate claims on leadership withdrew from community activities or posed
challenges which led to protracted litigations and deep strife which undermined the basis for self-sustaining collective action in those societies. This
was a very serious problem especially among the Vai (Holsoe 1967).[29]

As a result of the establishment of interior administration, the nature
of indigenous leadership was transformed. The major responsibilities of
chiefs were to maintain order, recruit labor and collect taxes. As an
incentive for tax collection, chiefs were paid a commission which was a
percentage of their collection. Thus, far from serving to stimulate the self-
organizing capabilities of indigenous societies, most chiefs became major
instruments of control and, in many cases, predation in the new system
of local administration.[30]

The expansion of the interior bureaucracy coincided with the introduction of plantation economy. This development produced mixed economic
results. While the plantation economy incorporated a large number of
people of central and eastern Liberia into the money economy, the transformation of farmers into plantation workers and the pattern of migration
from villages coupled with the labor demands of the Liberian government
produced a complex social situation. While, in some parts of the country,
villages were left desolate as a result of labor recruitment, in other parts,
plantation migration was adapted as an integral part of village social
processes (McEvoy 1972).

The most positive consequence of the establishment of the interior
bureaucracy was the curtailment of communal violence which had always
plagued the region even before the establishment of the Liberian state. A
related consequence was that the creation of the interior administration
provided the first opportunity for the delimiting of Liberian territory and
ensuring respect of Liberia's territorial integrity by the colonial powers
(Buell 1928).[31] Overall, however, the labor, tax and other demands made
on indigenous communities as a result of the establishment of interior
administration proved debilitating to most interior communities (League
of Nations 1930; Jones 1962; McEvoy 1972).[32]

Interior Administration and the Emergence
of Presidential Authority

At the national level, the creation of an interior bureaucracy clothed
with executive and judicial authority and responsible solely to the president
constitutionally, made the president the highest executive and judicial
official in the country. Through this bureaucracy, the president acquired
enormous levers which affected the nature of proprietary control. The era
of deconcentration of power in the hands of local bosses had come to an
end. With the decline of trade, patronage through the new bureaucracy and
the higher echelons of the Frontier Force became the important resource
available to ensure control. These sources of patronage were only available

to the president. District commissioners presided over vast areas of the interior, collected taxes and requisitioned food and other resources from the people at will. Officers of the Frontier Force also benefitted from predation. Customs duties gradually became less important. The main source of government revenues was corporate taxes and rent from Firestone and later the mining concessions. These were paid directly into the coffers of the central government and not through any local intermediaries. With substantially increased revenues and improving physical infrastructure, the central government's authority steadily reached deeper into the hinterland.

Meanwhile in the coastal cities and towns, further measures were taken to strengthen presidential authority over local administration. In 1922, the municipal charter of Monrovia was revoked by the legislature on the recommendation of the president. Within the next 10 years virtually all municipal charters were revoked (Buell 1928).[33] Municipalities were changed to "commonwealth districts" and managed by boards appointed by the president. Poor management and lack of accountability were reasons given for the revocation of municipal charters. Also, at this time, all local tax collectors were put under the direct and sole control of the bureau of internal revenues of the department of the treasury in Monrovia. Taxes were thereafter desposited in the central treasury and remittances made to local administrations by directives of the president. While these measures were ostensibly designed to make tax collection more efficient and to curtail misuse of public funds, they drastically reduced the levers available to local sub-proprietors and altered the nature of their relationship with the center. The era of the local county boss had come to a close. Aided by the interior bureaucracy, the president emerged as the sole patron.[34]

The impact of the involvement of the central government in the development of social infrastructure at the levels of the counties and cities was strongly felt as revenues from rubber increased in the 1930s and 1940s.[35] It is a debatable question as to whether local patron-client networks funded with such resources could have made such accomplishments. It does seem clear, however, that neither the decaying system of local proprietary control nor the emerging system of presidential control provided the stimulation for the development of local initiatives and self-organizing capabilities. The abuses of human resources and the alienation of land which are well documented attest to the shortcomings of the new interior bureaucracy as a facilitator of human social and economic well-being.[36]

Local Administration and Development

The introduction of Firestone and later the involvement of other multinational corporations in iron ore and timber extraction after the second World War opened new sources of government revenue which did not depend on the efficiency of customs officials and tax collectors. Corporate profits, ground rent, and dividend sharing became the new sources of revenues and the basis for new prosperity in Liberia. With such new resources at its disposal, the presidency not only became more powerful, it became more self-sufficient and personalized.[37] These developments coupled with the emergence of African independence and other factors created the imperative of socio-economic development. Local administration was, therefore, perceived as an instrument of development.

The first step in the use of local administrative structures as an instrument of development was the reorganization of interior administration. In 1964, new counties were created out of hitherto subjugated hinterland provinces. A single system of local administration was put in place. All counties were headed by superintendents who were assisted by county commissioners, assistant commissioners and chiefs. In addition, all of the other types of officials such as judges, magistrates, justices of the peace, sheriffs, clerks of court, township commissioners, collectors of customs and internal revenues, and scores of others who were part of the coastal patronage network but not part of the interior bureaucracy were also to be appointed in the new counties by the president. The patronage powers and economic control of the president increased tremendously as the local administration bureaucracy grew bigger. The further penetration of local administration bureaucracy into rural society produced more disruptions of indigenous social and production patterns. Opportunity for a government position lured many individuals away from farming. Many productive local farmers now sought the status carried by such positions as justice of the peace, sherrif, stipendiary magistrates and procurement officer in county, township and district administrations.

The National Planning Agency was created at this time. It was upgraded to a full department of government in 1966. The National Planning Council consisting of a specific set of government agencies and headed by the president was organized to become the focal point of "development planning." One of the innovations introduced by the council through budgetary reforms was the formulation of the "development budget."[38]

More changes were made in the early 1970s in response to the introduction of the "integrated rural development" approach which was promoted by the World Bank (Ministry of Planning and Economic Affairs 1976). Decentralization was said to be the new administrative strategy for promoting rural development. At this point, new administrative structures were added to the local administration infrastructure. For example, a position of assistant superintendent for development was created.[39] In addition, several levels of "development councils" were established.[40] Municipal charters were restored as a further means of stimulating local involvement in development. Community development officers were appointed to urban communities as specialists and animators. (See Ministry of Local Government, Urban Reconstruction and Rural Development, *Annual Report* 1974.)

Operating as an instrument of development, the machinery of local administration was effective in implementing large-scale development projects such as the construction of roads and highways. For example, between

1967 and 1977, more than 3000 miles of secondary and feeder roads were constructed, more than twice as many as had been previously constructed. While a large portion represented roads constructed by externally funded agricultural schemes and logging companies, a considerable effort was made by county development agencies with the use of monies and other resources mobilized by community and county development committees. (See Ministry of Rural Development, *Annual Reports* 1976–1979; van der Kraij 1983.)[41]

More often, unfortunately, government-directed development agencies have penetrated community-based organizations and perhaps, inadvertently, diminished the latter's self-organizing character. Frequently, the presence of government animators, liaison officers or development officials in these organizations have disrupted the structure of discourse and decision-making within them with negative consequences on their self-governing character.[42]

In the rural areas, far from stimulating "integrated rural development" or achieving a measure of "decentralization," the new arrangements created a larger bureaucracy, required considerable coordination at the national level and produced as many politically motivated projects as "development projects."[43] The new "development councils" provided new platforms for the politically ambitious. Armed with the latest political slogans, they could mobilize a political base, formulate a "self-help" project and invite political leaders to the launching ceremonies. In many such cases, a manipulation of the people became the strategy for launching political careers.

Setting aside "development projects" which are inspired by the private ambitions of local political entrepreneurs, there are still fundamental conceptual and operational problems with the government's development program. Reports of government agencies are replete with suggestions that development is conceived almost exclusively as the construction of physical and social infrastructural facilities: the construction of market sheds, feeder roads and the provision of drilled wells by the government. The role of local communities is essentially only to mobilize unskilled labor and, sometimes, raise a portion of the funds for the projects. (See *Annual Reports* 1973–1979 Ministry of Local Government, Urban Reconstruction and Rural Development.) The importance of the development of self-sustaining, self-organizing capabilities does not always feature in the official calculus of development.[44] The decisions determining the nature of the projects and how they should be implemented are usually made in a central planning exercise with the possibility of donor funding a strong consideration in decision-making.

Amid the political-oriented schemes and the narrow conception of development, there are some communities which took advantage of the atmosphere facilitated by the government's pronouncements on rural development to initiate community development projects. Such genuine community development projects are usually initiated from within the communities by highly regarded local individuals who have distinguished themselves through years of solid community service and have won the trust and respect of the community. Such individuals who may be the school teacher, physician assistant, or nurse are likely to be the major catalyst of community development. Development projects undertaken under such auspicies are different from the other types by their reliance on local resources primarily, and the use of such indigenous institutions as voluntary associations, clan associations and youth clubs.[45] Unfortunately, the survival and sustained performance of such local self-organizing institutions can be precarious unless they can develop channels of effective communication within the larger structure of authority and are nested in a wider framework of federated authority relations (Elinor Ostrom 1985). The probability of success is minimal for any unit of collective action which operates on the basis of its own self-organizing and self-governing capabilities within a larger framework which is driven by the promulgation of directives and decrees from the top.[46]

A reconceptualization of the role of local administration as an instrument of development was begun in the mid–1970s. This exercise sought to promote a strategy of "regionalization" of development administration and the relocation of decision-making authority from the center to the regions.[47] Although a plan for implementation had been fully developed, the exercise was never implemented.[48] However, it is doubtful that the new initiative would have created opportunities for local self-government.

Public discussions about the reconstitution of the political order after the military takeover of 1980 focused considerably on the question of local self-government. This concern was reflected in the numerous suggestions from individuals and community associations from all of the counties that county superintendents should be elected. Unfortunately, concerns about the cost of operating local deliberative bodies and the perceived need to preserve the unitary character of government were among factors which prevented the implementation of this proposal.[49]

The militarization of local administration has been a major development of post-coup political order in Liberia. Even after the promulgation of a new constitution and the ostensible return to civilian rule, the role of the military in local administration has remained significant. For example, in 1987, six out of 13 county superintendents were military men in active service. The minister of defense and other military and para-military officers of the joint security command are actively involved in tax collection and in investigations of allegations of fraud and corruption in local and national administration. Soldiers from military garrisons in the counties are deployed to close down local courts and coerce local residents to do farming. Local commanders of these garrisons frequently impose themselves as arbiters of personal disputes between individuals in these communities.

Conclusion

This essay has shown that political authority in Liberia has, over time, been exercised as proprietary control and local adminstration as an instrument of control. Transformations in the nature of proprietary control have been accompanied by changes in the structure of local administration. In the 19th century, political authority was exercised as proprietary control by merchants, and local administration consisted of a network of patron-client relationships concerned largely with control of customs duties, ports of entry, and related matters. These local patron-client relationships together with other factors such as persistent conflicts with indigenous communities, an unscientific pursuit of trade, and external colonial pressures created conditions under which self-sustained, self-organizing capabilities at the community level could not fully develop.

New revenues from rubber and, later, iron ore provided opportunities for the concentration of authority in the hands of the president. An interior bureaucracy was developed and utilized first as an instrument of control. It was periodically refurbished to increasingly serve as an instrument of "development." With the assistance of the international community, the government, employing structures of local administration, has administered an assortment of projects that have achieved modest improvements in the conditions of physical and social life of local communities in most parts of the country. Nevertheless, there is very little evidence of the development of local institutions which are capable of stimulating the self-organizing capabilities of local communities so that development as a process of social learning and self-sustained collective action can be well grounded in the society.

Unfortunately, given the historical context within which structures of local administration have developed and their initially exploitative role at the local level, considerable efforts are required to remove the cloud of suspicion with which their activities are usually perceived, especially in hinterland communities. Moreover, and more importantly, there is an inherent incompatibility between the center-directed, top-down conceptual and operational approach to the question of development and the stimulation of self-sustaining, self-organizing local capabilities. The former is an essential element of authority relations in a unitary system of governance while the later is the foundation upon which systems of self-governance are developed.

It seems essential, therefore, that the pursuit of development be percieved first and foremost as requiring a significant transformation of authority relations so that decision-making and the demand for accountability at the local level can be increased. This requires a fundamental restructuring of the constitution of order so that such effective institutions of collective action as youth associations, mutual loan societies and others which are usually perceived to be tangential in the formal consideration of development strategies are permitted to play mainstream formal roles commensurate with their effective roles in their societies.

In nurturing self-organizing capabilities, it is important to begin with local communities as they are. Capacities for self-organization are also capacities for adaptation. Adaptation involves learning, growing and self-actualization. The sad truth is that political and social processes which operate as the personal domain and proprietorships of leaders are incapable of permiting or coping with such adaptations. Nonetheless, it is also an essential truth that although the building of the African state has proceeded from the top down, the development of self-sustaining African nations will have to proceed from the bottom up. In the case of Liberia, the unitary system of authority will require serious critical review.

Notes

1. M. B. Akpan (1973) has described the imposition of Liberian government authority over what is now Liberian territory as black colonialism comparable with European colonial domination elsewhere in Africa.

2. I subscribe to the distinction between local government and local administration. The former has to do with local decision making and control while the latter refers to structures facilitating central control. See Olowu (1987).

3. See Bendix (1960) for a summary of the original Weberian discussion of patrimonial rules.

4. The pattern of change in Africa has consisted of sequential movements involving neo-patrimonial rules in which ethnic based and military-led proprietary rules suceed each other. The net effect is a situation of increasing poverty and despair which has been documented by the OAU (1980) and the World Bank (1983) and other international agencies. In the case of Liberia, the government itself has declared its incompetence and inherent corrupt nature. See Ministry of Planning and Economic Affairs (1983) Country Economic Memorandum.

5. Proponents of this alternative included a mix group of religious leaders, public officials, and southern gentlemen. Repatriation was not intended to end slavery but to reduce the social tensions and apprehensions derived from the presence of a growing number of free blacks whose status required definition and whose existence presumably provided a threat to slave holders. The repatriation idea was widely embraced until the early 1830s when the abolitionist movement grew in strength. See Alice Dana Adams (1964).

6. The ACS consisted of many of the most influential individuals of government and of the church. The Reverend Robert Finley, the convenor of the organizing meeting, was a reputable Presbyterian clergyman from New Jersey, Judge Bushrod Washington was a Supreme Court judge, The Honorable Henry Clay was a member of Congress, and Mr. Elias Caldwell was an officer of the Supreme Court. These are a few of the prominent persons who organized the ACS (Stebbins 1853; Staudenraus 1961).

7. Spraggins (1957) has suggested that the promotion of US trade and the gaining of an economic foothold were also prominent considerations behind repatriation.

8. Those blacks who supported emigration conceived of schemes headed and directed by blacks and not by a white-dominated society. A wealthy black trader called Paul Cuffe from Massachusetts was the first to repatriate blacks to Africa. In 1815, at his own expense, he repatriated 38 blacks to Sierra Leone. Cuffe envisioned a black outpost of Christianity and civilization in Africa linked to blacks in the United States in an effort to terminate the slave trade, emancipate slaves in the United States and uplift black people everywhere. See Sherwood (1923).

9. Manumitted slaves had been released purposely for deportation to Africa. Recaptured Africans were persons who were recaptured from slavers after the

abolition of slavery trade in 1809. Such persons were already enroute to slavery but were returned to Africa and merged with the settlers of Liberia.

10. A fourth cluster, the colony of Maryland in Africa, joined Liberia in 1857 to become Maryland county in Liberia.

11. From 1819 to 1830, the ACS received $264,710 through Congressional acts to support emigration to Liberia. By the mid-1800s, the ACS had raised more than two million dollars from donations mainly from private sources (Akpan 1975). Support for the ACS began to decline as of the 1830s when abolitionists such as William Lloyd Garrison took the offense in the debate about colonization. See Garrison (1968).

12. In 1847, Liberia declared her independence. A constitutional convention which met that year drafted a constitution which provided for a strong executive president, a bicameral legislature and a judiciary. The president was given broad powers of appointment of all officials except legislators. No provision was made for local self-governance.

13. See Government of Liberia (1869) *Act Defining Payment of Duties,* and Government of Liberia (1875) *Act Providing for Support of General Government.*

14. An example from Sinoe is instructive. In 1894, as factions developed within the local proprietorship in Sinoe and the influence of the dominant merchant, J.J. Ross, was under challenge, the superintendent ordered an audit of the accounts of the county treasurer. The treasurer refused to submit to an audit and to appear before the superintendent and his local officials. The superintendent then, without the approval of the president, dismissed the county treasurer to replace him with a more loyal person. The county treasurer rejected his dismissal and obtained an injunction from the judge who was sympathetic with the county treasurer's faction to prevent his replacement from taking over. The superintendent ignored the injunction and installed his own man as county treasurer. Angered by the arbitrary action of the superintendent, the president ordered him to reinstate the dismissed county treasurer. The dispute ended in a stalemante. Months later, the superintendent requested the president to relieve the former of his position. The president then replaced the superintendent with the latter's closest ally in the local proprietary network (Sullivan 1978). Examples like this one make it clear that in nineteenth century Liberia, local administration was, in fact, local proprietary control exercised by county bosses with whom the central government interacted through processes of conflict and accomodation.

15. The passage of ports of entry laws dated as far back as 1825 and continued throughout the nineteenth century. These laws were ineffective because of the inability of the government to enforce them.

16. Such other factors as growing European imperial encroachments and economic domination and world market price fluctuations combined with the proprietary rule to stifle local potentials (Buell 1928; Brown 1941; Syfert 1977).

17. For example, from 1875 to the turn of the century, settler as well as indigenous communities in Cape Palmas were embroiled in one armed conflict after another (Martin 1968). In Sinoe, intermittent conflicts among Kru communities, between Kru and local settler communities and between Kru communities and the Liberian government continued until 1936 (Davis 1968, 1975; Sullivan 1978, 1988). Similarly, in western Liberia, settler communities such as Robertsport remained on the brink of disaster from mid-1850s to the turn of the century (Holsoe 1967).

18. From 1847 until his death in 1876, free-born merchant Roberts was the chief patron in Liberia. He served as first president of Liberia from 1847 to 1855 but continued to preside over Liberian society after his presidency. A major figure

in the deposition of E.J. Roye in 1871, Roberts returned to the presidency to restore stability. He served until 1875. When Roberts died in 1876, the mantle of leadership was bestowed on Hilary R.W. Johnson, son of one of the earliest settlers to serve as vice agent under the ACS. Johnson was secretary of state and a confidante of Roberts during the latter's second tenure as president. Although Johnson did not become president until 1883, his was undoubtedly the most influential voice in Liberia from 1880 until the turn of the century. Arthur Barclay took over from Johnson. Like Johnson, Barclay had been a young protege of Roberts. He had served as private secretary to Roberts in 1874. Barclay dominated the political process from the early 1900s until his death in 1938, serving as president for 12 years as of 1904 (Liberty 1977).

19. For example, see Sullivan's (1978) description of communities in Sinoe and Buttikofer's (1890) observations on settler communities in the late nineteenth century.

20. The Mel-speaking people include the Gola and Kissi; the Mande include the Vai, Mandingo, Loma, Kpelle, Gbande, Mende, Mah, and Dan, and the Kwa include the Dey, Belle, Bassa, Kru, Grebo, and Krahn.

21. The major confederation was the Condo confederation in the heartland of what is now western Liberia. Condo had been founded by Sao Boso through conquest, alliance formation, and shrewd annexations (Holsoe 1966). The major trade routes of most of what is now western and central Liberia were controlled by Condo. A similarly organized but smaller confederation had been organized by Zolu Duma in Vai and Gola country near the western coastal area of what is now Liberia. Zolu Duma's confederation controlled the region bordering the ports of the Gallinas, an area of intensive slave trading in the eighteenth and nineteenth centuries (Holsoe 1974). In most of the areas which are now southern and eastern Liberia, an assortment of Kwa political communities existed. Among some of the coastal Kwa communities, the position of chief did not exist at all. It was the Liberian government which imposed hierarchies on some of these communities when the interior bureaucracy was organized at the turn of the twentieth century (Davis 1968; Sullivan 1978). Coastal Kwa communities struggled among themselves for favorable trade positions and against interior groups which sought to displace them. No major, sustained association existed among them at the time of the intervention of the settlers.

22. Among the reasons for the decline of Liberian role in coastal trade were the following: (1) introduction of steam ships by European trading establishments and the failure of Liberian merchants to adapt the new technology; (2) the development of synthetic substitutes for camwood and other natural dyes depressing the price of Liberian supplies; (3) decline in the price of coffee due to the availability of Liberian coffee (coffee Liberica) from other sources; the establishment of colonial authority along the coast made available to Europeans new sources of commodities formerly supplied by Liberian merchants; (4) business malpractices by Liberian merchants (Brown 1941; Akpan 1975).

23. The national disapproval of the conditions of the loan of 1871 was an important factor leading to the forcible removal of the president from office. The loan of 1906 was contracted in part to meet the obligations of the 1871 loan. It was not until 1926 when as part of the agreements with Firestone Rubber Company, a loan of five million dollars was obtained to clear all external and internal government obligations. For many years from 1906 to 1930, the European and American financial receivers performed oversight functions in customs collections to ensure repayment of loans.

24. It is important to remember that the interior constituted more than 70 percent of the territory claimed by the Liberian government and more than 80 percent of Liberia's population. Control over interior administration constituted control over virtually all of Liberia except the coastal enclaves. Interior administration was, indeed, national administration.

25. The Liberian Frontier Force was established along lines similar to the Sierra Leone Frontier Force which had earlier been established by the British as an instrument of colonial domination. British military officers were provided to assist the Liberian government in organizing the Liberian Frontier Force.

26. As of the 1880s certain Liberian officials assisted by a few chiefs of indigenous communities were engaged in contract labor transactions with European agricultural and commercial enterprises in Africa. Liberian labor was also recruited during the construction of the Panama Canal (Kuhn 1975). In 1926, the Liberian government signed an agreement with the Firestone Rubber and Tire Company of Akron, United States. One of the stipulations of the agreement committed the Liberian government to recruit labor to work rubber plantations to be established by Firestone in Liberia (Brown 1941).

27. In 1921, for example, the plan was made more elaborate so that interior administration was divided into two jurisdictions namely, county jurisdiction and interior jurisdiction. Those districts which fell within the confines of the counties were to be headed by county commissioners who were to report to the county superintendents. Five hinterland districts were delimited. They were to be headed by district commissioners who were to be assisted by assistant district commissioners and station agents and were to report to the secretary of the interior through a commissioner general. See Buell (1928).

28. The last major Kwa resistence was on the Kru Coast in the 1930s. As a result of this uprising, a detachment of soldiers of the Liberian Frontier Force was permanently stationed in the area (Davis 1975).

29. The manipulation of indigenous societies through "elections" of paramount chiefs saw the installation of a former orderly to an influential interior administrator as paramount chief of the Kissi Chiefdom and a domestic servant of a missionary physician as paramount chief of a Mano political jurisdiction. Both cases resulted in protracted communal disputes and weakened communal solidarity for a time.

30. Even the institution of the Poro was regulated by the government to the extent that its survival required major adaptations which radically changed its character. Many senior officials of government became honorary members of the Poro. The President became the chief patron. Today, all Poro officers require certification from the Ministry of Local Government. See Annual Report, Ministry of Local Government, Urban Reconstruction and Rural Development (1974).

31. Although Liberia was founded in 1847, the fulfilment of requirements related to the exercise of territorial control was only possible after the establishment of the interior administration by the third decade of the twentieth century.

32. Despite the constant labor recruitment and heavy fines for constructing roads, the results of road construction efforts were minimal. It was not until 1947 that the first major trunk road reached Ganta, a distance of about 150 miles north of Monrovia. A considerable portion of this road was constructed by United States Army engineers to secure American interests during the Second World War (van der Kraaij 1983).

33. Municipal government consisted of a mayor and councilmen, all of whom were formally elected. However, in reality, mayors and councilmen were part of the patronage available to sub-proprietors. As of 1917, the president began complaining

about corruption within municipal governments in the country. City government was funded in much the same way as county government: a portion of revenues collected in the municipality was made available to the mayor by the superintendent upon the authorization of the president.

34. Interestingly, about this time, superintendents were now unofficially referred to as vicegerents. Their link and responsibility to the president was now direct.

35. The first government-organized secondary education and health care program was begun. A secondary school and a hospital was constructed in every major coastal city at that time. The first set of local young men from the major cities were recruited for training as professionals (teachers, engineers and medical doctors). Despite such auspicious beginnings, the government's school and clinic programs were still supplementary to church-operated schools and clinics which constituted the core of Liberian social infrastructure until the 1960s. Up to 1950, at least 50 percent of all students were enrolled in church-sponsored schools and 60 percent of all teachers taught in those schools. Church-sponsored schools and clinics were always supported by foreign mission boards (Clower et al. 1966).

36. See League of Nations (1930), Buell (1928), Sundiata (1980) for details about labor recruitment practices under the interior administration and the Frontier Force. The alienation of communal land for plantation purposes is one of the numerous problems surrounding the question of property rights in rural Liberia. The selective application of indigenous customs pertaining to land ownership and the question of rights of inherentance of women are among the issues which are still unresolved in property relations in Liberia. See Carter and Mends-Cole (1983).

37. For a fuller discussion of the personalization of presidential authority in Liberia, see Liebenow (1969), and Sawyer (1988a).

38. The "development budget" was a special set of financial appropriations designated strictly for what were called "development projects." These projects were to be decided upon by the superintendent and local people but implemented by resident technicians representing the various agencies of the national government in the county.

39. The assistant superintendent for development was meant to be a regional planner and the technical coordinator of development projects.

40. These included the county development council, district development council, and chiefdom development councils. In urban areas, township development councils were also organized. The county development council was headed by the superintendent and included the county attorney (the county's legal officer appointed by and responsible to the Minister of Justice), the legislators of the county to the national legislature, the commander of the military detachment, county, and township commissioners and mayors—a position which was restored in the early 1970s, paramount and clan chiefs and representatives of the business community. In theory, county development councils were to aggregate and coordinate plans and projects of the various districts, chiefdoms, townships, and municipalities within the county.

41. The best known and one of the most successful of these county-based efforts has been the Lofa County Development Committee.

42. An interesting example from the urban area is the case of the involvement of the West Point Community Association with the Monrovia City Corporation and the Monrovia Marketing Association. The West Point Community Association had been struggling since the late 1960s to install basic facilities in the community. It had struggled with road maintenance and flood control during the rainy season, had opened a school in the community and was trying to build latrines and install

pipe-borne water. Without consultation with the community association or the marketing association, the prospective users of the new facility, the Monrovia City Corporation decided in the mid-1970s that a new market shed was needed in the area of the general market in the West Point community. Over the protest of the community, the corporation built an expansive concrete shed, at a cost of several hundred thousand dollars, deep in the community far removed from the normal commercial area and on the site of the new school the community proposed to build. For more than two years the new shed remained unused. The intended users of the new facilities found them too isolated and resented the city's plan to control their use. The West Point Community Association also organized an effective campaign against the use of the market shed. Eventually, the shed was re-possessed by the contractors, another government agency, and put to other uses. Shortly after this incident, government-employed community workers were assigned to the West Point Community Association, its leaders were given high profile in the machinery of the ruling political party, and its character of community participation underwent a drastic change as its leaders took instructions from agencies outside the community and served as local animators for the party.

43. In the 1960s, "development projects" had included the construction of presidential lodges in the counties and a military academy. In the 1970s, substantial road construction projects were undertaken. School and clinic projects were also undertaken. The integrated rural development projects were less successful. One of the major demonstration projects was located in the area of the president's personal farm.

44. Commenting on community participation in a community development project having to do with the digging of wells, the Ministry of Local Government, Urban Reconstruction and Rural Development had this to say: "Diggers were usually provided by the community, or when one is hired, a dollar per foot charged, which is paid by the community. Fiscal year 1979/80 provided higher salaries for well diggers starting July, 1979. This is intended to relieve the communities of the financial obligation" (Annual Report, 1979, p. 59). Regarding community participation in drilling wells, the report said, "the communities have been helpful in providing the drill crew with lodging and, sometimes, food. In other cases, they have provided sand and gravel for gravel packing of wells before the pump is installed" (p. 58).

45. For an example of one such rural community development effort, see Sawyer (1988b).

46. For excellent elaborations on this point, see Korten (1980) and Bryant and White (1982).

47. These efforts were undertaken by the United Nations sponsored Rural Development Task Force.

48. The final executive order authorizing implementation had not been issued by the president at the time of the military takeover. Since the military takeover, there has not been a discussion of the plan.

49. The National Constitution Commission rejected the proposal and attempted to formulate an arrangement appointed by the president upon the recommendation of a county council which will also be vested with oversight responsibilities of the superintendent's activities. These arrangements were rejected by the Constitutional Advisory Council which reviewed the draft constitution prepared by the Commission. See Sawyer (1987).

References

Adams, Alice Dana. *The Neglected Period of Anti-Slavery in America, 1808-1831.* Reprint. Gloucester, Mass.: P. Smith, 1964.

Akpan, M. B. "Black Imperialism: Americo-Liberian Rule Over the African Peoples of Liberia, 1847-1964." *Canadian Journal of African Studies* 7 (2) (1973): 217-236.

———. "The Liberian Economy in the Nineteenth Century: The State of Agriculture and Commerce." *Liberian Studies Journal* 6 (1) (1975): 1-24.

Alexander, Archibald. *A History of Colonization of the Western Coast of Africa.* Philadelphia: William S. Martien, 1846.

Bendix, Reinhard. *Max Weber: An Intellectual Portrait.* Garden City, N.Y.: Doubleday, 1960.

Beyan, Amos. "The American Colonization Sociate and the Socio-Religious Characterization of Liberia: A Historical Survey, 1822-1900."*Liberian Studies Journal* 10 (2) (1985): 1-11.

Blamo, J. Bernard. "Nation-Building in Liberia: The Use of Symbols in National Integration." *Liberian Studies Journal* 4 (1) (1971): 21-30.

Brown, George W. *Economic History of Liberia.* Washington, D.C.: The Associated Publishers, 1941.

Bryant, Coralie, and Louise G. White. *Managing Development in the Third World.* Boulder, Colo.: Westview Press, 1982.

Buell, Raymond L. *The Native Problem in Africa.* Vol. 2. London: Frank Cass, 1928.

Buttikofer, Johan. *Reisebilder aus Liberia.* 2 vols. Leiden: E. J. Brill, 1890.

Carter, Jeanette, and Joyce Mends-Cole. "The Legal Status of Women in Liberia." Monrovia: USAID, Liberia, 1983. Mimeo.

Clapham, Christopher. "The Politics of Failure: Clientelism, Political Instability and National Integration in Liberia and Sierra Leone." In *Private Patronage and Public Power: Political Clientelism in the Modern State,* edited by Christopther Clapham, 76-92. New York: St. Martin's Press, 1982.

Clower, Robert, George Dalton, Mitchell Harwitz, and A. A. Walters. *Growth Without Development: An Economic Survey of Liberia.* Evanston: Northwestern University Press, 1966.

Davis, Ronald. *Historical Outlines on the Kru Coast, Liberia, 1500 to Present.* Ph.D. Dissertation. Bloomington, Ind.: Indiana University, 1968.

———. "The Liberian Struggle for Authority on the Kru Coast." *International Journal of African Historical Studies* 8 (2) (1975): 222-265.

D'Azevedo, Warren L. "Some Historical Probelms in the Delineation of a Central West Atlantic Region." *Annals of the New York Academy of Sciences* XCVI (1962): 512-538.

———. "A Tribal Reaction to Nationalism." Part 1. *Liberian Studies Journal* 1 (2) (1969): 1-21.

Douglass, Frederick. *Douglass Monthly.* Vol. 1, No. 9. Rochester, New York, 1857.

Eisenstadt, S. N., and Rene Lemarchand, eds. *Political Clientelism, Patronage and Development.* Beverly Hills: Sage, 1981.

Foley, David M. "British Policy in Liberia, 1862-1912." Ph.D. Dissertation. London: The University of London, 1965.

Garrison, William Lloyd. *Thoughts on African Colonization.* Reprint. New York: Arno Press, 1968. Originally published in 1832.

Gellar, Sheldon. "State-Building and Nation-Building in West Africa." In *Building States and Nations: Models, Analyses, and Data Across Three Worlds*, Vol. 2, edited by S. N. Eisenstadt and Stein Rokkan, 384–426. Beverly Hills: Sage, 1973.

Government of Liberia. *Act Defining Payment of Duties*. Monrovia: The Legislature of Liberia, 1869.

––––––. *Act Providing for Support of General Government*. Monrovia: The Legislature of Liberia, 1875.

Gurley, Ralph R. *The Life of Jehudi Ashmun*. 2nd printing. New York: Robinson and Franklin, 1839.

Harris, Kathrine. "The United States, Liberia, and Their Foreign Relations to 1847." Ph.D. Dissertation. Ithaca, New York: Cornell University, 1982.

Holsoe, Svend E. "The Condo Federation in Western Liberia." *Liberian Historical Review* 3 (2) (1966): 1–28.

––––––. "The Cassava-Leaf People: An Ethnohistorical Study of the Vai People with a Particular Emphasis on the Tewo Chiefdom." Ph.D. Dissertation. Boston: Boston University, 1967.

––––––. "The Manipulation of Traditional Political Structures Among Coastal Peoples in Western Liberia During the Nineteenth Century." *Ethnohistory* 21 (2) (1974): 159–167.

Hyden, Goran. *Beyond Ujamaa in Tanzania*. Berkeley: University of California Press, 1980.

Jackson, Robert H., and Carl G. Rosberg. *Personal Rule in Black Africa: Prince, Autocrat, Prophet, Tyrant*. Berkeley and Los Angeles: University of California Press, 1982.

Jones, Hannah Abeodu. "The Struggle for Political and Cultural Unification in Liberia, 1847–1930." Ph.D. Dissertation. Evanston, Ill.: Northwestern University, 1962.

Kasfir, Nelson. "Designs and Dilemmas: An Overview." In *Local Government in the Third World: The Experience of Tropical Africa*, edited by Philip Mawhood, 25–47. New York: John Wiley, 1983.

Korten, David C. "Community Organization and Rural Development: A Learning Approach." *Public Administration Review* 40 (5) (September/October 1980): 480–511.

Kuhn, Gary G. "Liberian Contract Labor in Panama, 1887–1897." *Liberian Studies Journal* 6 (1) (1975): 43–52.

League of Nations. *Commission's Report* (International Commission of Inquiry in Liberia). Geneva: League of Nations, 1930.

Liberty, Clarence E. Zamba. "Growth of the Liberian State: An Analysis of Its Historiography." Ph.D. Dissertation. Palo Alto, Calif.: Stanford University, 1977.

Liebenow, J. Gus. *Liberia: The Evolution of Privilege*. Ithaca, N.Y.: Cornell University Press, 1969.

Little, Kenneth. "The Political Functions of the Poro." Parts 1 and 2. *Africa* 35 & 36 (1965, 1966): 349–365, 62–72.

McEvoy, Frederick D. "History, Tradition and Kinship as Factors in Modern Sabo Labor Migration." Ph.D. Dissertation. Eugene, Ore.: The University of Oregon, 1972.

Martin, Jane J. "The Dual Legacy: Government Authority and Mission Influence Among the Glebo of Eastern Liberia, 1834–1910." Ph.D. Dissertation. Boston: Boston University, 1968.

Miller, Randall. "'Home as Found': Ex-Slaves and Liberia." *Liberian Studies Journal* 6 (2) (1975): 92–108.

Ministry of Local Government, Urban Reconstruction and Rural Development. *Annual Report.* Monrovia, 1973-1979. Mimeo.

Ministry of Planning and Economic Affairs. *National Socio-Economic Development Plan, July 1976-June 1980.* Monrovia: Government of Liberia, 1976.

———. *Country Economic Memorandum.* Monrovia: Government of Liberia, 1983.

Ministry of Rural Development. *Annual Report.* Monrovia: Government of Liberia, 1976-1979.

Nettl, J. P., and Roland Robertson. *The International Systems and the Modernization of Societies.* London: Faber, 1968.

Olowu, Dele. "Local Institutions and Development: The African Experience." Unpublished paper. Ile-Ife, Nigeria: University of Ife, Department of Public Administration, 1987.

Organization of African Unity (OAU). *Lagos Plan of Action.* Addis Ababa, Ethiopia: OAU, 1980.

Ostrom, Elinor. "The Rudiments of a Revised Theory of the Origins, Survival and Performance of Institutions for Collective Action." Bloomington, Ind.: Indiana University, Workshop in Political Theory and Policy Analysis, 1985.

Ostrom, Vincent. *The Political Theory of a Compound Republic: Designing the American Experiment.* Rev. ed. Lincoln, Neb.: University of Nebraska Press, 1987.

———, Charles M. Tiebout, and Robert Warren. "The Organization of Government in Metropolitan Areas: A Theoretical Inquiry." *American Political Science Review* 55 (December 1961): 831-842.

Roth, Guenther. "Personal Rulership, Patrimonialism, and Empire-Building in the New States." *World Politics* 20 (2) (1968): 194-206.

Sawyer, Amos. "The Making of the Liberian Constitution: Major Issues and Dynamic Forces." *Liberian Studies Journal* 12 (1) (1987): 1-15.

———. "The Development of Autocracy in Liberia." In *Rethinking Institutional Analysis and Development: Some Issues, Alternatives, and Choices,* edited by Vincent Ostrom, David Feeny, and Hartmut Picht. San Francisco: Institute for Contemporary Studies Press, 1988a.

———. "The Putu Development Association: A Missed Opportunity." In *Rethinking Institutional Analysis and Development: Some Issues, Alternatives, and Choices,* edited by Vincent Ostrom, David Feeny, and Hartmut Picht. San Francisco: Institute for Contemporary Studies Press, 1988b.

Schmidt, Steffen W., Laura Gausti, Carl H. Lande, and James C. Scott, eds. *Friends, Followers, and Factions: A Reader in Political Clientelism.* Berkeley: University of California Press, 1977.

Schmokel, Wolfe W. "The German Factor in Liberia's Foreign Relations." *Liberian Studies Journal* 7 (1) (1976): 17-42.

Sherwood, Henry Noble. "Paul Cuffe." *Journal of Negro History* 8 (April 1923): 153-229.

Shick, Tom. *Behold the Promise Land: A History of Afro-American Settler Society in Nineteenth Century Liberia.* Baltimore: Johns Hopkins University Press, 1977.

Spraggins, T. L. "Economic Aspects of Negro Colonization During the Civil War." Ph.D. Dissertation. Washington, D.C.: American University, 1957.

Staudenraus, P. J. *The African Colonization Movement 1816-1865.* New York: Columbia University Press, 1961.

Stebbins, G. B. *Facts, Opinion Touching the Real Origin, Character and Influence of the American Colonization Society.* Boston: J. P. Jewett, 1853.

Sullivan, Jo Mary. "Settlers in Sinoe County, Liberia, and their Relations with the Kru, 1835–1920." Ph.D. Dissertation. Boston: Boston University, 1978.

_____. "The Kru Revolt, 1915: Causes and Consequences." Paper presented at the 20th Conference of the Liberian Studies Association, University of Akron, March 17–19, 1988.

Sundiata, Ibrahim K. *Black Scandal: America and the Liberian Labor Crisis, 1929–1936*. Philadelphia: Institute for the Study of Human Issues, 1980.

Syfert, Dwight Nash. "A History of the Liberian Coasting Trade, 1821–1900." Ph.D. Dissertation. Bloomington, Ind.: Indiana University, 1977.

The Observer. Newspaper published in Monrovia, Liberia, October 1880.

van der Kraaij, F. P. M. *The Open Door Policy of Liberia: An Economic History of Modern Liberia*. Bremen, West Germany: Bremer Afrika Archiv, 1983.

World Bank. *Sub-Saharan Africa: Progress Report on Development Prospects and Programs*. Washington, D.C.: World Bank, 1983.

Zolberg, Aristide R. *Creating Political Order: The Party-States of West Africa*. Chicago: Rand McNally, 1966.

8

Centralization and Development in Eastern Africa

John W. Harbeson

The thesis of this book is that overcentralization is a fundamental domestic flaw in the political structure of contemporary African states, one that is an important explanation of the all-too-prevalent political disarray and economic stagnation on the continent. Further, the argument of the book is that overcentralization corrodes the formation and maintenance of organizations through which African peoples may define and refine their social and political orders. Its hypothesis is that diminished political centralization will encourage the flowering of such social organization and mores. Therefore, the argument goes, more effective political structures will result which will, in turn, support improvement in the pace and quality of socio-economic development.

This chapter will present a preliminary examination of these propositions in the light of the experience of three eastern African states: Ethiopia, Kenya, and Tanzania. Together they represent a significant arena for the testing of the book's central propositions. Political authority is markedly centralized in all three states, but they differ from each other very significantly in their working ideologies, political structures, political histories, development strategies and development performance. One question is whether it can be said of such a diverse albeit small set of states, that they have indeed been overcentralized. A second question is whether such overcentralization is the primary domestic factor inhibiting more robust patterns of economic development and more stable and legitimate political structures.

This chapter will note, first, that centralization as employed in this book is in fact a composite of several related variables which have differed in their relative strength within the three eastern African countries considered here. Second, the chapter will argue that the elements of this composite variable have interacted in a complex fashion with a range of other variables in explaining these eastern African countries' records of political and economic development. Third, the chapter will argue that while some elements of centralization may have been essential in promoting what political and economic development these countries have achieved, others have encouraged practices that have been counterproductive to these ends. Fourth, the chapter will conclude that African regimes' decisions concerning whether and how to reform these practices will significantly influence the fundamental structures of the states within which they rule.

Definition of the Problem

The observed phenomenon of overcentralization, as conceived in this book, refers to a range of variables which together add up to authoritarian governments acting to confine the authoritative allocation of social values to a relatively small number of actors at the central level (Easton 1979). Such authoritarian governments seek then to impose their will on their subjects to such an extent as to inhibit the self-actualization of these subjects in political, economic, and spiritual terms.

But what are these variables? First, newly independent countries such as Kenya, left by retiring colonial powers with constitutions delegating considerable decision-making to regional authorities, acted to cancel such *delegation*. In this respect they returned to the practices of the colonial powers themselves at home and replicated in their colonies throughout much of their pre-independence history. Second, even with political authority safely concentrated in central governments, many countries' rulers have to varying degrees declined to permit even *deconcentration* of decision-making so that a broad range of officials from center to locale might have significant input in the formation and implementation of given policies.

A third variable concerns both the nature and extent of their *democratic accountability*. A few such as Botswana have maintained multi-party systems, others have turned to single parties, and still others have effectively abolished political parties altogether. Where parties have been maintained, they have varied greatly in the strength of their influence on political decision-making and in the extent to which they have governed themselves democratically internally. Fourth, central regimes have varied greatly in the extent to which they have encouraged *informal democracy*, i.e., participatory structures outside the framework of government itself through such vehicles as cooperatives, unions, farmers associations or auxiliaries to political parties, e.g., women's and youth associations.

Fifth, at central levels themselves there would appear to be significant if sometimes subtle differences in the extent of authority in *horizontal concentration* of power; i.e., the extent to which authority is concentrated in the hands of a single individual or dispersed more broadly among a number of actors or institutions at that level. Sixth, central African and other governments vary in the *scope of control* they seek to exercise at the grassroots level; i.e., the extent to which they seek to restrict the capacity of local social and economic institutions to function formally or informally independently of such central governments.

Central regimes in eastern Africa and elsewhere also differ from each other on a range of other political variables that influence the extent and consequences of centralization; e.g., their official ideologies, features of their political structures other than the nature and degree of their centralization, the nature of their development strategies and the manner in which such governments manage their development efforts and other public business. The distinctive political history of all three eastern African countries in this sample before and since independence (or the end of Haile Selassie's government in Ethiopia) is both cause and consequence of the interaction of these several variables. Lastly, it scarcely requires restating that the character of African socioeconomic and cultural institutions varies enormously as does the nature and extent of their influence on formal political decision-making processes.

The central question is, therefore, in what ways the complex centralization variable has positively or adversely affected the political and economic development of Ethiopia, Kenya, and Tanzania within the framework of these several other relevant operative variables. Phrased somewhat differently, the question is to what extent have these governments relied excessively upon elements of the composite centralization variable, and thereby, in conjunction with other variables just identified, have adversely affected these countries' political and economic development.

Centralization in East Africa

A full accounting of the political and developmental history of Ethiopia, Kenya, and Tanzania is self-evidently beyond the scope of a single chapter. However, some effort to identify patterns in these countries that are relevant to the hypotheses of this chapter and of this book is clearly necessary. In general terms all three countries have exhibited elements of centralization though in quite different forms and in varying degrees. Equally, they have differed significantly from each other on the other variables identified and in their development performance. This section will compare the three countries in terms of each of these variables identified in the preceding section.

Delegation

There has been little formal delegation of political power from central to more local levels before or since independence in Kenya and Tanzania and before or since the revolution in Ethiopia.[1] Centralized colonial rule in Tanzania by both Germany and Britain was frustrated by the absence of traditional political institutions above the district level through which events and practices could be directed at the local level.[2] Not long after independence, the Tanzanian government abolished local cooperatives whose evolving economic power appeared, in President Nyerere's view, to threaten his government's African socialist designs for the country. A decentralization policy promulgated in 1972 went largely unimplemented.[3] The Kenya constitution established by the retiring colonial power, at the insistence of European settler communities, did provide for extensive delegation of power to regional levels as well as extensive "checks and balances" at the central level. However, the Kenyatta government after independence used its large parliamentary majority to undo most of these provisions by means that the constitution itself provided (Harbeson 1973).

After a period of near total collapse of central government authority in Ethiopia between the last part of the eighteenth and the first half of the nineteenth century, emperors from Tewodros to Haile Selassie sought with some considerable success to increase and consolidate their authority at the expense of the feudal princes who each controlled large sections of the realm.[4] During Haile Selassie's rule the emergence of parliamentary and cabinet institutions signified what was to be unrealized potential for transformation of imperial institutions into those of constitutional monarchy. However, these embryonic structures did not include provisions for any appreciable delegation of authority the emperors had wrested from the princes to local levels (see Clapham 1968; Markakis 1974). Indeed, the Emperor proceeded to undo Eritrean regional autonomy established through the mediation of the United Nations, provoking a civil war that has continued with no sign of ending for more than a quarter of a century.[5] The successor government of Mengistu Haile Mariam has warred with Ogaden, Tigrean, and other regional movements as well as Eritrean liberation groups to prevent any formal or defacto delegation of significant authority to regional levels.[6]

Deconcentration

Significant degrees of deconcentration of political authority have existed in all three countries over much of their modern history. They differ sharply, however, in the direction of their current policies on this subject. Despite the unquestioned personal authority of the Emperor, provincial and local governors exercised considerable authority in his name. While the independent authority of the princes of the realm had largely been curtailed through the exertions of Haile Selassie and his modern predecessors, the informal influence of these traditional elites remained very considerable. As both great and lesser landlords, they were dominant figures in the lives of ordinary Ethiopians, especially in the rural areas (see Clapham 1968; Markakis 1974). It has been the policy of the Mengistu government to restrict very greatly any formal or informal deconcentration of governmental responsibility beneath the level of the chairman himself and a small group of largely military officers who work most closely with him (Harbeson 1988).

In both Tanzania and Kenya, provincial and district commissioners carried very considerable authority and influence within the colonial administrations of which they were a part. The same pattern continued well after independence in both countries. An important difference between Kenya and Tanzania was, however, that in Tanzania regional officials of the governing party, whose complex relationship with civil servants is beyond the scope of this chapter, also exerted substantial influence (Bienen 1967; Samoff 1974).[7] On its own and in response to pressure from international donors, Tanzania has acted in recent years to strengthen further these local officials, and it has also permitted the restoration of the district level cooperatives that had previously been abolished. Kenya, for its part, has taken the most direct measure to deconcentrate governmental authority through its District Focus policy. Under this policy the authority of provincial administrators is to be sharply curtailed as part of the goal of strengthening authority and capacity at district levels to participate in the planning and implementation of development measures[8] At the time this is written it is still too early to estimate how significant and substantial this policy of deconcentration will prove to be in practice. However, as in the case of Tanzania, such steps toward deconcentration have clearly been taken in the view that more effective development planning, implementation, and progress will result.

Central-Level Decision-Making

There are perhaps subtle but nevertheless significant differences among the three eastern African states in the distribution of decision-making authority at the central level. At one extreme, political power in Ethiopia appears to be more concentrated in the hands of a single individual than in either of the other countries. A military committee of more than one hundred members completed the liquidation of the imperial order. However, in the course of the ensuing transformation, the committee, or *Derg* in Amharic, rapidly shrunk in size and power came increasingly to be concentrated in the hands of Mengistu Haile Mariam alone. His concentration of power extended to the formation of the Workers Party of Ethiopia (WPE) which formally assumed power in September, 1984. A careful reading of the constitution for the democratic republic ratified in February 1987 and scheduled for inauguration in September 1987 suggests that it, too, will express Mengistu's undivided authority in a new form more than it will alter it (Harbeson 1988).

Kenya and Tanzania have both preserved the forms of presidential democracy, although the presidency remains the overwhelmingly dominant political institution in both countries. Parliaments continue to function in both countries and to debate public policies though their influence on reshaping government initiatives has been at best limited. Particularly in Kenya, dissenting voices have been heard in the Parliament, sometimes with severe official reprisals. Within the cabinets in both countries individual ministers have clearly appeared to exercise significant authority on their own while still remaining very much the agents of the president. Moreover, in both countries senior civil servants remain informally very influential despite their formal positions as lieutenants of their particular ministers. In Tanzania, also, the official party, the Chama cha Mapinduzi, C.C.M., has appeared to be substantially more influential on its own than its counterparts in many other African countries including both Kenya and Ethiopia. It has appeared to be the main defender of the country's official commitment to African socialism, for example, in the face of contemporary pressure from international donors for policy reform (Harbeson 1983).

Democratic Accountability

All three countries have relied upon the institution of a single official party to maintain the appearance and at least some of the reality of democratic accountability. If the absence of competitive parties is treated as an indication of overcentralization, then all three countries suffer from this malady. Of the three countries, Kenya has experienced the most electoral party competition, first in the last years before independence and, second, two years after independence when Kenya People's Union emerged to challenge the Kenyatta government's policies. However, the governments of all three countries would insist that through their single official parties democratic accountability has been effectively maintained. Julius Nyerere was one of the principal exponents of the idea of single party democracy in Africa (Nyerere 1968). During his twenty years as president of Tanzania, parliamentary elections were regularly held and turnover of members was frequent, including cabinet ministers on a few occasions. The same has been true in Kenya, although allegations of corruption and interference with electoral processes have appeared to be more frequent.

The formation of the Workers Party of Ethiopia and its formal assumption of the reins of government in 1984 has represented that country's first experience with party government, although four general elections for parliamentary seats occurred on a non-party basis in the last two decades of Haile Selassie's rule. Political parties themselves were unknown in Ethiopia until 1976 when the military government permitted the emergence of all parties not dedicated to restoration of the *ancien regime* (Hess 1964). The military government intended that all such non-reactionary parties would eventually form the basis of a single socialist party such as eventually emerged in the form of the WPE (see Provisional Military Government of Ethiopia 1976). However, controversies over the course of the post-imperial transformation of the Ethiopian state shipwrecked this effort and precipitated several years of quasi-civil war in addition to the on-going wars with regional liberation movements and the conflict with Somalia over the Ogaden. At this writing it remains to be seen how electoral accountability under the constitution ratified in February and inaugurated in September, 1987 will be maintained. It also remains unclear whether members of the new parliament will prove to be any less subordinate to, and dependent upon Chairman Mengistu than those of the earlier parliaments were with respect to Emperor Haile Selassie.

Informal Limits on Centralization

A major issue in assessing the degree of political centralization in a country is the extent to which socioeconomic formations outside formal political structures effectively limit the working authority of governments. Once again, important variations are visible among the three eastern African countries in this survey. In revolutionary Ethiopia there are few if any such structures which can so influence government policies. Agricultural producers and industrial workers, women and youth, are organized within rather than outside the framework of government. All major industrial and commercial firms have been nationalized, and there is little indication that non-nationalized smaller firms have exercised any independent influence as a group. High school and university students, a potent force in mobilizing support for revolutionary change under the Emperor's regime, have become very quiescent in the wake of bitter struggles during the revolution in which many of their number died, suffered imprisonment, or were forced into exile.

Kenya presents quite a different picture. The linkages between public political and private economic power have always been extensive and deeply rooted. Farmers organizations have continued to play an influential role in shaping agricultural policy. Labor unions, including those of civil servants, have scarcely maintained their independence of the government. However, they have been able to bring visible public pressure on the government in matters affecting their interests. Large industries, many of them multinational, have a freedom of action not found in countries where most such firms have been nationalized, although the presence on their boards of directors of high public officials has rendered their relationship to the government more complex. The existence of parastatals and public corporations has further complicated the relationships between public and private power. Though by no means independent of government, they do appear to represent some diffusion of power at the national level. Further, church leaders in Kenya have been increasingly outspoken in recent years and appear to be able to mold public opinion in ways that the government has come on occasion to find quite disturbing.

Extensive nationalization in Tanzania has limited the influence of private structures upon those of government as in Ethiopia. However, on its own and under pressure from international donors, Tanzania has allowed joint-venture companies to reappear, encouraged private enterprise in other ways, and has restored agricultural cooperatives at local levels. In such ways, Tanzania has taken cautious steps to permit private socio-economic formations, which may acquire some capacity outside of formal governmental structures, to have an influence on governmental policies.

Centralization and Governance at the Grassroots Level

As the introductory chapter observed, centralized governments are not always strong governments. Goran Hyden and other students of African politics have recorded the capacity of communities at the grassroots level to resist incorporation in the structures of the official economy (Hyden 1980, 1983). Indeed vibrant informal economies have been a fact of life in all three countries. Of the three, the Mengistu government in Ethiopia has made the most strenuous efforts to curb such informal political and economic independence at the grassroots level in ways quite unprecedented in the country's long history. It has undertaken to transform peasant associations created by the initial 1975 land reform into fully collectivized producers' cooperatives and to move them from isolated hamlets into official organized villages for purposes of political control as well as economic development and provision of social services. Tanzania's comparable effort to villagize its rural citizens by force in the early 1970s ran aground, leaving in its wake an ebullient informal economy and the peasant independence of which Hyden and others have written. Since independence, local self-help organizations called Harambee (or unity) societies, have been a characteristic and important feature of social life at the grassroots level in Kenya with clear official approval. While government has made considerable effort to guide and limit their activities, they still remain significant and potent forces at the local level (see Barkan and Okumu 1979).

Beyond these formal organizations at the grassroots level, there is little evidence that concentration of political power in the three countries has by itself undermined the continued existence of traditional local social institutions. In one respect, colonial regimes did have an important influence upon such structures. Through both action and inaction, particularly in Kenya, colonial governments greatly influenced local institutions in their capacity to regulate land tenure, though not necessarily because such colonial regimes were highly centralized. Beyond that, however, local savings, credit, market, and mutual assistance groups continue to exist and to function. Without question they have been greatly affected by broad patterns of change associated with the imposition and eventual expulsion of colonial rule in Kenya and Tanzania. It is less than clear, however, that the centralizing tendencies of governments in these two countries have been uniquely or particularly responsible for disrupting or altering the character of these local informal social structures and centers of power.

What has not occurred, however, is any substantial initiative in any of the three countries to invest traditional social structures, any more than formal local governments, with measures of local self-governance. They have not treated them as critical agents in ensuring the appropriateness, validity, and sustainability of development initiatives. Even local structures created by governments in the name of local self-governance, e.g., peasant associations and cooperatives in Ethiopia and village structures in Tanzania, have not been permitted or encouraged to assert such local political responsibility (Hyden 1980; Fortmann 1980). Neither Ethiopia nor Tanzania have specifically recognized the legitimacy and importance for the broad outlines of their rural development policies to be fine tuned to the circumstances of particular locales by any existing local institutions.

However, there is persuasive evidence that local organizations should indeed be allowed to play such roles in the interests of effective development. Fifty-six impact evaluations, specially commissioned by the United States Agency for International Development[9] to gauge the long-term consequences of its projects in a number of different sectors, have almost uniformly testified to the proposition that grassroots level organizations of producers must be able to shape development projects to their particular local circumstances if development projects are to be both successful and sustainable.

The conclusion emerges that there have been significant if subtle differences in patterns of centralization of authority in eastern Africa. While in the most general terms it would appear that the concentration of political and economic power, centralization as it is defined in this book, has been the most pronounced in Ethiopia and least so in Kenya, it should be apparent from the foregoing that such a generalization is too simplistic. In the first place, all three are highly centralized and, in the second place, the specific ways in which power is and is not concentrated in the three countries are of great importance in properly understanding their systems. Before proceeding to the question of how specific aspects of the concentration of political power have affected patterns of economic development in these countries, it is appropriate to review briefly those patterns of development.

Development

Notwithstanding very important differences in development ideologies and strategies among the three countries, all remain among the ranks of low income countries according to conventional indicators. Though all three remain among the world's poorest countries, there have been important differences in their development records.[10]

Development Ideology and Strategy

After overthrowing the regime of Emperor Haile Selassie, the successor military regime committed the country to a socialist future, an expressly scientific socialist future since about 1979. The Mengistu government has conceived and implemented revolutionary social and economic measures to nationalize rural and urban land. It has administered development at the grassroots level through peasant organizations enshrining differing degrees of collectivization and increasingly villagized local communities (Cohen and Koehn 1977).[11] It has nationalized all major industrial and commercial firms. The regime has established new structures for centralized development planning and promulgated a number of measures to give its policies the force of law. These are to be implemented strictly on pain of criminal penalities. Though the existence of hierarchies of peasant associations and urban *kebelles* (or neighborhood associations) are formally organized to permit broad participation in shaping the design and implementation of development initiatives, in fact, development policies are enacted and implementation is attempted in strictly top-down fashion.

Through such structures the government has effected a marked increase in levels of literacy, increased access to educational opportunities at all levels, and has sought to protect the environment through reforestation. As a result, literacy levels have been increased from less than 10 percent to more than 60 percent, and international development agencies credit the government with at least limiting if not completely controlling the use of forest resources. In great measure, the regime has relied upon state farms and upon the production of only three or four regions to sustain the agricultural economy. These state farms have produced the quantities of food necessary to feed urban populations and sustain the army but at the widely acknowledged cost of extreme inefficiency. It has struggled with partial success to restrict and limit the activities of private traders, but its important incentives to induce rural producers to accept increased collectivization have been broadly resisted. While a high percentage of rural producers have accepted membership in peasant associations and service cooperatives envisaged by the initial land reform proclamation, only slightly more than 2.2 percent of rural households have been persuaded to create more collectivized producer cooperatives after nearly a decade of official efforts toward that end (Ministry of Agriculture). The regime's present ten-year development plan contemplates very rapid rates of economic growth, increases in education and health care, rapid increases in industrialization, and increased reliance upon state farms and producer cooperatives in rural areas. Even observers sympathetic to the regime's socialist orientation consider the plan to be unworkably ambitious (Government Printer 1984). However, the promulgation of such an ambitious plan has been employed by the government as a major rationale for still more draconian measures to try to compel improved grassroots level development performance.

Until the later years of Julius Nyerere's presidency in the early 1980s, Tanzania was perhaps the foremost exemplar of African socialism. Differences between Tanzania's official concept of African socialism and Ethiopia's scientific socialism were perhaps more pronounced than differences in the two countries' development policies and implementation strategies. The degree of collectivization undertaken in the *Ujamaa* villagization campaign in the early 1970s was somewhat less than that sought through producers' cooperatives in Ethiopia. However it was greater than that envisaged in the formation of peasant associations in the *first* phase of Ethiopia's land reform. Tanzania has relied more upon parastatal organizations for organizing production, marketing, distribution functions in agriculture than upon state farms.

Despite structures seeming to invite local producers' participation, Tanzanian administration of development initiatives at the grassroots level allowed very little such input from that level. Frustrated by the limited voluntary response to the government's calls for villagization, it resorted to force to achieve this end. By contrast, the available evidence indicates that Ethiopia has relied upon official persuasion backed up by strong economic incentives to gain acceptance of producer cooperatives. Similarly, Ethiopia appears not to have resorted to coercion to achieve villagization as of the beginning of 1988.

A further distinction in the administration of development policies between Ethiopia and Tanzania has been the latter's greater reliance upon the official party to implement the government's policies at least until 1984 when the WPE took formal control of the Ethiopian government. Even today there appear to have been degrees of division of power and of political responsibility between civil service and party officials in Tanzania that have been less characteristic of Ethiopia. In Ethiopia, party and administrative officials have been integrated within the same implementation structures at subnational levels. Development policies also appear to have been the subject of more visible and open debate in Tanzania within the party and among the party, ministries, parastatals and other governmental structures. Clearly, moreover, Tanzania has maintained civilian government since independence, while Ethiopia's military rulers have behaved less like civilian political elites than other military regimes throughout the continent (Harbeson 1987).

Kenya's initial official ideology of African socialism thinly veiled its working commitment to a more open, market-driven economy than that found either in Tanzania or in Ethiopia since the revolution (Government of Kenya 1965). However, Kenya's encouragement of private domestic and foreign investment has not proven a barrier to substantial official involvement in direction of the economy through parastatal organizations, land reform and settlement efforts, restrictions on private trade in certain agricultural products, official marketing structures, heavy regulation of local cooperative societies, and substantial overlap between the boards of directors of private businesses and the country's political leadership.

Development Records

While all three countries remain among the ranks of the world's least developed nations, there have been important differences in their developmental achievements on the evidence of conventional indicators. In per capita income, Ethiopia has remained the poorest country in the world. Tanzania, at least up until 1985, has continued to lag behind Kenya. The per capita income of both countries, however, has remained nearly three times that of Ethiopia. The World Bank has estimated that Kenya's average annual rate of growth in GNP between 1965 and 1985 has been 1.9 percent compared to nearly zero average annual growth rates for both Ethiopia and Tanzania and a record for low income countries (other than China or India) of 0.4 percent.

More than 80 percent of the population obtains a livelihood from agriculture in all three countries. In common with other low-income countries, Kenya, Tanzania, and Ethiopia have all suffered declines in agricultural productivity in the 1980s. However, only Kenya has maintained a rate of agricultural growth above the low-income average. Kenya's slipped from 4.9 percent for the period 1965 to 1980 and to a rate of 2.8 percent between 1980 and 1985; the corresponding figures for Tanzania were 1.7 percent and 0.7 percent and for Ethiopia 1.2 percent and -3.4 percent. All three have shown long-term declines in agricultural production per capita. All three have struggled to grow at a faster rate than the rate of population increase. Kenya's current rate of population growth is the highest in the world at just over 4.0 percent; Tanzania's has been a high 3.5 percent, while Ethiopia's has been a somewhat slower 2.5 percent. Except for Kenya prior to 1980, economic growth in all three countries has lagged behind population growth since the mid-1960s.

Ethiopia's life expectancy has barely changed between the mid-1960s and the mid-1980s while both Tanzania and Kenya have recorded increases of nearly 10 years to about slightly over 50 years for both countries. Availability of health care facilities has clearly improved in Kenya over the same twenty year period, but the picture is mixed in both Tanzania and Ethiopia. Availability of doctors has sharply decreased in Ethiopia (though their distribution may have improved) while availability of nurses has increased; the opposite has been the case in Tanzania. Daily calorie supply has on average improved measurably in Tanzania while it has declined somewhat in both Kenya and Ethiopia. In common with trends for low-income countries as a group, access to educational opportunity has increased sharply in all three countries, except for Tanzania in the area of secondary education.

The link between political structure and development progress is not an easy one to pinpoint, and any such relationship is made still more difficult to discern by the influence of associated variables such as ideology, development policy and development strategy. Specifically, while the three countries have embraced widely differing philosophies of political economy, the preceding section demonstrated that the differences in governmental structure have been less pronounced and more complex than the countries' self-asserted images have projected. Similarly, Kenya's economic performance has, as is commonly asserted, been among the stronger ones on the continent and generally superior to those of Ethiopia and Tanzania. However, in some respects the differences are relatively modest. Moreover, the positions of these countries in economic terms *vis-a-vis* each other appear to have changed relatively little in the twenty years during which they have taken their different developmental paths. This suggests that the differences in their economic performance may relate as closely to broad historical differences in their patterns of political economy as to the character of their political structures in more recent times. Nevertheless, with these important qualifications one may conclude that on balance Kenya's development performance has been the strongest of three countries. Since Kenya is also the most decentralized of the three countries according to the criteria employed in this essay, and subject to the important qualifications already noted, a possible positive correlation emerges between development and decentralization.

Why has Kenya taken a course of at least marginally greater decentralization than the other two countries? Such incrementally greater decentralization as has occurred has *not* been the result of any conscious policy such as that articulated but never implemented in Tanzania. Neither of Kenya's first two presidents have been inspired by socialist visions that have seemed to carry a high degree of centralization as a predictable corollary. The not insignificant interventions of their governments appear to have been the product of pragmatic, practical considerations of poltical advantage and perceived economic imperatives in individual instances. The District Focus policy, the country's most dramatic decentralization initiative, appears to have been motivated both by an officially perceived need for greater economic belt tightening in the face of external pressures from the World Bank and other agencies, and by a political determination that the often great political power of provincial governors had become too great a hindrance to the Moi government's exercise of its powers. Thus, apparent increased district level development responsibility at the district level in Kenya, under the District Focus policy, may have been more a consequence than a deliberate official objective of the Kenya government. Decentralization may have emerged primarily in the interstices of policy initiatives undertaken with very different ends in view.

Political Foundations for Development

The preceding sections have suggested that Kenya has maintained a less centralized political system, in terms of the several variables identified, than either Tanzania or Ethiopia. Further, on balance Kenya's development record has been superior to those of both the other countries. The question arises, therefore, how plausible is the resulting apparent correllation between decentralization and developmental progress. A second question is, if this correllation is plausible, why it should be so. The third question is the implications of such a positive correllation for the political economy of development in Africa as a whole.

The first question is not an easy one for, as the Kenya evidence suggests, one cannot dismiss the importance of ideology, development strategy, organizational structure, development management methods and several other important variables in any development equation. Moreover, to be really convincing, any such generalization should be based on some longitudinal evidence so that one could say, for example, that over time as centralization has increased development performance has tended to be less robust. Testing of such propositions is well beyond the scope of this chapter. In the absence of such testing, however, one may certainly suggest that variables associated with political centralization, as the term is understood in this book, are *one* important if not necessarily controlling set of political variables influencing the nature and pace of developmental progress.

The second question is a somewhat more manageable one: why are variables' association with political centralization and those defining developmental progress *ceteris paribus* likely to be inversely related to one another? Part of the answer to the question must clearly be that such an inverse relationship obtains only beyond a certain point. This is because there are well researched, valid reasons for some measure of centralization in general and in Africa in particular. There are public goods to be managed, economies of scale to be realized, and external challenges to be met to mention only some of the most important of those reasons. The question then becomes at what point excessive political centralization has occurred and why such overcentralization contributes to restraining development progress. What can be said regarding this last question?

There is strong, empirically grounded evidence to support the proposition that development initiatives at the grassroots level are more likely to succeed the more the people for whom they are intended participate in shaping their design and implementation. Such participation is facilitated when local institutions engage people affected by official development initiatives in rendering them appropriate and valid in the circumstances of particular communities. This much is the overwhelming evidence of the United States Agency for International Development impact evaluations mentioned earlier. These are reinforced by similar observations made by other bilateral and multi-lateral development agencies, and research by scholars as well as practitioners of development management.[12] It follows logically that government development initiatives at local levels are more likely to succeed to the extent that implementing officials are formally vested or informally able to assert the discretion necessary to encourage participation by local organizations for this purpose.

If the literature on development management offers a rationale for the possible empirical correlation between decentralization and development performance suggested by the East African experience, this same evidence suggests that some elements of decentralization may be relatively more important than others in producing this relationship. On the one hand, some elements of decentralization have been clearly shown to be important in encouraging strong development performance; i.e., the administrative deconcentration and encouragement of democratic processes in official and unofficial local institutions just discussed. For these processes to function with real integrity, unofficial social institutions involved with development projects locally would appear to require a degree of political independence. On the other hand, the same evidence suggests that the other aspects of decentralization as understood in this book (formal delegation, horizontal dispersion of power centrally, and electoral accountability) may be desirable but possibly not essential conditions for strong development performance. Sufficient local participation, institutional autonomy, and administrative deconcentration to bring about important development have on at least some occasions occurred in countries that have been weak on horizontal disperson, formal delegation, and electoral accountability. Among the salient examples have been the Philippines, Honduras, Liberia, and Thailand (AID Impact Evalutions Nos. 1, 4, 14, 17, 27 18, 30, 31, 52, 53).

All three countries in this study, like most countries in the developing world, have ample room for improvement in broadening the scope for local participation and official flexibility in promoting development. Ethiopia and

Tanzania, however, over the course of the last twenty years have traveled relatively less far down this road than has Kenya. A careful examination of Tanzania's widely acknowledged failure in the Ujamaa villagization campaign suggests that much of the problem may have stemmed from failure to permit the very local self-reliance that was the hallmark of Nyerere's vision of African socialism. Had the importance of local participation and governmental deconcentration been as apparent at the time as it is a decade and a half later, and had Tanzania chosen to incorporate the lessons, very different results might have obtained (Harbeson 1983). Similarly, the revolutionary reforms introduced by the Mengistu government in Ethiopia have included the creation of structures through which local participation and governmental deconcentration might be practiced. The political dynamics of Ethiopia's revolutionary course have, however, led the Mengistu regime in an opposite direction. The preliminary evidence indicates that lack of developmental progress, especially in rural areas, is at least in part attributable to this state of affairs (Rahmato 1985).

By contrast Kenya has made considerably less stringent development demands upon its subjects than the other two countries, and has on balance over the course of the last two decades allowed more open political and economic competition. Within such an overall framework of greater openness, however, the Kenya government has nevertheless imposed what appear to be increasingly stringent regulations governing economic and political behavior. Thus, the differences between Kenya's approach to political and economic development, on the one hand, and those of Tanzania and Ethiopia, on the other hand, should not be exaggerated though they have been nonetheless real and significant. At the same time, it has not necessarily followed that all the consequences of Kenya's incrementally greater decentralization have been positive in terms of development. Kenya's political course has been accompanied by what nearly all observers have recognized to be a high degree of corruption, sustained or perhaps increased inequality, and blatant use of personal political power for personal economic ends and vice versa. Kenya's degrees of decentralization have not appeared to restrain these unfortunate patterns even if decentralization cannot be assigned as their cause.

The Constitutional Issue

To the extent that African countries have come to accept the importance of grassroots level participation and administrative deconcentration to successful development, they do indeed confront fundamental issues concerning the constitution of their post-independence states. The nature of this constitutional crisis is sometimes misconceived because of unexamined assumptions concerning linkages between patterns of political economy at macro- and micro-levels in given countries. Much has been written elsewhere to the effect that only more market-driven economies in conjunction with more competitive political systems can yield significant improvements in developmental progress. But the Kenya evidence suggests at best an imperfect correlation between such macro-level structures of political economy and the presence of micro-level requirements such as political deconcentration and grassroots level participation that have been found to be essential to effective development progress. At the same time, it may not necessarily be the case that all forms of socialism necessarily exclude fostering such micro-level requisites.

The real constitutional crisis may perhaps better be identified as one of political culture than of political structure. First, small producers who are the backbone of most African economies now and for the foreseeable future, are nevertheless politically peripheral in most African countries exhibiting all manner of ideological coloring. Second, the preponderance of the evidence suggests strongly that such producers respond favorably to a range of political and economic incentives to engage them, more than they do to structures which entrench command-based development. Such command-based development orientations and the often parallel approach of indifference to the concerns of small producers, are both unhelpful legacies of the colonial era not yet completely dispatched. Recognition by public officials of these legacies for what they are, would appear to be a necessary precondition for instituting greater decentralization in the interests of development. Such recognition would in turn appear to await the appearance of a generation of African leaders who perceive elements of decentralization as instrumental in a second phase of weaving national fabrics of political identity begun by those who led the way to independence. Such a new generation of leaders would come to see that broadening political participation in development at the grassroots level might speed processes of nation building and national renewal which, in many countries, have rapidly weakened and declined since the euphoria of political independence faded more than a quarter-century ago.

Notes

1. Basic works on the post-independence development of Kenya's political economy include Gordon 1986; Kitching 1980; Swainso 1980; Wasserman 1976; Leys 1975; Rothchild 1973; Harbeson 1973.

2. Among the principal sources on colonial Tanzania are Austen 1968; Iliffe 1969; Brett 1972; Pratt 1976; Ingle 1972; Young and Fosbrooke 1960.

3. Principal sources on post-independence Tanzania include Hyden 1980; Resnick 1981; Coulson 1982; von Freyhold 1979; Fortmann 1980; Yeager 1982.

4. Among the major sources on pre-revolutionary Ethiopia from the restoration of the imperial office in the mid-nineteenth century are Rubenson 1976; Markakis 1974; Jones and Monroe 1955; Marcus 1975; Darkwah 1975; Levine 1965, 1974; Greenfield 1965; Clapham 1968; Gilks 1975.

5. Among the major sources on the Eritrean problem have been Sherman 1980; Trevaskis 1960; Selassie 1980; Erlich 1983.

6. Major sources on the Ethiopian revolution have been relatively few in number. On the earlier years see Ottaway 1978; Hall 1977; Lefort 1983; Molyneux and Halliday 1981; Harbeson 1988.

7. Two careful examinations of this relationship at the local level are Bienen 1967; Samoff 1974.

8. For a discussion of District Focus see Republic of Kenya, *District Focus for Rural Development* (Government Printer 1983) and a recent discussion by Cohen and Hook, *District Development Planning in Kenya* (Kenya Ministry of Finance and Planning, 1986).

9. Since 1979, the Agency for International Development has undertaken a series of in-depth, comprehensive impact evaluations of projects. The purpose has been to gauge the long-term sustainability and replicability of these projects and their significance for the basic objectives outlined in the foreign assistance legislation. Fifty-six of these evaluations have been published by the Studies Division, Office of Evaluation, Bureau of Policy and Program Coordination, AID. These evaluations support the participation thesis strongly. A major work on the subject is Norman Uphoff and Milton Esman, *Local Organizations in Rural Development* (Cornell 1984).

10. The quantitative data are from the World Bank's 1987 *World Development Report* (Oxford, for the World Bank 1987).

11. On the land reform legislation see Cohen and Koehn, "Rural and Urban Land Reform in Ethiopia." *African Law Studies,* Vol. 14, No. 1 (1977), pp. 3–62. Very little fieldwork has yet been possible on the impact of the land reform at the grassroots level. One important study of the villagization process in one province is John M. Cohen and Nils-Ivar Issakson *Villagization in the Arsi Region of Ethiopia* (Report prepared by SIDA consultants, Swedish University for Agricultural Sciences, Uppsala, 1987).

12. See, for example, Uphoff and Esman 1984; Lindenberg and Crosby 1981; Moris 1981; Honadle and Klauss 1979; Bryant and White 1982).

References

Austen, Ralph. *Northwest Tanzania under German and British Rule.* New Haven, Connecticut: Yale University Press, 1968.

Barkan, Joel, and John Okumu, eds. *Politics and Public Policy in Kenya and Tanzania.* New York: Praeger, 1979.

Bienen, Henry. *Tanzania: Party Transformation and Economic Development.* Princeton, New Jersey: Princeton University Press, 1967.

Brett, E. A. *Colonialism and Underdevelopment in East Africa.* Fair Lawn, New Jersey: Oxford University Press, 1972.

Bryant, Coralie, and Louise G. White. *Managing Development in the Third World.* Boulder, Colorado: Westview, 1982.

Cohen, John M., and Peter Koehn. "Ruran and Urban Land Reform in Ethiopia." *African Law Studies* 14 (1) (1977): 3–62.

———, and Nils-Ivar Issakson. *Villagization in the Arsi Region of Ethiopia.* Report prepared by SIDA consultants, Swedish University for Agricultural Sciences, Uppsala, 1987.

Clapham, Christopher. *Haile Selassie's Government.* New York: Praeger, 1968.

Coulson, Andrew. *Tanzania: A Political Economy.* London: Clarendon Press, 1982.

Darkwah, Kofi. *Shewa, Menelik, and the Ethiopian Empire 1813–1889.* London: Heinemann, 1975.

Easton, David. *A Systems Analysis of Political Life.* Chicago, Illinois: University of Chicago Press, 1979.

Erlich, Haggai. *The Struggle over Eritrea 1962–1978.* Stanford, California: Hoover Institution, 1983.

Fortmann, Louise. *Peasants, Officials and Participation Rural Tanzania: Experience with Villagization and Decentralization.* Ithaca, New York: Center for International Studies, Cornell University, 1980.

Gilkes, Patrick. *The Dying Lion: Feudalism and Modernization in Ethiopia.* New York: St. Martin's, 1975.

Gordon, David. *Decolonization and the State in Kenya.* Boulder, Colorado: Westview, 1986.

Government of Kenya. *African Socialism and Its Application to Planning.* Nairobi: Government Printer, 1965.

Greenfield, Richard. *Ethiopia: A New Political History.* New York: Praeger, 1965.

Hall, Marilyn. "The Ethiopian Revolution: Group Interaction and Civil-Military Relations." Unpublished Ph.D. dissertation, George Washington University, 1977.

Harbeson, John W. *Nation-Building in Kenya: The Role of Land Reform.* Evanston, Illinois: Northwestern University Press, 1973.

――――. "Tanzanian Socialism in Transition: Agricultural Crisis and Policy Reform." *Universities Field Staff International Report* No. 30, 1983. Hanover, New Hampshire: Universities Field Staff International, 1983.

――――. *The Military in African Politics.* New York: Praeger, 1987.

――――. *The Ethiopian Transformation: The Quest for the Post-Imperial State.* Boulder, Colorado: Westview, 1988.

Hess, Robert. "The Ethiopian No-Party State." *American Political Science Review* 58 (1964): 947–950.

Honadle, George, and Rudi Klauss. *International Development Administration: Implementation Analysis for Development Projects.* New York: Praeger, 1979.

Hyden, Goran. *Beyond Ujamaa: Underdevelopment and an Uncaptured Peasantry.* Berkeley: University of California Press, 1980.

――――. *No Shortcuts to Progress.* Berkeley: University of California Press, 1983.

Iliffe, John. *Tanganyika under German Rule.* London: Cambridge University Press, 1969.

Ingle, Clyde. *From Village to State in Tanzania: The Politics of Rural Development.* Ithaca, Cornell University Press, 1972.

Jones, A., and E. Monroe. *A History of Ethiopia.* London: Clarendon, 1955.

Kitching, Gavin. *Class and Economic Change in Kenya: The Making of an African Petite-Bouroeoisie.* New Haven, Connecticut: Yale University Press, 1980.

Lefort, Rene. *Ethiopia: An Heretical Revolution?* Trenton, New Jersey: Zed, 1983.

Levine, Donald. *Wax and Gold: Tradition and Innovation in Ethiopian Culture.* Chicago: University of Chicago, 1965.

――――. *Greater Ethiopia: The Evolution of a Multicultural Society.* Chicago: University of Chicago, 1974.

Leys, Colin. *Underdevelopment in Kenya: The Political Economy of Underdevelopment.* Berkeley: University of California Press, 1975.

Lindenberg, Marc, and Benjamin Crosby. *Managing Development: The Political Dimension.* West Hartford, Connecticut: Kumarian Press, 1981.

Marcus, Harold. *The Life and Times of Menlik II.* London: Clarendon Press, 1975.

Markakis, John. *Ethiopia: Anatomy of a Traditional Polity.* London: Clarendon Press, 1974.

Molyneux, M., and Fred Halliday. *The Ethiopian Revolution.* London: Verso, 1981.

Moris, Jon. *Managing Induced Rural Development.* Bloomington, Indiana: International Development Institute, 1981.

Nyerere, Julius. *Freedom and Socialism: A Selection from Writings and Speeches 1965-1967.* London: Oxford University Press, 1968.

Ottaway, Marina and David. *Empire in Revolution.* New York: Africana, 1978.

Pratt, Cranford. *The Critical Phase in Tanzania 1945-1968.* New York: Cambridge University Press, 1976.

Provisional Military Government of Ethiopia. *National Democratic Revolutionary Program,* April, 1976.

Rahmato, Dessalegn. *Agrarian Reform in Ethiopia.* Trenton, New Jersey: Red Sea Press, 1985.

Resnick, Idrian. *The Long Transition: Building Socialism in Tanzania.* New York: Monthly Review Press, 1981.

Rothchild, Donald. *Racial Bargaininig in Independent Kenya.* Fair Lawn, New Jersey: Oxford University Press, 1973.

Rubenson, Sven. *The Survival of Ethiopian Independence.* London: Heinemaan, 1976.

Samoff, Joel. *Tanzania: Local Politics and the Structure of Power.* Madison: University of Wisconsin Press, 1974.

Selassie, Berekhet Habte. *Conflict and Intervention in the Horn of Africa.* New York: Monthly Review, 1980.

Sherman, Richard. *Eritrea: The Unfinished Revolution.* New York: Praeger, 1980.

Swainson, Nicola. *The Development of Corporate Capitalism in Kenya.* New York: Monthly Review Press, 1980.

Trevaskis, G.N.K. *Eritrea: A Colony in Transition.* London: Oxford University Press, 1960.

Uphoff, Norman, and Milton Esman. *Local Organizations: Intermediaries in Rural Development.* Ithaca, New York: Cornell, 1984.

von Freyhold, Michaela. *Ujamaa Villages in Tanzania: Analysis of a Social Experiment.* New York: Monthly Review Press, 1979.

Wasserman, Gary. *The Politics of Decolonization.* New York, New York: Cambridge University Press, 1976.

World Bank. *World Development Report 1987.* New York: Oxford University Press, 1987.

Yeager, Rodger. *Tanzania: An African Experiment.* Boulder, Colorado: Westview Press, 1982.

Young, Roland, and Henry Fosbrooke. *Smoke in the Hills: Political Tension in the Morogoro District of Tanganyika.* Evanston, Ill.: Northwestern, 1960.

9

Centralization, Self-Governance, and Development in Nigeria

Dele Olowu

Introduction

Nigeria, by virtue of her history, size, political culture and the style of her economic development policies, occupies a unique position in Africa. With a population equal to about a fifth of the continent, she has served since her independence in 1960 as Africa's major experiment in operating a federal polity. Even the military, which has ruled the country for more than half of the period since independence, has had to concede aspects of this federalist political structure as well as the country's commitment to popular government and the rule of law. Economically, in spite of growing state interventionism since the late 1960s, the private sector has remained the prime mover of economic growth, not only in traditional agriculture but also in such modern sectors as construction, transportation and commerce.

These economic and political values: federalism, democracy, and a tolerably open economy, are products of Nigeria's unique pre-colonial and colonial history as well as the size and diversity of her peoples. A major theme in this book concerns the progressive centralization of political power in African countries and the consequences such a political strategy has created in social and economic realms. This Nigerian case-study is particularly appropriate from this viewpoint in that it dramatizes very clearly how political and economic values shared widely by the country's leadership (and to some extent her people) and the accompanying institutions to which they gave rise in the pre-independence and the immediate post-independence period in 1960, were transformed into more centralized values and institutions by another leadership group. The tension between political realities and the choice of political strategy in the post-independence period has been great, leading to severe economic and political problems. I shall try to demonstrate in this chapter how this situation emerged and the nature of the tensions created, and I will suggest by way of conclusion how the present tension may be eased.

In the first section of the chapter, I shall discuss salient elements of the centralized and decentralized approaches to development. Next, I shall examine the Nigerian socio-political environment which led to the adoption of federalism and other liberal institutions at independence. In a third section, I shall review the efforts made thus far to overturn these institutions and their supporting values through the superimposition of a centralized political management strategy. I shall, in the fourth section, review the implications of these developments for the Nigerian economy and polity and, in a final section, suggest possible directions for easing the tension between social reality and strategy.

Approaches to Development:
The Centralized and Decentralized Models

It has been alleged with good reason that development is probably one of the most debated terms in the social sciences (Independent Commission 1980). In spite of this, however, some consensus seems to have emerged. Development is now generally regarded as bi-focal involving both socio-economic transformation or improvement of the material conditions of the people as a whole, and nation-building. The latter denotes increasing effectiveness and institutionalization of the political system (Heady 1979: 244). For economists, "socioeconomic progress" is by consensus measured by two indices: economic growth as reflected by the annual growth of the Gross National Product, and the spread of its benefits (the distribution of income or welfare or both). On the other hand, "nation-building" as a measure of political change has presented greater problems of definition for students of political science. A number of scholars have challenged the authenticity of the "tribe-to-nation" approach which such conceptualizations have often presumed (Gellar 1972). Others have suggested other concepts such as national integration, political system capacity, effectiveness and political participation (Pye 1971; Huntington and Nelson 1976).

The exact relationship between economic and political development (as defined above) has continued to be as contentious as ever. Must economic modernization precede political modernization as some have contended? The lessons of economic history in the West, the East and the more recent breakthroughs in the Far East seem to suggest that socioeconomic transformation in terms of rapid economic growth seems to constitute the prerequisite for the establishment of participatory political systems (Emerson 1971; Rostow 1971: 98–183). Indeed, some political scientists characterized political development as the ability of the political leadership to control and "mobilize" the people in a period of rapid socioeconomic change (Apter 1965; Riggs 1964; Huntington 1968). Economic development theories have also presumed authoritarian control as inevitable for the management of the economic growth process (Illchman and Bhagava 1970). The apparent ease with which some socialist as well as newly industrializing countries in Asia and the Middle East carried out the very rapid industrialization of their economies seems to provide the full proof for this position. Thus there developed a preference for dominant mass-party regimes or even dictatorships, either civilian or military.

As a result it came generally to be accepted that some sort of authoritarian coercion was essential for economic growth and economic development. This was regarded as a pre-condition for popular government (Rostow 1971; Black 1971; Nordlinger 1971; Ward 1971). A conviction was generally shared both by the intelligentsia in the Third World and their foreign advisers and aid-givers: economic development required political stability which only authoritarian governments could guarantee. The socioeconomic conditions of the new states were frequently likened to that of Europe during the war years when democracy had to be temporarily suspended in several countries to undertake successful prosecution of the war (Zolberg 1966). As a corollary, it was expected that as a country "matured" economically and her peoples' social conditions improved, her political system would become more responsive, thereby guaranteeing stability. A number of country-cases within the Third World seem to vindicate the position that authoritarianism was more appropriate to the rapid social changes associated with modernization.

As it worked out in Africa over the last three decades, however, this model of development was beset by several major flaws. First, there was the tendency for the state to progressively assume responsibility for all or at least what it considered to be "the commanding heights" of the economy. For this, massive bureaucratic systems were required which, given the environment in which they operated and the relatively short histories of such state systems, were not been able to operate as effectively as they should, either as structures or in terms of their relationship with the public. They distorted incentives within the private sector (both modern and traditional) and undermined political contributions that might have been made by the people to the development process.

Second, African mass party regimes or military dictatorships evinced a tendency to exterminate institutions ensuring accountable performance. They thereby created opportunities not only for radical social change but also for political and bureaucratic corruption. Finally, for a country with the size and diversity of Nigeria, a centralized strategy of this type elevated too many issues to the national level, ones often not resolvable at that level given the complex nature of the society.

These constitute elements of "premature centralization" which were alluded to in Chapter 4. This is not an argument against all centralization *per se;* some measure of centralization is probably an inevitable aspect of the modernization process. In particular, given the pre-colonial antipathies between Nigeria's major ethnic groups and the brief history of colonial rule, some central authority to facilitate and help integrate ongoing relationships among her peoples must be regarded as part of the processes of state consolidation. However, centralization processes in Africa have not generally worked as frameworks to integrate existing diversities, but instead have tended more to repress the diverse and basic organizations needed to play constructive roles in the development and integration process.

An alternative approach which draws on a relatively less developed body of theory than the first sees the activity of a diversity of organizations as essential to the process of economic growth and social development. These organizations grow from (or are stifled by) the institutions which govern a people. Institutions, as discussed in Chapter 1 and developed further in Chapter 12, are the systems of rules which structure how communities of people make and take collective decisions and actions (Buchanan and Tullock 1962; Olson 1965; Ostrom 1973; Ostrom and Ostrom 1977). The national government constitutes only one—albeit an important one—of the actors in this context. Without institutions which create and sustain a diversity of viable organizations to faciltate the broad and flexible human organizational patterns necessary to produce an increasing variety of complex goods and services, neither capital, technology nor energetic public activism will avail in bringing about social transformation. Centrally managed, directed or coerced organization, in this framework, while capable of producing limited goods, is seen as rarely flexible, adaptable or closely enough attuned to variable and changing human needs and motivations to be able to sustain a complex and diverse economy. Stagnation results instead.

Economists have begun to pay greater attention to this critical issue. This resulted from questions generated by the failure of the application in the Third World of the Marshall Plan economic policies (of injecting massive external capital by way of aid) which had proved successful in post-Second World War Europe. The most famous economic theories which supported the reapplication of the Marshall Plan type policies in the Third World was the capital constraint model, a combination of Rostow's economic growth stage model and the Harrod-Dommar savings-capital theory. However, according to Todaro, the critical institutions, organizations, and attitudes which must activate capital and new technology were simply absent (Todaro 1981: 16). These would include: effective systems of contract, credit, and money markets; municipal services including public education, health, and transportation; effective systems of weights and measures; institutions for transmitting and exchanging information cheaply; an effective public bureaucracy; and institutions for the discovery and adaptation of new ideas. These cannot be sustained by a single, central organization but are activated through collaboration among diverse individuals in the pursuit of their individual and collective interests: implied in this logic is the importance of choice rather than coercion. These are just as necessary to the development process as capital and technology (Owens and Shaw 1972).

This aspect is often overlooked in interpreting the economic history of the industrialized Western nations as well as the newly industrializing nations of east Asia. It, for instance, explains why neither aid nor windfall revenues arising from the extraction of minerals or agricultural products have in themselves provided the stimulus towards rapid socioeconomic transformation in African countries (Borgin and Corbett 1982). Our approach emphasizes the need for each people to build upon its available social "technology" for creating and sustaining institutions so they may take on new tasks and pursue new shared needs and goals. Only with this in place and under appropriate incentives can a developing country make sustained use of an infusion of modern capital and technology. This seems to have been the path taken by most industrialized economies and it is difficult to see how this process can be bypassed without severe distortions (Aitken 1959; Holt and Turner 1966; Ruttan and Hayami 1984). We return to this issue again in the final chapter.

If institutions which encourage and facilitate a diversity of human organizations are essential for the stimulation of economic growth and development, they are equally essential for political development. Political development may be understood as a process of increasing sophistication in the technology of consensual human association on the basis of rules. In Africa, however, most countries were brought together. by the force of colonial power. Colonial force was used to sustain rule, however, only for a relatively short period until alternative courses of action were taken by Africa's peoples which ultimately resulted in political independence. Still, what seems to have happened in most African countries was that instead of seeking systems of broad social organization and activity which might work to sustain the inherited state structures by an emerging, working consensus, resort was made instead to the deployment of force or the purchase of support in the name of building nation-states and rapid economic growth. This stifled opposition and limited policy options. More importantly, it led to various forms of violence such as civil wars, coups, counter-coups, etc. (Zolberg 1966).

The failure to seek viable rule systems to sustain inherited political territories through consent diverted Africa's peoples from the genuine process of economic and social development: from building on and expanding their peoples' "self-organizing" capabilities. Governments spent a disproportionate amount of their scarce resources to beef up state security apparatus, prosecute civil wars or engage in futile rounds of constitution-making which took a highly centralized, control-oriented political system for granted. Very little genuine attention, as described in Chapter 4, was devoted to the encouragement of self-governing institutions which could form the basis for peaceful and consensual association among the variety of multi-ethnic groups which exist in Africa, and energize broad grass-roots based development activities. A structure to facilitate this is needed.

The federal principle of concurrent units of self-governance within a nation-state raises the ideal of a self-governing polity to the highest possible level. It is equally possible to have unitarily governed countries which grant wide latitudes of autonomy to their local communities and hence employ federal principles within the framework of a formal unitary constitution (V. Ostrom 1973; Krane 1986; Elazar 1987).

Federalism creates two important opportunities, one political, the other economic. First, it provides a framework for the political union of diverse units which would otherwise have been separately constituted. Moreover, power can be delicately balanced to ensure that concurrent powers among the diverse units are used to check proclivities to excesses at all levels within the system. In this way the art of self-governance is continually taught and disintegration is avoided. Secondly, it enables the federating states to benefit from the economic opportunities of large and small operations at diverse levels beginning with the most basic. These unique opportunities which the federal structure provides for a country undergoing a process of modernization have not been fully analyzed partly because the study of federalism has been dominated by lawyers and political scientists, and partly because political scientists have recently tended to be more enamored with political mobilization strategies which rely almost exclusively on centralized, modernizing elites.

The point, of course, is that the federal contract was entered into by the industrialized federal countries of today in part as a strategy to deal with political and economic under-development. In each case, these countries (the United States in 1787, Switzerland in 1848, Canada in 1867) were relatively underdeveloped both economically and politically at the time of the contract (Wheare 1963; Riker 1964; Dikshitt 1975). We might add to this list late federations such as Australia (1900), Brazil (1891), and India (1950). One student of the subject notes that:

> All modern federations were at their inception, political unions covering unprecedently large areas with scattered centres of populations and comparatively underdeveloped communications . . . and federalism seemed the necessary form of government primarily for this reason (Parker 1940: 1).

The federal contract provides an umbrella under which various nationalities might pool their resources for economic and military advantage while at the same time ensuring that the human drive for self-organization in the provision and maintenance of a range of goods and services is not extinguished. The peculiar advantage of federalism is that because of its relatively loose constitution, it enables a political system to maximize the advantages both of small and large political organization.

According to Daniel Elazar, basic to the federal idea is what he termed "contractual non-centralization":

> Contractual non-centralization—the structured dispersion of power among many centers whose legitimate authority is constitutionally guaranteed—is the key to the widespread and entrenched diffusion of power that remains the principle characteristic of an argument for federal democracy. Non-centralization is not the same as decentralization. Decentralization implies the existence of a central authority, a central government. The government that can decentralize can recentralize if it so desires. Hence in decentralized systems the diffusion of power is actually a matter of grace not rights, and

as history reveals, in the long run it is usually treated as such (Elazar 1976: 12–13).

It is important that the fundamental political integrity of the separate polities within the overarching political organization which is federalism be maintained and respected. This is not to suggest a static notion of federalism. Indeed, it has been argued that federalism is a process rather than a design (Friedrich 1968). It is equally valid to argue that federalism is an institutional design which makes varying changes (differentiation or integration) possible in a diverse or "federal" society (Jinadu 1979; V. Ostrom 1987). Federalism provides a device by which these "federal" qualities of society are articulated and protected (Livingston 1956: 2; see also Dikshitt 1975; Dubey 1975). It is one, though by no means the only, method of dispersing power and thereby sustaining rule-based relationships as discussed in Chapter 12.

The keys to economic prosperity in this framework are the guaranteed peace and the advantages of a large economic union which federalism makes possible, as well as the many routine activities of self-governing political communities which constitute the realm. Here each individual is presumed to be the best judge of his own interests and needs (Tocqueville 1966). The key role of central authorities is to provide a framework or structure which discourages individual choices which would disrupt productive social relations. Thus, an individual makes decisions to involve himself or to withdraw from collective activity on the basis of his perceptions of "goods" and "bads." From this central principle results a range of public goods and services which are produced not by a central public administration system, but by a number of public authorities depending on the choices of the individuals living in the society. Various characteristics of goods (exclusiveness, jointness of production and/or use, technology of production, divisibility, etc.) can also be taken into account, and the variety of human choices and the diversities of scale economies result in a large number of organizations: large and small, in cooperation or conflict, to satisfy public needs and preferences (Ostrom and Ostrom 1977).

The advantage that this arrangement has over the central provision by a central bureaucracy is that goods and services produced can be more finely tuned to better reflect public needs and preferences. More importantly, while reducing or eliminating the pathologies of over-grown bureaucracies which include overmanning and various other forms of goal displacement, economies of scale are realized by the multitude of public enterprises arranged on different scales (Buchanan and Tullock 1962; Landau 1969; Wolfe 1979).

The federal model is particularly appropriate to countries with diverse cultures, and one of its essential elements is that it institutionalizes social divisions by creating mechanisms for the articulation of such diversity in the hope of forging unity through diversity. It should to be noted that war, modernization, and other social upheavals pose major challenges to federalism and change the nature and dimensions of intergovernmental relations within a federal system. Nevertheless, the main distinctiveness of the federal and covenantal notion is that the institutional integrity of the multiple polities is considered as necessary to the effective functioning of a federal system of government. This has been retained in most genuinely federal states even with these developments (Wheare 1963; Birch 1955; Watts 1970; V. Ostrom 1973). Indeed some long-standing unitary states are adopting federal properties of organizational discontinuity (Krane 1986) while a few others have begun to examine the possibilities of the federal system. This is a far cry from the position of some Third World scholars who contend that organizational diversity cannot be regarded as an essential attribute of the federal system (Ramphal 1979: xvii) or that a federal polity can coexist with totalitarian regimes (Jinadu 1979: 23; Oyovbaire 1985).

This chapter will now suggest that a federal system of government provides unique opportunities for relatively rapid political and economic development within multi-ethnic societies such as Nigeria. This potential contribution of the federal system of governance seems to have been evident to Nigeria's leaders up to the independence period, but lost on those who replaced them.

A Profile of Nigerian Society:
Historical, Political, Economic, and Social

Nigeria's option for the decentralized approach was dictated both by the circumstances of her historical evolution to statehood and the preferences of her leaders. Modern Nigeria came into existence in 1914 with the amalgamation of Northern and Southern Nigeria by the British Colonial Administration led by Lord Lugard. The Northern and Southern Nigeria Protectorates had been separately incorporated into British spheres of influence beginning from the middle of the nineteenth century through the activities of British chartered companies, the most famous of which was the Royal Niger Company. By 1900, these charters were withdrawn and the three separate British administrations in Nigeria—the Lagos Colony, the Oil Rivers Protectorate and the Royal Niger Protectorate came under the British colonial service as Northern and Southern Nigeria Protectorates.

Modern Nigeria contains a wide diversity of peoples, a multiplicity of complex governmental systems, and a long history before European contact, much of which is available only in oral tradition. The old kingdoms include the kingdoms of Bornu, Ife, Benin, the Empires of Oyo and the Fulani, the city-states of the Hausa and the Niger delta, besides the acephalous societies of the middle belt and the southeastern provinces. Estimates of the country's ethnic diversity vary between 250 and 400 groups. Table 9.1 contains the list of major population groups.

Each of the major ethnic-linguistic-cultural groups and communities had developed its own system of social organization and order by the time of the formal establishment of colonial administration in 1900. None of these units was characterized by an indigenous, strong, central authority. Even

TABLE 9.1 Major Ethnic Groups in Nigeria

Ethnic Units by 1960 Regions	Estimated Population	Estimated Ethnic Percentages
Northern		
Hausa-Fulani	15,370,000	29.0
Tiv and Plateau Cluster	4,860,000	9.0
Kanuri	2,484,000	5.0
Idoma-Igala-Igbira	1,404,000	2.6
Bororo (Pastoral Fulani)	957,000	1.5
Nupe	682,000	1.2
West		
Yoruba	10,800,000	20.0
Edo	1,784,000	3.3
East		
Igbo	9,180,000	17.0
Ibibio and Semi-Bantu	3,240,000	6.0
Ijaw	1,083,000	2.0
Others Unclassified	3,830,000	3.4
Total	55,670,000	100.0

Source: National Population Census (1963). Abstracted from T.O. Odetola, *Military Politics in Nigeria: Economic Development and Political Stability* (New Brunswick: Transaction Books, 1978), pp. 165–168.

where relatively large empires existed, as in Yorubaland, Benin, in the Hausa city-states or along the Coast, "native society was remarkable for its fragmented state" (Akpofure and Crowder 1966). The only exception to this rule in precolonial Nigeria came with the Islamisation of vast regions of Northern Nigeria by Fulani Jihadists from across the Futa Djallon highlands, now modern-day Senegal. They evolved a centralized form of government based on Islamic fundamentalism and feudalism. Even then, this part of Nigeria was organized as a loose confederacy of states (emirates) whose leaders owed a spiritual allegiance to the commander of the faithful based in Sokoto. The Sultan of Sokoto, in his capacity as the spiritual and temporal head of the caliphate, could appoint or depose an emir, sometimes without consulting the local council of electors. Beyond this, emirate rule was patterned after that of the caliphate: absolute, despotic, and extortionary.

In the Yoruba states on the other hand, no Yoruba oba could be a despot, even though his domain might cover a fairly wide territory. His rule was more ceremonial than real, and various checks and balances prevented a drift towards autocracy and personal rule (Atanda 1973). The Yoruba oba was made to share his authority with chiefs and with secret or professional societies with clearly defined functions. Power was carefully separated both at the centre and in the relationship between the centre and provinces. Religion provided an additional institutional safeguard against autocracy. The pattern in Yorubaland also obtained in the Bini Kingdom.

In the acephalous societies of the middle belts of Northern Nigeria and the eastern parts of Nigeria, each village was relatively autonomous and was the largest political unit. Cooperation for common defense was typical among such villages. Gerontocracy was the basis for village leadership, though opportunities also existed for the emergence of community leaders on the basis of their meritorious performance in war or commerce. Decisions were taken in the various village units in matters relating to the public and the clan by "a collectivity of those who had attained the ripe status" (Afigbo 1973; 1974; Okonjo 1974).

It was on top of this mix of political arrangements that British colonial administration was imposed through the famous Indirect Rule system after 1900. The system was first applied with relative success in Northern Nigeria up to 1913. After the amalgamation in 1914, the principle was extended into the Southern Protectorate. Indirect Rule was a modest success in the Bini and Yoruba states which had some form of centrally administered political system. However, notably in Oyo and other Yoruba states where the tenets of indirect rule made the Oba (in the case of Oyo, the Alafin) much more powerful vis-a-vis other chiefs who shared power with him, and in Egbaland which by that period had received independence from Britain, complete with separate legislative and executive councils and various departments of government, the system posed fresh problems. For the Egbas, Indirect Rule was retrogression, not progress. And the system was a disastrous failure in the Tiv lands and the southeastern parts of Nigeria. Two major reasons were responsible for failure. First, this was the part of the country which continued to present problems for the British with respect to effective occupation. Some parts were not subdued until 1918; even afterwards, punitive expeditions continued to be necessary. Second, no indigenous administrative system of the type on which British administration could extract taxes existed. Therefore, the British colonial officers raised "warrant" chiefs through whom they exercised power. In 1929, there was a major revolt against the system, led by women protesting taxes, as well as the corruption which went with the manner in which warrant chiefs performed their judicial functions in the native courts (Jones 1979: 54–55).

The amalgamation of Nigeria in 1914 formed the basis for the evolution of Nigeria's federalism. Amalgamation was a pragmatic move by the British "administocracy" in Nigeria. It allowed use of the rich resources of the Southern Protectorate (mainly revenues generated from alcohol) to bail out the niggardly Northern Protectorate administration, and to integrate administration and control in specific respects. The only departments that were amalgamated were: Treasury, Railways, Surveys, Judiciary, Army, Posts and Telegraphs and Audit. All other aspects of administration, including budget, were separated between Northern and Southern Protectorates. A deliberate policy of limiting intercourse between the Northern and Southern Protectorate peoples was promoted by British colonial administration (Nicolson 1969). The two consolidated protectorates continued to form the basis of Nigerian politics and administration in subsequent years rather than the motley collection of linguistic or ethnic differentiations which the colonials met during their early encounters. In 1939 the Southern Protectorate was split into two, and the three units thus produced were referred to as Northern, Western and Eastern Regions. In spite of intense minority representations for recognition and a number of policy moves in this direction, this tripartite division formed the basis of the first federal constitution of 1951 and subsequent ones in 1954, 1960 and 1963.

Both within the colonial bureaucracy in Nigeria and the Colonial Office in London, the preference for a decentralized or federal structure was based on the sheer size of the country, broad ethno-linguistic differences, and the administrative history of Nigeria up to 1900 (Okafor 1981: 131–147; Awa 1964). Support for federalism, however, came not only from colonial officials but also from the key nationalist figures (Awolowo 1960; 1966; Azikiwe 1943; Coleman 1958; Eleazu 1977). There were differences only with respect to the number of units within the federating system: Azikiwe was for eight, Awolowo for eighteen. And according to the late Chief Awolowo, when the people of Nigeria in 1951 were given an opportunity to indicate through their representatives at native authority, provincial and regional levels which constitutional arrangement they preferred, they unanimously rejected the unitary alternative in favor of a federal constitution (Awolowo 1966: 8).

A unitary system was indeed imposed on the country under the Richard's Constitution in 1946. But this constitution was roundly condemned by all parties and sections of the country as having failed to take full cognizance of "the diversity of cultures of the people of Nigeria" (Awa 1964: 23). The Richard's Constitution thus gave way, from 1951, to a quasi-federal constitution (which required state legislation to be approved by the national executive), and subsequently to a federal constitution in 1954. The independence and republican constitutions of 1960 and 1963 respectively thus contained provisions for a federal system of government, parliamentary democracy and mixed economy. However, even though the regions were granted considerable powers over resources and responsibilities in the constitution vis-a-vis the general government, these federal constitutions were flawed in two important respects. First, emergency powers were given to the Nigerian federal parliament to suspend the division of responsibilities contained in the constitution. This ultimately proved fatal for the constitution when the federal government used this emergency power to suspend the government of the Western Region, which was the political base of the federal government's leader of opposition. A second fundamental weakness was that the territory was partitioned artificially, on mainly administrative grounds rather than on linguistic, ethnic, economic or cultural considerations, and into three large regions. One of these regions had 79 percent of the federal territory and 55 percent of its population. Third, these artificial regions rather than the people of Nigeria were widely regarded by most of the politicians and legal pundits of the period as the repository of "original sovereignty."

These three factors made the Nigerian federal system highly unstable (Ayoade 1973; Olorunsola and Elaigwu 1983; Jinadu 1985). The situation led to and was compounded by three additional problems. First, the repression of demands for the creation of additional states based on ethnic solidarity (one, the Midwest state, was conceded in 1963, more to spite the federal government's opposition party which controlled Western Nigeria than as an act based on principle). Second, the regional governments themselves increasingly became centralized, generally reducing or withdrawing powers of self-governance given earlier to local governments in the 1950s. The violence and instability occasioned by these factors provided the circumstance for military intervention in 1966.

A third factor was the region-based single-party system which emerged in Nigeria after the Second World War. The struggle among these parties to win and control federal powers from 1959 when the first nation-wide direct elections were held, compounded the problems of Nigerian federalism (Awa 1964; Dudley 1982). The tri-part single-party system emerged not as a result of constitutional requirements, but due to the intolerance for opposition in each of the regions and later at the federal level (Adamolekun 1975).

It is important to emphasize that at least up to 1960, the trend since 1922 when the first constitution was written had been progressively toward democratizing an otherwise highly autocratic colonial system of government. Power was increasingly shared by a legislative branch which progressively gained more responsibility and prestige up to 1945 when for the first time, government officials were in the minority compared to non-official members (Okafor 1981). In 1954, self-government was granted on a Westminster political and administrative model (Nicolson 1969; Adamolekun 1986). Also, even though the state had begun to play a more visible role in the country's economic and social development, away from its *laissez-faire* role up to the 1920s, at independence the overall involvement of government within the economy was much less dominant than it became in the late 1960s and 1970s (Olaloku 1979).

Centralization Pressures and Trends

Though Nigeria's key political leaders favored a decentralized political structure such as was inherited at independence, the structure proved to be highly unstable for the reasons advanced in the last section. While there existed many differences among key political actors on the issue, there was considerable unanimity as to the crucial integrating roles which were to be played by the federal government. However, shortly after independence, a new class of elites had emerged both from the right and left whose orientations and ideas were best articulated by members of the academic community, federal public servants, and relatively younger elements within the military. They saw the relatively decentralized federal structure itself rather than its peculiar problematics as the source of instability. They became increasingly convinced of the need for a stronger, dominant, central government. This is evident from the writings of key leaders within the academic community. Ultra-nationalism, certain presuppositions about development, and their strong preference for a socialist or neo-socialist political order, all help to explain this kind of elite behavior.

None of these traits can be said to be peculiar to the Nigerian environment. It has been long recognized by political scientists, for instance, that modernizing elites tend to perceive a socialist order with its promise of radical change, coordinated planning and elite leadership as offering a more realistic and short-cut strategy for their countries' transformation (Lipset 1971; Shils 1971). Though Nigerian socialist academics have an ambivalent posture toward the state in a post-colonial economy, their preference was for a much stronger state which would promote the activation of nationalist and possibly socialist interests (Williams 1980; Ake 1984). Even among the non-ideologues however, there was a preference for a much more centralized state. This was particularly strong among economists who had a greater opportunity to influence policy (Akeredolu-Ale 1985: 35–41), although it was not exclusive to them. The failures of development planning were blamed on the federal structure (Aboyade 1968; Ayida 1968), and the dominance of the modern sectors of the economy by foreign private capital and management (over 60 percent of all shares in early 1970s) was regarded as a threat to national economic growth (Teriba et al. 1972).

Among non-economists as well, the preference was and is for an increasing role for the central government. A leading Nigerian geographer recently prescribed a "big-push" rural development strategy which is both comprehensive in scope and speedy in execution through the state as the only solution to rural under-development in developing countries (Mabogunje 1980: 118–148). For models of development, policy-makers and their advisers either looked towards socialist China or Tanzania (Ogunsanwo 1970; Mabogunje 1980; Nigeria 1981), Japan (Gobir 1970; Dudley 1970), or lately to Brazil (Forrest 1986). Many political scientists were particularly irritated by the niceties of liberal democracy and federalism which they saw as obstacles to national development. Egite Oyovbaire, a leading scholar on Nigerian federalism, argues persuasively in a recent book that the federal idea of concurrent collectivities of self-governance together with their concomitant liberal ideals of representative institutions and limited government is irrelevant for a developing country like Nigeria:

> In the second half of the twentieth century, these precepts and their assumptions are unrealistic in the case of post-colonial, ethnically heterogenous and rapidly developing societies (like the Nigerian one) for which an assertive and *dominant* role by the federal government is both desirable and necessary—desirable for national integration, necessary for the socio-economic transformation of the economy (Oyovbaire 1985: 19–20, emphasis added).

This statement captures the main-stream presuppositions of Nigerian political scientists (see Akinyemi et al. 1979; Dare 1979; and *Quarterly Journal of Administration* 1980). Few of them will, however, go to the extent to which Oyovbaire goes, denying that there exists any historical basis to Nigerian federalism (Oyovbaire 1985: 17).

The Nigerian military was the last of the major institutions to be Nigerianized. This was not only with respect to its personnel (over half of its commissioned and warrant officers were British in 1961) but also with respect to their core values. These core values stressed subordination of the military to their political masters and a purely instrumental role for the military. The senior ranks of the military were also long dominated by expatriates and Nigerian combatants who rose from the ranks. From 1960, however, the top ranks of the military were opened to Nigerian university graduates. Some of these saw the military as an instrument for achieving political transformations of their dreams. One of the architects of the first military *coup d'etat* in Nigeria recounts his experience as follows:

> My first impression which really distressed me was that it was *not* a nation-alistic organization and it was far from being revolutionary. A nationalistic army would first of all be ideological. Secondly, it would be political. Thirdly, it would be patriotic. . . . Ideologically, the core of the revolutionary officers had agreed on a programme of action to be implemented if we had successfully taken the reins of power into our own hands (Ademoyega 1981: 27, 33).

This "core" of revolutionary officers intended to change not just the military but the nation as well. Their "plan" included an abolition of the federal system, a rejection of Nigeria's "extreme form of capitalism," the abolition of traditional institutions and the creation of a new social order based on socialist precepts (Ademoyega 1981: 33–48).

This group of officers (mostly colonels) within the military were suc-cessful at bringing about the country's first military coup, but could not rule. Senior military officers led by General Aguiyi-Ironsi arrested them and seriously considered returning power to the discredited civilian rulers. From 1966 the military ruled Nigeria until the inauguration of a new constitution in 1979, and again after four short years (1979–83) until the present time. The country is currently preparing for another civilian con-stitution which is to be operational in 1992.

Virtually all students of Nigerian politics and public administration agree that the entry of the military brought about a centralization of the country's political and administrative system (Nwosu 1980; Smith 1981; Jinadu 1985; Oyovbaire 1985; Olowu 1987a). The different dimensions of this process will be examined shortly, but in essence it implied that the non-centralized political system (underlaid by federalism) was transformed into a hierarchical one with federal officials at the top. This process was encouraged not only by the academic and military elites but also by senior civil servants at the federal level. Some of the latter advocated perpetual military rule under General Gowon before the latter was overthrown in a palace *coup d'etat* in July 1975 (Ayida 1973; Dudley 1982; Adamolekun 1986). The pattern which centralization has followed in Nigeria is not the familiar one of swings of the pendulum between centripetal and centrifugal forces, but a tendency, effectively, to move toward abrogating the country's federal status. "Federal" is still used to describe the country, but it is unclear how accurate this claim is (Olowu 1987a).

As our discussion shows, it is important to underscore the fact that some of the problems caused by the structural flaws of the Nigerian federal system discussed above made *some* aspects of centralization brought about by the military supportive of national integration. There was a need to consolidate and balance the Nigerian national space, install certain basic national infrastructure (especially interstate roads, basic education, undertake land reforms, stimulate inter-regional mobility of goods and services, etc.), and to ensure uniform standards of certain key rules throughout the country. The central question, however, is whether all these have been carried out at the expense of destroying federalism in Nigeria and, while solving some real problems, created a number of serious new ones?

Dimensions of Centralization

Military rule effectively reversed the decentralist strategy in Nigeria. It is important to note, however, that a process of gradual centralization of power at the federal level had commenced under civilians, and was achieved through a process of bargaining among politicians who were experienced at working the federal system. For instance, the federal government's planning powers increased as it improved its own apparatus for coordinating regional plans. At the administrative level, even though the constitution did not provide for cooperative institutions, a number of such institutions had emerged by mutual agreement. These included institutions on establishment matters (National Council on Establishment), on the economy (the National Economic Council), and several consultative bodies including the National Universities Commission and the Manpower Board. Similarly, federally collected tax yields (especially from customs and excises) increased much faster than regional sources (personal income and produce sales taxes), though a substantial portion of federally derived revenues were turned over to the regions as statutory allocations. Indeed without an emerging consensus of the need for a relatively effective federal government capable of playing integrating roles in the federal system, the position of head of government at the federal level would not have been created in 1959. This gradual process, however, was put out of gear by military rule.

Perhaps military rule would not have mattered so much for Nigerian political and administrative organization had it not been for its length (17 out of 27 years of independence) and the manner in which it left its great legacies to succeeding civilian administrations. The first military administrator at the national level, believing that the problems of the country were caused by the federalist decentralized political strategy, announced a decree (the famous Decree 34) in 1967 by which Nigeria ceased to be a federal republic and instead become a unitary polity. The regional/state units were to become "groups of provinces" under military prefects. This action led to serious social unrest in the northern parts of the country and ultimately to the removal of General Ironsi through a second military coup. The federal constitution was restored, but this did not stop the increasing centralization of political, economic, and administrative power.

Political Centralization

Military rule centralized political power in two important dimensions. First, it altered very appreciably the balance between the federal, state and local governments. Second, it also altered the balance between the three arms of government: the legislative, judiciary, and executive. We take these in turn.

Nigerian legislative houses at both the national and regional levels have had a much shorter period of existence than the executive and judicial branches of government. At independence, it was the least mature among the three national institutions of government. As a result, its performance was mediocre and at best perfunctory. During the First Republic (1960– 61) it sat irregularly (forty days in a year) and was unable to act as an effective check on the executive (Adamolekun 1975). The legislature is normally one of the first institutions that is disbanded by the military as it proclaims its revolutionary government and suspends the constitution. This is what occurred in Nigeria. The legislative branch was reintroduced during the Second Republic (1979–1983), but was again the first to be scrapped by the military at its second coming. The common practice under military rule in Nigeria is to fuse the executive and legislative roles in the executive. The Supreme Military Council, comprised mainly of military officers, becomes the supreme law-making body at the federal level (E. Olowu 1977). The same model is replicated at the state level.

The judiciary, however, has not usually been abolished. Military rule in Nigeria has coexisted with the judicial institution. Nevertheless, its role is effectively circumscribed. Usually, laws passed by military governments (decrees at the federal level, edicts at the state level) cannot be challenged in a court of law. The judiciary also has no autonomous operational management or financing. Even though the Nigerian judicial system has shown some resilience, its development and confidence have been stunted by military rule (see Aremu 1980; Obasanjo and Shyllon 1980).

The result was to leave substantial power in the hands of the executive, power that was not always used responsibly by those military officers as the several revelations of corruption by military officers have conclusively proven (Nigeria 1976b; Dudley 1982: 116–120).

Military rule also altered the balance between the federal and state governments. Even though the ambition of Aguiyi-Ironsi to have a national government with unified public and judicial services and a centralized budget was aborted by the 1967 military coup, the essential characteristics of a unitary relationship have developed and have been maintained since then. All military governments in Nigeria have utilized his Constitution (Suspension and Modification) Decree No. 1 of 1966 (Elaigwu 1987). This decree gives to the federal government the power to make laws for all parts of Nigeria "with respect to any matter whatsoever." The decree suspends the entrenched clauses in the constitution. These entrenched clauses protect the basic federal principles of the constitution and prohibits the federal government from undermining them unilaterally. These included the state system, revenue allocation, division of powers, etc. Moreover, the regional governments could legislate on any matter only after consulting with the federal government. These military governors were in any case appointed by the head of the federal government. Their budgets and development plans were subject to final approval in Lagos. While it is true that not all military governments showed the same degree of centralized control over the states, the difference in degree has not been considerable (Olowu 1987a). It must be remembered that the extent of constitutional centralization desirable for the federal system constituted one of the key issues which led to the three-year Biafran Civil War of 1967 to 1970 (Akpan 1971; Kirk-Greene 1975).

Administrative Centralization

Once the federal system was undermined constitutionally, a number of administrative consequences followed. First, the federal government reorganized the regional system into a twelve-state structure in 1967. Some twelve years later, in 1979, the states were restructured into 19. In 1987, two additional states were created to make the total 21. These efforts to restructure the federal system helped to ease some of the structural problems noted earlier.

Several responsibilities of the regional and indeed local governments were taken over by the federal government. Certain responsibilities such as higher education, agricultural marketing, police and prisons, which were in the concurrent legislative lists, were transferred to the exclusive legislative list. Those in the residual list such as primary and secondary education, basic health services, urban development, housing, youth and sports were all transferred to the concurrent list (Nigeria 1978; Olowu 1981; 1987a). Marketing board systems were nationalized as were all universities established by the states, and the fiscal system underwent fundamental changes which made the federal government's revenue sources dominant in the national system. Income and sales taxes were harmonized nationally by the federal government. State government revenues and expenditures fell drastically compared with federal revenues and expenditures. As the federal government received all the revenue accruing from oil, which began to dominate public sector revenue from the early 1970s, it took an increasing share from the states. Whereas the federal government retained only 46 percent of nationally collected revenue at independence in 1960 and only

30 percent in 1965, federal retained revenue rose to 65 percent in 1967. It reached 72 percent in 1976 at the creation of 19 states, and stood at 77 percent before the military handed over power to the civilians in 1979.

State government revenues were 78.5 percent of federal revenues in 1960; they were 30 percent between 1975 and 1980. State expenditures were 199 percent of federal expenditures in 1960. The ratio fell to 44 percent during the Third National Development Plan between 1975 and 1980. The Revenue Allocation Law of 1981 attempted to revise this position in favor of the states, but was preoccupied with revenue sharing rather than the redefinition of tax handles. As a result, state governments remain heavily dependent on federal statutory grants, and the administration of these grants could be and is easily manipulated by the federal government (Ayeni and Adelowokan 1988; Philips 1988). Whereas the states raised 40 percent of their revenues in 1968, the percentage for the 1980–85 period was only 13 percent.

In 1975, a major administrative reform of the country's public service pegged jobs at the state level one step below those of their equivalents at the federal level on a 17-point salary grading system which was adopted nationally. Similarly, in 1976 a national reform of the local government system was promulgated by the federal government (in consultation with the states). It had mixed results, however, as it complicated the question of direct federal government contact with local governments. Before, local government was a matter which the states had traditionally regarded as their exclusive responsibility (Gboyega 1987; Adamolekun 1984; Omoruyi 1985; Olowu 1986). An important aspect of this reform of local government is its creation of a niche for local self-governing institutions (distinct from field administrations of state government) within Nigeria's federal governmental system. This development must be regarded as a positive one, even though the gains have been complicated by other factors.

Economic Centralization

One major factor which assisted the military in centralizing power was the growing importance of oil as a revenue earner in the Nigerian economic system. Most of the proceeds from oil royalties and mining rights accrued to the federal government. This enabled it to increase its direct production activities through the creation of parastatals which totalled almost 300 by 1980. Even within the mainline civil service, the emphasis was on the creation of a development-oriented service, one that was capable of managing the development process (Nigeria 1974; 1975).

Moreover, the federal government also embarked on measures which indirectly increased central government control of the economy. One was the effort to indigenise ownership and control of Nigeria's modern private sector. In several instances in which private indigenous capital was not available, the federal government had to take control or buy controlling shares in a large array of foreign-owned businesses (Ezeife 1981). The philosophy which informed the second and third national development plans (1970–74 and 1975–80), was one in which the state took the control and management of the "commanding heights" of the economy (Collins 1980). This was incorporated into the 1979 Constitution.

One indication of the increasing control of the modern sectors of the economy by the government is indicated by the role of public and private sector investment in the planning process. Whereas the private sector made an investment of approximately 45 percent during the first national development plan (1962–68), the fifth and last national development plan (1981–85) expected only 14 percent from the private sector. Central government expenditure as a percentage of the gross domestic product has also risen from 9 percent (1962) to 38 percent in 1976 and 55 percent in 1979 (Okigbo 1979; Forrest 1986). The private ownership of land was abolished by a land use decree of 1978 which vested land in the state government.

The Balance Sheet on Centralization

The centralization of the Nigerian polity had both positive and negative consequences. On the positive side, Nigeria's military rulers have been accorded acclaim in that some believe they hastened the pace of the nation's economic growth. Onyejekwe, for instance, concluded that the evidence is overwhelming that the military regime of General Gowon during the period 1970–1975 achieved a higher rate of economic and social development than the preceding civilian regime (1960–66). He demonstrated that this was true "whether we looked at gross indicators such as the GDP or whether we looked at sectoral growth and development such as agricultural, industrial, transport, communications, educational and health sector" (Onyejekwe 1981: 215).

Similarly, one of Nigeria's leading sociologists, argued the case for a positive correlation between coercion and development by submitting with respect to Nigeria that:

high militarization can be associated with high (levels of) development. For example, in Nigeria between 1964 and 1966 during a civilian regime the GNP was 4.2, but between 1969 and 1971 during the military regime it jumped to 9.1 and in 1972 to 12.1. . . . By some statistical calculation I tried to remove the contribution of oil and the figure was still as impressive as 6.1 (Odetola 1985: 17).

While it would have been interesting to have access to the methods with which the role of oil revenues was statistically discounted by the above-mentioned author, there was no doubt that growth was impressive. The economy grew between 1960 and 1968 at 4 percent. From 1970 to 1974, the growth rate was about 10 percent and fell only to 8 percent between 1974 and 1980.

It is also possible to argue that the military introduced basic changes to the structure of the federal system which civilian politicians would have found difficult to embark upon. They created new state units: 8 in 1967, and 7 additional units in 1976 to bring the total units within the federal system to 19. In addition, they restructured the local government system and attempted to involve them in the social and economic development programs of the federal government. Their decision to shift the federal capital from Lagos to Abuja continues to remain controversial.

There are those, however, who do not agree with this positive assessment. That the economy was fuelled largely by the growth in oil revenues (especially from 1973 with the Arab oil embargo when the price of oil quadrupled) rather than "better management" is evident from the fact that oil revenues contributed between 90 and 95 percent of foreign exchange earnings from 1977 to the early 1980s. Moreover, the economy has tended to rise and decline with the swings in the market for oil, creating a moderate recession in 1977 and a major one since the early 1980s. The economy declined by 6.0 percent between 1980 and 1983, by 1 percent in 1984. In per capita terms, the decline was 8.6 percent (1983), 3.5 percent (1984) and 1.5 percent (1985).

Some believe that the military government's strategy of modernization was reckless, spendthrift, inconsistent and sowed the seeds of economic crisis which have aggravated the severe recession from which the economy suffers presently. Table 9.2 shows that agriculture contributed 64.4 percent of the GDP in 1958–59; its percentage contribution fell to 18 percent in 1979–80. The three most significant contributors today are mining (26 percent from 1.1 percent), transportation and communication, and construction. Agriculture's contribution fell not only in percentage but also in absolute terms. J. Gus Liebenow (1985: 135) argues that the military's venture into agriculture in Nigeria was a disastrous failure. Other scholars share this viewpoint (Kasfir 1977) and some have also indicated that military rule led to a faster expansion of defense, far above the growth of development expenditures (Adekson 1981: 67).

Both the International Labour Office (ILO) and Frances Stewart believe that while there has been an impressive overall growth of the Nigerian economy, the spread of that growth has been minuscule. Conceding the fact that notable efforts were made in educational, health, and transportation infrastructure, the ILO report noted that Nigeria's huge expenditures had relatively little impact on the conditions of the majority of the population. It noted continuing heavy incidence of diseases and poverty, widening inequalities, greater regional imbalance, inadequate urban facilities and continuing dependency on oil accompanied by the decline of other economic sectors notably agriculture (International Labour Office 1981; see also Olatubosun 1975; Filani 1981). Similarly, Frances Stewart, in a summary of her report of Basic Needs achievement in Nigeria in the period dominated by military rule claimed:

> Despite the dearth of good statistics, enough can be deduced to be confident about the broad picture of Basic Needs (BN) in Nigeria. All the indicators of health—life expectancy, infant mortality and morbidity—show a very poor state of health among most Nigerians.

TABLE 9.2   Sectoral Distribution of Gross Domestic Product in Nigeria, 1958–1979 (selected years in percentages)

	1958/59	*1960/61*	*1966/67*	*1973/74*	*1979/80*
1. Agriculture, Forestry & Fishing	64.4	64.1	51.9	34.1	18.0
2. Mining	1.1	1.2	6.9	17.8	25.9
3. Manufacturing	4.7	4.8	7.9	8.9	6.7
4. Electricity & Water	0.2	0.3	0.7	0.8	0.5
5. Building & Construction	4.2	4.0	5.3	8.1	11.1
6. Distribution	12.5	12.7	12.8	10.8	5.1
7. Transport & Communication	4.8	4.6	4.7	4.3	19.2
8. General Government	3.0	3.2	3.4	7.9	7.7
9. Education	2.5	2.6	3.6	3.0	
10. Health	0.5	0.5	0.8	1.2	5.7
11. Other Services	2.1	2.0	2.7	3.3	
Total	100.0	100.0	100.0	100.0	100.0

Sources: F.A. Olaloku, ed. *Structure of the Nigerian Economy* (London: Macmillan Press, 1979), pp. 6–78; Henry Bienen, *Nigeria: Absorbing the Oil Wealth* (London: Euromoney Publications, Ltd., 1982), p. 8.

Nigerian health compared badly with some other African countries such as Kenya and Tanzania whose per capita income is significantly lower. All studies of nutrition in Nigeria suggest that Nigeria is on the margin of suffering a protein and calorie deficiency *on average*. Such an average situation suggests that there must be many people suffering from malnutrition, some of severe proportions. This is borne out by more micro-studies. Food production appears not to have kept pace with population increase during the past fifteen years or so; nutrition certainly has not improved over this period; the most optimistic interpretation of the figures is that nutritional standards have not deteriorated. Educational achievements among the adult population are very poor, with perhaps as few as 10 percent literate. But education has expanded rapidly recently and achievements are much greater.

The education sector is the one BN sector which has received substantial resources in recent years. Nigeria has spent rather little on health in relation to her income; within the health sector there has been a strong bias towards curative medicine and towards the urban areas. The Guidelines to the Fourth Plan conclude that only 25 percent of the rural population is covered by medical services. Water has received a negligible quantity of funds; throughout Nigeria water supplies are very poor in both quantity and quality (Stewart 1985: 130).

These were, moreover, not the only negative effects of centralized governance under military rule. Centralized rule led to a dangerous dependency on the center within the national economic system. The private sector as well as the states were heavily dependent on the federal government, the first for capital expenditure, the latter for revenue sharing. Federal expenditure on construction and transportation constituted almost a third of the GDP (Table 9.2). While these activities were carried out through private enterprise contracting, they led to their own abuses, including overinvoicing, cost inflation, etc. Private sector activities in the "modern" sector revolved around these activities and the federal government's powerful role here

(Dudley 1982; Aina 1982; Olowu 1983). The federal government was also heavily involved in control and management of the oil mining industry, also a source of top-level corruption scandals (Turner 1978). In addition, centralized governance ensured that the nation's urban system became more parasitic: it received the lion's-share of the nation's resources even though a majority of the people lived and worked in rural settlements, and the majority of national wealth was produced in those rural areas (Mabogunje 1968; Bates 1981; Filani 1981).

Putting military rule in perspective with respect to corrupt practices, Billy Dudley sums up the position as follows:

> Under military rule, with no constituents to conciliate and no electorate to be accountable to—in however weak a sense one interprets the notion of accountability—the effect of the oil boom was to convert military political decision-makers and their bureaucratic aides into a new property-owning, rentier class working in close collaboration with foreign business interests with the sole aim of expropriating the surpluses derived from oil for their private and personal benefit.
>
> The collaboration took a variety of forms, one of which was to ensure that a particular foreign interest was a valuable government construction contract for which a suitable reward was then made to the official or officials in a position to influence the award of contracts. Another method was to arrange for bulk purchases . . . with highly remunerative kick-backs built into the supply price. Yet another method was participation in a joint enterprise (Dudley 1982: 116–117).

Even though some changes were made in the Nigerian public finance systems, ultimately state and local governments became heavily dependent on the monthly allocations from the federal revenue account. Now, this dependence on oil as the engine for growth proved disastrous in two important respects. First, it was highly unstable as both prices and production oscillated on a monthly basis. It made the planning of governmental expenditures almost impossible. Second, and more importantly, it led to a concentration on "sharing" national resources rather than on the creation of new wealth. This psychology, among other consequences, fuelled the demands for more states and local governments and indeed constituted the basis for policies which were designed to eliminate or reduce other revenue-earning taxes and measures (Smith 1982; Philips 1987; Olowu 1987b).

With the increased dependency on non-tax revenues there came a tendency to enlarge the bureaucracy. The Nigerian public service grew from some 200,000 workers in 1960 to 2 million by 1980. By 1983 the public service had a size of 3.2 million employees representing 65 percent of total modern sector employees. The majority of these officials were at the federal and state levels, local governments having an estimated 10 percent of the national percentage. Even at the federal and state levels, most of the officials were to be found at the headquarters. At the federal level, 40 percent of all officials were in Lagos State; this compares with some 10–12 percent of American federal officials in Washington in about the same period

(Nigeria 1983a; 1983b). Agencies as well as officials were multiplied without any observable increase in governmental services, efficiency or effectiveness (Balogun 1975; 1983). Indeed, the few studies that exist show that at least in agriculture, the police, electricity and postal services, there has been a decline in overall governmental performance (Balogun 1983: 214–231).

The foregoing is not to suggest that civilian governments were better than the military. If anything, the civilian administration of the Second Republic was worse, perfecting the excesses of the military especially in respect to corruption and mismanagement (Forrest 1986). What I have attempted to show is that military rule led to an extremely centralized approach towards the management of what was earlier considered to be a federal society. Rather than dismantle this legacy of military rule at the return to civilian government, many of these "gains" were incorporated into the constitution, and help explain the social and economic disorder that characterized the Second Republic from 1979 to 1983 when the military returned themselves to power. What then are the main elements of this military legacy for the civilian?

First, as earlier pointed out, the philosophy whereby the national government took "control of the commanding heights" of the economy was incorporated into the constitution. While this does not preclude a strong private sector, it means that the government could, if it wished, maintain a tight hold on the economy. This provision alone (Section 16) of the constitution has led some legal scholars to conclude that the 1979 constitution tends more towards a socialist state than the mixed economy with which Nigeria has been traditionally associated (Nwanbueze 1979: 24, 28). Moreover, a large proportion of governmental responsibilities was given to the federal government under the 1979 constitution. The desire for a strong federal authority was such that the constitution drafting committee (hand-picked by the military, many of whom came from the universities) recommended the existence of only one long list of federal responsibilities with the federal government determining what states could or could not legislate. This position, however, was rejected by the Constituent Assembly which was elected to endorse the constitution. They managed to encase twelve groups of subjects under the concurrent list, but this still left the federal government with a very comprehensive exclusive legislative list covering virtually every aspect of economic and social endeavour—from banking, borrowing, mining, incomes and corporate taxation and agricultural commodity exports, to antiquities, technical and vocational education, minimum educational standards at all levels, etc. In case there was any other thing in which the federal government might wish to be involved but was not empowered by the constitution to do, a general competence clause was inserted in favor of the federal government.

This led to a situation whereby the public sector not only had a disproportionate share (65 percent) of total modern sector employment, but one in which the federal government alone by 1984 wholly owned and managed 14 manufacturing and construction companies, held majority shares in 20 others, a significant share in 15 and minority shares in 5. The companies ranged from those producing steel, fertilizer, and newsprint to those handling film distribution, groceries, beer manufacturing, automobile assembly, etc. This was in addition to its holdings in financial institutions such as banks, insurance companies, and all 16 companies connected with petroleum prospecting, refining and marketing, the latter of which were all wholly federally owned. The Federal Government's equity shares in these companies totalled N8.3 billion or some 60 percent of total investments of approximately 13 billion naira (Sanda 1986). Government thus became a big business which secured considerable access for those who controlled it not only to benefit themselves legally or illegally, but to seek to use state power to benefit their business ventures and ethnic clientele. This factor complicated politics during the Second Republic as each party sought desperately to control this huge federal largess (Joseph 1983; Forrest 1986).

The problem was compounded by a second legacy: the dominance by oil revenues of the national public finance system. Besides the instability which this meant for all levels of government to which we have already referred above, high dependence on customs revenue led to the under utilization of non-oil revenue sources at all levels; a demand for more institutions such as states, local governments, river basin development authorities, and higher educational institutions; and the collapse of financial discipline within the public sector. The Senate authorized thirty requests of additional states, but was forestalled only by the preparations for the 1983 federal elections. Local government units were increased from 301 to 781, six new federal universities were created and there was talk of creating one federal polytechnic in every federal constituency. Expensive and highly bureaucratized river development authorities were established to promote irrigation and an "agricultural revolution." In addition, agricultural revolution committees were established by the federal government throughout the states as were presidential liaison offices.

Uncompleted housing projects today litter all state capitals with the state governments making additional requests for federal money. The states also embarked on a range of hastily executed programs of public housing, free education and health services, and integrated rural development programs. Local governments were dominated by state government appointees and generated little revenue of their own. Both state and local governments' internal revenues fell in relative and absolute terms (Smith 1981; 1982; Olowu 1987b). All these organizations were heavily bureaucratized with the result that several agencies, especially at the local and state levels, could not pay the salaries of their staff without incurring loans from banks, external sources and the federal government. State governments had an outstanding debt of 13.3 billion naira in December 1983, when the military returned to power.

A third legacy from the military is the mechanism for resolving some of the problems brought forth by centralized rule in a federal society. The choice of mechanism was primarily some form of quota. The federal military government had developed an informal rule of ensuring "balance" between "North" and "South" in terms of appointments to positions— executive or advisory. It also created the Joint Admissions and Matriculation Board to ensure that entry into institutions of higher learning reflected the country's regional spread (Rothchild 1985: 86–88). The 1979 constitution specifically provides for appointments of both political and administrative types in order to reflect the federal character. The section (14:4) states that:

> the composition of the Government of the Federation or any of its agencies and the conduct of its affairs shall be carried out in such manner as to reflect the federal character of Nigeria and the need to promote national unity, and also to command national loyalty thereby ensuring that there shall be no predominance of persons from a few states or from a few ethnic or other sectional groups in that government or in any of its agencies (Nigeria 1979: 14).

The same provisions were applicable at the state level with respect to each state's local government area. How this was to be implemented was nowhere clarified, and different governments and agencies within the government adopted different interpretations (Gboyega 1984; Musa 1985).

Most debates during the Second Republic thus revolved around how to "share" jobs, revenue, salaries, institutions, etc., rather than how to produce. How to shake up the wobbling economy was really not explored (Adamolekun 1985; Falola and Ihonvbere 1985). Each of the political parties was also seriously engaged with "zoning" and "balancing" its spoils of office. There was complete obliviousness to the dangers faced by the economy. As late as 1982 the President's Economic Adviser announced that the Nigerian economy was as "resilient as ever." By the time the dangers to the economy were recognized and stabilization measures imposed, the civilian administration was nearly buried by the clamor for more on the part of its beneficiaries as well as by mismanagement and corruption (Olowu 1985b; Iyayi 1986).

Another effect of centralization was the heightening of social unrest. The civil war, as already pointed out, revolved around this issue. With the conclusion of the war on the federal side, the process of centralization was considerably enhanced, but at great costs. A host of issues which could have been resolved in a federal society at the state and indeed local level became the subjects of hot national debates—agriculture, housing, education, television, health, control of religious activities and organizations, local government and rural development to mention a few. Given the high level of centralization of social resources, it is inevitable that the central government should be involved with these questions. However, the effect has been to raise too many issues to levels where they divide the country rather than focus on those issues which might unite a federal society (Watts 1970; Elaigwu and Olorunsola 1983).

One other affect of centralization was to raise the stakes involved in securing control of central government resources. This has been particularly evident in the seeming powerlessness of states against irresponsible federal acts and the constant recourse to judicial redress during the Second Republic (Adamolekun 1982). It is also evident in the desperation for political power at the center which led to arson, murder and other election abuses in 1983 (Adamolekun 1985). Going by the Nigerian experience alone, one can argue that centralization in a complex society leads inevitably to institutional breakdown as it makes it more difficult to achieve consensus without coercion. This paves the way for military rule and further centralization, completing the cycle, but solving no underlying problems.

The military returned to power in a dawn coup on December 31, 1983, to "save" the country from complete collapse. Some of the worst excesses of overbureaucratization and overdependence on a single revenue source have been mitigated, but only to some extent. Even though an IMF loan was rejected by the vocal majority, the government took an important initiative, with the assistance of the World Bank, in order to restructure the economy. A 400 percent devaluation of the currency through a second exchange market was undertaken in 1986. The bureaucracy has been reduced by an estimated 100,000; a number of organizations (especially newly created universities) have been merged; and the new local governments created by state governments since 1979 were dissolved and proposals for new states were shelved. In September 1987, two new states were created out of Kaduna and Cross-River States respectively following the recommendation of a political bureau which collated ideas for the Third Republic. The political bureau had suggested the creation of six new states. Currently, preparations are underway to return power to civilians again in 1992. Yet little or no attention has been paid in the current constitutional proposals to the fundamental contradiction between centralization and the large and complex Nigerian society which we have attempted to address in this chapter.

Toward the Future

While many in Nigeria will readily agree that the extreme centralization to which the Nigerian system has been exposed over the last two decades has not solved many of the problems of which it was thought capable, few are ready to concede the possibility that its underlying presuppositions may be invalid. Nevertheless, the foregoing should not be construed to mean that strong objections have not been raised in Nigeria to these centralizing trends. Such objections surface again and again either in moments of crisis, at constitutional conferences, or on the pages of technical reports such as those on revenue allocation in 1978 and 1980. These voices, however, have become rather weak and muted. At other times, such as after the elections of 1983 or the increasingly northern orientation of the Buhari government in 1984, they seem to be expressions of frustration and have lacked clear analysis.

We have tried in the earlier sections of this chapter to show that underdevelopment, multi-ethnicity and an open economy need not preclude economic growth and development. Many of the industrialized countries of today were in a similar position when they saw in the federal model a logic which could be used to transform these seeming complications into advantages. The federal model constitutes a creative piece of human architecture designed first to provide an opportunity for plural societies to sustain a permanent union; then to provide specific economic advantages; and finally to provide an environment for contestation which forms the basis for law and social order in a modern democracy. This is a different strategy from a unitary system. The latter has its own logic and limitations, but is certainly not suitable for large, heterogeneous democratic societies such as is being built in Nigeria. The tendency towards extreme centralization in a complex polity like Nigeria represents political and economic suicide, as it overloads the central government with more responsibilities than it can cope with while at the same time setting forth dangerous competition among various groups for the control of the central governmental system.

Most of the expected benefits of centralized management have failed to materialize. Rather, it has produced fresh problems. There is perhaps no clearer demonstration of this truth than with respect to economic development planning. Before 1967, the consensus was that the poor results of planning were traceable, at least in part, to the federal, decentralized institutional framework. But the centralized planning framework which emerged after 1970 has failed to cure this poor performance. Rather, it has created fresh problems (Nwosu 1977; Adedeji 1980; Filani 1981). Similar arguments can be made with respect to police services. Centralization seems to have led to greater insecurity as high-ranking policemen collude with armed robbers against the citizens. In several communities, community *vigilante* groups are relied upon for security more than the national police system. Unfortunately, it is disheartening that scholars continue to recommend even further centralization of the political system to mitigate the system's failure. (See for instance Smith 1982: 12.)

One of the major problems confronting Nigeria's constitution-making efforts is the difficulty of identifying the limits of centralization. Centralization had seemed under military rule to be the cure to all the nation's ills. There is no doubt, as we have shown above, that centralization of virtually all modern economic and social activities has produced substantial results in some areas, helped along by easy (oil) money and military rule. Its great problems are twofold: first, it encouraged inefficiency, waste, corruption and a focus on distribution rather than growth at the center; and second, it failed to offer an institutional structure to encourage and sustain the broad and deep collective action needed to spread the benefits of development across the country.

This is not to argue that there are no limits to decentralization. Excessive decentralization to the large regional units of the pre-1966 era led to local excesses and political fragmentation which made military rule almost inevitable. The alternative model which we have advocated in this chapter is based on a recognition of the strengths and weaknesses of both excessive centralization, decentralization and non-centralization in a country at Nigeria's stage of economic and social development. It is discussed in Chapters 4 and 12, and is based on the logic of concurrent sovereignties which has been reasoned to underpin federalism (V. Ostrom 1987: 104; Elazar 1987: 166).

Summary and Conclusions

Nigeria is a country with great, but as yet unfulfilled, potential. Most close watchers of the events in that country believe that the greatest problem hindering that potential is managerial. I have argued in this chapter, instead, that the roots of the problem are structural and constitutional.

The structural problem has been solved to a large extent: the federal units (states) are more balanced and diverse than at independence in 1960, and a niche has also been found for local governments within the federal system. However, the inappropriateness of the choice of a centralist constitutional strategy for the governance of the Nigerian federal society is not yet fully understood. I have attempted here to call attention to this second problem confronting the Nigerian federal system. The outlines of an alternative system have also been suggested.

We are not arguing here that a rigid dualism between the federating units and the federal government is the ideal. Modernization brings about substantial, though uneven, homogenization, integration and centralization of any society. But this is a long-run and discontinuous process, and a viable federal system is an effective institutional strategy for the inevitable swings between centralization and decentralization which will occur as well as the discontinuities among various policy areas. The present drive towards centralization can thus be easily overdone if it is not counterbalanced by arrangements that ensure continuity of a system of rule which accommodates multiple systems of governance. Federal arrangements help do just this. Even though some structural changes have been effected within the Nigerian political system with positive effects, virtually all the problems which brought the "revolutionary" officers out of their barracks to undertake the January 1966 *coup d'etat* have been aggravated by the centralization occasioned by military rule: massive corruption, political intolerance, and economic mismanagement. What must now be done is to see how multiple, concurrent institutions of human collective action and accountability are the only mechanism by which these problems can be resolved.

References

Aboyade, O. "Relations Between Central and Local Institutions in the Development Process." In *Nations by Design: Institution-building in Africa,* edited by Arnold Rivkin, 83–118. New York: Anchor Books, 1968.

Adamolekun, L. "Parliament and the Executive in Nigeria: The Federal Government Experience 1952–1965." In *Ife Essays in Administration,* edited by C. Baker and M.J. Balogun, 62–69. Nigeria: University of Ife Press, 1975.

―――. *Public Administration: A Nigerian and Comparative Perspective.* London: Longman, 1982.

―――. "The Idea of Local Government as a Third Tier of Government Revisited." *Quarterly Journal of Administration* 18 (3 & 4) (1984): 113–138.

―――. *The Fall of the Second Republic.* Ibadan: Spectrum Books, 1985.

―――. *Politics and Administration in Nigeria.* London: Hutchinson, 1986.

Adedeji, A. "The Preparation of the Third National Development Plan." In *Administration for Development in Nigeria,* edited by Paul Collins. Lagos: African Education Press, 1980.

Adekson, J. Bayo. *Nigeria in Search of a Stable Civil-Military System.* Boulder: Westview Press, 1981.

Ademoyega, A. *Why We Struck: The Story of the First Nigerian Coup.* Ibadan: Exams Publishers, 1981.

Afigbo, E.A. "The Indigenous Political Systems of the Igbo." *Tarrikh* 4 (2) (1973): 13–23.

―――. *The Warrant Chiefs: Indirect Rule in South-Eastern Nigeria 1891–1929.* London: Longman, 1974.

Aina, S. "Bureaucratic Corruption in Nigeria: A Search for Causes and Cures." *International Review of Administrative Sciences* 48 (1) (1982): 291–294.

Aitken, Hugh G.J., ed. *The State and Economic Growth.* New York: Social Science Research Council, 1959.

Ake, Claude. *A Political Economy of Africa.* Essex: Longman, 1984.

Akeredolu-Ale, E.O. "Values and Underdevelopment." In *Nigerian Public Administration 1960–1980: Perspectives and Prospects,* edited by L. Adamolekun, 31–44. Ibadan: Heinemann, 1985.

Akinyemi, A.B., P.D. Cole, and W. Ofonagoro, eds. *Readings on Federalism.* Lagos: Institute of International Affairs, 1979.

Akpan, N.U. *The Struggle for Secession in Nigeria, 1966–1970: A Personal Account of the Nigerian Civil War.* London: Frank Cass, 1971.

Akpofure, Rex and Michael Crowder. *Nigeria: A Modern History for Schools.* London: Faber and Faber, 1966.

Apter, D. *The Politics of Modernization.* Chicago: University of Chicago Press, 1965.

Aremu, L.O. "Intergovernmental Relations in Nigeria: A Legal Overview." *Quarterly Journal of Administration* 14 (2) (1980): 133–140.

Atanda, J.A. "Government of Yorubaland in the Pre-Colonial Period." *Tarrikh* 4 (2) (1973): 1–12.

Awa, E.O. *Federal Government in Nigeria.* Berkeley: University of California Press, 1964.

Awolowo, Obafemi. *The Autobiography of Chief Obafemi Awolowo.* London: Cambridge University, 1960.

―――. *Thoughts on Nigerian Constitution.* Ibadan: Oxford University Press, 1966.

Ayeni, V., and A. Adelowokan. "The Administration of the 1982 Revenue Allocation Law." In *The Nigerian Federal System,* edited by Dele Olowu. Ibadan: Evans Press, 1988.

Ayida, A. "The Contributions of Politicians and Administrators to Nigeria's National Economic Planning." In *Nigerian Administration and Its Political Setting,* edited by A. Adedeji, 45–55. London: Hutchinson, 1968.

―――. *The Nigerian Revolution 1966–76.* Ibadan: Ibadan University Press, 1973.

Ayoade, J.A.A. "Secession Threat as a Redressive Mechanism in Nigerian Federalism." *Publius* 3 (1) (Spring 1973): 54–74.

Azikiwe, N. *Political Blueprint of Nigeria.* Lagos: African Book Co., 1943.

Balogun, M.J., ed. *Managerial Efficiency in the Public Sector.* Ile-Ife: University of Ife Press, 1975.

———. *Public Administration in Nigeria: A Developmental Approach.* London: Macmillan, 1983.

Bates, Robert H. *Markets and States in Tropical Africa: The Political Basis of Agricultural Policies.* Berkeley: University of California Press, 1981.

Birch, A.H. *Federalism, Finance and Social Legislation in Canada, Australia and the United States.* London: Oxford University Press, 1955.

Black, C.E. "Phases of Modernization." In *Political Development and Social Change,* edited by J.L. Finkle and R.W. Gable, 436–454. New York: John Wiley, 1971.

Borgin, Karl, and Kathleen Corbett. *The Destruction of a Continent: Africa and International Aid.* San Diego: Harcourt, Brace, Jovanovich, 1982.

Buchanan, James M., and Gordon Tullock. *The Calculus of Consent.* Ann Arbor: University of Michigan Press, 1962.

Coleman, James S. *Nigeria: Background to Nationalism.* Berkeley: University of California Press, 1958.

Collins, Paul. *Administration for Development in Nigeria.* Lagos: African Education Press, 1980.

Dare, L. "Perspectives on Federalism." In *Readings on Federalism,* edited by A.B. Akinyemi, P.D. Cole, and W. Ofonagoro, 26–35. Lagos: Nigerian Institute of International Affairs, 1979.

Dikshitt, R.D. *The Political Geography of Federalism: An Inquiry into Origins and Stability.* Delhi: Macmillan, 1975.

Dubey, A. *Yugoslavia: Development with Decentralisation.* Baltimore: Johns Hopkins University Press, 1975.

Dudley, B. "Japan." In *Nigeria in Search of a Viable Polity,* edited by M. Tukur and T. Olagunju, 8–17. Zara: Ahmadu Bello University, Institute of Administration, 1970.

———. *An Introduction to Nigerian Government and Politics.* Bloomington, Ind.: Indiana University Press, 1982.

Elaigwu, J.I. "Federalism and the Military: Nigerian Experience." In *The Nigerian Federal System: Administrative Problems Under Civilian and Military Governments,* edited by Dele Olowu. Ibadan: Evans Press, 1987.

——— and V.A. Olorunsola. "Federalism and the Politics of Compromise." In *State Versus Ethnic Claims,* edited by D. Rothchild and V.A. Olorunsola, 281–303. Boulder: Westview Press, 1983.

Elazar, Daniel J. "Federalism vs. Decentralization: The Drift from Authenticity." *Publius* 6 (4) (1976): 9–20.

———. *Exploring Federalism.* Tuscaloosa, Alabama: University of Alabama Press, 1987.

Eleazu, U.O. *Federalism and Nation-Building: The Nigerian Experience.* Ifracombe: Stockwell, 1977.

Emerson, R. "The Prospects for Democracy in Africa." In *The State of the Nations: Constraints on Development in Independent Africa,* edited by M.F. Lofchie, 239–257. Berkeley: University of California Press, 1971.

Ezeife, Emeka. "Nigeria." In *Indigenization of African Economies,* edited by Adebayo Adedeji, 164–185. London: Hutchinson, 1981.

Filani, M.O. "Nigeria: The Need to Modify Centre-Down Development Planning." In *Development from Above or Below? The Dialectics of Regional Planning in Developing Countries,* edited by W. B. Stohr and D.F. Fraser-Taylor, 283–304. Chichester: John Wiley, 1981.

Forrest, Tom. "The Political Economy of Civil Rule and the Economic Crisis in Nigeria, 1979–84." *Review of African Political Economy* 35 (May 1986): 4–26.

Friedrich, C.J. *Trends of Federalism in Theory and Practice.* New York: Praeger, 1968.

Gboyega, Alex. "The 'Federal Character' or the Attempt to Create Representative Bureaucracies in Nigeria." *International Review of Administrative Sciences* 50 (1) (1984): 17–24.

_____ . "The Performance of Local Government." Paper delivered at Workshop on "Improving Performance in the Public Sector in Nigeria." University of Ife, Ile-Ife. Mimeo (1969).

_____ . *Industrialization in an Open Economy: Nigeria 1945–1966,* Cambridge: Cambridge University Press, 1987.

Gellar, Sheldon. *State-Building and Nation-Building in West Africa.* Bloomington, Indiana: International Development Research Center, Indiana University, 1972.

Gobir, Y.A. "The Economic Growth of Japan: Are These Any Lessons for Nigeria?" In *Nigeria In Search of a Viable Polity,* edited by M. Tukur and T. Olagunju, 1–7. Zaria: Ahmadu Bello University, 1970.

Heady, Ferrel. *Public Administration: A Comparative Perspective.* 2d ed. New York: Marcel Dekker, 1979.

Holt, R.T., and E. Turner. *The Political Basis of Economic Development.* Princeton, New Jersey: Van Nostrand Coy, 1966.

Huntington, S.P. *Political Order in Changing Societies.* New Haven: Yale University Press, 1968.

_____ and Joan M. Nelson. *No Easy Choice: Political Participation in Developing Countries.* Cambridge, Mass.: Harvard University Press, 1976.

Ilchmann, Warren, and R.C. Bhagarva. "Balanced Thought and Economic Growth." In *Frontiers of Development Administration,* edited by Fred Riggs, 247–273. Durham, N.C.: Duke University Press, 1970.

Independent Commission on International Development Issues. *North-South, A Programme for Survival.* London: Pam Books, 1980.

International Labour Office. *First Things First: Meeting the Basic Needs of the People of Nigeria.* Addis Ababa: Jobs and Skill Program, 1981.

Iyayi, Festus. "The Primitive Accumulation of Capital in a Neo-Colony: The Nigerian Case." *Review of African Political Economy* 35 (May 1986): 27–37.

Jinadu, A. "A Note on the Theory of Federalism." In *Readings on Federalism,* edited by A. B. Akinyemi, et al., 13–25. Lagos: Nigerian Institute of International Affairs, 1979.

_____ . "Federalism, the Consociational State, and Ethnic Conflict in Nigeria." *Publius* 15 (2) (Spring 1985): 71–100.

Joseph, Richard A. "Class, State and Prebendal Politics in Nigeria." *Journal of Commonwealth and Comparative Politics* 21 (3) (1983): 21–38.

Kasfir, N. "Soldiers and Policy-Makers in Nigeria." *Fieldstaff Reports* 7 (3) (1977).

Kaufmann, Otto K. "Swiss Federalism." 1985, Mimeo.

Kirk-Greene, A.H.M. *The Genesis of the Nigerian Civil War and the Theory of Fear.* Research Report No. 27. Upsalla: Scandinavian Institute of African Studies, 1975.

Krane, Dale. "The Effects on the Public of Centre-Local Relations: A Cross-National Study." *International Political Science Review* 7 (1) (1986): 39–53.

Landau, M. "Redundance, Rationality and the Problem of Duplication and Overlap." *Public Administration Review* 29 (July/August 1969): 346–358.

Liebenow, J. Gus. "The Military Factor in African Politics: A Twenty-Five Year Perspective." In *African Independence: The First Twenty-Five Years,* edited by G. Carter and P. O'Meara, 126–159. Bloomington, Indiana: Indiana University Press, 1985.

Lipset, S. M. "Political Cleavages in 'Developed' and 'Emerging' Polities." In *Political Development and Social Change,* edited by J.L. Finkle and R.W. Gable, 502–518. New York: John Wiley, 1971.

Livingston, W.S. *Federalism and Constitutional Change.* London: Oxford University Press, 1956.

Mabogunje, A.L. *Urbanisation in Nigeria.* London: Oxford University Press, 1968.

———. *The Development Process: A Spatial Perspective.* London: Hutchinson Press, 1980.

Musa, Shehu. "Developments at the Federal Level." In *Nigerian Public Administration 1960–80,* edited by L. Adamolekun, 111–120. Ibadan: Heinemann, 1985.

Nicolson, I.F. *The Administration of Nigeria, 1900–1960: Men, Methods and Myths.* Oxford: Clarendon, 1969.

Nigeria, Federal Republic. *Main Report.* Vol. 1. Lagos: Public Service Review Commission, 1974.

———. *White Paper on the Report of the Public Service Review Commission,* Lagos: Public Service Review Commission, 1975.

———. *Government Views on the Federal Assets Investigation Panel 1975.* Lagos: Ministry of Information, 1976a.

———. *Guidelines for Local Government Reform.* Lagos: Government Printer, 1976b.

———. *Report of the Technical Committee on Revenue Allocation.* Vol. 1. Lagos: Government Printer, 1978.

———. *Constitution of the Federal Republic of Nigeria, 1979.* Lagos: Federal Ministry of Information, 1979.

———. *Fourth National Development Plan 1981–1985.* Vol. 1. Lagos: National Planning Office, 1981.

———. *Report of the Study Team on the Management of Intergovernmental Relations in Federal Systems.* Lagos: Federal Government Press, 1983a.

———. *National Manpower Survey 1981.* Lagos: National Manpower Board, 1983b.

Nordlinger, E.A. "Political Development: Time Sequence and Rates of Change." Reprinted in Finkle and Gable, eds. *Political Development and Social Change,* 455–470. New York: Wiley, 1971.

Nwanbueze, Ben. *Government Powers in Relation to Economic Affairs and the Economy Under the Constitution.* Lecture Series 25. Lagos: Nigerian Institute of International Affairs, 1979.

Nwosu, H.N. *Political Authority and the Nigerian Civil Service.* Enugu: Fourth Dimension, 1977.

———. "Intergovernmental Relations in Nigeria: The Increasing Dependency of the State Governments on the Federal Government." *Quarterly Journal of Administration* 14 (2) (1980): 197–206.

Obasanjo, O., and F. Shyllon. *The Demise of the Rule of Law in Nigeria Under the Military: Two Points of View.* Ibadan: Institute of African Studies, University of Ibadan, Occasional Publication, No. 33, 1980.

Odetola, T.O. *Guns, Pens and Words: The Military, the Politicians and the Intelligensia in the Process of Political Mobilisation.* Inaugural Lecture. Ile-Ife: University of Ife, 1985.

Ogunsanwo, A. "Institutional and Administrative Perspectives for National Development: The Case of Tanzania." In *Conference on Institutional and Admininistrative Perspectives for National Development,* edited by M. Tukur and T. Olagumju, 24–34. Zaira: Baraka, 1970.

Okafor, S.O. *Indirect Rule: The Development of Central Legislature in Nigeria.* Survey, Thomas Nelson, 1981.

Okigbo, P.N.C. "Ideological Perspectives of Public Sector Role in the Nigerian Economy." In *Public Sector Role in Nigerian Development,* 1–15. Lagos: Nigerian Economic Society, 1979.

Okonjo, M. *British Administration in Nigeria 1900–1950: A Nigerian View.* New York: Nok Publishers, 1974.

Olaloku, F.A., ed. *Structure of the Nigerian Economy.* London: Macmillan, 1979.

Olatubosun, Dupe. *The Neglected Rural Majority.* Ibadan: Nigerian Institute of Social and Economic Research, 1975.

Olorunsola, V.A., and J.I. Elaigwu. "Federalism and the Politics of Compromise." In *State Versus Ethnic Claims: African Policy Dilemmas,* edited by D. Rothchild and V.A. Olorunsola, 281–303. Boulder: Westview Press, 1983.

_____, ed. *The Administration of Social Services in Nigeria: The Challenge to Local Governments.* Ile-Ife: Local Government Training Program, 1981.

_____. "The Nature of Bureaucratic Corruption in Nigeria." *International Review of Administrative Sciences* 49 (3) (1983): 343–352.

_____. "Bureaucratic Corruption and Public Accountability in Nigeria: An Assessment of Recent Developments." *International Review of Administrative Sciences* 60 (1) (1985a): 7–12.

_____. "Nigeria: Local Government Changes." *West Africa.* London, 1985b: 2,210–2,211.

_____. "A Decade of Local Government Reform in Nigeria: 1976–1986." *International Review of Administrative Sciences* 52 (3) (1986): 287–299.

_____. "Nigeria: Federal and State Transfers to Local Governments, 1970–1987." Washington, D.C.: World Bank Background Paper, 1987a. Mimeo.

_____, ed. *The Nigerian Federal System: Administrative Problems Under Civilian and Military Governments.* Ibadan: Evans Press, 1987b.

Olowu, E.O. "The Legislative Process Under the Military: The Nigerian Experience." *Quarterly Journal of Administration* 15 (2) (1977).

Olson, Mancur. *The Logic of Collective Action.* Cambridge, Mass.: Harvard University Press, 1965.

Omoruyi, O. "Beyond the Local Government Reform of 1976." In *Nigerian Public Administration 1960–1980,* edited by L. Adamolekun, 183–194. Ibadan: Heinemann Books, 1985.

Onyejekwe, Okeyh. *The Role of the Military in Economic and Social Development: A Comparative Regime Performance in Nigeria 1960–1979.* Washington, D.C.: University Press of America, 1981.

Ostrom, Vincent. "Can Federalism Make a Difference?" *Publius* 3 (2) (Fall 1973): 197–238.

_____. *The Political Theory of a Compound Republic: Designing the American Experiment.* Rev. ed. Lincoln, Neb.: University of Nebraska Press, 1987.

_____ and Elinor Ostrom. "Public Goods and Public Choices." In *Alternatives for Delivering Public Services: Toward Improved Performance,* edited by E.S. Savas, 7–49. Boulder, Colorado: Westview Press, 1977.

Oyovbaire, S.E. *Federalism in Nigeria: A Study in the Development of the Nigerian State.* London: Macmillan, 1985.

Parker, R.S. "Australian Federation: The Influence of Economic Interests in Political Pressures." *Historical Studies in Australia and New Zealand* 4 (1940): 1–24.

Philips, A.O. "Fiscal Goals and the Revenue Allocation System." In *Federalism and Military Rule: The Nigerian Experience,* edited by Dele Olowu. Syracuse, New York: Maxwell School of Citizenship and Public Affairs, forthcoming 1989.

Phillips, Dotun. "Revenue Allocation." In *The Nigerian Federal System,* edited by Dele Olowu. Ibadan: Evans Press, 1987.

Pye, Lucian. "The Nature of Transitional Politics." In *Political Development and Social Change,* edited by J.L. Finkle and R.W. Gable, 538–550. New York: John Wiley, 1971.

Ramphal, S.S. "Keynote Address." In *Readings on Federalism,* edited by A.B. Akinyem, et al., xiii–xxv. Lagos: Nigerian Institute of International Affairs, 1979.

Riggs, F.W. *Administration in Developing Countries: The Theory of Prismatic Society.* Boston: Houghton Mifflin, 1964.

Riker, William H. *Federalism: Origin, Operation and Significance.* Boston: Little, Brown and Company, 1964.

Rostow, W.W. *Politics and the Stages of Growth.* London: Cambridge University Press, 1971.

Rothchild, D. "State-Ethnic Relations in Middle Africa." In *African Independence: The First Twenty-Five Years,* edited by A.M. Carter and P. O'Meara, 71–96. Bloomington, Ind.: Indiana University Press, 1985.

Ruttan, V.W., and Y. Hayami. "Toward a Theory of Induced Institutional Innovation." *Journal of Development Studies* 20 (July), 1984.

Sanda, A.O. *Minimum Government and the Sociology of Nigeria's Public Administration.* Inaugural Lecture Series 16. Nigeria: University of Ife, 1986. Mimeo.

Shils, Edward. "The Intellectuals in the Political Development of the New States." In *Political Development and Social Change,* edited by J.L. Finkle and R.W. Gable, 249–276. New York: John Wiley, 1971.

Smith, B. "Federal-State Relations in Nigeria." *African Affairs* 80 (320) (1981): 355–378.

––––––. "The Revenue Position of Local Government in Nigeria." *Public Administration and Development* 2 (1) (1982): 1–13.

Stewart, Frances. *Basic Needs in Developing Countries.* London: Longman, 1985.

Teriba, O., E.C. Edozien, and M.O. Kayode. "Some Aspects of Ownership and Control Structure of Business Enterprise in a Developing Economy: The Nigerian Case." *Nigerian Journal of Economic and Social Studies* 14 (1) (1972).

Tocqueville, Alexis de. *Democracy in America.* Edited by J.P. Mayer. New York: Doubleday Anchor Books, 1966.

Todaro, M.P. *Economic Development in the Third World.* 2d ed. New York: Longman, 1981.

Toyin, Falola, and Julius Ihonvbere, eds. *The Rise and Fall of Nigeria's Second Republic 1979–84.* London: Zed Press, 1985.

Turner, Terisa. "Commercial Capitalism and the 1975 Coup." In *Soldiers and Oil: The Political Transformation of Nigeria,* edited by K. Panter-Brick. London: Frank Cass, 1978.

Ward, Robert E. "Authoritarianism as a Factor in Japanese Modernization." *In Political Development and Social Change,* edited by J.L. Finkle and R.W. Gable, 478–484. New York: Wiley, 1971.

Watts, Ronald L. *Administration in Federal Systems.* London: Hutchinson Educational, 1970.

Wheare, K.C. *Federal Government.* 4th ed. London: Oxford University Press, 1963.

Williams, Gavin, ed. *State and Society in Nigeria.* Idanre: Afrografika Publishers, 1980.

Wolfe, Charles. "A Theory of Non-Market Failure: Framework for Implementation Analysis." *Journal of Law and Economics* 22 (1979): 107–139.

Zolberg, A. *Creating Political Order: The Party-States of West Africa.* Chicago: Rand McNally, 1966.

10

The Problem of Sovereignty
in Human Affairs

Vincent Ostrom

Human beings are fated to live in a realm of ideas and to attempt to make the best of their circumstances by using ideas to shape their relationships both with the material conditions and resources of the world and with other human beings. Wherever ideas are used to take some thing or some relationships into account and transform it into other things or relationships, we can view the experience as artisanship and what is created as artifacts. Artifacts, then, are human creations drawing upon ideas or conceptions to fashion or create something. In studying the realm of the artifactual, an important element for human understanding is an awareness of the ideas and techniques that are used in the creation of any artifact and of the purpose to be served by any creative effort.

The objects used in human artisanship have their distinctive qualities; and how they reveal their potentials requires a knowledgeable awareness and skill on the part of any artisan. The quality of what is fashioned depends upon the sophistication and skill of artisans including that level of sophistication which conveys a sense of an aesthetic appreciation to others.

When human artisanship turns to the structuring of relationships among human beings, it is human beings who are both the materials being acted upon and the artisans who are involved in conceptualizing and creating patterns of relationships as ways of life in human societies. Such structures may be so deeply imbedded in habits and traditions that they are assumed to be natural and to have an organic quality of their own. Generations of people come and go; but patterns of organization that are constitutive of distinctive ways of life come to be identified as distinguishing peoples, cultures, and societies that persist apart from the coming and going of particular generations of individuals.

Whenever peoples of different cultural traditions and ways of life interact with one another, they develop some measure of conscious awareness of the differences in ways that people think, feel, and act in relation to one another in different societies. In the course of time, human beings have come to give critical scrutiny to the way that ideas and beliefs permit human beings to relate to one another both in the accomplishment of different tasks and in fashioning ways of life that reflect qualitative considerations of basic importance for human beings. Life has meaning in the realm of ideas for what people do and accomplish, how they relate to one another, and for what feelings are evoked by some ultimate sense of achievement represented by such concepts as grace, honor, virtue, freedom, justice, equality, and well-being.

With the development of written languages and the amplification of human knowledge that has accrued as a consequence of writing, increasingly large domains of human relationships have been subject to conscious human efforts to order relationships in explicit ways. Since the dawn of history, these efforts have gained expression in efforts to establish empires in one form or another. The Egyptian, Babylon, Chinese, Persian, Macedonian, and Roman empires are among the more ancient of these traditions. So are the Mayan, Incan, Ghanaian, Mali, Songhay, and other traditions. The German, Russian, Turkish, Spanish, Portuguese, British, French, Dutch, and Japanese empires are more recent manifestations of imperial traditions that extend into modern times.

The disintegration of the first German (Holy Roman) empire at the beginning of the nineteenth century, the Spanish empire through the nineteenth century, and the Austrian, British, Dutch, French, and Portuguese empires, and the second and third German empires in the twentieth century have been accompanied by efforts to conceptualize political orders that are identified as nation-states. To the extent that the concept of nation has a distinctive referent, it is to a people who share a common language, literature, and cultural tradition. It is the concept of state that has become increasingly important in the organization of human societies following the collapse of British, Dutch, French, German, Japanese, and Portuguese empires with World War II and the period immediately following that war.

The concept of state can in some basic sense be viewed as constitutive of human societies in the modern era when the peoples of the world are organized as nation-states in a global family of nations. This concept has been especially important in the organization of European states growing out of what had been called the Holy Roman Empire, the Latin American states and the Phillippines growing out of the Spanish Empire, and the African and Asian states growing out of the British, French, Portuguese, and Dutch empires. As an artifact which, in human hands, has a perhaps unique capacity to impose and sustain itself among many peoples, some attention to its theoretical roots may be useful in understanding both its positive and negative implications for human beings.

In the global family of nations, the concept of state is usually associated with a theory of sovereignty which presumes that each state is fully independent of each other state and each state is fully responsible for the governance of its own internal affairs. Sovereignty means authority to govern. If each state is sovereign, it is independent and has authority to govern within its territorial domain. According to this conception, each state is exclusively responsible for what goes on within its own borders. The working institutional attributes associated with sovereignty in the organization of particular nation-states within the family of nations have been subject to significant disputation among the peoples comprising those nation-states, however. Thus, any given expression of sovereignty within a given nation-state refers to the authority to govern a particular population, growing from its particular experience.

The disputation about patterns of order in human societies is grounded in a fundamental tension which needs to be examined first. That issue will be treated in the next section on the problem of order. Three ways in which human beings have attempted to resolve the problem of order will then be considered. One is to rely upon a single sovereign (a single authority) that rules over society. Another is to rely upon a sovereign authority that is confined by certain social and legal processes within a society. A third is to rely upon the reiteration of principles of self-government in a system of constitutional rule.

When viewed from this perspective, the problems of centralized African states are not something uniquely African. While the source of these problems is inherent in the conceptions that are used by any people to create order in their society, these solutions to the problem of order are grounded in the human condition more generally rather than in any peoples' unique condition. Thus parallel problems and failures of other peoples may enable African peoples to discern the causes of their troubles and conceive of remedies which may enable them to better order their relationships with one another. Similarly, other peoples' successes with these same problems may help Africans select conceptions, principles, and institutions from their own rich history to address these problems, just as Africans' ultimate solutions may open new doors to other peoples of the world.

The Problem of Order

To begin, let us assume that human beings are able to relate to one another in two fundamentally different ways. One is evoked by threat of aggression where there is a tendency for conflict to escalate into hostility, enmity, and violence. Another is evoked by patterns of respect and reciprocity. The one might be characterized as warfare and the other as peace. Given certain assumptions of human fallibility, limited resources, imperfect socialization, etc., the conditions of peace can be achieved only within the bounds of mutual understanding where people can bind themselves to act in conformity with that mutual understanding.

Shared expectations about the appropriate limits to respectful relationships among human beings can be conceptualized with reference to rules. Some patterns of conduct are beyond the limits of propriety and are proscribed as improper. Other patterns of behavior are conceived as being within the scope of respectful relationships and are thus allowable or permitted. However, temptations always arise for some not to act in conformity with these mutual expectations. If rules cannot be made binding in human relationships, the advantages that accrue from mutually respectful relationships will give way to threats, enmity, and hostility.

All human societies, therefore, confront the task of how to maintain the rule-ordered relationships necessary for mutually respectful communities of relationships. To do so requires that rules be made binding in human relationships; and this condition, in turn, depends upon potential recourse to sanctions when rules are violated and human beings offend the norms of propriety for maintaining respectful relationships in human societies. Maintaining acceptable standards of human relationships always depends upon potential recourse to some form of sanction, punishment, or coercion.

This is the fundamental dilemma that arises in all human societies. Mutually respectful relationships cannot be maintained if some are free to pursue temptations to prey upon others. Those devoted to peace and goodwill must have recourse to instruments of coercion to defend themselves from those who would prey upon and exploit others. This is a source of tension that can never be fully resolved in human societies and must always be a subject of discussion and disputation among the peoples comprising nation-states. As we will suggest below, solving the problem in any one way means that the basic tensions are likely to manifest themselves in characteristic ways.

This problem is greatly magnified as human beings attempt to maintain configurations of rule-ordered relationships that affect millions of people over extended geographical domains. The rule-ruler-ruled relationship is the primary focus of what is referred to as institutions of government in human societies. It is these institutions that are the primary object of attention in the organization of nation-states and the key linkages in the organization of international relationships in the global structuring of human societies.

As large populations and territories are organized by reference to rule-ruler-ruled relationships, basic questions arise about patterns of governance in human societies. Different patterns are possible. The basic theory of sovereignty (i.e., authority to govern), as formulated by Thomas Hobbes, is associated with the rise of the modern state through the absolute princes and absolute monarchs of Europe. That doctrine was contested on two fronts. One was based upon a conception of the organic character of society that demanded respect for the autonomy of certain institutions within the society. The other source of contestation was the differentiation of legislative and judicial prerogatives from executive functions in establishing a rule of law. This is the foundation for what Germans call a *Rechtsstaat*. A third conceptualization is associated with federal republics where institutions of government are themselves formulated and governed by reference to constitutions as fundamental law. Each will be considered in turn, since many tensions and puzzles in history and in contemporary Africa can be understood in light of these considerations.

The Absolute Sovereign

The theory of the absolute sovereign is based upon the presupposition that peaceful relationships in human society require limits that can only be achieved through commonly accepted rules that can be made binding in human relationships by recourse to some form of coercion. In Hobbes's expression, "covenants (commonly accepted rules), without the sword, are but words, and of no strength to bind a man at all" (Hobbes 1960: 169; my parentheses). If human beings are to be bound to observe rules of law, it is necessary to have recourse to rulers who will wield the sword of justice to secure the enforceability of law.

To make rules binding in human relationships requires recourse to a fundamental inequality in human societies where rulers enforce rules in relation to those who are ruled. In achieving a resolution to this problem, Hobbes presumes that any system of law must be a coherent body of law that is consistent in its various provisions. This presumes a unity of law. To achieve a unity of law, Hobbes further presumes that there must be a unity of power. The unity of a commonwealth depends upon a unity of law; and the unity of law depends upon a unity of power. There must be a single ultimate source of authority that has the last say in formulating, enforcing, and adjudicating law and exercising the prerogatives of government if the multitude of people forming a commonwealth are to achieve peace and concord.

A unity of power implies a monopoly over the powers of government including the powers of the sword that are necessary for the maintenance and enforcement of rules of law. A unitary centralized state implies some single center of ultimate authority which is the source of law, determines the application of law, and enforces law throughout a society. A basic puzzle arises when it is recognized that such an ultimate source of law cannot itself be held accountable to a rule of law. Instead, as the source of law it is above the law. From this formulation, it follows that the prerogatives of rulership in a society are unlimited, inalienable, absolute, and indivisible. A unity of power implies a monopoly of authority relationships in a society and the basic characteristics of a monopoly are that it is indivisible, absolute, unlimited, and inalienable with those who exercise monopoly prerogatives.

These circumstances yield the anomaly that the sovereign, as the source of law, is above the law and cannot be held accountable to a rule of law in the governance of a society. This same authority exercises control over the lawful instruments of coercion in a society as represented by the police, the sword of justice, and the military forces. The inequality between rulers and those who are subject to their rulership under such a constitution is extreme. One center of authority has a legal monopoly of the instruments of coercion in the society and all others are subjects.

This gives rise to the extraordinary opportunities for those who exercise the prerogatives of government to use the instruments of coercion at their disposal to rig the laws to their own advantages and to use those instruments of coercion to exploit and oppress others in a society. Both law and the sword of justice can be turned into instruments of exploitation where those who exercise rulership prerogatives do so to their own advantage and to oppress and, if necessary, to war upon their subjects. The centralization of all authority in a single hand can yield disastrous consequences for a society.

Hobbes recognizes this potential and warns that those who exercise sovereign authority will be subject to natural punishment for offending against the conditions for maintaining peace and concord in society:

> And hereby it comes to pass, that intemperance is naturally punished by diseases; rashness, with mischances; injustice with the violence of enemies; cowardice, with oppression; negligent government of princes, with rebellion; and rebellion with slaughter (Hobbes 1960: 241).

The conditions of peace grounded in a mutually respectful community of understanding, thus, again gives way to war.

So long as great opportunities exist for some to exploit others, we can expect some human beings to be attracted to those opportunities like bees to a pot of honey. Some rulers may exercise their prerogatives with a gentle hand, but there will be others who use laws as traps for money and contribute to pervasive patterns of corruption. There will be others who exercise the powers of the sword on behalf of sovereigns who will themselves turn and seize the prerogatives of rulership. Instead of achieving peace and concord where human beings take advantage of each others capabilities to create a prosperous society, the prerogatives of rulership can be used to permit some to prey upon others and gain increasing dominance over society. The commonwealth, instead of becoming a common source of wealth and prosperity, becomes a predatory and increasingly totalitarian state which exploits, oppresses, and wars upon its subjects when rulers succumb to the temptations of securing great wealth and power over others. It is this model of sovereignty, however, which has guided and molded the global state system of the twentieth century.

The Struggle Against Absolutism

Jean-Jacques Rousseau recognized that the rule-ruler-ruled relationship in human societies is likely to yield perverse consequences:

> Man was/is born (to be) free, and everywhere he is in chains. One who believes himself the master of others is nonetheless a greater slave than they (Rousseau 1978: 46; my parenthesis).

Temptations inherent in the prerogatives of rulership to acquire wealth and power over others can lead both to the destruction of much of the social infrastructure in society and to an erosion of a rule of law where laws serve more as opportunities for self-enrichment on the part of a few rather than as rules for mutually productive communities of relationships.

Much of world history has been preoccupied with struggles against absolutism. Absolute centralized authority, such as Louis XIV, Hitler, or Stalin exercised, has never been sufficient to achieve peace and concord: the potentials for advantage-taking juxtaposed against fallible human nature seem always to bring about conflict. The conditions of peace require vigilance and struggle grounded in a deep understanding of what it means to be free rather than to be either masters or slaves. Since, however, the struggle can never be regarded as over, peoples who have recently escaped one absolutist master (i.e., colonialism) must stay wary of new masters, both domestic and foreign. This problem grows from the fundamental human condition, transcending culture, and might be expected to apply to human beings everywhere, including Africa. Indeed, once Africans have completed their decolonization process, they may be able to offer the rest of the world new answers in its quest, such as those suggested by Goran Hyden in Chapter 11.

The European struggle against absolutism focused upon the assertion of: (1) an autonomy for social infrastructures which were assumed to be an autonomous part of society as a social organism and (2) distinguishing aspects of governance so as to separate processes of law making and adjudication from those that pertained to law enforcement. When both of these developments are taken together, they imply the need for substantial limits to the exercise of sovereign prerogatives. The latitude for the exercise of sovereign authority, the prerogatives that applied to *raison d'etat*, have thereby been severely constrained.

The concept of society as a social organism arises from the apparent continuities of human organization that persist despite the coming and going of generations of individuals and successions of rulers. If one assumes these continuities of social life and of human civilization are desirable and ought to be maintained, then the integrity of the basic institutions within a society which structure and transmit them need to be recognized and maintained. If those institutions are seriously disrupted, the continuity of the society itself may be threatened. They are tangible expressions of deeply held norms of social life, the vehicles which revise and transmit these norms, the context of moral reasoning, and the very tools of daily life. If absolute sovereigns become sufficiently predatory, they may threaten the continuity of the society itself.

In the struggle against despotism, a variety of different institutional arrangements were asserted to be essential infrastructures that were organic to society itself and entitled to substantial autonomy from state authorities. Perhaps first among these was the family as an institution that had to do with human reproduction and the interdependencies associated with succeeding generations in the cycle of life. Another such institution was the church. From the eleventh century onward, the church in Western Europe maintained an autonomous standing and claimed to exercise judgment about the proper discharge of secular authority. Fundamental tension between the exercise of ecclesiastical authority and secular authority has persisted through centuries of European history. Similar claims were asserted on behalf of merchants who claimed a right to trade and engage in commerce in the domains of different sovereigns. This was substantially reinforced by the existence of free cities throughout most of European history. The free cities were the operating base for guilds and merchant companies and gave substantial leverage to merchants in fashioning the commercial law of Europe. This was significantly reinforced by Roman law concepts that treated commercial law and property relationships as being within the domain of "private" law subject to adjudication in civil courts that had autonomous standing apart from the imperial courts of the sovereign. In addition, many European societies claimed the right of local self-government or local self-administration so that the affairs of local communities were conducted by locally selected officials rather than imperial officials of a central bureaucracy. In some European states, the independence of municipal bodies has seriously eroded, but in many other European nations local governments have continued to exercise substantial autonomy in the governance of local affairs.

As some European states pressed toward absolutism, those efforts were met with significant resistance on the part of those who have sought to maintain the autonomous standing of basic social infrastructures ranging from family structures, churches or religious associations, commercial relationships, and local government. Periods of darkness in Europe, such as Germany during the Third Reich and Russia under Stalinist and Tsarist rule, have coincided with the successful suppression of these social infrastructures. Otherwise, contestation and disputation in the realm of ideas have rarely been eliminated in European societies; and public opinion has achieved an independent standing from those who exercise the prerogatives of government. The relationships have been tense, and the struggle continues.

European thinkers have long recognized, as John Locke (1952: 82) did, that placing the power of making law in the same hands that have the power to execute law creates "too great a temptation to human frailty." When such happens, those who have the power of enforcing law can "exempt themselves from obedience to the laws they make, and suit the law, both in the making and execution to their own private advantage, and thereby come to have a distinct interest from the rest of the community contrary to the end of society and government. . . ." The differentiation of both legislative and adjudicatory processes as distinguished from executive processes of government has been based upon Lockian presuppositions about the separation of powers. The executive can then be bound by the requirements that an exercise of authority be based upon previously established standards of law. In turn, the taking of executive action is subject to a judicial judgement by independent courts of law that must concur in the validity of a charge before the exercise of executive sanctions.

By distinguishing legislative and judicial processes, those who exercise executive authority find their discretion limited both by a rule of law and the concurrence of the judiciary with regard to proper exercise of executive discretion. Under these circumstances sovereign authority is substantially limited. In the absence of autonomous legislative and judicial processes, those who exercise sovereign prerogatives as Locke recognized can make and suit the law to their own private advantage and to the disadvantage of others in a society.

These observations and principles of political architecture face the disadvantage of an almost contemptuous familiarity. Their logic and structural implications must not, though, be dismissed on such grounds, because they lack *avant garde* appeal, or offer no simple guarantees of a "new age" as do Marxist-Leninist and other centralist traditions. The separation-of-powers tradition offers only the prospect that the struggle to maintain human freedom in the context of political order can continue as an unending struggle.

Constitutional Rule

A different resolution to the organization of government in human societies can be achieved by building upon the foundations of a democratic society, rather than interposing limits upon those who presume to exercise sovereign authority to rule over society. Much the same results are achieved, but the logic for conceptualizing and designing such a system of government is different.

Hobbes recognized that three forms of government might exist. A monarchy existed when one individual exercised sovereign prerogative. An aristocracy is the form of government where one assembly of a few exercise sovereign prerogative; a democracy where one assembly of all citizens govern a society. In the last case, a puzzle occurs which suggests how human societies might construct a form of government where those who exercise the prerogatives of government can be made subject to a rule of law.

This puzzle arises from the circumstance that for there to be government by an assembly of all citizens, there must necessarily exist a shared common understanding about the rules that apply to the conduct of an assembly and what it means to rule by assembly. Rule by an assembly in governing a society requires rules of assembly in setting the terms and conditions that apply both to the organization of an assembly and in the conduct of its proceedings. We might then distinguish between the rules that apply to the terms and conditions of assembly as against those rules enacted by an assembly to apply to the ordinary exigencies of life outside an assembly. The former is constitutional in character; the latter is ordinary law. If the former can be made enforceable with regard to the exercise of governmental prerogatives, constitutional law might be enforced in relation to those who exercise governmental prerogatives. We might then think of a system of constitutional government as one where constituting rules, or "constitutional law," can be enforced in relation to those who exercise governmental prerogatives.

Montesquieu (1949: 126–127) conceptualized how small democratic societies might be formed into confederate republics (Montesquieu 1949: Book IX) and the Americans who formulated the Constitution of the United States in 1787 conceptualized how processes of constitutional choice might be reiterated to create a federal system of government where each unit of government would be subject to a general theory of limited constitutions so that all exercises of governmental authority could be subject to limits and no one would exercise unlimited authority (Hamilton, Jay and Madison, n.d.). Such a system of government is subject to a structure of authority relationships where processes of constitutional decision making are separated from governmental decision making. Ultimate authority to set the terms and conditions of government is exercised by the people acting in their constituting, i.e., constitutional, capacities. The authority of government is limited with reference to the prerogatives of persons and citizens to exercise basic powers in the government of their own affairs: their right to constitute and reconstitute forms, processes and powers of collective choice; their authority to associate with others by mutual agreement; and their rights to due process of law. Through this, the jurisdiction of different units of government is limited. Within each unit of government the prerogatives of making, enforcing, and adjudicating law are each assigned to distinguishable decision structures and subject to limits. A system of governance is then established where all exercises of governmental authority are subject to limits and a people is thereby empowered (Ostrom 1987).

Such a system works by what is sometimes referred to as "checks and balances." These achieve equilibrating tendencies where power is used to check power. The operation of government depends upon the concurrence of legislative, executive, and judicial bodies under circumstances where the operation of law and the conduct of officials is subject to open public scrutiny. High levels of contestation and disputation prevail, but the temptations for some to make and suit the law to their own private advantage is greatly constrained. In such a system, which may take a variety of forms, citizens retain the capacity to organize to engage in collective action at multiple levels, including to constitute and reconstitute new regimes of law to solve new problems. Though some might argue that Africa needs a greater concentration of authority to develop, the evidence of success of such centralized regimes is weak, as Chapter 3 of this volume suggests. Some might also argue such balanced systems are alien to Africa. However, the political traditions which Africa's people draw from are diverse, and it is difficult not to find precedents for a large variety of regimes, including constitutional ones with balanced powers. The centralized state seems more typical of Western than African traditions (Sklar 1985).

This equilibrating system works well when citizens have developed a level of shared common understanding about what it means to be free and to govern one's own affairs with proper regard for the interests of others. Under these circumstances, people can relate to one another as equals, maintain relationships with one another based upon mutual respect, develop new structures to provide for new needs, and integrate broader communities than hitherto existed, while at the same time recognizing each other's liberty to disagree and to maintain their own autonomy as free persons. Such shared understandings can serve as a mechanism to both legitimize and bound the claims of individuals in a community upon one another and thereby help protect against the despot who would manipulate one against another.

When individuals offend against the liberty of others, they must stand culpable for their wrong-doing with obligations to remedy any wrong done if any system based on free association among people is to survive. When such conditions prevail with regard to the rightful exercise of governmental prerogative, the ability of officials to lawfully use the prerogative of office to their own private advantage is limited. A system of constitutional law depends upon citizens who are willing to resist the unlawful exercise of authority by officials and press for constitutional, legal, and political remedies that will hold officials to account for their proper discharge of public office. The very process of contention that results allows for the restatement, clarification, and evolution of the underlying normative order: it sustains the process of normative reasoning which legitimizes, empowers, and regulates political institutions. At its best, it acts to enhance learning, so that human beings as fallible creatures can constrain temptation strategies and reinforce an understanding of their mutual obligations over time to extend across generations.

Conclusion

The concept of the state has a highly ambiguous place in relation to human development. The simple concept of sovereignty which presumes that the unity of a commonwealth depends upon a unity of law and a unity of law upon a unity of power yield a condition where there is one ultimate center of authority which has the last say, rules over society, and is not accountable to society. This generates an anomoly where sovereignty is inalienable with a sovereign, absolute, unlimited, and indivisible. This entails a monopoly of power which rules over society.

Such a structure of dominance yields temptations for those who are sovereign, or for those who can usurp sovereign prerogatives, to use the coercive powers of the state to oppress and exploit others. A sovereign state under these circumstances easily becomes a predatory state where laws are used as opportunities for self-enrichment and instruments of coercion are used to oppress and war upon subjects (Scott 1972; Ekpo 1979; Gould and Amaso-Reyes 1983; Olowu 1988). These conditions can be expected to prevail wherever those who are in rulership positions can make and suit the law to their own private advantage.

Where people are subject to exploitation and deprivation by others, resistance will occur. When that resistance becomes an effort to challenge those who exercise the instruments of coercion in a society, we can expect the patterns of organization that rely upon a unity of power, strict secrecy, and strict discipline to prevail in the organization of a revolutionary movement itself. Should such a revolutionary struggle be successful, those who led the revolution become the new sovereigns, and demand the right to exercise all powers on behalf of the revolution. A new absolute sovereign replaces the old sovereign. In this way, Lenin's revolutionary party became the new sovereign authority in the Soviet state creating a new ruling class whose power was "more complete than the power of any other ruling class before in history" (Djilas 1957: 38).

The basic tension associated with the creation of order in human societies is one that cannot be resolved and put aside as a problem that has been "solved." Rather, the problem is one that pervades all human relationships and requires a continuing struggle on the part of human beings to maintain proper limits upon the exercise of authority. The long and persistent struggle among the peoples of Europe against absolutism has yielded limits both in recognition of the autonomous standing of basic infrastructures in society and in relation to the application of a rule of law to the exercise of executive prerogative as being limited both by legislation and by judicial processes. These principles can be extended where the prerogatives of government are subject to processes of constitutional choice and a distribution of authority so that all exercises of governmental prerogatives are subject to enforceable rules of constitutional law. These principles of design may be useful and adaptable to other regions of our world, and deserve careful consideration.

Where limits upon governmental authority cannot be maintained, temptations will then exist for those who exercise governmental prerogatives to make and suit the law to their own private advantage. If that advantage is conceived to be great wealth and power over others, we should not be surprised that some who exercise rulership prerogatives will acquire great wealth and power. The use of that power will be directed toward exploiting others. Wealth then accrues to some by impoverishing and oppressing others. Yet, those who hold such wealth are prisoners of the authoritarian systems they have built: they can hardly walk freely among their peoples, nor relax their hold on power, even for a moment. It is these circumstances that enable one to appreciate why Rousseau's puzzle is true: "Man was/is born (to be) free, and everywhere he is in chains. One who believes himself the master of others is nonetheless a greater slave than they" (Rousseau 1978; my parentheses).

It is only when men learn what it means to be free, and struggle to maintain proper limits upon the exercise of authority so that no one is allowed to become the master of others that human beings have the possibility of creating relationships which they may freely enter and leave as they seek mutually productive patterns of human development. Absolute sovereignty creates an overwhelming temptation for some to exercise an unlimited power to make and suit the law to their own private advantage, as John Locke long ago recognized. All countries are potentially plagued by circumstance that officials will be tempted to make and suit the law to their own private advantage and to the disadvantage of others in the society. This possibility can be constrained only as people achieve the capabilities for scrutinizing the performance of officials and struggle to maintain proper limits on the conduct of officials.

The highly centralized unitary state is likely to become a predatory state. The predators may have had their beginnings as petty politicians, soldiers, or erstwhile revolutionaries. They have every incentive to increase the authority of the government and expand the coercive instrumentalities of government. They shed crocodile tears about poverty of the people, live in luxury, and build fortunes in Swiss bank accounts. But, they never look to Switzerland as the model of a society that closely limits the prerogatives of officials to critical public scrutiny by broadly enpowering the people with constitutional authority, and sustaining diverse social, economic, and political institutions in a free society.

When people use the concept of a state to fashion the patterns of organization which are appropriate to nation-states in the modern world, they need to look closely at the configuration of relationships that apply to the ordering of relationships within nation-states. The patterns of imperial authority in colonial systems are not an appropriate basis for creating a free society where people exercise a significant voice in the governance of their own affairs, or are able to organize themselves in diverse ways to provide for ever changing needs, wants, and problems. Rather than the authority system typical of Europe's imperial tradition, one might better look at the European peoples' struggle against absolutism and the efforts to establish constitutional constraints as part of the struggle for human development. These struggles have gone on for centuries in Europe, North America, Latin America, Asia, *and* in Africa. Yoruba, Ibo, and Akan societies, for example, each have experienced these struggles and addressed them in their own ways.

The task of fashioning ideas that are appropriate for constituting systems of government that are compatible with mutually respectful relationships is not compatible with patterns of dominance where some exercise power over others. The task is to fashion multiple structures of governance where people can exercise power with one another; in many situations African people engaged in and learned from these struggles in acephalous societies during the pre-colonial era. The challenge for Africans today is to discover in their own history, values, experience and traditions, a path that leads away from the highly centralized state and toward self-governance. This implies construction and sustenance of a variety of institutions to facilitate the pursuit of diverse collective goods, to relate diverse people to one another, to check central power, and to sustain the process of normative inquiry and moral choice that rely upon reasoned inquiry rather than raw power. Under those conditions, commonwealths can facilitate mutually productive relationships that enhance the aggregate wealth of the community rather than creating predatory states where some use the instruments of coercion to exploit others.

Certainly recent analyses of personalism and the erosion of constitutional government in Africa have conclusively demonstrated that even societies more communitarian in their ethics and values than the West are nonetheless vulnerable to despotic rule (Jackson and Rosberg 1982; Bates 1981). Indeed, a tradition emphasizing unity and cooperation in community affairs may be more vulnerable to the abuse of a despot than a tradition emphasizing dissent and individual freedom. Be that as it may, the challenge is real, and the task remains.

Unless people learn how to place appropriate limits upon governmental authorities and how to exercise the power and responsibility of governance themselves, they will have to endure being the prey of officials who make and suit the law to their own advantage and use instruments of coercion to exploit others. We must go beyond concepts of the state to understand the potentials for human development; we must understand what it means to engage in self-governance, and what is required *for* a people, and *of* a people that this might be done. Opportunities always carry their commensurate obligations.

Bibliographical Note

The analysis advanced in this essay draws upon standard references that are familiar items in European political thought from the seventeenth century onward. What is of critical importance is the focus upon a constitutional level of analysis which is concerned with the terms and conditions of governance in human societies and the possibility of constitutional choice where people might deliberate and set the fundamental laws applicable to the terms and conditions of governance. In the absence of deliberation and choice, the terms and conditions of government will be shaped by accident and force through war, military coups, and violent revolutionary struggles. Too frequently political scientists have viewed constitutions as mere formalities; but this circumstance applies to all law. Words on paper are mere formalities. The problem is *how* to build the conditions that make words on paper binding in human relationships, and how to confine what gets formulated as words on paper to that which can be made effective.

Hobbes's *Leviathan* is the standard account of a theory of sovereignty. Locke, Montesquieu, and Rousseau provide contrary formulations that advance the possibility of constitutional government, particularly if Rousseau's general will is viewed as the shared common understanding to be articulated as the foundation for constitutional government. The Scottish philosophers, especially David Hume and Adam Smith, contributed basic foundations for thinking about problems of constitutional choice in their emphasis upon sympathy or fellow-feeling as foundation for moral considerations that apply to freedom and justice. *The Federalist* by Alexander Hamilton, John Jay, and James Madison, explains the calculations that went into the design of the United States Constitution. Vincent Ostrom's *The Political Theory of a Compound Republic: Designing the Political Experiment* articulates the basic theory in *The Federalist* to explain the U.S. Constitution. When Tocqueville's *Democracy in America* is juxtaposed to his *The Old Regime and the French Revolution,* we find an analysis of the difference between a self-governing society organized in accordance with principles of constitutional rule and a state-governed society organized in accordance with principles of central dominance.

Three contemporary works give added perspective. Harold J. Berman's *Law and Revolution* gives an important historical account of the development of western law. To this should be added Hans Albert's *Freiheit und Ordnung* to afford a complementary historical perspective about Europe and the taming of power. The implication of the growing complexity of modern life for human governance and development is rather fully elaborated in *Guidance, Control, and Evaluation in the Public Sector* edited by F. X. Kaufmann, G. Majone, and V. Ostrom. This volume is the product of a multinational, multidisciplinary research group organized by the Center for Interdisciplinary Research at Bielefeld University (West Germany) to explore problems of public sector organization in light of concerns about the effectiveness of the modern state.

The Marxist-Leninist tradition can be viewed from these same perspectives. Lenin's emphasis upon the unity of leadership in a revolutionary party is equivalent to Hobbes's emphasis upon the unity of power. When Lenin's vanguard party exercises a unified leadership of a dictatorship of the proletariat, a single center of sovereign authority exists. The basic argument is advanced in Lenin's *What is to Be Done?* and in *State and Revolution.* Whether the state will wither away or whether Lenin's revolutionary party becomes the new sovereign, is at issue in Marx's explanation of a state as against Hobbes's explanation. Milovan Djilas's critique lends support to Hobbes's formulation. Socialist societies, such as Yugoslavia, have become increasingly preoccupied with the development of self-managing and self-governing capabilities and, in doing so, constitutional considerations again come to the forefront of attention.

Somewhat similar circumstances exist in the African heritage. African societies have been both organized as extended empires and as stateless societies. Anthropologists have distinguished between cephaleous societies (i.e., societies with heads) and acephaleous societies (i.e., societies without heads). Some of the African empires worked out constraints that yielded a taming of power; others manifest a high degree of arbitrary authority. Europe too had its cephaleous societies best illustrated by imperial France, Spain, Prussia, and by Bismarck's German empire. Switzerland and the Netherlands most closely approximate acephaleous societies. The case can be made that Europeans have more to learn by using the Swiss experience as a model than Bismarck's Reich. Africa too may have much to learn from its acephaleous societies if the challenge of the future is to fashion self-governing societies rather than state-governed societies. Amilcar Cabral's emphasis in *Return to the Source* rightly recognizes that the African peoples must draw upon their own resources to fashion their ways of life while doing so in light of the experience of other peoples in other lands. This is the circumstance confronting all mankind; and peoples in other lands will be enriched as African peoples move ahead in their own efforts to develop self-governing capabilities.

References

Albert, Hans. *Freiheit und Ordnung.* Tuebingen, Federal Republic of Germany: J.C.B. Mohr, 1986.

Bates, Robert. *Markets and States in Tropical Africa: The Political Basis of Agricultural Policies.* Berkeley: University of California Press, 1981.

Berman, Harold J. *Law and Revolution.* Cambridge, MA: Harvard University Press, 1983.

Cabral, Amilcar. *Return to the Source: Selected Speeches of Amilcar Cabral.* New York and London: Monthly Review Press, 1973.

Chardin, Pierre Tielhard de. *The Phenomenon of Man.* New York: Harper and Row, 1961.

Djilas, Milovan. *The New Class.* New York: Praeger, 1957.

Ekpo, M. U., ed. *Bureaucratic Corruption in Sub-Saharan Africa.* Washington, D.C.: University Press, 1979.

Gould, David J. *Bureaucratic Corruption and Underdevelopment in the Third World: The Case of Zaire.* New York: Pergamon Press, 1980.

_____ and J. A. Amaso-Reyes. *The Effects of Corruption on Administrative Performance: Illustrations from Developing Countries.* Washington, D.C.: World Bank Staff Working Papers, No. 580, 1983.

Hamilton, Alexander, John Jay, and James Madison. *The Federalist.* Edward Mead Earle, ed. New York: Modern Library, n.d.

Hobbes, Thomas. *Leviathan or the Matter, Forme and Power of a Commonwealth Ecclesiasticall and Civil.* Michael Oakeshott, ed. Oxford: Basil Blackwell, 1960.

Jackson, Robert, and Carl Rosberg. *Personal Rule in Black Africa: Prince, Autocrat, Prophet and Tyrant.* Berkeley: University of California Press, 1982.

Kaufmann, Franz-Xaver, Giandomenico Majone, and Vincent Ostrom, eds. *Guidance, Control, and Evaluation in the Public Sector.* Berlin and New York: Walter de Gruyter, 1986.

Lenin, V. I. *What Is to Be Done?* In *Selected Works,* Vol. II, 25–192. New York: International Publishers, n.d.

_____. *State and Revolution.* New York: International Publishers, 1932.

Locke, John. *The Second Treatise of Government.* Thomas P. Peardon, ed. New York: Liberal Arts Press, 1952.

Montesquieu, Charles Louis de Secondat. *The Spirit of the Laws.* New York: Hafner, 1966.

Olowu, Dele. "Bureaucratic Morality in Africa." *International Political Science Review* 9 (1) (1988): 215–229.

Ostrom, Vincent. *The Political Theory of a Compound Republic: Designing the Political Experiment.* Revised edition. Lincoln, Nebraska: University of Nebraska Press, 1987.

Rousseau, Jean-Jacques. *On the Social Contact.* Edited by Roger D. Masters; translated by Judith P. Masters. New York: St. Martins Press, 1978.

Scott, James. *Comparative Political Corruption.* Englewood Cliffs, New Jersey: Prentice-Hall, 1972.

Sklar, Richard L. "The Colonial Imprint on African Political Thought." In *African Independence: The First Twenty-Five Years,* edited by G. Carter and P. O'Meara, 1–30. Bloomington, Ind.: Indiana University Press, 1985.

Tocqueville, Alexis de. *Democracy in America.* Phillips Bradley, ed. New York: Alfred A. Knopf, 1945.

_____ . *The Old Regime and the French Revolution.* Garden City, New York: Doubleday, 1955.

11

Reciprocity and Governance in Africa

Goran Hyden

Introduction

The last of continents to be gripped by the drive for independence, Africa is still engaged in exploring the parameters of governance. This search for viable independence started off in an exuberant mood. Having been born into a world characterized by its faith in progress, Africa's first steps towards sustainable *uhuru* were inevitably influenced by the spirit that gripped the rest of the world. Compared to Asia and Latin America, Africa was viewed as having a special opportunity to make rapid and steady progress because it was believed to lack the oppressive social structures and cultural impediments that observers saw present on the other two continents (Hunter 1969).

In this climate, the temptation of African leaders to ignore the past and treat their societies as "clean slates" was understandably great. They wanted their countries to catch up with the more industrialized parts of the world as quickly as possible and chose the most positive features from their experience. Consequently, the model of progress was foreign and modern rather than domestic and traditional.

Having just emerged successful from a struggle against external occupation and exploitation, the prevailing expectation was to develop their societies without the pains and strains that had accompanied the march to modernity in other parts of the world. Political systems were set up accordingly. Rapid progress required national unity and unity, in turn, demanded a one-party system, the argument went. Politics became an instrument of social engineering; the state an engine of change.

Against this backdrop, it is not surprising that the first decades of independence have been a period of endless, sometimes shameless, experimentation with the continent being treated much like an empty box. Pet notions of development from both the East and the West have been applied to Africa with little regard for constraints and opportunities on the continent, usually at the expense of domestic values and institutions.

Thirty years after Sudan (1956) and Ghana (1957) initiated the wave of political independence in Africa it is clear that it was an imaginary expectation that the transfer of power from imperial nations to sovereign states would usher in an era of rapid economic growth, a broadening of social development programs, an upliftment in living standards of the masses of the people, and a combination of effective and democratic governments. Progress has proved much harder to achieve than Nkrumah held out when counseling fellow nationalists in the late 1950s to "seek ye first the political kingdom and everything else will be added unto ye." Today Africa knows that there is nothing magic about the political kingdom. If anything, as this chapter will argue, it is the root of the present development crisis facing the continent.

Thus, this chapter starts from the assumption that the current African malaise can be best understood by a critical examination of the conditions of governance in Africa. By "governance" we mean here the use of political authority to promote and enhance societal values—economic as well as non-economic—that are sought by individuals and groups. It refers to the processes whereby values in society, at different levels, are being realized. The concept is broader than "government" in that it presupposes that values are being allocated and defended by structures other than the government or the state. More specifically the chapter wishes to highlight the dilemmas of governance that exist in societies where the growth of pristine states was aborted by colonial conquest, and a set of secondary state structures with no organic roots in African society were created in their place.

The Conditions of Governance in Africa

To fully appreciate the conditions of governance in Africa and the constraints and opportunities contained therein, two major modifications in our theoretical and methodological outlook are necessary at this point. The first is that endogenous factors are as important as exogenous ones and that informal processes are as significant as formal ones. More specifically, for example, the question of governance in Africa has to transcend the conventional state/market dichotomy. The second is the need for a reconceptualization of the actor/structure dichotomy that has characterized the political science literature in recent years in order to better grasp what the prospects for changes in styles and forms of governance might be. A complimentary task would be a reconceptualization of the state which reflected and was consistent with the implications of this analysis. The last is the overall goal of this volume.[1]

The Relevance of Endogenous Phenomena

One of the most striking features of the debate about Africa in the past few years has been the "discovery" of the potency of indigenous African values and organizations. While formal structures—both governments and markets—have been collapsing in many countries, the resilience and vibrancy of things African have stood out particularly sharply. The growing recognition thereof in the academic literature has more recently had its spinoff effects in the thinking of the international donor community. There is at last respect for the importance of community-based, organic growth.

This "discovery" is evident in many fields: in the growth of interest in local farming systems; in the burgeoning literature on the informal sector; in the expanding research on gender and household issues, etc. These studies point in a similar direction: modernization is not a unilinear process; customary institutions have a life of their own and combine with modern values in new and often surprising ways; economic processes and social relations rarely resemble those prescribed in capitalist or socialist blueprints; and government agencies often fumble in darkness when attempting to implement development policies.

Sara Berry (1985), for instance, demonstrates in a well documented study that agricultural accumulation in Western Nigeria in the past three decades did not entail dispossession, nor did it create a rural proletariat, a middle peasantry, or a class of capitalist farmers. Instead, access to land and the control of labor were organized in terms of descent-group and community relations. Such relations also determined their entry into rural commerce and into the tertiary sector. The persistence of descent-based relations did not prevent differentiation from taking place; indeed, it has become one of the most obvious features of contemporary Nigerian society. The point of her study, however, is that it occurs on terms and in disguises that are very different from those that the earlier literature suggested. Other recent research on the rural economies of Africa (Guyer 1981; Jewsiewicki and Letourneau 1985; and Forrest 1986) makes it clear that peasant production and exchange remains principally oriented toward use-values, that the consumption imperative and kinship obligations more fully than the commodity exchange dictate the logic of the rural economy, that the "unofficial" economy is generally predominant in Africa and enables peasants to articulate with the capitalist trading sector in order to satisfy peasant-specific interests. Sixty to eighty percent of peasant labor time in East Africa is reported to be devoted to farming for direct household consumption (Lele and Chandler 1981: 111). Even in one of the most highly commercialized cash cropping areas of West Africa—the groundnut basin of Senegal and Gambia—cultivators are above all determined to maintain their rice fields or millet crops, as this remains the primary means of feeding the family (Guyer 1981: 115). Intercropping, so characteristic of peasant household production throughout sub-Saharan Africa, is another case in point. Mixing food crops intended for household consumption with commodity crops is a way of relying on cash income for food purchases in case the food crops fail and, conversely, to be able to turn to home-grown foods should the cash crops prove insufficient (Richards 1985: 26–28).

The priority of obtaining household necessities is extended to trading. The African peasants, by and large, enter market relations mainly in order to obtain items that will be consumed or supplied by relatives; its prime purpose is to obtain use-values. The principal mechanisms through which peasants engage in exchange is unofficial trade, i.e. barter or cash exchanges that take place outside the state marketing system and apart from the officially condoned private channels. African peasants have increasingly turned to unofficial trade in the past ten years because of the failure to provide satisfactory terms of trade to producers and the underdevelopment of the private trading sector. In a number of cases, particularly in West Africa, this has meant a revival of systems of barter and of monetary exchange networks that functioned well in precolonial times, never quite disappeared in colonial days, and are now serving as an alternative means of obtaining food, material necessities and liquid capital. These unofficial trade circuits have been absorbing an increasingly high percentage of the cash crops produced, as much as 90 percent of the surplus food crops and the vast majority of the household-fabricated artisanal goods (Bates 1981: 82–85; Lele and Chandler 1981: 101–105; and Hart 1982: 87).

I have suggested elsewhere (Hyden 1980; 1983) that these phenomena cannot be treated merely as peripheral. They all derive from a social logic that is still predominant in societies where the peasantry has not yet been effectively captured by other social classes. Non-capitalist values are alive in these settings because the whole economy is based on principles that have little in common with either capitalism or socialism (in its modern trappings). Thus, since the African economies are still dominated by small-holder producers, dependent on family labor to satisfy their levels of consumption and subject to taxation by a distant authority, one can legitimately talk of the presence of a peasant mode of production. The reason why it should be called a "peasant" mode as opposed to a "familial" or "tributary" mode is that its organization transcends family boundaries and that its principal characteristic is not merely the payment of tribute to a ruling caste. The peasant mode, by contrast, is characterized by the fact that the producers themselves largely determine and approve the basic features of the economy. For instance, although it is well known that land tenure patterns vary tremendously in Africa, distribution of land and organization of production are decided either by those who till the land or by community leaders (Guyer 1981: 91–92). Berry's study (1985: 64–67) confirms that among the Yoruba of Western Nigeria, ownership and regulation of land is based strictly on kinship, with access to land being regulated through membership in descent groups. Even where conscious efforts have been made to capture the peasantry, this pattern has not changed. Thus, for instance, in Tanzania, where some five million peasants were affected by a compulsory villagization program in the mid-70s, peasant households continued to wield direct control over the production process (Bernstein 1981: 60; Bryceson 1982: 558).

Controversy has arisen around the question of whether peasants cease to be peasants when they are uncaptured by the state or those who control it (Kasfir 1986). How can they continue to be peasants if in the definition one element is their subordination to a distant revenue-collecting authority? The point is that surplus appropriation does not necessarily cease with non-existent or ineffective revenue collections by the state nor with peasant withdrawal into unofficial trade. Funds are still appropriated—though in a more informal fashion—and keep circulating within networks that are specified by relations of affection. These relations are rarely supportive of specific bourgeois class interests or government objectives. It is in this sense that such withdrawal from state control or the formal economy is real and subversive of official policy.

The peasant mode of production, thus, gives rise to economic activities that revolve around personalistic and affective ties, involving the immediate or extended family, lineage relations, village or community bonds, and religious obligations. This economy is not necessarily egalitarian—capital is appropriated and circulated in ways that defy the logic of either capitalism or socialism—but it differs from either of the other two (or feudalism, for that matter) by virtue of not being differentiated primarily by class but by various types of affective ties. The difference between rich and poor is still one of degree rather than kind: it is still characterized more by one person having more than the other of the same thing (land, cattle, wives, etc.) rather than by one person owning the means of production and the other being without access to it at all. Thus, for instance, while members of poor peasant households increasingly supplement their income by offering their labor to richer farmers, these labor exchanges are usually not "naked" market phenomena but pursued within the context of specified affective relations. The emerging class differentiation in rural Africa is encapsulated in the economy of affection.

The social relations that make up the economy of affection are determined by a logic that serves to enhance mutual security and reward individuals or groups according to specific performance criteria. In this economy, "private" and "collective" are not dichotomized as in capitalist or socialist economies. As a result, neither contract nor monopoly constitute principles on which the understanding of mutual rights and obligations is based. The prevailing principle in the economy of affection is the "covenant"—a more diffuse—usually tacit—expression of commitment among members of a given community. At the same time, these affective ties are solidified by the emotional and historical bonds that provide members of these units with a real sense of belonging. Thus, in the absence of a predominant conflict between capital and labor, these ties constitute the equivalence of the relations of production. In Marxist terminology, they are in the context of the peasant mode of production, the "determinant" relations. This is particularly apparent in patterns in land tenure, intra-community distribution and in various forms of reciprocal exchanges within as well as between communities.

The principal differences between capitalism, socialism and the economy of affection can be summarized as follows: (see Table 11.1).

TABLE 11.1 Contrasting Models of Social Organization in Three Types of Economic Systems

Differentiating Category	Capitalism	Socialism	Economy of Affection
Organizational Principle	Market	Hierarchy	Community
Allocative Principle/ Basis for Sanctioning	Exchange Contract	Redistribution Monopoly	Reciprocity Covenant
Presumed Social Behavior	Selfish	Compliant	Solidarity

The significance of the economy of affection and the fact that market and state (or hierarchy) are not the only variables determining social behavior are hard to appreciate as long as our studies are conceived in conventional actor/structure terms. It is to the limits of that dichotomy that I now turn.

The Limits of the Actor/Structure Dichotomy

The dualism between individual voluntarism and structural determinism has been a central notion in Western political thought for a long time. It has had far reaching both epistemological and methodological implications for social science analysis. Ever since Marx and Durkheim, the notion of "structure" has been associated with a natural science model, in which structure as constraint is compared to the impersonal forces of nature. Although Marx implied a definite scope for voluntarism when predicting the revolutionary overthrow of capitalism, he not only confined such an opportunity to specific historical conjunctures but also assumed that the latter were the outcomes of structural contradictions that were largely independent of human action and rather the outcome of the "functional" needs of the capitalist system. Marxist theory is structuralist and deterministic to the extent that in its application to capitalist society it argues that there are structural contradictions—one may wish to call these a "suicidal bent"—built into such a society in the form of an historic law. Such theory is voluntarist and deterministic in its treatment of post-revolutionary society. Here all constraints on human action are removed and enlightened decisions that benefit everybody in a similar fashion are possible. Darkness has been replaced by light; constraint by opportunity. Nowhere else is this dichotomy as dramatically illustrated as in this theory.

It is, of course, replicated, though in a less explosive fashion, in liberal theory. Here the original emphasis is not on structure but on voluntary action: on the notion that individuals are capable of making rational choices in their own interest. In its neo-classical economic version, the typical reference is to opportunity rather than constraints; to incentive rather than power. In the same way as Marxist scholars have difficulty in disengaging from the normative bias of their theory in favor of revolution, and thus out of wishful thinking apply it to circumstances that hardly resemble those originally assumed, their liberal counterparts often "upscale" their choice theory to fit studies of decision situations that have little in common with the contexts in which the theory originally developed. In the field of development studies, as the paradigmatic pendulum has swung away from neo-Marxist towards public choice theories, the tendency has been to "write off" structures and instead stress only the possibilities that exist in voluntary individual action. This kind of theoretical "ping pong game" however, takes us nowhere. To overcome the shortcomings inherent in the dichotomy discussed above, at least two modifications are needed: (1) structure and agency are inseparable; and (2) systems, and the structures associated therewith, are present not only at the level of the nation-state or the globe but also at lower levels.

Structure does not exist independently of human beings. It is not merely like a wall that puts limits on what can be achieved. Structure is both the medium and outcome of the practices which constitute social systems. The concept of the duality of structure connects the production of social interaction, as always and everywhere a contingent accomplishment of knowledgeable social actors, to the reproduction of social systems across time and space. For instance, the economy of affection is a social system whose structures are shaped and modified through repetitive social interactions, each one producing a specific outcome while simultaneously reproducing the system at large. This is the fundamental postulate of Giddens' structuration theory (Giddens 1984). Systems of social interaction, reproduced through the duality of structure in the bounded context of rationalizing specific actions, are constituted through the interdependence of actors or collectivities. Interdependence refers to the degree of "systemness" that is involved in any mode of system reproduction. "Integration" can be defined therefore as regularized ties, interchanges, or reciprocity of practices between either actors or collectivities. "Reciprocity of practices" has to be understood as involving regularized relations of relative autonomy and dependence between the parties concerned. As such, "systemness" is not synonymous with "cohesion" or "consensus." According centrality to the notion of social reproduction does not imply emphasizing stability at the expense of radical discontinuities in system organization. The inherent relation between production and reproduction involved in the idea of the duality of structure carries with it the implication that the seeds of change are present in every moment of the constitution of social systems across time and space. To conceive of interaction as occurring across time and space is to emphasize that social actors do not just "adapt" to the "functional needs" of the institutions which they themselves produce and reproduce in their interaction, yet not exclude recognition of the fact that institutions are important as retrievers of human history as it escapes from human interactions in the form of unintended consequences and unacknowledged conditions.

The notion that structure and actor are interdependent has several important implications for the study of governance in Africa. The first is that treating the nation-state as the "given" system is misleading. Interdependencies between state and community are much weaker than those holding specific communities together. African countries are "bottom-heavy." Their resources, both material and symbolic, are concentrated and circulated in the periphery. Instead of being able to penetrate these communities, the state is being used by them. These "systems within the system" constitute the building blocs of governance, guided by their own normative structures. African societies are de facto poly-constitutional. Current state systems, however, have not built on this; instead they have generally battled against it.

The second implication is that formal structures constitute only part of the scene of governance. In the same way that economists now increasingly acknowledge the significance of the "informal sector," political analysts need to pay greater attention to the influence of non-official agencies on political processes. Take for example the case of land tenure in Africa. There is growing evidence (Noronha 1985) that systems of land tenure are being reproduced less by common law than by customary practices prevailing within given ethnic communities. A "legalistic" approach to governance is clearly inadequate in the context of African societies where the processes of statecraft are nascent and where governance continues to be highly circumscribed by non-political factors. Issues of governance, therefore, should be viewed in the broader context of the entire "constitutive" process, i.e. the ways and means by which norms are institutionalized as a result of the application of effective power in society.

The third implication is that structure is not only constraining but also enabling. The notion that structures are merely confining—so common in Africa in the present economic crisis—is both crude and misleading. And this is not just an academic point. There is a tendency in Africa to derogate the lay actors and treat them as "cultural dopes" or "bearers of the mode of production" with no worthwhile understanding of their surroundings or the circumstances of their action. As a result, their views tend to be disregarded in any practical development program and little interest is shown in their activities and social interaction by academic analysts. Yet, through their action they make an ongoing contribution to the production and reproduction of one set of structures as opposed to another. Their lack of involvement in civic structures should not be construed as evidence of total powerlessness. African peasants are not just at the "receiving end" of the power structure. By being involved in local community structures, they help reproduce a poly-constitutional set-up that poses a special challenge to and opportunity for governance.

A fourth implication is that the normative constitution of interaction, i.e., the actualization of rights and the enactment of obligations, is an integral part of the modality of structuration. Culture is created by the continuous confrontation between objectives and the resources—knowledge, power, talent, trust, and others—that are necessary to achieve the objectives. Politics as the allocation of scarce values is not about material things only. It is as much about the institutionalization of rights and obligations that arise out of such confrontations between values and resources or conflicts of interest in society.

To be sure, culture is both constant and changing and the analyst must recognize this distinction. Following Elinor Ostrom and Larry Kiser (1982: 206–218), an analysis of the role of culture in governance may be facilitated by the distinction between three levels of institutional analysis. The first— the operational level—refers to actions that individuals can take without prior authorization from other individuals because they are derived from existing institutional arrangements. A case in point may be the African farmer tilling his land, a right bestowed on him by his clan. The second level refers to collective decisions taken by officials to determine, enforce, continue, or alter actions authorized within institutional arrangements. A group of clan elders deciding on who is entitled to inherit a piece of commonly owned clan land may illustrate the type of decisions taken at that level. The third level refers to collective choices about rules governing future collective decisions to authorize actions—the constitutional level. An example would be the same council of elders making a decision to alter the rules under which land is being allocated and inherited among members. An issue is usually elevated to the third level in situations where actors experience constraints and are induced or forced to consider changing "the rules of the game." A study of the constitutive process involves tracing the conditions in which a given issue enters that process, the factors determining the institutionalization of new rules and their reproduction in the form of structures, and the outcomes produced by these structures.

The final section of this chapter will be devoted to the question of what kind of conceptual and theoretical framework might provide a particularly useful starting point for the study of issues of governance in Africa. How can we get a better theoretical handle on governance in a society where non-capitalist values are most prevalent and influential?

The Concept of Reciprocity

The challenge here is to identify a concept that captures the nature of African realities, yet relates to other concepts in use in the study of politics; in other words, to find a concept that enables us to universalize the African experience, however anomalous it may appear at first sight. We are assisted in this pursuit by the growing dissatisfaction with conventional rational choice theory which presupposes a utilitarian individualism without any normative restraints (E. Ostrom 1987), and the consequent emerging interest among these critics in the concept of reciprocity. The latter featured in the writings of several philosophers, notably Hobbes and Hume, who reflected on the issues facing Europe in its transition from a precapitalist to a capitalist society. It has been largely ignored in modern political theory where, instead, the liberal-utilitarian strand has come to dominate. Reciprocity was rediscovered this century by anthropologists and economic historians writing on "traditional" societies and their role in the social transformation of the world in the past hundred years (Polanyi 1945). Although it has remained a core concept in social practice in Africa to this day, it was swept off the academic agenda first by the positivist-inspired literature on modernization and subsequently by the materialist, neo-Marxist upsurge in the late 1960s and 1970s. Both schools had the tendency of regarding the concept as part of a historical phase already passed by humankind. Any attempt to treat it as part of "development studies," therefore, was seen as romanticizing Africa's past.

This view is hard to sustain today. As this chapter has tried to demonstrate, the most intriguing thing about contemporary Africa is the resilience of its indigenous social organization and the growing marginalization of things "modern." It is in this context that a renewed focus on reciprocity becomes particularly significant. Reciprocal practices are more central to politics in contemporary Africa than elsewhere. This does not mean that pre-colonial ideals are still in operation, but a focus on reciprocity permits us to incorporate dimensions that are excluded by the assumptions underlying conventional rational choice theories, derived from neoclassical economics. It also allows the study of governance in Africa to relate to a growing body of literature on collective choice developing in Europe and North America.

Reciprocity and Exchange

Much of what passes today as "political economy" is attempts to understand politics in terms of exchange. Political scientists, at least in part out of envy of the methodological precision that economists can achieve by building their discipline around the concept of exchange as a basic mode of human interaction, have developed decision theories with universal claims centered on "exchange" rather than "power." To understand fully how "reciprocity" relates to this literature, it is important to compare the concept to "exchange."

While both concepts refer to interactions consisting of mutually beneficial transfers (Boulding 1973), they do differ with regard to two important attributes: (1) a *quid pro quo* and (2) simultaneity in performance (Oakerson 1983). An exchange is a fully contingent relationship: each part agrees to perform only on condition that the other perform. Similarly, exchange is also assumed to exhibit simultaneous performances between parties. The exchange is conceived as a single event, in which there is no doubt as to whether one will receive as well as give. While exchange represents the combined presence of a *quid pro quo* and simultaneity, reciprocity is defined by their combined absence. In a reciprocal relationship, each party expects a return, but there is no guarantee. Contingency in reciprocity develops only over a series of reciprocal acts, as both parties cease to participate because their expectations are not fulfilled. In this situation, of course, no reciprocity will occur. Reciprocity is also characterized by a time lag between performances. Whether one will get a return from ones contribution is potentially problematical. A formal definition of reciprocity, then, can be given as a mutual transfer in the absence of both a *quid pro quo* and simultaneity. The contribution that each party makes to the welfare of the other is with an expectation of mutual performance. Reciprocity occurs only if these expectations converge.

The process of reaching an agreement is also different between exchange and reciprocity. Bargaining, the principal strategy used by parties to an exchange, is inappropriate in a situation where a *quid pro quo* is lacking (Boulding 1973: 116). The instrument of agreement in exchange is contract. In cases of reciprocity, it is the convenant. Unlike contracts which are concerned with precise terms and conditions, the covenant represents an agreement about norms governing future conduct. As such, it draws as much on moral reasoning as upon economic calculation. It presupposes shared perspectives or the ability of actors to consider the interests of others, as opposed to a purely self-interested orientation.

The inclusion of reciprocity in our analysis has the theoretical advantage of allowing us to understand more fully why individuals may decide to cooperate even if there is no immediate gain as implied in the conventional exchange model used, e.g., by Olson (1965). Reciprocity extends more easily than exchange to an unlimited domain of persons because precise negotiations of terms and conditions do not occur. Individuals can contribute with a single act to the welfare of numerous others and sustain expectations of mutual return. This is the essence of the economy of affection: individuals contribute with an expectation that others will do likewise because there is a deep legacy to that effect which is too costly for each individual actor to ignore. Political economists have been primarily concerned with refining models of social action in which the assumption is that individuals engage in bargaining to secure disproportionate gains for themselves. Such models overlook the fact that where reciprocity prevails, "freerider" problems arise far less frequently and collective action is usually possible without either coercion or "selective incentives." This becomes clear if we scrutinize more closely the model of man associated with the economy of affection. It fits neither the simple maximization of subjective utility nor the altruism model, the two most common in the literature on collective action. The problem with both of these is that they assume too much; in fact, they assume away precisely the kind of behavior that characterizes the economy of affection. Take, for example, the maximizing model used by most economists, including Olson. The presumption that individuals will freeride is taken for granted. If the opportunity is there, it will be taken. In other words, the inclination toward freeriding is built into the set of assumptions from which predictions are derived. Reciprocity is impossible in that scenario. The same methodological problem holds true for altruism. If we assume that individuals behave altruistically, reciprocity is not problematical. It is just another case of prediction being guaranteed from the choice of assumptions.

To enlarge the scope of analysis of collective behavior we must recognize that individuals can participate in patterns of reciprocity without necessarily being worse off. Self-interest does not have to be the same as maximizing personal utility. In the model of man associated with the economy of affection, reciprocity enables each individual to realize a return on his or her own contribution. The benefits of participating in a reciprocal relationship exceed its costs. Thus, both individuals and collectivity make gains. The notion that participation in a reciprocal venture is inefficient and involves self-sacrifice, so commonly held in conventional rational choice theory, is unknown in those situations where the economy of affection still prevails. There is no irreconcilable contradiction between "individual" and "collective" because self-interest in the affective context does not mean "selfishness." Borrowing from Oakerson (1983:16), we may say that in this model man is not a maximizer but a satisficer of a certain sort: he is satisfied with a return that leaves himself better off and prefers such a behavior over one that implies maximizing his own returns at the expense of others. In the economy of affection, man both desires and expects reciprocity of others and knows what the penalties are if he himself fails to practice it. To be sure, reciprocity does not come automatically. It depends on learning and judgement and not every participant in affective relations is necessarily practicing it as conscientiously as others. In Africa, however, those who are seen to maximize as opposed to satisfice, and thus are regarded as greedy and selfish, usually come under strong community pressure to reform their behavior. If they ignore such pressures, the community usually decides to ostracize them. These pressures toward reciprocity are much stronger in the economy of affection than they tend to be in modern capitalist or socialist economies where the dichotomy between "individual" and "collective" is much more pronounced and the philosophical legacy in these countries leaves people much more uncertain about one another's readiness to practice reciprocity. Yet, the latter is crucial to effective governance also in capitalist and socialist countries.

The Conditions of Reciprocity in Africa

What we are suggesting here is that reciprocity is likely to be easier to practice in some conditions than in others. We cannot take it for granted in every situation. Reciprocity is reversible. After all, individuals may want the benefit of freeriding or they may fear that others will seek that option. So, in what conditions can we expect reciprocity to flourish?

Reciprocity is more likely to develop in situations where each person lives close to the margins of survival and believes he does not possess the technological means to survive a hard year on his own. Making a contribution to somebody else or to the community at large with the expectation of receiving something in return at some later point is sensible in such circumstances. With reference to Southeast Asia, James Scott (1976) has referred to this kind of behavior as the "moral" economy. His main argument is that peasants are risk averse and as a result have collectively developed social insurance mechanisms. These are reinforced by the ethic of subsistence, i.e., the right of the peasant to subsist. He further argues that patron-client relations in peasant societies are regulated by an ethic of reciprocity, whereby the respect of the peasants for their elites and the payments made to those elites are supposed to be balanced by a return flow of justice, protection, and subsistence insurance. Popkin (1979), while sharing with Scott the assumption about the "safety-first" goals of the peasants, argues that they are household utility maximizers, and as such will behave according to their self-interest rather than the village's. In his scheme, it is individual rather than collective rationality that determines peasant behavior.

Reference to this Scott/Popkin debate is made here because much of the analysis of peasant behavior in Africa has been influenced by it, yet conditions in the latter continent are different from those prevailing in Asia in at least three important respects. African land tenure systems are the products of relative abundance of land cultivated largely under rain-fed conditions, while in Asia such systems are the outcome of irrigated cultivation usually under high levels of population density. Secondly, and partly related to the first point, is the fact that neither land nor labor has been commoditized to the extent that it has in Asia. Above all, no social class of landlords has yet risen to power via outright alienation of land from the peasantry. This leads us to the third difference with Asia (and in this case most of the rest of the world): the basis for economic and political integration in Africa tends to be predominantly social rather than territorial. It rests on the community rather than the state. It centers on relations among human beings rather than the relation between man and a given productive system.

As a result, reciprocity takes on a theoretical as well as practical significance in Africa that goes well beyond what has been the scope of the debate about the "moral" economy. The latter presupposes a dichotomy between individual and collective interests that is yet to materialize in the African countries. To be sure, such a dichotomy is not wholly absent, but it is not a central issue for the very reasons listed above. This means that the conditions of governance in Africa are fundamentally different from those assumed by the various theoretical approaches discussed in the first part of the chapter.

The day-to-day language as well as the political idiom of African societies tends to be geared towards developing and maintaining reciprocity. For instance, both stress symbols of togetherness and commitment to the common good. The language—if not the act—of exchange and bargaining is foreign to these societies. Ordinary language is usually intended to suppress such notions as "strategic bargaining." It is also apparent in the political language used. "Ndugu" (brother) is preferred over the impersonal "comrade." Political authority is described and legitimized in the language of parental authority. Built into it is the notion that leaders and followers have a reciprocal duty toward each other: an obligation is solicited today in anticipation of an unspecified benefit at some later point (Martin 1986).

Reciprocity cannot survive without mutual trust. It is only in situations where trust prevails that individuals are willing to make a contribution in return for an unspecified benefit at some future point. Such trust develops with experience and is likely to be institutionalized particularly in face-to-face communities where people know each other and where escape is both difficult and costly. Although such trust is particularly prevalent within relatively narrow lineage systems, it usually stretches beyond such micro units to encompass whole clans or ethnic groups. There are also examples of such relations of trust developing across ethnic boundaries. A good example is the *sama manila* (strange farming) system of the West African region of Senegambia which involves a migrant's supply of labor to a host's plot in exchange for a temporary exclusive use of a plot of land. These migrants come from far away and engage in a system of tenure that a Westerner would call sharecropping. That is a misnomer, however, as the migrant gets a plot of land in return for labor services. As such it is an attempt to break a bottleneck in production on the host's land. Secondly, there is no specific contract and no central enforcement agency in case of dispute. Instead, the transaction is couched in the language of reciprocity, as a system of mutual benefits with self-enforcing mechanisms. Mutual trust may initially be low but the migrant's access to land makes him a "hostage" in the new situation. Eventually, therefore, the boundaries of trust are extended to incorporate the "strange farmers" (Swindel 1978).

This example points to the fact that reciprocity also demands accountability. The accounting required is not precise, nor focused on specific contributions as in the case of exchange. Instead, individuals are held accountable for their adherence to general norms of conduct. For instance, in the old days, members of a given community would make donations to an elder or a chief—a form of voluntary taxation—in anticipation of his protection and support in case of an emergency. This is the basis of clientelist politics (e.g., Eisenstadt and Lemarchand 1981) and it takes on special importance in Africa because patrons there do not usually control the means of production on which their clients are dependent. Put in other words, African patrons have less leverage than patrons in other contexts. They lack the coercive means of a landlord or capitalist owner, and by virtue of being the representative of a genuine and living community, African patrons cannot afford to ignore—at least for long—the principle of accountability. To be sure, each patron tries to augment his autonomy by securing as strong a material base of his own as possible; hence the drive towards what in Marxist terms usually is called the capital accumulation of the "petty bourgeoisie." This label, however, is overly simplistic as it denotes the private accumulation without reference to the social pressures under which such accumulated resources have to be applied.

The more trust and accountability go together, the more likely that a community will be able to understand and accept mutual criticism. In precolonial Africa, criticism of leaders was not unusual. Within community boundaries, enough trust existed to enable members to engage in accounting of each other's behavior. This is what African leaders today often refer to as "constructive criticism." The latter has proved extremely difficult to institutionalize at the governmental level in African countries. It does survive, however, within specific communities where trust is still strongly rooted.

In Olson's theory of collective action, the presence of trust and account-ability is explained by size of group or organization. Collective action becomes more difficult as the size of the relevant entity grows. Thus, in his schema, voluntary cooperation is possible only in small groups, prob-lematic in intermediate groups, and impossible in large ones. In the small and intermediate groups, individuals are sufficiently close to each other to become acquainted and thus develop a mutual trust. Further, they can monitor one another more easily and hold each other accountable for their conduct. Thus, is organizational size a reason why African states cannot accommodate today the kind of "constructive criticism" that was (and still is) such a prominent feature of the African community?

The answer is that looking at size alone is misleading because in Olson's theory its significance follows from the basic assumption that individual actors are utility maximizers. In Africa's largely non-capitalist conditions, such a model of man makes little sense. It does not mean that Africans are not rational, only that their behavior tends to be rational in terms that Weber described as "substantively" as opposed to "formally" rational. What this means is that in the model of man prevailing in Africa, decisions are not made in calculative terms but in response to specific forces that shake the basic fundament of social action. In this model, where individual self-interest is embedded in reciprocity, there appears to be greater elasticity in the inclination to voluntarily cooperate with others, at least in certain circumstances, than the conventional collective choice theory suggests. The boundaries of communities in Africa, even those of ethnic groups, are not encased in stone (Kasfir 1979). They are flexible and usually wax and wane with circumstances. Thus, for instance, when faced with a common external threat, community boundaries can expand as happened in Africa's liberation wars when fighting guerrillas were given hospitality, protection and support by ordinary peasants to whom they were strangers, yet shared a community that neither party usually would call into question. Neither a utilitarian calculus nor a coercive management was needed in this situation. There was no contract signed formalizing rights and obligations. The common ground for collective action was opposition to colonial occupation, the prospect of independence, and the distant goal of a better future, hardly a "selective incentive." In Africa, where covenantal as opposed to contractual obligations prevail, group or organizational boundaries are generally less formalized than in capitalist or socialist settings.

As suggested above, this phenomenon can in certain circumstances be a great strength, but it can also be highly problematic as is the case when Africans are expected to perform in the context of organizations built on contractual principles. Nowhere else is this conflict more apparent than at the state level where the indigenous principles of reciprocity expressed in covenantal terms constantly run up against the received norms of a "contractual" state, as implanted by the colonial powers in the past hundred years. This issue is at the core of African governance: how can the African state continue to be a viable member of the international community (with its insistence on contractual obligations) while at the same time utilize the strength that follows from the prevalence of a reciprocal ethic?

It is to this question that I finally turn in this chapter.

Reciprocity and Governance

The assumption that the longer term viability of the African state depends on a closer examination of the pros and cons of reciprocity as currently practiced in political and economic contexts on the continent will be explored with reference to four key aspects of governance: (1) relating community to state; (2) institutionalizing rule; (3) improving public management; and (4) enhancing social justice.

Relating Community to State. This is a particularly critical issue because norms regulating the allocation of scarce values are more effectively embodied in the community than in the state. Reciprocity, and thus trust and accountability, is more strongly articulated in the "primordial" than in the "civic" realm (Ekeh 1975). In this sense, as we have noted above, the African polities are genuinely poly-constitutional. Yet, the overwhelming post-colonial trend in Africa has been towards discouraging local government and instead strengthening central authority. This apparent paradox may be best understood by examining the special problems of sustaining viable "superstructures" in societies where reciprocal norms are already institutionalized at the community level.

Because the African state is not the organic outcome of a process of endogenous growth, and thus the result of an indigenous class of rulers establishing control over a given territory, it sits, as I have argued elsewhere (Hyden 1980), suspended in "mid-air" above society. In this situation, the tendency has been to "blow up the balloon" so as to reach maximum size, i.e., to make the state as large as possible so as to accommodate competing community interests that do not lend themselves to reconciliation through some form of utilitarian calculus. Making the state appear omnipresent and omnicompetent, therefore, has been a way of reducing the risk of internal conflict. This is because such a strategy has enlarged the scope for the kind of policy-making that follows when the principle of reciprocity is applied to the state level: the advocacy of populist policies that do not threaten existing community norms but instead drain resources from state organizations that exist independently of affective communities. The result has been the emergence in Africa of a state centralized in language, law and aspiration, but ineffective or "soft" in reality. The consequent failure to enhance state capabilities has more recently reached such proportions that the international community, through its financial watchdog, the International Monetary Fund, has been forced to intervene in order to reverse the practice of using the state primarily as an agency to satisfy patronage demands made in the name of given communities.

The important thing to note here is that while the move towards a greater reliance on the market mechanism may have the effect of reducing the significance of clientelist politics, it is not in and of itself sufficient to enable African states to enhance their longer term viability. At the core is the question of how political authority may be distributed differently so as to take advantage of community strength, yet avoid the break-up of the state. Such a move towards greater self-governance would, as other chapters in this volume also argue, be desirable on many grounds, but it presupposes that African countries would be ready to move from a collective level of choice—where things are taken for granted—to that of constitutional choice, where public debate about the rules guiding politics is allowed. Few countries in Africa have considered that they can afford to do so and, when they have, it has usually been after the arbitrary abrogation of a former constitution.

Institutionalizing Rule. This takes us to the second issue: how rule may become institutionalized in African countries. Much has been written about it. Callaghy (1984), for instance, regards "patrimonialism" as the strategy that African leaders prefer. Jackson and Rosberg (1982) tend to accept the inevitability of personal rule in societies where the state was inherited, more or less like an empty shell, from a colonial power. Rothchild (1986) refers to the preference among African political leaders to engage in "hegemonial exchanges," i.e. conflict management by means of reciprocal interchanges.

A theory of reciprocity may help us in getting a better understanding of this issue by highlighting the conditions of governance in societies where reciprocal practices prevail and covenant rather than contract sets the parameters of political action. The former, as noted above, represents an agreement as to what norms or principles should guide future conduct. It does not "pin down" the political actor to the kind of specific terms or conditions associated with the contract. The result is that he has potentially much greater discretion vis-a-vis his constituents than is the case in a constitutional democracy. It is this discretion that gives the overall impression that African politics is so "personalized."

When confined to the community, this reliance on covenant is usually not a problem because there are usually sufficient moral pressures to keep the political actors within what the members consider acceptable bounds. It becomes much more problematic at the state level where the political head typically has to resort to dependence on his own political machinery to counteract the centrifugal pressures of individual community patrons. This strategy to institutionalize rule has increased arbitrariness and paved the way for a broad range of state interventions that have only caused the alienation of local communities. "Softness" and "arbitrariness" are equally harmful consequences of trying to apply the principle of reciprocity to the state level without further examination of what the pros and cons of such an action might be in the longer run, or what the fundamental constitutional implications of such a strategy might be. For instance, while there has been much support for the notion of decentralization in Africa in the past fifteen years, moves in such a direction have all been in the form of deconcentration, i.e., delegation of authority within existing government institutions rather than to autonomous local government units. The latter, as Wunsch and Olowu demonstrate in their introductory chapter of this volume, are responsible for only a minute percentage of the overall allocation of public resources. Yet, institutionalizing rule may in the long run depend on the readiness of African governments to provide greater scope for self-governance at the community level. To the extent that such local governance has evolved informally in African countries since independence, it has been largely successful. Kenya's *harambee* movement is a case in point.

In order to confront the problem of institutionalization of governance in Africa, the implications of the important role played by the organizing principles implicit in the economy of affection must be considered.

For example, the centralized or Hobbesian concept of sovereignty and state is comfortable with either the capitalist or socialist conceptions of social organization and exchange. However, it does not fit as well as the "economy of affection" as a principle of social organization because the key principles that organize the latter, community, covenant and solidarity, all exist outside its control, without need for its sanction, and potentially in opposition to it (see Table 11.1). Reciprocity is similarly out of the control of the centralist state's direct or customary indirect tools of control (i.e., economic management through either blueprints and bureaucracy, or through manipulation of commodity and currency markets). The centralized state, in the face of economies of affection, risks either drifting into irrelevance or, in frustration, edging into despotism. Both patterns can be seen in contemporary African history.

Patron-client systems based on central resources serve to offer some control to the center, but are deeply vulnerable to corruption as well as dearly expensive since no effective measures of accountability have developed. The organizational principles of the economy of affection do not appear able to constrain the patrons, whose access to resources depends upon their control of a state apparatus organized on contractarian and hierarchical principles, and sanctioned by international conventions (Jackson and Rosberg 1982).

In order for contemporary African statecraft to move beyond this trap, it is essential to develop a paradigm of governance that allows space for the economy of affection to operate, and opportunities for members of that economy to broaden its linkages and productive capacity as new opportunities and needs appear. As the economy of affection has already well proven its capacity to organize complex human endeavors over large spaces, such a paradigm of governance would properly emphasize a critical "framing" or constituting role for the state. In this, the state would focus on providing a framework which would undergird, protect, facilitate and sustain existing structures of collective action, and expedite their integration to undertake new productive relations and avoid conflict.

Improving Public Management. The state, unlike the community, is an arena where investments to build trust have to be made. Regime management, therefore, necessitates the use of public funds for "maintenance" purposes. Because political patrons in Africa tend to be leaders not of secondary organizations, such as cooperatives, trade unions or professional associations, but of primary organizations, i.e., communities, access to which are controlled not by the state but by the patrons themselves, management of public resources tends to be highly "politicized." For instance, to play the reciprocal game effectively, the supreme political leader usually requires access to untied resources that can be given in return for support on a given issue. When such untied resources are not immediately available, the supreme leader may make a sudden and arbitrary reallocation of already tied public funds so as to ensure continued support in the future.

On the surface, this may look no different from the kind of "horse-trading" that goes on in the United States Congress. Particularly in recent years as the party organizations have lost much of their former influence at state and lower levels of political action, similar tendencies to ignore the longer term consequences of commitment of public funds have become apparent. Yet, there is at least one significant difference: public management in the U.S. is shared by a broad range of institutions drawn from both the private and voluntary sectors in addition to the public one. A move in a similar direction may be the only way African countries can go in order to deal with the current "deadlock" of public management. From a development point of view, sharing responsibilities for public activities with local and intermediary institutions as well as encouraging diversity in organizational form should have the effect of strengthening societal capacity and thus national self-reliance. Among other things, such a strategy could have the effect of channeling demands on the public sector away from individual political patrons towards other agencies—both private and voluntary—and thus help strengthen horizontal linkages that cut across existing community boundaries. Such linkages may be a prerequisite for any move beyond exclusive reliance on clientelist politics and the development of interest articulation through secondary as opposed to primary organizations.

The question here is how far incumbent political leaders are ready to share power with others and how far they are ready to open the doors to a public debate on this and related issues. Ironically, the non-capitalist principle of reciprocity may prove a stumbling-block here: readiness to voluntarily elevate these issues to the constitutional level comes only with the acceptance of a utilitarian outlook and thus the use of formal or legal rationality. Constitutional changes of political systems have historically proved possible only in societies where such an outlook is prevailing. Thus, the question that I have raised elsewhere (Hyden 1983) arises: is constitutional governance, including greater scope for self-governance, feasible in contemporary Africa without a concomitant rise of a bourgeoisie ready to defend those principles?

Enhancing Social Justice. Under this final sub-heading, we will treat the question of what the prospects are in contemporary Africa for enhancing respect for human rights and strengthening social justice. The conventional approach to human rights issues assumes the existence of inalienable and unyielding qualities of interaction between persons and groups, and between the latter and the state, and even among states. The assertion that human rights are universal has encouraged a research approach based on the auditing of human rights violations in Africa and the consequent discussion of ways in which African governments can assure greater compliance with these prescriptions (Howard 1986). In other words, human rights progress lies in the greater acceptance of Western concepts and practices. Although possibly useful in the long run, this ethnocentric approach involves such a myopic vision of African conditions and trends that they are sure to produce endless attacks, defenses and counterattacks rather than a realistic appraisal of the important problems and directions of development within the human rights realm (Cohen 1987).

To get a better appreciation of the dilemmas associated with enhancing human rights in Africa, it is likely to be more fruitful to start from the other end—the processes that help constitute conceptions of justice and fairness in the African societies. This approach rejects the notion that such conceptions are static. For instance, many customary rights are today being questioned. A study of governance needs to highlight the conditions under which rights issues are being shifted from a collective to a constitutional level of choice. Human rights emerge from conflicts, mediation and evaluation of society by influential individuals. A theory of reciprocity may help us understand where African societies come from, illustrating both the strength and weakness associated with covenantal agreements. Especially interesting is an examination of the effects of abuse of such agreements: does it lead to a redefinition of the conditions of trust and accountability, to a rejection of the basic principles underlying reciprocal practices, or merely to a shift in loyalty from one actor to another. Richard Joseph's recent study (1988) of democracy and "prebendal" politics in Nigeria addresses this set of issues.

Nigeria is interesting in the context of African governance in that it shows that an arbitrary, patrimonial form of rule is not inevitable. The more competitive, prebendal form of politics, in spite of its shortcomings, brings the tension between contractual and covenantal obligations into the open, and thus forces the political actors to consider the adequacy of existing institutional arrangements to an extent that does not take place in the more closed patrimonial form of rule. As a result, the Nigerian polity is not only more open than other political systems in Africa but also more likely to encourage actors to shift issues from the collective to the constitutional level of choice. The point about the duality of structure, i.e., that it is both the medium and the outcome of social practice (and thus potentially both confining and enabling) comes across strongly in the Nigerian context. It is helpful not only for analytical purposes but also to illustrate that the options for alternative forms of governance in Africa are more varied than an examination of only patrimonial systems of rule would suggest.

The conclusion to draw here is that while patrimonialism may provide stability in the short run, it tends to block the road to constitutional development and reform. Fundamental issues of governance tend to be "frozen" at the collective level of choice. As a result, changes in the system are difficult without resorting to unconstitutional means. The task of institutionalizing human rights and other social justice concerns is adversely affected. Where prebendal politics prevails, by contrast, and competitive community demands are brought out into the open, instability may be the short term result, yet in the longer run emerging concepts of justice and fairness are being institutionalized and the scope of civic rights broadened: institutions or "rules" (as discussed in Chapter 12) are emerging that *transcend* organizations, and thus a constitutional *state* is developing, rather than one which is merely patrimonial. Nigeria already appears to be further along this road than other African countries. For instance, it is hard to imagine that a despot—or even a well-meaning, paternalist ruler—could do to Nigeria what Amin or Nyerere (in their own different ways) did to their respective countries.

The relative peculiarity of Nigeria in the context of African governance is usually explained with reference to such factors as its size and the absence of a heavy colonial legacy. While these factors are of some significance, there is reason to concentrate greater attention to the dynamics of its political system. The creative tension between indigenous and foreign values provides a particularly useful context for further studies on the constraints and opportunities associated with the concept of reciprocity and its implications for governance in Africa. Similarly, the applicability of a theory of reciprocity may be tested there under more congenial conditions than elsewhere on the continent. Finally, though the scope for "constitutional engineering" in Africa may be more limited than it was in North America at the time *The Federalist Papers* was written and the U.S. constitution was first brought into existence, Nigeria's experimentation with a federal system of government is already an important move towards greater respect for self-governance. As Vincent Ostrom (1971), by going back to the original intentions behind the U.S. constitution, argues in his theory of a "compound republic," the capacity for self-government can be enhanced by the concurrent existence of multiple communities of interest, and the simultaneous energizing and equilibrating tendencies they generate.

The challenge of governance in Africa is how the concurrent interests of its multiple communities can be reconciled in institutional arrangements that simultaneously enhance both the viability and strength of the African nations in the international arena, and the community rights, energies, and interests within the state. As this volume is trying to demonstrate, the most promising venue for dealing with this dilemma of governance may be a greater push for the notion of self-governance, i.e., a rule-based expansion of the capacity of African's to engage in legitimate collective action which, among other things, broadens the role of lower level organs of policy-making in the development responsibilities currently monopolized in most African countries by an over-extended state.

Conclusions

I wish to draw three principal conclusions from this reflective and at the same time prospective analysis. The first is that at the conceptual and theoretical levels, there is emerging within comparative politics a greater interest in "reciprocity" and its implications for understanding collective behavior. It is apparent particularly in the new school of institutional analysis (E. Ostrom 1987; V. Ostrom, Feeny and Picht 1988). It questions the atomistic, utilitarian assumptions underlying the theory of collective action in the past two decades. It provides analytical scope for more diverse forms of human behavior, including a recognition of reciprocity as a key variable in shaping collective decisions. Thus, there may be the beginning of a new paradigmatic shift in comparative politics.

The need to differentiate between "exchange" and "reciprocity" becomes especially important in the study of governance in Africa. In the absence of any marked cultural differentiation, social separation and political opposition between the ruling elites and the masses, reciprocity is the basis of political integration, as it was at similar historical junctures in other societies (Eisenstadt 1963). As long as private and collective conceptions of property remain undifferentiated and covenantal rights and obligations prevail over contractual ones, the basic assumptions underlying conventional exchange theories of collective action make little sense. Social progress may eventually change these conditions, but for some time to come, economic decisions in Africa are likely to be embedded in the relations of affection. Reciprocity, then, is at the core of governance in Africa, and will be for the foreseeable future.

Current principles of statecraft applied in Africa do not build on covenantal logic, flowing as they do out of an essentially European tradition. States so organized atop covenantal societies have difficulty "engaging" their societies, and tend to develop into patrimonial systems with some tendencies toward both irrelevance and despotism. A system of governance allowing both "space" for covenantalism to work, and structure to encourage greater integration is necessary. Developing a theory of reciprocity for the purpose of a better understanding of the process of governance in Africa thus makes a lot of sense.

It must be recognized that reciprocity constitutes a phenomenological dilemma to African political actors because they are forced to operate in the context of a "received" (from the colonial powers) state organization in which the differentiation between private and collective as well as covenantal and contractual obligations are taken for granted. This lack of fit between societal and state norms is at the root of the failure of the

African state. Patrimonial rule, by far the most common in Africa since independence, has proven particularly inadequate to the task of resolving this dilemma. It has justified overcentralization of power and a growing alienation of the state from society. To build on this logic, one must begin developing the operational implications of such concepts as "self-governance" to explore whether and how it might help Africa's peoples overcome their economic and political weakness and thus increasingly make progress initiated and sustained by themselves.

Notes

1. Since the begining of comparative politics in the late 1950s, two approaches, *structural functionalism* (Almond and Coleman, 1960; *Almond and Powell, 1966*) and *neo-Marxist political economy* (Baran 1957; Frank 1969; Leys 1975; Rodney 1972) have stressed the role of structure as an independent variable. One approach, public and collective choice (Hardin 1968; 1971; Olson 1965) has stressed the independent role of actors. At this point, neither of these three research traditions seems to provide much guidance for comparative politics. That is why the search for a new paradigm is relevant.

References

Almond, G. and Coleman, J. S., eds. *The Politics of the Developing Areas*. Princeton, N.J.: Princeton University Press, 1960.

———— and Powell, B. *Comparative Politics: A Developmental Approach*. Boston: Little Brown, 1966.

Baran, P. *The Political Economy of Growth*. New York: Monthly Review Press, 1957.

Bates, Robert H. *Markets and States in Tropical Africa: The Political Basis of Agricultural Policies*. Berkeley: University of California Press, 1981.

Bernstein, H. "Notes on State and Peasantry." *Review of African Political Economy* 21 (May-September) (1981): 44–62.

Berry, Sara. *Fathers Work for Their Sons*. Berkeley: University of California Press, 1985.

Boulding, K. *The Economy of Love and Fear*. Belmont, California: Wadsworth, 1973.

Bryceson, D. "Peasant Commodity Production in Postcolonial Tanzania." *African Affairs* 81 (325) (1982): 547–558.

Callaghy, T.M. *The State-Society Struggle: Zaire in Comparative Perspective*. New York: Columbia University, 1984.

Cohen, R. "Prolegomena for the Understanding of Human Rights Issues in Africa." Unpublished paper, Center for African Studies, University of Florida, Gainesville, 1987.

Eisenstadt, S. N. *Political Systems of Empires*. New York: Alfred Knopf, 1981.

———— and Lemarchand, R., eds. *Political Clientelism Patronage and Development*. Beverly Hills: Sage Publications, 1981.

Ekeh, P. "Colonialism and the Two Publics in Africa." *Comparative Studies in Society and History* 17 (January) (1975) 91–112.

Forrest, J. "The Peasant Mode of Production in Africa." Unpublished paper, Department of Political Science, University of Wisconsin, Madison, 1986.

Frank, Andre Gunder. *Capitalism and Underdevelopment in Latin America.* New York: Monthly Review Press, 1969.

Giddens, A. *The Constitution of Society.* Berkeley: University of California Press, 1984.

Guyer, J. "Household and Community in African Studies." *African Studies Review* 24 (2 and 3) (June-September) (1981): 87–137.

Hardin, G. "The Tragedy of the Commons." *Science* 162 (December) (1968): 1,243–1,248.

Hardin, R. "Collective Action as an Agreeable N-Prisoners' Dilemma."*Behavioral Science* 16 (5) (September) (1971): 472–481.

Harrison, Paul. *The Greening of Africa.* London: International Institute of Environment and Development, 1986.

Hart, K. *The Political Economy of West African Agriculture.* Cambridge: Cambridge University Press, 1982.

Howard, R. *Human Rights in Commonwealth Africa.* Totowa, New Jersey: Rowman and Littlefield, 1986.

Hunter, G. *The Modernization of Peasant Societies.* Oxford: Oxford University Press, 1969.

Hyden, Goran. *Beyond Ujamaa in Tanzania.* Berkeley: University of California Press, 1980.

_____. *No Shortcuts to Progress.* Berkeley: University of California Press, 1983.

Jackson, R. H., and Rosberg, C. *Personal Rule in Black Africa.* Berkeley: University of California Press, 1982.

Jewsiewicki, B., and J. Letourneau. *Mode of Production: The Challenge of Africa.* Ste-Foy, Canada: Safi Press, 1985.

Joseph, R. *Democracy and Prebendal Politics in Nigeria.* New York: Cambridge University Press, 1987.

Kasfir, N. "Explaining Ethnic Political Participation." *World Politics* XXXI (3) (April) (1979): 365–388.

_____. "Are African Peasants Self-Sufficient?" *Development and Change* 17 (2) (1986): 335–357.

Lele, U., and W. Chandler. "Food Security: Some East African Considerations." In *Food Security for Developing Countries,* edited by A. Valdes. Boulder, Colorado: Westview Press, 1975.

Leys, C. *Underdevelopment in Kenya.* Berkeley: University of California Press, 1975.

Martin, D. "Political Idioms in Tanzania." Unpublished paper, Centre d'Etudes et de Recherches Internationales, Paris, 1986.

Noronha, R. "A Review of the Literature on Land Tenure Systems in Sub-Saharan Africa." Discussion Paper, Research Unit, Agriculture and Rural Development Department, The World Bank, Washington, D.C., 1985.

Oakerson, R. J. "Reciprocity: The Political Nexus." Unpublished paper, Marshall University, 1983.

Olson, M. *The Logic of Collective Action.* Cambridge, Massachusetts: Harvard University Press, 1965.

Ostrom, E. "Micro-Constitutional Change in a Multi-Constitutional Political System." Paper presented at the conference on "Advances in Comparative Institutional Analysis." Inter-University Center of Postgraduate Studies, Dubrovnik, Yugoslavia, 1987.

_____ and Larry Kiser. "The Three Worlds of Action: A MetaTheoretical Synthesis of Institutional Approaches." In *Strategies of Political Inquiry,* edited by Elinor Ostrom. Beverly Hills: Sage Publications.

Ostrom, Vincent. *The Political Theory of a Compound Republic.* Rev. ed. Lincoln, Neb.: University of Nebraska Press, 1987.
_____, David Feeny, and Hartmut Picht, eds. *Rethinking Institutional Analysis and Development: Some Issues Alternatives and Choices.* San Francisco: Institute for Contemporary Studies, 1988.
Polanyi, K. *The Great Transformation.* London: Victor Gollancz, 1945.
Popkin, S. *The Rational Peasant: The Political Economy of Rural Society in Vietnam.* Berkeley: University of California Press, 1979.
Richards, P. *Indigenous Agricultural Revolution.* London: Hutchinson, 1985.
Rodney, W. *How Europe Underdeveloped Africa.* London: Bogle L'Ouverture Publications, 1972.
Rothchild, D. "Interethnic Conflict and Policy Analysis in Africa." *Ethnic and Racial Studies* 9 (1) (January) (1986): 66–86.
Rothchild, D., and N. Chazan, eds. *The Precarious Balance: State and Society in Africa.* Boulder, Colorado: Westview Press, 1989.
Scott, J. C. *The Moral Economy of the Peasant: Rebellion and Subsistence in Southeast Asia.* New Haven, Conn.: Yale University Press, 1976.
Swindel, K. "Family Farms and Migrant Labour: The Stranger Farmers of the Gambia." *Canadian Journal of African Studies* 12 (1) (1978): 3–17.

12

Beyond the Failure of the Centralized State: Toward Self-Governance and an Alternative Institutional Paradigm

James S. Wunsch

Introduction

This book has so far argued that many of Africa's contemporary problems can be understood in significant measure as products of the over-centralized state so characteristic of post-independence Africa. The tendency to eviscerate local structures of government; to centralize all public management in centrally directed, hierarchical bureaucracies; to concentrate control of the economy in a national planning system; to take control of key industries through monopoly, parastatal enterprises; to absorb legitimate political activity in single parties; to reduce the independent latitude of action by unions, cooperatives, private firms, and the media; and to concentrate legislative and executive power in the hands of a president or military government, have worked to slow economic progress, to weaken the capacity of Africans to make and implement collective choices, and to intensify social conflict. How this occurred has been discussed throughout the volume.

This book has taken an approach to development which has emphasized the need for flexibility, accountability, adaptability and learning in complex human organizations, and the critical role played by humans' self-organizing capabilities in accomplishing these things. Drawing on both theoretical and empirical studies, it has considered the limits of monocratic and hierarchical organizations in producing complex economic, social and political goods, as well as our limits in knowledge which have led so many "blue-printed" programs and projects to disaster (Landau 1980; Mickelwait 1978; Wunsch 1986). It has, instead, argued for political arrangements that provide *space* for human organizational talents and cognitive abilities to develop and work, and *structure* to assure that these efforts did not lead to new instances of conflict, exploitation, and predation.

This chapter will explore organizational principles which might serve as a starting point in developing such a polity. Building on the logic of Chapter 10, it will consider two fundamental understandings human beings have had of the political relationship. It will show how those have been related to political choices and structures. In doing this it will review the "rulership" and "monocratic" paradigm of government so dominant in post-independence Africa, and present in contrast, a "self-governance" model of governance. The second, we believe, will serve Africans as a more fruitful *starting point* for discussion and experimentation than the monocratic paradigm has done given Africa's development challenge, its multi-ethnic heritage, and the mixed but still generally strong traditions of local social and political organizations which Africa has.

The purpose of this chapter is not to "draft" or to suggest the transfer of "model" "constitutions" from one cultural experience or environment to another. It does not presume that such a task can be done. It certainly does not presume that the solutions to Africa's political problems can be reached by "rewriting" constitutional documents. It does, however, assume that certain principles of political structure occur and reoccur throughout human history, are products of human choice, and thus can have relevance across time and space. An analytical discussion, such as we attempt here, of two contrasting political paradigms may be of use to Africa's peoples as they return in the 1990s to the task they began some thirty to forty years ago: fashioning working political rules that meet their needs. It is to this discussion that we now turn.

Paradigms of Governance

A critical turning point for African leaders in the post-independence era was their understanding of what were the building blocks of the state. In their understanding, drawing from the sociologically focused paradigms then dominant in both academic and official circles, African leaders saw the task of political development to be the task of building strong and viable organizations quickly. These organizations would be able to mobilize domestic and international resources rapidly and authoritatively, command loyalty, and bring about economic development. They sought, in general, to construct parties and executives substantially autonomous from institutional and other constraints: first, from the colonial regime, and then from those members of African societies who would have questioned, slowed or compromised the leaders' goals. Organizations, in other words, were consciously constructed and/or operated to triumph over existing legal constraints in the interest of rapid, revolutionary change (Jackson and Rosberg 1986).

Because of this, post-independence government in Africa has largely been consistent with a monocratic and hierarchical conception of the state and of sovereignty. In this perspective, a center which monopolizes all use of legitimate coercion is understood to be "the state." While it might in some ways be seen as springing from the people, all organized political life is explicitly understood as occurring at the center and operating only on its authorization and sufferance. This is largely consistent with the model of the state articulated by Thomas Hobbes (Hobbes 1960).

As discussed in Chapter 10, in this tradition the concepts of state or government presuppose absoluteness and determinacy. A state exists so certain actions may be authoritatively determined to be obligatory, prohibited or allowed. It exists to rule. The consistency implied by this suggests that decisions must be made (or at least subject to review) at a single, known, predetermined and consistent point. All this leads to the idea of a single locus of sovereignty (be it found in a monarch, parliament or other central point); to single monopolistic organizations for administration of public affairs; and to the idea that some men "govern" others. At least implicitly, it suggests that without such a locus there would be general disorder, and thus suggests the idea that social order grows from an institution we normally call (in singular terms) "the Government" (V. Ostrom 1986a; 1986b). Such a conceptualization was implied in the past by the logic of Hobbes; today it is implied by a logic which equates development generally to economic development, and argues that centrally managed economic development will produce optimal results. The critical role many African leaders saw for themselves in this task was reinforced by the organizational model of Lenin, and the Marxist tradition that a single "solution" to social problems existed (Lenin 1969). Once discerned, what possible reason could there be to leave its implementation open to question by a pluralistic, democratic process (Nyerere 1968; 1973; Nkrumah 1973)?

Political elites reflected this conception of politics and government in the roles they chose. As the occupiers of the center, they saw themselves as critical to the attainment of their respective utopian goals, or even to the very survival of the state (Gellar 1972). They looked to centrist and blue-printed solutions for problems of political and social order, rather than to socially rooted and experiential solutions (see Chapter 3, this volume). In retrospect they appear to have had little regard for the sense or capacity of the general populace (Sklar 1985).

A second broad tradition of governance emphasizes dispersing and sharing political authority among multiple actors—to facilitate more broadly participative governance. The state in this paradigm exists to facilitate the peaceful pursuit by the people of their various conceptions of the good. It can be contrasted to the centralist-rulership paradigm on a number of criteria, including its stress on citizen empowerment, policy and program heterogeneity, self-organization by the public, protection of individual choice, polycentricity, compounded institutional arrangements, the rule of law (i.e., rules dominating organizations), and the ultimate basis of the state on normative choice. So far this volume has attempted to show how a public life built on these qualities would be more likely to encourage development in Africa. The next section of this chapter will elaborate more fully on how self-governance regimes differ from regimes of rulership, and begin to discuss some of the institutional prerequisites of sustaining these differences.

Self-Governance Regimes
and Institutional Arrangements

Perhaps the most immediately clear difference between regimes of self-governance and regimes of rulership lies in the roles reserved for citizens in the former. Individual citizens and corporate entities retain political prerogatives which allow them, in effect, to share in the process of governance. Rights of suit and of local autonomy, and rights to make contracts and to establish sub-national juridical entities, etc., are seen as essential prerogatives of citizenship in this tradition (Berman 1983). Those who occupy particular political roles are not "rulers" by virtue of that, but are agents or trustees for a broader community of persons.

It is in part because of the implications of these last relationships that regimes of self-governance require the achievement of agreement on certain fundamental principles of proper and improper actions. The implied assumptions of classical Western liberalism (balanced interests will protect citizen rights) are seen in this paradigm as unlikely to maintain such limits on the actions of powerholders without a core of normatively based beliefs and understandings regarding people's obligations (both "oughts" and "ought nots") to one another (Lowi 1979).

Such a perspective has deep roots in political theory, deeper ones than are often acknowledged in contemporary positivist political science. For example, the polity as conceptualized by Aristotle is a political "community." It comes into existence as men find they agree on certain fundamental norms and principles of social life, and is animated by their need to make binding decisions upon themselves regarding their ongoing collective affairs (Lord 1984). A similar view is reflected by the Swiss, in their use of the concept of "Genossenschaft" rather than the Prussian "Herrschaft," to refer to government (V. Ostrom 1986a). In this tradition, government is regulated by and has its procedures defined from those fundamental agreements, and by citizens' experience in solving their collective problems over time.

A third important distinction between the monocratic-hierarchical tradition and this second or "self-governance" tradition is the central role played by the "working rules" in the latter. In the monocratic tradition, a *ruler* governs or rules a people. That ruler might be a monarch, a parliament, a charismatic leader, a revolutionary cadre, or some other figure or council with absolute power over the *subjects*. Who or what composes the ruler is less important than the logic of its unlimited, ultimate authority (V. Ostrom 1986a). Neither other actors nor rules limit his choices, at least not in any institutionalized sense.

This role does not exist in any simple way in the second tradition. Instead, a body of fundamental agreements "constitutes" a set of political relationships and working rules among *citizens* of the polity. Those rules define, empower and limit those who may act with the authority of the state as well as defining upon whom, under what conditions, and regarding what questions. The emphasis on *rules* to organize such political relationships makes it possible to disperse broadly the authority to act. The diversity which may be presumed generally to exist in contemporary society then can serve as a vested interest to sustain self-governance. That diversity must also be presumed to be bounded by agreement on certain broad norms of social and political organization. While this last question cannot be *a priori* resolved, discussions such as Professor Hyden's in this volume (see Chapter 11) and this chapter, below, suggest there may be the foundation for such agreement in many African states.

The logic of "self-governance" is also important in that it allows space for many access points and rule-based organizations which permit citizens to join with one another to take collective action: to tax, contract, hire, fire, borrow, mandate, and face the consequences of these choices. Similarly, it can facilitate many rule-based organizations which allow citizens to act in a mediating position between individuals and the sovereign actions of government. It is thus *"polycentric."*

The second tradition also provides a structure to allow for what has been described as a *"compounded"* governmental system (V. Ostrom 1986a; 1987). If governance occurs through working rules which establish political relationships among citizens, and does not require that one organization, group, or person have absolute authority over a defined space, then there is no reason why several processes of governance cannot occur simultaneously among a people. Constituting agreements can establish multiple organizations and rules of action to provide for varying needs and goods. Each organization and process can be held separately accountable to its respective community of interest according to rules established by that community (Ostrom et al. 1961; Oakerson et al. 1987). Such a system helps to balance autonomous local governance with effective national authority. Therefore, the entire nation is governed by a single body of *rules*, manipulable by the nation through known procedures. Within those rules, national, regional and local organizations are allowed to take on certain tasks and responsibilities. Once again, rulership is replaced by self-governance. Maximizing the populace's self-organizing capabilities under regimes of law becomes a goal and key role rather than an obstacle for central state organizations (V. Ostrom 1986a; 1986b; 1987; Tocqueville 1966; Oakerson 1985).

In large and diverse polities, as most of Africa's are, where there exist diverse communities, such self-governing arrangements can allow for the simultaneous operation of alternative sets of political relationships based on regimes reflecting diverse norms, as well as other, more encompassing political relationships based on regimes which reflect more generalized and shared norms. The latter can work to resolve the interdependencies which exist among the several communities. In contemporary government, such arrangements are generally labeled as varieties of "federalism"; however, this must be understood generically (V. Ostrom 1983; 1987). Federal-like relationships can be established in what are essentially unitary states through the instrument of devolution (see Chapters 4 and 9, this volume).

For such a polycentric and compound system to be sustained over time, distinctions among "levels" of rules must be understood and protected (E. Ostrom and Kiser 1982). At the most basic level are those rules which: establish fundamental personal rights and immunities from political action, and define when, where and how political organizations are established and modified (rules of "constitutional" choice). At a second level are rules which define when, where, how and with what limits those organizations may establish political obligations, prohibitions, etc. (rules of collective choice; see Chapter 10, this volume).

The organizations so established are the routine working units of political life, and they pass legislation, issue orders and reach judgments which are used to construct, reconstruct, and modify the patterns of daily social and economic life. However, to be sustained, the organizations must remain subordinate to the "constituting" rules which gave them life, and which remain the prerogative of the people as a whole. In regimes of self-governance the "State," and all the awe that term carries, is best understood as being those rules, and not the organizations they spawn. Otherwise, those who occupy powerful positions in these organizations can quickly move to complete dominance of the polity, redefining citizen rights and obligations, and revising their permissable scopes of action to fit their interests. In such circumstances polycentric and compound features will be severely challenged. Predation may replace the citizens' ability to protect themselves (V. Ostrom 1986c), and may preempt their incentive to work co-operatively to better their lives. Let us discuss these latter points further.

Organizations and Institutions

While all organizations must have some authority to define the rules under which they operate, few if any are in control of all or even most of those rules. More or less "total" organizations, such as the military may have more control, particularly under war-time conditions. Others such as schools are closely circumscribed by rules over which they have little or no influence. In general, organizations which are not based on rules established "outside" of them have the potential to behave as social "rogues." Separated from systematic control by external organizations or persons, they are literally "irresponsible." As well as possessing the ability to unilaterally choose to commit great harms against others, they have the potential to become irrelevant, as their separation from society's systematic communication and control mechanisms (rule systems and other organizations) suggest they may become normatively and operationally out-of-touch, or even destructive. The "prophetic" and "tyrannical" leaders of Jackson and Rosberg, or the military in factional regimes as discussed by Decalo perhaps best fit this description (Jackson and Rosberg 1982; Decalo

1976). Such an analysis also nicely fits Zolberg's description of the life-cycles, declines, and final fates of the "one-party states" of West Africa (Zolberg 1966).

The extent to which organizations control their own rules of collective and constitutional choice and can unilaterally revise rules of individual behavior for their members is important in part because organizations inevitably are limited in membership. This leads to significant asymmetries of influence between those who are members and those who are not. When organizations control coercion, such asymmetries are explosive. Rules, when properly designed, can work to empower a broad proportion of a society and thereby ensure control over organizations (V. Ostrom 1985; 1986b). Organizations which, on the other hand, are accountable only to themselves violate a fundamental rule of political justice: no one is fit to judge a cause to which he is an interested party (Hobbes 1960). The ability to unilaterally redefine the rules of political life, the obligations of citizens, and the limits upon governors are precisely what we attempted to show were so detrimental to Africa in Chapter 3. It is, in Robert Jackson and Carl Rosberg's analysis, the single most powerful explanation of Africa's political instability since independence (Jackson and Rosberg 1982).

Because human beings are the "artisans" of their own public lives, the way they understand public life to work will affect powerfully the world they construct (V. Ostrom 1986a; 1986b). For example, if one conceptualizes social order as provided by the actions of "a government," and if one conceives of the "state" as those persons with the authority to "rule" the citizens, even if one also adheres to ideals such as popular sovereignty, democratic elections and so forth, there is a tendency to concentrate rules, power and decision-making processes so that the few will indeed be able to govern the many. One will centralize and face the problems we have discussed in this volume. Alternatively, if one conceptualizes government as "governance" and as involving a "polity," where society works peacefully upon itself to define rules in a context of fundamental agreement on certain norms of proper and improper action, and through many organizations based on rule systems, then one will tend to create and sustain dispersed, decentralized, participative government (Tocqueville 1966).

Generally, political theory has reflected a tension between the values of these two conceptualizations: power focused into single organizations appears to make possible radical social change, but leads to terrible policy errors and cataclysmic violations of human rights as well. The dispersion of participation and control made possible by keeping organizations subordinate to rules leads to continuity of social order, but sometimes to continuities of social injustice as well. The potential for rapid change of both good and evil is generally regarded as limited in the second tradition. This is because sovereign authority is shared and multiple organizations usually share task domains when rules are beyond the reach of single organizations or persons who might dominate such organizations. The second tradition, however, is one more likely to encourage the relationships of reciprocal restraint and respect which we have argued in this volume are necessary for development to occur (see Chapters 9, 10, 11, this volume) (Oakerson, 1983).

Like all complex political relationships which attempt to balance the central capacity to act with dispersed public power, "compound" or "polycentric" institutions are vulnerable. Structural imbalance, erosion through ignorance and neglect, the apparent claims of "emergencies," and *coup* can all be threats. Furthermore, there is no sure preventative against these dangers.

However, the more a people understands the nature of political relationships, the nature of a compound/polycentric polity and what is at stake in their defense of it, and the more broadly power is dispersed by such a polity the safer it will be. In that regard, "living" the polity is its own best defense: once it becomes imbedded in a peoples interests and "mores," it will be difficult to dislodge (Tocqueville 1966).

It is important in all this to bear in mind that there are a variety of ways one can establish constituting rules which frame polycentric and compounded regimes and help to protect them from the power of political organizations. For example, in Africa, histories and myths regarding the founding of a political community in an area tend to ascribe sacred importance to certain organizing political principles which were, in effect key constituting rules (Mair 1962). Similar approaches can be seen in contemporary states, particularly Islamic ones, which choose principles and rules drawn from religious tradition. Ideology has played a similar role in many states, particularly socialist and Marxist ones. In the latter, of course, the sanctity of constituting principles is simultaneously challenged by the doctrine of the dominance of the revolutionary cadre. Nonetheless, the design principle remains valid, even though the execution here is flawed.

Many states have chosen the vehicle of the formal, written constitution and the doctrine of judicial review to distinguish constituting rules from operational rules, and to protect the former from working political organizations. Others, most clearly the United Kingdom, have neither, but instead hold as unchallengeable certain customs, agreements and well established parliamentary acts.

The key point here is that elements of rule-based political systems can be found in many places and have been protected in a variety of ways. Because even most imperial political structures, at least until the totalitarian states of the twentieth century, ruled only loosely over their subject peoples, most of the world's peoples have heritages of working polycentric and compounded polities. In contemporary Africa, for example, the. Yoruba, Tiv, Ibo, Nuer and others have precedents for polycentric and compounded systems, where enduring rules of public life structure the procedures and organizations used in public life. Once a people begins to conceptualize order and integration as growing from a multi-centered political life, it can begin to seek such principles in its own heritage.

Tensions and Vulnerabilities of
Self-Governance Regimes

In a world of fallible human beings, limited information and uncertain knowledge, one must assume any political architecture will face vulnerabilities. The overcentralized state, we have attempted to show, has been vulnerable to problems of abuse of power, poor communication between center and periphery, rigid and ineffective policy-making and implementation, and underutilization of indigenous, grassroots-level social infrastructure and knowledge.

The self-governance state must also be assumed to have vulnerabilities. Given the relaxation of close central control and the broad political empowerment such a system implies, one would expect that some of these will deal with controlling conflict and encouraging cooperation among the various units of government organized under the aegis of the national regime. One might also expect vulnerability to reduce accountability by the multitude of organizations made possible by polycentric/compound regimes. Finally, one might expect, as discussed in the previous section, some vulnerability of constitutional and collective choice rules to powerful political organizations with authority to make collective choices (E. Ostrom and Kiser 1982; V. Ostrom 1986a).

To all of these vulnerabilities, the first buttress is understanding. Africans pushed toward highly centralized regimes as the most likely successful development modality. Africans who come to understand and believe in self-governance regimes must similarly work to explain, improve and protect them. As human beings we create, in some measure, our worlds from our own understanding (V. Ostrom 1980). As political artisans who grow to understand alternative paths to social order and human development, we can have an incalculable affect on their survival by our understanding and active support of their key features.

Even individuals of good faith, however, must be expected in a world of limited knowledge and understanding, to understand differently the obligations and prohibitions of law and the opportunities and limits of development. Fallibility contributes to this as well (V. Ostrom 1986c). From these different understandings will come creative, varying, and adapting organizations pursuing human development. There will also emerge conflicts among units, threats to basic human rights, and deviations from accepted sound and honest administrative practice. Such instances appear to demand redress and thus incline central organizations to reimpose central control.

When that central control is exercised through conventional administrative hierarchies, the centripetal tendencies of central power (growing from controls over budgets, personnel, legal authority, police power, and other resources such as status, wealth and visibility) will tend to strip localities of the autonomy needed to act as viable political organizations, and to gradually erode the working instruments of self-governance polities.

Courts of law, as working entities in one form or another, however, can provide needed integrating and regulating functions without such dramatic centripetal dangers. Lacking authority over budgets and personnel, lacking immediate control over police forces, and lacking the general powers of national legislatures and executives, courts can be the enforcement mechanism which link national rule-based provisions to local organizational activity. With bodies of law defining criminal actions, establishing civil liability, and establishing general parameters of organization, operation and policy, courts can be the key linkage between the center's need for "macro"-management, and the periphery's need for "micro"-independence. If courts are accessible to individual citizens, so much the better: each person can serve as a sentinel for his or her locality. Furthermore, rules of civil liability provide an incentive for local authorities to correct damaging behavior earlier rather than later (V. Ostrom 1976; 1983; 1986a). The stubborn survival of independent African judiciaries, even at times within military and single-party regimes, indicates that outlining such a role for the courts in Africa is not merely wishful thinking (Legum 1985).

Accountability is generally seen as another vulnerability for self-governance systems. We would suggest this danger has been exaggerated. Lacking hierarchical supervision, the worry goes, to whom are the multitude of civil service personnel accountable? Local elections can be a key system to deal with this problem. Local elections close "feedback" loops much more tightly, and can encourage civil servant orientation to locality needs. Functioning, competitive parliamentary elections in both Kenya and Tanzania suggest that electoral politics, too, is *not* beyond the ability of Africans. The powerful role voluntary organizations, often structured by elections, have played in development activities throughout West Africa suggests electoral systems can also work in local affairs (Little 1966; Smock 1971; Wunsch 1974). Once considered, it seems most fears for "accountability" are really for "accountability" to (i.e., control by) the center.

Needless to say, concerns of professionalism, competence and honesty remain very much a part of people's worries in such a system. General (central) parameters over such matters as training, licensing, compensation, security, etc., can co-exist with substantial local control through local councils with hiring, taxing, firing and spending powers. Court systems can further serve to safeguard critical parameters while avoiding close hierarchical supervision from the center. Overall regulations plus a role for the courts can encourage systemic integration, while elections can be used to encourage accountability to local desires and needs.

Basic human rights are also of concern in self-governance regimes. While the effectiveness of monocentric regimes in guaranteeing human rights has certainly been open to question, one must presume that where many loosely linked organizations are developing and pursuing politics, violations will occur. This issue is critical both because of its intrinsic importance and because certain elementary rights of personhood are clearly necessary if elections are to work locally to assure accountability, and if persons are to be able to work at all levels to protect rules of constitutional and collective choice (Ely 1980). Here again a functioning courts system is essential. And again, as noted above, a broad dispersion of political power is probably necessary to provide an animated social interest in *having* and sustaining such a courts system.

Leadership and Public Policy

In many ways, the understanding and effectiveness of leadership will be critical to the survival and success of a self-governance system. This is because the nominal institutional or "rule" provisions are only the starting point in developing true *working* rules which sustain these political relationships. Such working rules can derive (and have derived) from a variety of nominal provisions; it is the working reality which is critical. It is in part leadership that chooses to build institutions which brings this about. For leaders seeking rapid development, however, this poses some dilemmas.

Leaders are obviously concerned with solving problems. However, general questions of direction and management are perplexing in regimes of self-governance. Leaders do not have the sort of absolute control they appear to have in a monocratic system. However, by working through and protecting the rules which define the structure of opportunities and constraints faced by the many organizations active in self-governing societies, leadership may be able to exert a far more powerful long-term influence: reciprocity, respect and restraint may lead to more productive long-term programs and policies (Oakerson, 1988).

Leadership properly understood in regimes of self-governance is primarily concerned with protecting and fine tuning the institutions (rules) which create the processes and organizations that operate throughout society. This differs from the attempt to control and determine in detail the outcomes of actions taken by the organizations brought to life by the state's legal structure. This does not deny the importance of specific policy outcomes. Specific policy outcomes are important because of their undoubted impact on human beings' lives, because they are critical information for assessing institutional performance, and because they are clues to use to redesign those institutions. However, leaders simply lack the leverage, either themselves alone or through dominant organizations, to control outcomes directly. The attempt to do so has repeatedly led to overwhelming avalanches of information and clogged decisions at the center, distorted information, damaging authority leakage, and to dangers of corruption, coercion, and abuse of power when dominating organizations are used to extend the ruler's faltering reach (Jackson and Rosberg 1982).

Instead, what leaders' information and influence makes them able to do is to pay close heed to the general behaviors elicited by the structures of incentives and disincentives which rules create, and to seek to modify these rules in ways which work to encourage self-organizing capabilities throughout society. Their "relative advantage" and key role (which no one else can perform) is in constructing and revising political frameworks.

When leaders allow local governmental organizations to make their own decisions and mistakes over a long time and over a substantial space, the universe of experience generated can be expected to become more diverse, creating more effective solutions to problems than any small circle of leaders could have possibly discovered on their own. At that point, manipulation of such legitimate authority which they may have over such rules as revenue authorizations, personnel standards, size of local governments and the like, may well effect the improvements they discover without suborning the autonomy, creativity or effectiveness of local government. Decentralization through rule-based institutions thus paradoxically can become a tool by which the power of local persons and of national governing institutions are simultaneously expanded. This is because a self-governance type constitution is positive-sum: it allows for the expansion of collective choice capacities throughout the state. While there will no doubt be conflict at times among the various levels, nonetheless, the energy available to the system has increased. As long as the existence of each level is protected, the normative agreement within society is proportionate to the authority to make choices allocated to that level, and there exist procedures to resolve the dispute, the conflict can probably be tolerated.

Similarly, leaders in self-governance regimes must heed the rules outlining their own processes or rules of action, as they attempt to manipulate the rules which influence the "world of daily affairs." While a given set of collective choice rules may at times impede progress toward what is seen by some as necessary collective choices, the existence of those constituting rules is an invaluable defense against personalism, arbitrary government, and what tend to become exploitative and fragile regimes (Jackson and Rosberg 1982). In general, the critical role for political leaders in such regimes is to understand and analyze institutions as frameworks which facilitate general outcomes, consider how well these frameworks are operating, how they may be refined to work more effectively (given generally chosen goals), and how to modify them through existing rule frameworks (Fuller 1981). Such change may come slowly, but the public support necessary to bring it about can serve to ensure its success.

Rules themselves, in such a state, can be seen as strongly influenced by the fundamental beliefs held by members of the polity regarding right and wrong. The state, in the logic of self-governance, grows from such norms, and if the center is to sustain self-governance, it will be limited by the type and extent of norms shared. State, in other words, is created by society in this model, and can continue as an enterprise in self-governance rather than an exercise in dominance only in so far as that relationship continues. This has important implications for the scale and pace of change that the center can assert. Revolutionary dogma and elite radicalism are each fundamentally irrelevant (though certainly dangerous) to creating and sustaining such a polity. Instead, the routine and repeated experiences of daily life, and the patterns of lessons of self-control, temperance, mutual respect, cooperation, tolerance, or the opposites prevailing in society, are critical to understand the sources and future of the polity. The "habits of the heart" of a society interact with institutions and material conditions to produce the social behaviors and politics which characterize it and change it over time (Tocqueville 1966).

Multi-ethnic or multi-national polities, history suggests, can be built on such bases if there is a core of shared values among the social groups involved, and if leaders take care that the security of various communities is protected. Measures of "consociation" such as those discussed by Lijphart can be usefully employed, both to avoid threatening component groups and to encourage favorable contact which gradually integrates the various parts (Lijphart 1977). Maxwell Owusu's study of multi-ethnic micro-politics in Swedru, Ghana, is an excellent example of such a working arrangement (Owusu 1970).

It is regarding these last issues, the patterns of daily life created by the polity, that leaders in a rule-focused self-governance-oriented state should pay particular heed. In this understanding of "state," the leaders' shared role in formulating and reformulating rules of individual conduct and collective action give them their most powerful lever to influence the path of social change. Society, in this paradigm is not "forced" into new directions by a dominant organization, but led by the types of relationships that are encouraged and discouraged among persons and communities. Rules which encourage advantage taking, violence, severe asymmetries in influence, lack of accountability and the like among persons, will stimulate conflict, exploitation, social-economic withdrawal and decay. As Chapter 9 suggested, such pernicious "circles" developed in Nigeria in the First Republic and led directly to its collapse. Leaders and citizens must therefore pay particular heed to the task of defining individual rights and obligations which produce behaviors conducive to the type of society they have chosen. Such a system can provide far more space for the reciprocity discussed in Chapter 11 as typical of African societies than centralized regimes can. Once the failure of the centralist state strategy is clear, it is equally clear that these questions are critically important because they are the way a people gradually chooses its own destiny: what sort of behavior will any given rule elicit, and what are the social implications of that behavior?

Africa and Self-Governance

The reader may justifiably wonder if this could really be applied in Africa, given its current conditions and apparent future. Is it sensible to expect that regimes, whose major problem is the absence of institutional government, will change by our simply demonstrating the logic and potential of such institutions? There are three answers to this. *First,* insofar as African leaders misunderstood the relative roles of organizations and institutions, rhetoric, policies and actions then led them directly to the center-dominant, organizationally restricted system characteristic hitherto of the overcentralized state. If leadership's understandings and behaviors were to change, then an environment where institutions or rules might flourish would be strengthened. While the discussion of this book has repeatedly referred to structures, rules and organizations, the authors are aware of the fact that these emerge from working rules, not from paper constitutions. Working rules are created by human beings. Revised understanding of the polity and what the implications of various choices of paradigms may be is the first step to developing such working rules, and then of building from them stable, enduring institutions which begin to carry the normative power of "law."

Second, and as suggested in Chapter 9's study of Nigeria, law, rules and institutions of self-governance flourish under circumstances of contestation and dispersion of power (also see Berman 1983). Once political life is granted to people and to a number of organizations by rules favoring organizational multiplicity and diversity under law, turning the clock back becomes increasingly difficult. The same dynamic that threw colonialism out after World War II could work to protect vital domestic politics and the rules that organize it, once reestablished (Mawhood 1983). It is instructive that in spite of her serious challenges, Nigeria has remained the African state with perhaps the most independent judiciary, and one with unusually stubborn, resilient civilian politics. The social and organizational diversity growing from her vast size and protected by her federalism has slowed (though not halted—see Chapter 9) centralization, and has worked repeatedly to bring her leaders back to rule through law rather than through dominant organizations. The pattern, as noted in Chapter 9, of her gradually increasing centralization, is a salutary reminder of the power of centripetal forces. Nonetheless, Nigeria remains Africa's least centralized polity, and one with forces still quick to protest arbitrary, lawless government.

Third, we are confident that the cultural basis for regimes of self-governance does exist in Africa. Many supporters of centralization have essentially argued that centralized, authoritarian governments are necessary for Africa because of its ethnic diversity. To be sure, and considering Africa in general, we would not dispute that great social diversity exists, nor would we deny the destructive force unleashed in ethnic conflict. Yet, we would offer several additional observations which may put these issues in perspective.

While Africans are diverse and spread across a broad continent, these differences are matters of degree, and peoples living in proximity often share important fundamental moral understandings. For example, Melville Herskovits, often regarded as the founder of African studies in the United States, has argued that much of the emphasis on particularistic differences among Africans was produced by colonialism and served imperialism's interests in justifying the arbitrary and casual carving up of Africa. Similarly, the down-playing of Africans' moral philosophy served other Western imperial interests. Instead, he argued, Africans possessed, then and now, a complex web of values, which, ". . . had stood the Africans in good stead as they adjusted to the internal or external innovations to which they had been exposed through the centuries." These values have included individual deference, loyalty and obligation to community, subordinating individualism to social cooperation, and deference to tradition (Herskovits 1958: 472).

In the dominant rationalist-individualist paradigm of Western civilization such values have been customarily dismissed as "primitive," and as impediments to building the "modern" nation-state. Quite commonly they are dismissed as "particularistic" and also are blamed for "tribalism." And yet, when the Western paradigm is understood as what it is: simply one culture's set of assumptions (among many cultures) about human nature on such questions as individualism vs. community, rationality vs. diverse sources of wisdom, and secularism vs. faith, then the cultural imperialism implicit in the bulk of development theory (including the centrist state modality) ought to be more clear. The illogic of assuming that complex working polities can be constructed only on the assumptions characteristic of the post-Enlightenment West should also be clear (Packenham 1973).

In fact, African values *are* different from the Enlightenment-era values dominant in the West since the eighteenth century. But that does not mean they do not exist, are not legitimate human values, nor that complex polities cannot be built upon them. Indeed, notable contemporary scholars and philosophers have come to question whether Western civilization can be sustained on secular, individualistic and rationalistic values alone (Nisbet 1975; 1983)!

Looked at from this perspective and with the history of the past three decades at hand, ethnic conflict can be seen to be produced more by the center's threatening actions regarding the various communities which sustain African's lives, than by any intrinsic hostility among Africa's peoples (Zolberg 1966; Schwarz 1969; Bates 1981; Rothchild and Olorunsola 1983). Indeed, the vast majority of African peoples have lived quite peacefully and sometimes harmoniously in close proximity and often well mixed among one another (Owusu 1971; Little 1966; Cohen 1969). They have generally remained aware of themselves as separate communities in some respects, but they have also joined together efficiently and effectively to address issues of joint concern particularly dealing with their peaceful and economically productive relationships (Hill 1970). Frequently they have developed formal institutionalized mechanisms to sustain these peaceful relations and resolve such conflict as arose among them. Indeed the working, local inter-ethnic polities that exist right now in most of Africa are powerful examples of polycentric and compounded systems (Little 1966; Wunsch 1974).

Great ethnic conflict has usually been caused by the capture, or apparent near capture, by one group of control over the *centralized* state, and the dangers of dominance this has foretold. Nigeria from independence to 1966, and in the events leading to its civil war may be the best example of this (Schwarz 1969; see Chapter 9, this volume). Sudan is a second tragic example.

The shared values of individual obligation to community, reciprocity, social cooperation, and deference to tradition are formidable norms, and rich resources upon which social relations are built. They are also powerful principles around which a polity may be integrated and working rules can be defined with broad and deep public support. Perhaps even more importantly, these are values which lend dignity and worth to all persons. Values such as these may be essential for regimes of self-governance to be sustained over time (Ostrom 1983). The success Africans have had in relating peacefully to members of other kin groups and ethnic communities suggests that such values can be used *both* to organize relationships within self-conscious communities *and* to organize effective working rules regulating the relationships among members of differing communities. It is from stable and effective working rules such as these that what are commonly referred to as "institutions" develop and the "rule of law" emerges (Commons 1959). What finally emerges may not look a lot like Western institutions. It is enough that they are generally agreed upon and reflect a deep value and respect for human dignity.

Few attempts to pursue this approach to human organization have been pursued. Decentralization, for example, as a means toward self-governance has generally been approached in a way that is certain to guarantee its failure and return to centralization. For example, as Chapter 4 illustrates, decentralization efforts have tended to be limited: they have been largely deconcentration, where fiscal, personnel, policy and programmatic authority have been maintained at the center. Ill equipped, either in resources or authority for their responsibilities, local governments have foundered. Similarly, lacking real authority to act, local governments have not generated the local political interest and commitment which theorists such as Tocqueville and scholars such as Mawhood (1983) and Kasfir (1983) have argued are necessary for local capacity to develop. Thus, decentralization has been preordained to defeat.

At the other extreme, and not without justifiable concern, the centralists point to numerous problems they believe will be intensified by substantial decentralization. Ethnic diversity will be sustained and intensified; regionalism will be encouraged; nationally oriented industrialization policies might be fragmented by inter-regional rivalries; resources will be spread too thinly; inter-ethnic and inter-regional equity issues will become more difficult to resolve; economic coordination will become problematic, and the like. A number of these concerns are noted in Chapter 8, on East Africa. Such concerns are real, but have been unnecessarily intensified by the tendency to see decentralization as an all-or-nothing proposition, where central organizations currently controlling sovereignty "deliver" that sovereignty to other, decentralized organizations. The latter, having naturally numerous and diverse perspectives on their local values and interests, are seen as beginning a process of political, social and economic fragmentation which appears never likely to end.

What is needed for self-governance to progress is to show how the concerns of those who understand the need for national policies and programs in certain areas can be met, yet al.so allow for genuine local autonomy in others where the interests and programs of localities' infringe little upon one another and local creativity and flexibility can bring real benefits. This chapter has argued that such a balance can be met once scholars, officials and citizens understand the paramount need for institutions or law in governance, the subsidiary role of organizations, the role that dispersed power plays in protecting rule-governed relationships, and once they begin to use those understandings to define working rules which create and sustain these self-governing relationships.

Of course, only Africa's peoples and its leaders can make the decision to turn from an overcentralized political system, and to build one which allows for, structures, and assists the growth of the multiple organization which we have argued would speed development. Were they to make such a decision, then a major intellectual and applied task of political engineering would confront them. While only they have their capacity to design such a system and to refine it to meet their specific conditions, we have attempted to show the important consequences implied in choosing between these two paradigms of human governance.

Development in Polycentric/Compound Polity

How could the abstract system described so far in this paper provide any improved prospect for speeding development to Africa's impoverished rural dwellers? What follows is a vignette of how this might work regarding a key problem: local government and rural development.

Decentralization to a large variety of local governments regulated by law makes possible the existence of a large number of flexible, diverse organizations. These, in turn, can allow persons, groups and communities to act collectively to pursue their various conceptions of the good. This provides several possible advantages, including: 1) the enhanced capacity to avoid and correct error associated with organizational redundancy; 2) the potential to reduce the intensity of political conflict; 3) the capacity to articulate programs more closely to community values; 4) and the potential to neutralize tendencies to concentrate and abuse power at all levels of government. Let us review the arguments.

Redundancy, duplication and overlap have been seen as important design strategies to improve organizational performance. As organizations make decisions, gather and process information, interpret meaning, test paradigms, and supervise programs, redundancy, etc., appears to help avoid error and to provide early detection and correction when it does occur (Landau 1969; 1986). Particularly in Africa (as in other LDCs) where theories of social and economic change are incomplete and data is almost always inadequate or in error, diverse sources of information and interpretation will be critical for political institutions to avoid serious error (Rondinelli 1982). Single-chain organizational systems are only as strong as their weakest link; redundant organizational systems, particularly where varying organizational models are used simultaneously, have the potential to compensate for their varying weaknesses.

Political conflict also may be eased by increasing the number and diversity of local governments. Dispersing the rewards of political success widely by maintaining many offices, governments, and private niches, reduces the costs of losing any single political contest. Many active organizations lower the likelihood that one organization can gain dominance over rule-generating institutions through control of personnel or of overwhelming rewards or punishments. Similarly, offering private citizens several avenues of organization, appeal and action reduces their stake in any single, official action. Spreading decision-making widely, including to such polycentric actors as an independent judiciary, separate units of local government, labor organizations, and private business, helps to ease the explosive costs and benefits of "winning" and "losing" in the political economy. This need not mean the abdication of the polity's right to regulate and supervise such areas as the economy so it operates consistently with collective values. These can be supported in multi-organizational systems by rules implemented by an independent judiciary, and through ongoing central-government roles such as those reviewed in Chapter 5 of this volume.

Increased organizational flexibility can also allow a closer fit between values, operating rules, and methods of collective choice. To the extent that law is accepted because it is consistent with people's values or because it has been adopted through rules which themselves reflect a people's values, the legitimacy of law is strengthened, and, it has been frequently hypothesized, it therefore becomes more self-enforcing and more effective (Fuller 1981). There is space in this approach for smaller units of governance, ones which can reflect varying norms and value systems. Larger units also exist when agreement is broader and/or policy consistency is truly critical. It allows for simultaneous layers of governance across any given locality.

Thus, communities might be authorized to establish multiple education organizations to reflect varying religious or ethnic values. A community might have one organization to provide for commonly desired physical facilities and public safety; perhaps two to provide for diverse representation in a more general unit of government; and be part of a larger unit established across several communities to provide for flood control, livestock health services, or a medical dispensary. Where values are divergent and pertinent to the production of a particular public service, separate jurisdictions may be established. People, of course, will live within multiple jurisdictions at any given moment, and that is in fact not a problem but an advantage. This is in part, as the literature on social relations in Africa clearly indicates, because the "traditional-modern" dichotomy of human social psychology model is fallacious. Instead, there is good evidence that people are "situation selectors" who find little difficulty in perceiving that they have multiple needs and that their support for a variety of organizations with varying populations are appropriate to help fill those needs

(Smock 1971; Wolpe 1974; Bunker 1987; Owusu 1970; Parkin 1969; Little 1966; Cohen 1969). Furthermore, many have argued that the existence of multiple identifications is an effective force for social integration and easing the stakes of conflict (Dahl 1963).

One of the advantages of such a flexible and diverse system is the use it can make of still thriving working rules of social political organizations often dismissed as "traditional," "ethnic," "backward," or "divisive." For, as we have argued in Chapter 1 of this volume, the bulk of Africa has endured both the colonial and independent eras with little social order provided by the center: policemen, lawyers, courts, etc., are virtually never seen in the rural areas where the vast bulk of the people live. Yet, in most areas social order is maintained, civil disputes do not arise willy-nilly, and when they do they are often resolved at the local level according to local rule systems and without reference to external actors or "national" rule systems (Little 1966). Local organizations have implemented complex, costly, long-term community improvement programs (Smock 1971). Rule systems like these, where they still exist, embody substantial wisdom about social relations, retain significant amounts of social legitimacy, and often enormous amounts of implicit social support. They are, right now, the bedrock of real governance in much of contemporary Africa; they could become a powerful source of legitimacy, popular support, and counterbalancing power for national organizations, were they supported by and integrated into the general or "national" institutions.

Finally, a large number of diverse organizations offers human beings methods to combine in order to protect their critical values and key interests. As Mancur Olson suggested two decades ago, the capacity to organize is not equally available to all groups: the largest, most dispersed and poorest face the greatest costs to organize at the same time that they have the fewest easily available methods of meeting those costs (Olson 1965). Recently, Robert Bates' analysis of the relative success in Africa of small farmers versus large farmers in capturing the spoils and protecting themselves from the depredations of governments has illustrated the pertinence of Olson's analysis (Bates 1981). The many small farmers regularly lose to the few larger farmers because the former lack structures through which they can organize to protect themselves. The ease with which earlier potentially polycentric and compounded systems fell before monocratic forces must be understood in large part as a problem of insufficient distribution of power throughout the state.

With viable, functioning local organizations addressing the many social issues and needs, national leaders will be more able to focus on the commanding heights of the economy: on national economic policy, debt management, natural resource development, higher and technical education, negotiation with foreign states and corporations, and evaluating the impact of national revenue, personnel, etc.

They will also be able to focus on national policies and frameworks to encourage better performance by these many local authorities. These latter are tasks which do need to be done, which local governments cannot do, and ones for which national governments have a relative advantage of position, resource and perspective. On the other hand, at the local level variations in organizational modalities can be pursued to fit local needs, experiences and circumstances. Some will fail and thus can be avoided, but other approaches may work surprisingly well, and lead to new organizations in the nation's institutional "repertoire." Moreover, the artful use of courts and a wide-spread right and capacity by individuals to bring suit can help remedy what "fragmented" corruption develops at the local level. And yet, one looks long and hard across Africa for such institutions of local government.

Conclusions

This chapter has argued that many of Africa's development problems have grown from a paradigm "problem": from the misunderstanding so powerful in the world today that governing is something done by governments rather than as a process carried on by citizens through diverse organizations empowered and limited by institutions or rules of law adopted and modified by a people. Once governance was so misunderstood, *organizations* rather than *rules, institutions* and *citizens* became the dominant structure of governance. Often pursuing the interests of their members, a few powerful organizations displaced, preempted, absorbed and occasionally destroyed the vast diversity of organizations that every society needs. Error, abuse of power and stagnation soon resulted.

Instead, I have argued that polities could be better understood as the relationships springing from the accumulated working rules or "institutions" of a people, and that attention to forming and molding these rules and institutions so they assure many diverse and flexible organizations is the essential prerequisite to development. Through these institutions national organizations can be empowered and limited to perform national functions, and lesser organizations can be empowered and limited to perform more local functions. Such a system would challenge African leaders to develop working rules which sustain self-governance and to support and refine these rules until they became institutions and developed the legitimacy of law. To construct such regimes of law and to work through them would be a slower but perhaps a more sure road to sustained development. It is a challenge to build institutions which will transcend personnel and time to become the tools of development for the people.

References

Bates, Robert. *Markets and States in Tropical Africa.* Berkeley: University of California Press, 1981.

Berman, Harold. *Law and Revolution: The Formation of the Western Legal Tradition.* Cambridge, Mass.: Harvard University Press, 1983.

Bunker, Stephen G. *Peasants Against the State: The Politics of Market Control in Bugisu, Uganda, 1900–1983.* Urbana: University of Illinois Press, 1987.

Cohen, Abner. *Custom and Politics in Urban Africa.* Berkeley: University of California Press, 1969.

Commons, John R. *Legal Foundations of Capitalism.* Madison: University of Wisconsin Press, 1959.

Dahl, Robert. *A Preface to Democratic Theory.* Chicago: University of Chicago Press, 1963.

Decalo, Samuel. *Coups and Army Rule in Africa: Studies in Military Style.* New Haven, Conn.: Yale University, 1976.

Ely, John Hart. *Democracy and Distrust: A Theory of Judicial Review.* Cambridge, Mass.: Harvard University Press, 1980.

Fuller, Lon. *The Principles of Social Order.* Edited by Kenneth Winston. Durham, N.C.: Duke University Press, 1981.

Gellar, Sheldon. *State Building and Nation-Building in West Africa.* Bloomington: International Development Research Center, Indiana University 1972.

Herskovits, Melville. *The Human Factor in Changing Africa.* New York: Vintage Books, 1958.

Hill, Polly. *Studies in Rural Capitalism in West Africa.* London: Cambridge University Press, 1970.

Hobbes, Thomas. *Leviathan or the Matter, Forme and Power of a Commonwealth Ecclesiastical and Civil.* Michael Oakeshott, editor. Oxford: Basil Blackwell, 1960.

Jackson, Robert, and Carl Rosberg. *Personal Rule in Black Africa: Prince, Autocrat, Prophet, Tyrant.* Berkeley: University of California Press, 1982.

———. "Sovereignty and Underdevelopment: Juridicial Statehood in the African Crisis." *Journal of Modern African Studies* 24 (1) (1986): 1–32.

Kasfir, Nelson. "Designs and Dilemmas: An Overview." In *Local Government in the Third World,* edited by P. Mawhood, 25–48. Chichester: John Wiley, 1983.

Kiser, Larry L., and Elinor Ostrom. "The Three Worlds of Action: A Metatheoretical Synthesis of Institutional Approaches." In *Strategies of Political Inquiry,* edited by Elinor Ostrom, 179–222. Beverly Hills: Sage Publications, 1982.

Landau, Martin. "Redundancy, Rationality, and the Problem of Duplication and Overlap." *Public Administration Review* 29 (July/August 1969): 346–358.

———. "On Decision Strategies and Management Structures: With Special Reference to Experimentation." Berkeley, CA: Institute of Governmental Studies, Mimeo, 1986.

Landau, Martin, Suchitra Bhakdi, Ledivinia Carino, Rolando Tungpalan and James Wunsch. *Final Report: Provincial Development Assistance Project.* Berkeley: Institute of International Studies, 1980.

Legum, Colin. "The Future of Democracy." *West Africa* (June 1985): 1110–1111.

Lenin, V. I. *What is to be Done?* New York: International Publishers, 1969.

Lijphart, Arend. *Democracy in Plural Societies: A Comparative Exploration.* New Haven, Conn.: Yale University, 1977.

Lindblom, Charles E. *Politics and Markets: The World's Political-Economic Systems.* New York: Basic Books, 1977.

Little, Kenneth. *West African Urbanization: A Study of Voluntary Associations in Social Change.* Cambridge: Cambridge University Press, 1966.

Lord, Carnes (translator). *Aristotle: The Politics.* Chicago: University of Chicago Press, 1984.

Mair, Lucy. *Primitive Government.* Bloomington, Ind.: Indiana University Press, 1962.

Mawhood, P. *Local Government for Development: The Experience of Tropical Africa.* Chichester: John Wiley, 1983.

Mickelwait, Donald, et al. *The New Directions Mandate: Studies in Project Design, Approval and Implementation.* Revised. Washington, D.C.: Development Alternatives, 1978.

Nisbet, Robert. *The Twilight of Authority.* New York: Oxford University Press, 1975.

———. *Community and Power.* New York: Oxford University Press, 1983.

Nkrumah, Kwame. *Revolutionary Path.* New York: International Publishers, 1973.

Nyerere, Julius. *Ujamaa: Essays on Socialism.* London: Oxford University Press, 1968.

———. *Freedom and Development: A Selection from Writings and Speeches, 1968–1973.* London: Oxford University Press, 1973.

Oakerson, Ronald J. "Fragmented Local Government: Toward a New Understanding." Bloomington, Indiana: Workshop on Political Theory and Policy Analysis, Indiana University, 1987. mimeo.

Oakerson, Ronald J. "The Meaning and Purpose of Local Government: A Tocquevillist Perspective." Washington D.C.: American Council on Inter-Governmental Relations, ACIR Working Paper, 1985.

Oakerson, Ronald J. "Reciprocity: A Bottom-Up View of Political Development." In *Rethinking Institutional Analysis and Development,* edited by Vincent Ostrom, David Feeny and Hartmut Picht, 141–158. San Francisco: International Center for Economic Growth, 1988.

Olson, Mancur. *The Logic of Collective Action.* Cambridge, Mass.: Harvard University Press, 1965.

Ostrom, Vincent. "The American Experiment in Constitutional Choice." *Public Choice* 27 (Fall 1976): 1–19.

———. "Artisanship and Artifact." *Public Administration Review* 40 (4) (July/August 1980): 309–317.

———. "Reflexions on Public Administration in Europe." In *The Development of Research and Training in European Policy-Making,* Papers presented at the Inaugural Colloquium of the European Institute of Public Administration, 122–169. Maastricht, The Netherlands: European Institute of Public Administration, 1983.

———. "Multi-Organizational Arrangements in the Governance of Unitary and Federal Political Systems." In *Policy Implementation in Federal and Unitary Systems,* edited by Kenneth Hanf and Theo A. J. Toonen, 235–265. Dordrecht, The Netherlands: Marinus Nijhoff Publishers, 1985.

———. "Constitutional Considerations with Particular Reference to Federal Systems." In *Guidance, Control, and Evaluation in the Public Sector,* edited by F. X. Kaufmann, G. Majone, and V. Ostrom, 111–125. Berlin and New York: Walter de Gruyter, 1986a.

———. "A Fallabilist's Approach to Norms and Criteria of Choice." In *Guidance, Control, and Evaluation in the Public Sector,* edited by F. X. Kaufmann, G. Majone, and V. Ostrom, 229–249. Berlin and New York: Walter de Gruyter, 1986b.

———. "Cryptoimperialism and Predatory States." Bloomington, Ind.: Workshop in Political Theory and Policy Analysis. Working Paper, 1986c.

———. *The Political Theory of a Compound Republic: Designing the American Experiment.* Rev. ed. Lincoln, Neb.: University of Nebraska Press, 1987.

Owusu, Maxwell. *Uses and Abuses of Political Power.* Chicago: University of Chicago Press, 1970.

Packenham, Robert. *Liberal America and the Third World.* Princeton, N.J.: Princeton University Press, 1973.

Parkin, David. *Neighbors and Nationals in An African City Ward.* Berkeley: University of California Press, 1969.

Rondinelli, Dennis. "The Dilemma of Development Administration: Complexity and Uncertainty in Control-Oriented Bureaucracies." *World Politics* XXXV (1) (October 1982): 43–72.

Rothchild, Donald, and Victor Olorunsola, eds. *State Versus Ethnic Claims: African Policy Dilemmas.* Boulder, Colo.: Westview Press, 1983.

Schwarz, Walter. *Nigeria.* New York: Praeger, 1969.

Smock, Audrey. *Ibo Politics: The Role of Ethnic Unions in Eastern Nigeria.* Cambridge, Mass.: Harvard University Press, 1971.

Tocqueville, Alexis de. *Democracy in America.* Edited by J.P. Mayer. Garden City, N.Y.: Anchor Books, 1966.

Wolpe, Howard. *Urban Politics in Nigeria: A Study of Port Harcourt.* Berkeley: University of California Press, 1974.

Wunsch, James. *Voluntary Associations: Determinants of Structure and Activity in Two Ghanaian Secondary Cities.* Ph.D. Dissertation. Bloomington: Indiana University, 1974.

————. "Administering Rural Development: Have Goals Outreached Organizational Capacity?" *Public Administration and Development* 3 (1986): 239–263.

Zolberg, Aristotle. *Creating Political Order: The Party-States of West Africa.* Chicago: Rand McNally, 1966.

13

Conclusion: Self-Governance and African Development

Dele Olowu and James S. Wunsch

This volume has reviewed theories, policies, and practices which advocate political and administrative centralization as the solution to Africa's development problems. We have conjectured that centralization has tended to increase rather than ease the continent's underdevelopment. Through a combination of historical and theoretical analyses (Chapters 1 through 5 and Chapters 10 through 12) as well as case studies of specific countries (Chapters 6 to 9), we have assessed the impact of political centralization on development and governmental performance. We have consistently sought general patterns in the search for theory and general solutions. We recognize there is great variability among African states, and note that our findings need to be adapted to each state's unique circumstances.

To avoid being misunderstood, it is important to state at this point what the book has not done. First, we have not argued that Africa's peoples have failed. Confronted by ecological, economic, demographic, and political crises, African countries have made some significant achievements since independence. At independence, some two to three decades ago, many countries had few indigenous senior officials. The whole of the French Central African Federation from which emerged four independent African countries had only five university graduates at independence. Conditions were much worse in former Portuguese and Belgium colonies (Tordoff 1984). Many African countries now have the basic core of a professional bureaucracy and an independent judiciary. As was explained in Chapter 2, colonial rule presented independent African states with some unfortunate legacies which many of them have had difficulty altering. Moreover, two to three decades is a rather short period in which to judge overall success or failure. The ability of Africa's peoples to rule themselves is not at issue. Indeed, even with flawed institutions of governance, they have accomplished much. Rather, we have argued that the centralized state *strategy* has failed and that many of Africa's genuine successes have occurred in spite of and have been limited by that strategy.

Second, we have not argued that African states are more centralized than other nations judged simply by the ratio of central government expenditures to the gross domestic product. As we have indicated in Chapters 1 and 5, African states may not be considered as centralized on the basis of such data alone. Rather, we have tried to demonstrate, especially through the country cases, that African states are institutionally overcentralized. The major elements of centralization on which we have focused are both economic and political: relative resource and expenditure levels between central and sub-national units, the relative importance of government in the national economy, and the levels of general civic capacity and constitutional concentration.

Third, we have not argued that the solution to these general problems is simply "decentralization." Instead we have tried to develop and show the power of the idea of "self-governance." By self-governance we mean, essentially, the institutionalized empowerment of the people, and the expansion of their ability to engage in collective choice and action at a variety of scales of human organization. Too often "decentralization," as discussed in Chapter 4 and in the case studies, has simply replaced one form of "tutelage" and rulership for another.

This volume examined at length the sources of the widely accepted presupposition that centralized political and administrative structures are more conducive to the development process. This core presupposition has been hitherto sustained by four widely held beliefs about African development, all of them influenced heavily by sources outside the continent. These are:

(1) the doctrine of elite superiority in consolidating and sustaining the social order;
(2) the promises of rationalism, science, and money for the transformation of underdeveloped societies (Hyden 1983);
(3) certain interpretations of the experience of continental Europe relating to the emergence of the state, modernization, and bureaucratization (Grimm 1986; Kaufmann 1986); and
(4) a heritage of colonial administration which emphasized the executive vis-a-vis other essential political institutions (Sellasie 1974; Young 1982).

Throughout this book, though especially in Chapter 3, we illustrated five developments which have tended to follow from these core presuppositions and how they have eroded development. The first is the replacement of competitive politics by a one-party system dedicated to national unity. With a few exceptions, this has been the norm in Africa. The second is the reliance on a single, bureaucratic structure accountable solely to the central executive, and extending into the countryside. This approach views development as a process which must be centrally planned and funded from above. The third is the struggle against ethnicity and ethnic consciousness through a unitary political order, one which precludes the existence of any autonomous local units of governance, modern or traditional. The fourth is the centralization of authority in the hands of the executive. And the fifth is a focus on the national budget as the primary instrument of development. In the sections which follow, we shall review how these presuppositions and developments produced counterintuitive results. We will also review what we believe to be a critical issue: how development has been conceptualized in Africa, and how that understanding led to the centralist strategy.

Development: An Institutional Problem

We noted in several chapters of this book that there is a broad consensus that "development," whose ultimate goals are material improvement in the peoples' condition of life and political integration including the opportunities for popular participation, constitutes a reasonable goal for African states. However, the strategy by which these desirable goals should be achieved enjoys no similar consensus. At the core of the centralist strategy are beliefs that industrialization holds the key to rapid economic growth, is the forerunner to both economic and political development, and that centralization by the state is the key to this industrialization.

Such a conception of development has led to the familiar situation in which state-run or state-supported import-substituting industries emerged behind high tariffs. Robert Bates has shown how the urban political class manipulated the prices paid for agricultural exports, imposed high taxes on farmers, and manipulated the exchange rate regime to ensure that sufficient resources were extracted from "traditional" agriculture to support "modern" industries. The latter, in fact, contributed very little to the overall development process (Bates 1981). Because of the cheap imports resulting from an overvalued currency, such industries have few backward linkages, operate at high costs, and turn out poor quality, shoddy products. This represented severe opportunity costs, particularly when one recalls how scarce resources were (and are) in these states.

The political implications of this development strategy were even more damaging. Most African leaders and their advisers believed that only the state had the capacity, the knowledge, and vision to bring about industrialization as well as the social transformations which go with it. Such beliefs were grounded in models of development which regarded the process of development as the application of modern science, capital, and technology to the African environment. This environment was regarded as replete with ignorance, tradition, and low productivity. African economies were understood to be dualistic, comprised of "modern" and "traditional" sectors. The modern sector was viewed as productive while the "traditional" sector was seen as a subsistence area, of low or even negative marginal productivity. This view was extended not just to the economy but also to all other aspects of society (Lewis 1955; Rostow 1961). As Goran Hyden

explained elsewhere (Hyden 1983), this naive faith in progress had implications for the political organization of development: a treatment of society
as a *tabula rasa* on which new institutions could be imprinted. This led
to the emergence of the one-party state. "Rapid progress required national
unity and unity, in turn demanded a one-party system. . . . Politics became
an instrument of social engineering; the state an engine of change" (Chapter
11, this volume).

Even where one-party states did not emerge, military dictatorships did,
and the results everywhere have been sadly disappointing. We have reviewed in the preceding chapters the type of results which this model of
development led to—great blunders in policy and management; inefficient,
ineffective but expanding bureaucracies; extermination or repression of the
opposition; forced or voluntary exile of key leaders; mass cynicism and
alienation of the people from government; the capturing of "monopoly
rents" by bureaucratic classes which these small economies could not
tolerate; and, in several cases, to civil war or breakdown of social order.
The overall effect has been counterproductive for development: resources
have been wasted, lives have been destroyed and, often, existing institutions
have decayed.

The question that must be raised, then, is why has this been the case
in Africa? Given the seeming success of highly centralized governmental
structures in some socialist countries and the newly industrializing countries
of Asia, why has the centralized state model failed so in Africa?

While centralized strategies have been pursued elsewhere, there are
important differences which help explain why such a strategy has fared
poorly in Africa. First, several annalysts have suggested that when strong
central governments were balanced by other viable organizations, states
have fared better than when the centralized state has attempted to capture
or eradicate all other organizations: India, Hungary, Yugoslavia and Thailand may fit the first category; Burma, Vietman and the Philippines probably fit under the second (Owens and Shaw 1972). Second, strong states
in Asia and East Europe generally were planted among a more highly
mobilized and organized populous and economy, better able to balance the
state's excesses and errors than has occurred in Africa (Brett 1986). Third,
and finally, no student of contemporary affairs can fail to note the movement toward decentralization and political pluralism occurring today across
Asia and Eastern Europe. Leaders in the Soviet Union, Yugoslavia, Hungary, South Korea, Taiwan, Poland and elsewhere are seriously questioning
significant aspects of the centralist strategy, if not altogether abandoning it
in the face of its problems. Perhaps it was not as successful as many once
thought?

This volume has suggested that the centralized state strategy in African
countries has suffered from a lack of propitious circumstances and leadership since the independence period. This can be seen in three ways.
First, some aspects of centralization in Africa are premature. What might
otherwise be reasonable elements of centralization and supportive of na-

tional integration, are far ahead of other evolving institutions of society and therefore have become obstacles to social progress. As we have observed in Chapter 5, the attempts to strengthen the state or the market structures which it controls only help to consolidate the power of a few elites rather than promote responsible government or competitive market systems.

Second, and more fundamentally, the centralized strategy depends too much upon having the appropriate leadership at the center. It also assumes that such power is always wielded without corruption, a tenuous assumption in societies marked by rapid social change and gross inequalities. Third, the centralized approach to governance fails to take into consideration the dire limitations of central command systems in societies with poor infrastructure, untrained manpower resources, pre-capitalist economies and "soft" state structures (Wunsch 1986).

We have argued in this volume that while the ultimate goal of development is material and social improvement and political integration, these cannot be achieved without institutions (rules of conduct) which promote and integrate a wide diversity of organizations—political, economic and social; central and local. If we are correct, the immediate task of development should be to discover and define institutions which stimulate and encourage people to work through these organizations to improve their social and material conditions. Given the well demonstrated capability of existing, indigenous organizations in Africa, we believe that a major task in the development process must be to assist the growth and development of "old" organizations as well as the creation of new ones. Instead, African governments have at times attempted to abolish or destroy organizations they regard as archaic and anti-developmental, particularly when they are not under the control of the state. Institutions (rule sets) which facilitate a large number of organizations are required: new and old; economic, social and political. Without the existence of institutions (i.e., legal frameworks as discussed in Chapter 12, this volume) which give birth to such a wide variety of organizations and activity, the problems of institutional overload, personalism, policy error and abuse of power, will only grow worse.

Unfortunately, however, the state, at least the way it is conceived and has developed in Africa, has tended to be one which designs institutions so the center dominates all other organizations. Whether they be markets, schools, universities, local or regional governments, trade unions or political parties, the center seeks control. Unity is confused with uniformity and all opinions contrary to those expressed by the state and its officials are regarded as threatening. As Chapter 4 illustrated, while much tinkering with "decentralization" has occurred, when all is said and done the "center" insists on continuing its detailed control over the "periphery." The results of this continued control have been reviewed throughout this book.

Fortunately, as we have shown in the preceding chapters, some economists and political scientists have come to realize that the state can hamper the development process in the absence of complementary organizations. In particular, the role of a wide diversity of organizations in the development process is becoming more clearly recognized (Todaro 1981; Ashford 1967; Hyden 1983; Rivkin 1968; Esman and Uphoff 1984; Brett 1986; Krane 1986).

That money is not the sole constraint to economic development, as was once eloquently argued by Rostow and other economists who subscribed to his capital constraint model, is perhaps evident by the fact that neither the availability of large aid funds nor windfall gains from mineral extraction or agricultural exports has been able to pull a country out of underdevelopment. As the examples of Nigeria (1970–80), Zaire, Zambia, or the oil states have shown, cash surpluses often create impediments to development.

One of the major paradoxes of African underdevelopment is the fact that extreme poverty coexists with vast human and material resources. According to some estimates, only 3 percent of the continent's hydro-electric power has been harnessed and only a half of its 220 million hectares of arable land is in cultivation. Yet inadequate food and energy supplies constitute two of the major dimensions of the African crisis (Brown and Wolf 1985; *Time* 1985). Why is this the case? This volume has attempted to show how these failures can be linked to overcentralization. We believe the evidence shows that Africa's problems are not so much ones of resource poverty as much as of lack of effective organization for development. Central governments which presume alone to promote development from the center have attempted the impossible.

A major element of this problem is the lack of accountability to the people that central organizations have had. Life-tenure presidencies, regime change through military coup, and single-party/executive dominant states have been difficult to call to account for their errors. The effects of so little central accountability have been intensified by the juridicial emasculation of the rest of the system. Communities which might be expected to take charge of such local problems as roads, schools, potable water, irrigation, markets and the like, have had the institutions necessary to do this denied or even taken from them. Accountability at the center and initiative at the periphery both appear to call for the same treatment: institutions of self-governance, so Africans can create and build their own destiny. Without them in effect, little genuine development can take place. A specific example may be useful here. Frequent calls for national fiscal self-discipline have been made in Africa, particularly just after military coups. Occasionally some regimes even appear to impose such discipline. However, such self-discipline rarely appears to become institutionalized into the polity, transcending a single strong leader. Nigeria's cycle of coups and short civilian rule appears to be a prime example of this.

If one leaves exhortations to fiscal self-discipline behind, one can see how spending the bulk of the funds at the national level makes the treasury into a giant common pool resource. All raid it as quickly as they can for the most personal use they can make of it before others do so first. Furthermore, no single person perceives himself as making a trade between this individualistic scramble and whatever public goods are preempted by it. The treasury is too immense to see clearly such a linkage; the trade-offs are too unclear; and the lost benefits (if any are perceived) are too diffuse to compete with the direct benefits provided by the myriad schemes which have developed. At times, discipline is imposed from above in spite of these perverse incentives. When the force imposing it is removed, the "discipline" is soon gone.

If instead much smaller units of collective action raise, allocate and spend funds on fewer, locally focused and chosen public enterprises, some persons will have an increased incentive to observe and track those funds, and hold those who spend them to public accountability. They will perceive robbery of the treasury as robbery from them, and seek to prevent it. This is precisely what Audry Smock found in the study of Ibo Community Associations in the late 1960s (Smock 1971).

Given all this, conventional theories of underdevelopment seem not as relevant to the African situation as once thought. Such theories include the capital-constraint model of Rostow, Harrod-Domar, Lewis and Kindleberger. We find the international structuralist models also only partially relevant to Africa's present conditions, as discussed in Chapter 5. However, we have also called for some caution in respect of simplistic application of neo-classical economic models to African situations.

All these models have a tendency to promote political centralization in the absence of complementary institutions. Yet the national or central government has been grossly deficient in the performance of tasks which it has assigned to itself. Institutions (rules) of property, authority, political participation, central planning, and bureaucratic dominance have arrogated power to the center and spawned weak organizations in all sectors. Their weakness, in turn, has left the state overburdened, prone to error, and prone to abuse its power. When it has attempted to be all and do all, it has been vulnerable to serious errors and abuse from those who held power, as discussed in Chapter 3. The problem was well captured by Arnold Rivkin's perceptive question: "Can the state in Africa be all things?" (Rivkin 1968: 31). In complete agreement with him and other scholars whom we have cited in this book, we and our collaborators in this volume have returned a negative verdict.

In the remainder of this chapter we shall try to suggest how institutions which promote self-governance are crucial to several goals espoused by all those interested in African development: economic growth, social welfare, human cooperation and peace, national integration, and democracy.

Economic Development

Any serious discussion of broadly based economic development in Africa must take agriculture as its starting point. This is because this sector alone provides employment for 72 percent of the continent's labor force, and constitutes the major foreign exchange earner for most African countries.

While not denying the fact that formidable problems of an ecological and international nature exist, the agricultural sector provides a clear demonstration of how inadequate organizational diversity has constrained development. As we have discussed, especially in Chapter 3, and as has been analyzed and discussed by other scholars, the domination of the agricultural sector by the central government and its subordination to the interests of those who control it has proved disastrous for all African countries (Bates 1981; World Bank 1981; Brett 1986). Governments have attempted to design and run agricultural systems in which all organizations connected with the agricultural sector, whether they be cooperatives, local governments, marketing agencies, pricing, credit or research institutions, were completely under its control. The result has been declining agricultural productivity, increasing food imports and ecological deterioration (Lofchie 1985; 1986). The correlation between governmental dominance of the agricultural marketing and agricultural decline has been demonstrated by the remarkable improvements which several African countries have witnessed since the adoption of structural adjustment programs which reduced state controls including the abolition of marketing boards. Nigeria is the best example of this; Ghana's recent record has also been encouraging. Palm, cocoa, and rubber trees which were once abandoned by farmers because of the poor prices they received in the past are now being rehabilitated across West Africa (*West Africa* 1987).

We have argued, however, that these policy changes, while producing important improvements in the agricultural sector, are not sufficient on their own to bring about lasting changes within the agricultural sector and the economy at large. Political change is also needed. That a country like Ivory Coast which has adopted an export-led agricultural growth policy currently faces severe economic and fiscal problems is an indicator of this. According to Neil Ridler, the current economic and fiscal problems are due not only to the falling price of coffee and cocoa (which were real: coffee by one-third, cocoa by one-half), but also to the inability or unwillingness of the government to reduce the growth of public expenditure when it was already evident that prices were falling (Ridler 1985). As we have argued in the preceding chapters, centralized bureaucracies have severe problems correcting their own behavior. This experience illustrates some of the weaknesses of overcentralization even for a government that has adopted a "reasonable" economic policy. Structural adjustment programs, this suggests, are likely to have limited long-term effects in the absence of diverse agricultural (credit, pricing, research, marketing, etc.) and political organizations which might encourage the emergence of a more generally flexible and adaptable policy-making process.

At the heart of the agricultural problem in Africa is the low productivity from which this sector suffers. But what sector would experience productivity growth when its capital was systematically bled off to fund a costly state which not only returned little to it, but also stifled that sector's capacity to organize itself for improvements? The productivity problem is

TABLE 13.1 The Structure of Production in Some African Countries*

Year	Agriculture	Industry**	Services
	Percent of Labor Force		
1960	82	7	11
1980	72	12	17
	Percent Distribution of Gross Domestic Product		
1960	47	17	36
1982	33	27	40

*Not all sub-Saharan countries are included, but sample more than two-thirds of all African countries.
**The "manufacturing" subsector of "industry" to GDP is much smaller: 7% in 1960, 8% in 1982.

Source: World Bank, Toward Sustained Development in Sub-Saharan Africa (Washington, D.C., 1984).

serious, since the agricultural sector employed 72 percent of the labor force, but was responsible for only 33 percent of the 1982 gross domestic product in sub-Saharan Africa.

To be sure, the contribution of industry and services to GDP are not insignificant. In 1982 they were 27 percent and 40 percent respectively, and they employed only 12 percent and 17 percent of the labor force (see Table 13.1). And yet, in spite of their growth there is no evidence that they have become sustaining forces for economic development in Africa. We have reviewed many of the arguments put forward to explain this paradox: a government-dominated services sector; industries which are poorly integrated into the rest of the economy; industries which produce shoddy products and cannot compete on the world market; and industries which survive by taking subsidies from genuinely productive sectors of the economy. Both the agricultural and industrial sectors seem sick. The question is, what can be done to stimulate them from their doldrums?

Recent thinking on the relationship between agriculture and domestic industry emphasize the links between the two (Owens and Shaw 1972). Michael Todaro states the matter succinctly in his appraisal of the economic development literature in this regard:

Traditionally, the role of agriculture in economic development has been viewed as largely passive and supportive. Based on the historical experience of Western countries, economic development was seen to require a rapid structural transformation of the economy from one predominantly focused on agricultural activities to a more complex, modern industrial and service society. As a result, agriculture's primary role was to provide sufficient low-priced food and manpower to the expanding industrial economy which was thought to be the dynamic, 'leading sector' in any overall strategy of economic development.

Today, development economists are less sanguine about the desirability of placing such heavy emphasis on rapid industrialization. Perhaps more importantly, they have come to realize that, far from being a passive supporting sector in the process of economic development and the handmaiden of industry, the agricultural sector in particular and the rural economy in general need to be viewed as the dynamic and leading elements in any overall strategy—at least for the vast majority of contemporary Third World countries. Without such agricultural and rural development, industrial growth will either be stultified or, if it succeeds, will create such severe internal imbalances in the economy that the problems of widespread poverty, inequality and unemployment . . . will become even more pronounced (Todaro 1981: 205).

If agriculture and rural transformation must play the leading role in the development process, this book has argued that this is a task which the national government acting alone cannot perform. Governments can assist the process through favorable economic policies, land reform programs when needed, and through the promotion and dissemination of research, and through appropriate regional development policies. But, given the diversity of tasks to be done and the well established weakness of central governments, a large number of other social, political and economic organizations would seem to be required to complement the central government's efforts. These would include market structures, local governments, voluntary local organizations, and the many others mentioned in this volume.

Others have argued that such organizations are essential prerequisites to agricultural modernization and rural development (Esman and Uphoff 1984; Owens and Shaw 1972). They help to pool local knowledge about soils and crops into useable forms for agricultural researchers (Richards 1985); provide social and financial infrastructure—rural roads, credits, basic health services, etc.—to complement central government efforts (Lonsdale and Enyedi 1984; Siebel 1986; Esman and Uphoff 1984); and act as political counterbalances to central governments which at times pursue the interests of the center rather than the nation (Owens and Shaw 1972). They also serve as intermediaries among the people and between the people and the government and help to resolve the problems of the imperfections of the market in a rural setting. In addition, they provide a framework for more effective management of common pool resources—grazing lands, fishing grounds, water sources, etc. That local persons are capable of making intelligent decisions that help to preserve rather than destroy common pool resources has been very well documented (Martin 1985; E. Ostrom 1987; 1988). Indeed, it has been demonstrated that the management of common pool resources by the collective choice activities of the local people themselves have often been more beneficial than their management by central government agents or the market (Blomquist 1987; E. Ostrom 1988). The constitutional challenge of designing institutions which encourage persons and organizations effectively to manage common properties may hold one of the most important keys to problems of deforestation, land degradation, and erosion of the topsoil on the continent. Below we indicate the range of organizations (working through different mechanisms and activities) that are required for genuine agricultural and rural development (Table 13.2).

The transformation of the agricultural and rural sectors of a country has important implications for industrialization. Higher agricultural incomes and productivity create a demand for non-agricultural products.

TABLE 13.2 Organizations Required for Rural Development

Principal Mechanism	Bureaucratic Structures	Market Interactions	Local Organizations
Decision Makers	Administrators and experts	Individual producers, consumers	Leaders and members
Guides for Behavior	Regulations	Price signals	Agreements
Criteria for Decisions	Policy/technically best means to implement it	Efficiency/best way to maximize profit	Interests of members
Sanctions	State authority	Financial loss	Social pressure
Mode of Operation	Top-down	Individualistic	Bottom-up

Source: Adapted from M.J. Esman and N.T. Uphoff, *Local Organizations: Intermediaries in Rural Development* (Ithaca: Cornell University Press, 1984), p. 20. Copyright © 1984 by Cornell University Press. Used by permission of the publisher.

Improvements in productivity release additional labor forces which could engage in diverse processes of rural industrialization—the processing of raw materials for export or for local industries. The development of infrastructure itself lays the foundation for industrialization. Above all, this infrastructure facilitates effective linkage between domestic industries and the agricultural and rural sector, particularly when backed by appropriate economic policies. There are thus many indirect contributions which organizations connected with rural development make to industrial growth.

A large number of organizations are also directly required for industrial growth. The 1987 *World Development Report* chose this as its theme. It advocated greater use of private sector initiatives rather than the more costly misadventure of government direct and indirect action in this critical area. It also emphasized the role of "informal" sector organizations which are not usually regarded as part of the "modern" private sector (World Bank 1987). This is in fact a welcome and startling development. Small-scale and informal producers have generally been regarded as "peripheral" (Leys 1975) and their activities have been usually seen as of zero marginal productivity (Lewis 1955). It is a sharp contrast to the general preference for large industrial projects of the 1950s and 1960s. Recent critiques of the earlier strategy in two countries are particularly revealing.

On Nigeria's capital intensive industrialization strategy, Kilby noted that:

> The large, capital-intensive soap factory, brewery, flour mill and so on have no visible 'carry-over' in Nigeria—they have remained technological enclaves. On the other hand, small modestly financed, individual or family-owned concerns (predominantly Levantine) employing the most rudimentary and unadorned production processes have spawned hundreds of Nigerian firms in soap making, metal working, sawmilling, rubber creeping, baking, umbrella assembly, singlet manufacture and construction. The reason for this is simply that earning is a continuous process, comparable to an individual climbing a

ladder in the sense that if too many rungs are missing, if the technological
gap is too great, upward progress ceases (Kilby 1969: 107).

Similarly, a recent report on the "Barefoot Revolution" in Africa commissioned by the Club of Rome notes the flowering of small scale projects
designed to solve common problems confronted by local people in different
parts of the Cameroon. This contrasts to the large projects, often managed
by economic experts, which brought nothing but "ruin and misery" to the
mass of the people (Mensing 1987: 20). These examples underscore the
importance and potential of small scale operations in the industrial sector
and are indicative of the nature of possibilities that exist once assumptions
concerning the exaggerated capacities of the formal sector and its partner,
the state, are relaxed.

Organizations in the small and informal sector have also been quite
effective in providing essential services. These have included inter- and
intra-city transportation, and municipal services such as water, schools,
electricity distribution, and even police services. Unfortunately, in many
African countries these services are managed by government monopolies,
or organizations that are under close government controls, leaving urban
enterprise handicapped by poor utilities. The lack of access to credit, to
inexpensive and effective judicial systems to adjudicate contracts, and to
effective public and municipal services severely hinders both sectors, and
are thus major obstacles to genuine industrial growth in Africa (World
Bank 1987; Marsden and Belot 1987; See also Chapter 5).

Political Centralization and Political Development

To understand the political path Africa's leaders have followed, one must
note two factors which were particularly disturbing to African leaders and
modernization scholars: the large number of ethnic groups brought together
by the accident of colonial rule, and the absence of an accepted political
authority and constitutional order. We will first discuss ethnicity.

One of the key goals of modernization was the integration of these
diverse ethnic groups (condescendingly referred to as tribes) through the
imposition of the dominant culture of a modernizing elite: intellectuals,
senior civil servants, and political officials (Rubin and Weinstein 1974).
They regarded any attempt to disperse power either at the "capital" (to
legislature, executive, judiciary instrumentalities) or on an "area basis"
(through federalism or local governance) (Maas 1959) before this process
was completed as likely to lead to disastrous results. Such actions might
fuel outright secessionist sentiments; even if they did not do this, they
would impede cohesion around the development plan (Riggs 1964; Huntington 1968). Thus, African states, as we have seen, have been inclined
toward a form of the Hobbesian *Leviathan* using two key instruments to
bring about unity and political integration: the single party and unitary
state model centered on the executive.

The single party has its variations—from the liberal form (as in the Cameroon, Ivory Coast, Kenya, at the regional level in pre-1966 Nigeria), to doctrinaire models (Zambia, Tanzania, Sekou Toure's Guinea), and to patrimonial forms (Malawi or Swaziland), to cite only a few examples (for more complete analysis see Sklar 1983; Decalo 1985; Ayoade 1986). Few African countries operate a multi-party system of government (Gambia, Senegal, Botswana, Mauritius, Zimbabwe, and Liberia), and even in some of these countries the ruling party has such an advantage over the others that it is virtually impossible to defeat it at an election. A major consequence of single-party institutions is to stunt the growth of autonomous organizations outside of the party which can both challenge and complement its policies. Whether it is trade unions, universities, civil services, or local governments, as Chapter 3 discusses, only institutions which are under the control of the single party are allowed to thrive in this circumstance. Arnold Rivkin sums up the situation in this manner:

Institution-building (by African governments) has meant dependent, circumscribed, controlled institutions. The history of universities, courts, civil services, parliaments—to say nothing of private or theretofore private voluntary groups—in Africa has been one of subordination, take-over, and destruction by the one party. The implications of this institutional pattern for state-building have been serious and direct. It has made it all but impossible for truly national institutions representative of and responsive to the total nation to develop and grow. It has also made the formal constitutional structures meaningless, as the party structure (notwithstanding propaganda to the contrary) has generally been a tightly held monopoly of a relatively small controlling group who can play musical chairs with formal constitutional institutions—consolidating ministries, dismissing ministers, and disregarding legislative prerogatives. (Rivkin 1968: 17, parentheses added.)

By repressing the growth of these autonomous organizations, the African state denied itself of two crucial elements of institutional development: criticism and legitimacy. Dissent was driven underground and voluntary or forced exile was the fate of those who could not conform to the mediocrity and sycophancy that resulted. The very organization, the party, that was expected to promote development itself suffered from the absence of incentives to develop as an organization or improve its performance. Public apathy and alienation toward the state grew. Ironically, today some African leaders complain about the poor quality of their news media, the performance of their civil services, judiciary, or local governments. But the very incentives toward performance—opportunities for citizen claim-making and participation, internal and external criticism, rewards for challenges that bring improvements, and the chance to make a difference through these—have been withdrawn (*West Africa* 1987; Olowu 1988). Rule systems organizing public affairs and business were designed which encourage organizations prone to error and prone to public distrust. Institutional decay rather than institutional development was the counterintuitive result of policies aimed at bringing about unity and integration.

This created the background to the incessant military interventions in the continent. Unlike popular institutions, the military has been difficult to subjugate by the party. Moreover, its officers have a nationalist and centralist orientation through their training. Confronted with the decline of other organizations it is easy for military officers to perceive themselves as the only organization capable of "saving" their country. However, with but rare exceptions, the military itself by organization and training cannot promote institution-building any more than the single party. It has a strong tendency to centralize all power in itself and perceive all other autonomous organizations as threats to "unity, peace and stability." Institutional provisions at the center which limited the rulers and protected space for other organizations to operate, such as the judiciary, have often been further circumscribed by the military. As Chapter 12 suggested, organizations which break out of constitutional constraints are prone to error, to rogue behavior, and to replacement through similar processes. The results are the recurring *coups* and *counter-coups* which many countries have suffered. Nigeria, Ghana, Sudan, Uganda, Benin, Togo, Congo, and Burkina Faso are prime examples of this pattern. In the end, the military is as ineffective as the civilians were. To prevent military coups, single-party regimes attempted to reduce or dominate the military (as in Tanzania), or they called on a foreign legion as the Togolese leadership did early in 1987.

Ethnicity is regarded with considerable embarrassment in Africa. As we showed in Chapter 2, several governments have gone as far as proscribing ethnic associations. This approach to ethnicity is rooted in part in the policy of separate development for the races and ethnic groups which prevailed in several colonies before independence (Mazrui 1983). It also grew from modernization theories which saw ethnicity as a transient phase in the evolution of the modern nation-state (Deutsch 1963; Gluckman 1966; Bates 1970). Finally, it also grew from scholarship which treats ethnicity as a consequence of capitalist development, a ready instrument in the hands of the privileged classes, and something can be resisted only by a centralized state (Nnoli 1978; Joseph 1983).

As a result of these considerations, most African leaders chose highly unitary constitutions. The aim was to promote unity by the imposition of a dominant culture rather than through cultural pluralism. The unitary model of governance is the dominant form in virtually all African countries in spite of the ethnic diversity of their populations. Several countries in Africa which came to independence with a federal or quasi-federal constitution such as Kenya, Uganda, Cameroon, and as we discussed in some detail, Nigeria, have changed their constitutions to unitary ones, either *de jure* (as in Kenya and Uganda) or *de facto* (as in Nigeria and the Cameroon). How has this been a mistake? What has it led to?

Ethnicity, is not peculiar to Africa. In fact it can constitute one of the building blocks for nationhood. Insofar as ethnicity reflects norms of cooperation and mutual assistance among peoples, it can speed the self-organizing capabilities we have discussed in this book. Much research suggests that ethnicity need not lead to conflict (Owusu 1970; Smock 1971). Indeed several scholars have pointed out that ethnicity and ethnic conflict may be less a function of modernization level than of state policy (Mughan 1979). Ethnicity remains a critical factor in the political experiences of many industrialized nations whether in the West (Switzerland, Belgium, the United Kingdom, the United States, Canada, or France), in the socialist countries (The Soviet Republics, Yugoslavia), or in the other developing countries (India, Malaysia, Indonesia, Brazil, and even tiny Singapore). More than one scholar has drawn our attention to the fact that ethnic groups in Africa will pass for nations in Europe (Bauer 1974; V. Ostrom 1973; 1987). Indeed, the different micro-ethnic nationalities related to one another as different nations (either in war or trade) before the imposition of colonial rule (Dudley 1982).

The forms and nature of ethnic association takes within a country can be often explained as a response to state policy. Ali Mazrui has pointed out that ethnicity does not constitute as much a problem in Francophone compared with Anglophone Africa because of differences in French and British colonial policy regarding ethnicity and modernization (Mazrui 1983). Recently, the high centralization of political authority occasioned by the adoption of unitary and executive constitutions encouraged different groups to associate with one another on the basis of the most likely possible winning coalition: to capture power at the center and to share in the fruits of political power. This would not have been different from what happens in other polities except that control of the state in these highly centralized systems has meant control of almost everything in the developed sector. This was reinforced by constitutional forms which placed control of the state in the hands of the executive and an informally selected circle of close associates. While some states have fared better in institutionalizing stable representation of key groups at the center (Senegal, Kenya), others have not, and at times intense conflict has been the result (Ghana, Nigeria, Uganda, Sudan). Highly centralized states with little institutionalization of rules of accession, representation and secession, are an explosive combination. Within such a system, disadvantaged groups have few options other than secession bids, as in the Sudan, Ethiopia, Chad, and Biafra in the late 1960s. At times this has led to open warfare.

Since ethnicity is a universal human characteristic, it should be remembered that there may be diverse approaches to resolving inter-ethnic problems. The single option of unitarism on which African leaders and their advisers have seemed fixed, precludes options that have worked elsewhere. These would include such approaches as federalism and consociation. They, in turn, like unitarism, come in different forms: unitary decentralized, unitary centralized, peripheral or centralized federalism, confederacy, etc. There is clearly a need for African societies to widen their range of constitutional choices. We have suggested in Chapter 9 that the federal model is one that should be carefully considered for Africa (Rothchild and Olorunsola 1983; Briand 1987).

A second general area where the problem of political centralization and political development can be seen is in the bureaucracy. In large measure growing from African leaders awareness of the weakness of their political authority and the absence of an established constitutional order, centralized administration through the Weberian model of bureaucracy was the primary instrument of state building which African leaders chose after independence (Zolberg 1966). Ironically, overcentralization asked too much of bureaucracy and has deeply damaged and at times discredited it. Once regarded as one of the monuments of modernity and the catalyst to the development process, it has recently been accepted that the bureaucracy in any African country might represent a major obstacle to development (Hyden 1983; Moris 1981; Brett 1986).

The African bureaucracy has not been able to fulfill its catalytic role in the development process for a number of at times conflicting factors. First, political organizations which ought to ensure its effective accountability were underdeveloped vis-a-vis the bureaucracy. Whereas the bureaucracy had its origins and character in the earliest periods of colonial rule, institutions establishing political functions and political organizations were introduced late, a few short years before independence, and have operated at varying levels of effectiveness since independence. Also, civil servants did not conceive their task as that of serving the people; rather the imperious attitude of the colonial administrative officials has persisted and been reinforced by the centralist strategy far into the post-independence period. Power, resources and opportunities have all been concentrated at the top, a situation responsible for a high level of centralization within the public service and poor performance in rendering public services. In fact, to the extent that the colonial bureaucracy placed fairly senior officials and support services in the rural areas, it was able to relate to the people much more effectively than occurs today. Post-independence African bureaucracies reversed that order, with the most able, competent and senior officials located at headquarters. Such a situation has been encouraged by the extreme centralization of the administrative system (Smith 1967; Murray 1978; Rweyemamu and Hyden 1975; Moris 1981).

Second, the Weberian values of meritocracy, efficiency, anonymity, and objectivity ran contrary to those prevailing in the African post-independence millieu from three fronts. The first problem is that the African bureaucracy adopted structures, methods, and values of the metropolitan colonial bureaucracies in an environment which is still organized on the basis of affection and traditional patterns of reciprocity (Hyden 1983; Brett 1986; also Chapter 11 in this volume). It is in this sense that some scholars have talked about African "premature bureaucracies" (Moris 1976; Okoli 1980) or "sala" bureaucracies (Riggs 1964; Kasfir 1969). A second source of value misfit is the tendency to politicize the bureaucracy in most African countries (Subramaniam 1977; Adamolekun 1986). African leaders' exclusive reliance on the bureaucracy for the implementation of their post-independence drive to development tended to emphasize personal loyalty over and above all other organizational values. The result has been a continuous tampering with the administrative machinery, often mass-retirement of officials with a change of government, and an undue emphasis on ethnic balance or regional representativeness within the bureaucracy.

A final source of misfit between African public bureaucracies and development is the nature of the task that had to be accomplished. The Weberian bureaucracy does best at settled or routine tasks rather than the complex and uncertain processes of development administration. According to Rondinelli:

> The Weberian model of organization has been especially inappropriate for developing countries because it overlooked or ignores the high level of uncertainty attending the implementation of development policies. It was primarily modeled on European government systems in which routine and standardized administrative procedures were suited to solving marginal and easily identified problems. But in developing countries the only certainty is that the course of development programs and projects is uncertain. Solving one aspect of the problem or set of problems uncovers or creates new ones, many of which cannot be anticipated and therefore be dealt with through routine and standardized administrative procedures (Rondinelli 1983: 119).

This same difficulty extends to planning. It has often been wondered why African countries continue to plan when past efforts have been so hobbled by the difficulty of effective planning in Africa. Planning presumes a good knowledge of both the past and clear expectations of the future. Neither is readily available in Africa (Waterston 1965; Agarwala 1983). Some countries like Nigeria do not even have a good idea of their population size—a basic input for the planning process—because of the fear by the different elite groups of the implications that an accurate census has for their bid for power and resources from the central government. Thus, the bureaucracy has fallen far short of the task.

Increasing evidence is emerging that what African countries (like their Third World counterparts) lack most is the basic infrastructure for development—the ability to manage small projects, solve local problems, sustain existing technological systems, energize human resources and maintain basic services. Without these in place, most efforts geared to economic growth seem doomed to fail (Todaro 1981; Ralston et al. 1983). Worse still, such a country may fall into the hands of well meaning but misguided leaders, or of charlatans who parade themselves as leaders serving the "national interest." But if the economy is stagnant and government is ineffective, then how is a developmental "break-out" to occur?

What we have advocated is a constitutional order which accommodates the dynamic interactions among complex and diverse self-governing organizations. We believe that is necessary in order to stimulate growth and reduce political instability. In other words, what is required in Africa is to strengthen the social order through a commitment to reconstituting the social system. This must allow the people to tackle as many of their problems themselves as they are able, while the state provides an overall structure, appropriate incentives and limits to complement those efforts. Only then, we believe, will the national bureaucracy be able to fulfill critical roles. If such a strategy is so necessary, then why have no African regimes adopted it? Let us turn to this last issue.

The Development Contradiction, Self-Governance and Prospects for Democracy in Africa

This volume has identified what some might regard as a development contradiction in Africa. Strong, centralized or autocratic regimes at the national level have been regarded as the only institutions capable of bringing about the process of modernization and industrialization. Furthermore, it is only when these later conditions are established that democratic forms are seen as able to succeed in Africa. This thesis is found generally in the writings of many authors both in the West as well as in Africa. In the political science literature this has almost come to be taken as a given, just as the belief is also strong among those who wield political power on the African continent. The thesis was cast in its most compelling form by Rupert Emerson:

> Democracy . . . is unlikely to establish itself as the generally prevailing form of government in Africa and will in fact appear only in relatively rare instances. More usually, even when it does appear, its life will be short and harassed (Emerson 1971: 239).

After listing the usual conditions for democracy which are marked by their absence in Africa (high levels of education, literacy and standard of living and social homogeneity) he concluded rather baldly:

> I believe it to be the case that hence forth development is almost sure to be undertaken, under authoritarian rather than democratic auspices, thus further strengthening the probability that the prospects for democracy in Africa within any time that one can now sensibly calculate are meagre indeed (Emerson 1971: 257).

A similar line of reasoning has been pursued by several other scholars (see for instance Lipset 1959; Rostow 1961; Huntington 1968; Oyovbaire 1978).

A belief that authoritarianism is essential to development helps explain trends toward centralization and the personalization of power and authority in Africa. Yet the consensus of many of those who have carried out careful analyses of the African development effort is that the authoritarian models imposed in much of Africa, either of the military or civil variety, have hindered rather than fostered development. The new structures of authority which were set up shortly after independence with the intent of replacing those democratic institutions bequeathed at independence in order to hasten the development process have proven everywhere to be counter productive.

We reviewed this problem in detail in the preceding chapters. We argued, especially in Chapters 1 and 3, that authoritarian regimes create too great a temptation to those who wield power to feather their own nests while effectively smothering all dissent. We suggested in those chapters that Africans are no different from other peoples of the world in this respect.

As a result, rather than solving the pressing problems of underdevelopment, African authoritarian regimes have aggravated them by imposing additional costs on their citizenry. This agrees substantially with the consensus of much serious thinking on Africa: while African leaders displayed great capabilities in bringing about political independence, they proved unequal to the subsequent task of using that political power to bring about desired social and economic changes. While conceding that the latter task was a far more difficult one than the former, the overall impression is that authoritarian or centralized African governments have been a dismal failure (Rivkin 1968; Adamolekun 1988).

We argued in this volume that centralization is a cause of underdevelopment in Africa. If this thesis is sustained, it is a rather clear contradiction of earlier writings on the issue. If so, one must ask: how could so many honest and concerned scholars and decision-makers be so wrong?

It would be unrealistic to suggest that we have all the answers. We do believe that some insight into this contradiction lies in three critical issues: the tendency to overlook fundamental institutions in comparative institutional analysis; the use of ambiguous concepts that simplify the task of comparative analysis but pose serious problems for the interpretation of real-life data; and the intellectual disposition of the West over the past three centuries to undervalue the "periphery" and overestimate the power and capacity of the "center."

One of the major faults of comparative institutional analysis is the tendency to focus exclusively on national level data. This is understandable given the diversity of subnational experiences and the large amount of data that must be accommodated in order to make more detailed comparisons of sub-national or micro-organizations. We, however, believe that the experiences that people acquire through working with and in organizations based on self-organizing capabilities are critical to the development process. In fact, we have referred to the diversity of organizations through which people achieve their daily needs as the basic *infrastructure* of development. When national governments damage the institutions which act as frameworks of rights, privileges, obligations and prohibitions and must nurture and sustain these diverse self-governing organizations, as they do in many African countries, they undermine the development process. The point is self-evident in commerce, business, and industry. Small businesses provide necessary experience and expertise for running large-scale businesses. In very critical ways, they also complement one another through the varying economies of scale they offer to correspond to the diversity of tasks that a developed economy calls for.

What is valid for business is also true here in the political realm. The experiences people derive at local levels in self-governance, in voluntary organizations, and in other associations, help to create essential attitudes and skills which complement the efforts of "national" political structures. In so far as governance is a normatively rooted process, and in so far as people learn, develop and apply norms through experience, the dearth of institutions which involve the people widely and help them gradually to develop and apply norms may be a key source of the endemic corruption of the contemporary African state (Ekeh 1975). It is doubtful though, whether such norms can be developed by proclaiming them from the top. We, and such theorists as Aristotle, Rousseau, Tocqueville and Cabral, believe that they are more likely to grow from the experience of self-governance by the people as a whole, where locally based and rooted norms are generalized upward as a people takes responsibility and accountability for governing itself in the diverse and numerous arenas of collective life. Unfortunately, governance and democracy is thought of largely in national terms. In the absence of institutions encouraging strong democratic organizations at the local and intermediate levels, such experiments have proved expensive and not very workable in African countries (Lindblom 1977; Kabongo 1986).

This takes us to the use of simplifying concepts, such as "democracy," "development," or "authoritarianism." In common understanding, for example, democracy means popular rule. But that understanding leaves aside a host of issues generally neglected in recent decades. Can the "popular" rule occur only at the center? How is the popular rule to be sustained vis-a-vis the tendency of power to act as a centripetal force? When there exists a diversity of popular desires, which group rules? Can "pluralism" co-exist with "popular rule?" Alternatively, what is "development?" Is it the possession of wealth (capital, a high GNP and modern technology)? Or is it better understood as the ability to produce these things? If so, what is required to produce them? The tendency to understand poorly and to oversimplify these concepts and to fail to use them in a critical fashion has led to policies and programs which have impeded African development. It is part of the reason why the flawed centralized-state strategy was adopted and sustained for so long.

In the case of "democracy," its simplistic application to Africa led to the importation of national-level institutions which fit poorly into African society and were soon cast aside. A failure by serious thinkers in recent years to delve into the complexities of democracy led most to miss that subtly which we have called "self-governance," and to fail to see its relevance for African development. Once the logic of self-governance is understood, Africans will, we believe, be able to seek and discover in their own institutions ways to encourage humans' self-organizing capabilities. This last point is a critical one, as a blind and careless inclination to simply import these complex institutional arrangements will probably lead to new cultural misfits and institutional failures. Instead, the *logic* of self-governance needs to be understood: people can govern themselves as persons and as members of communities, and the optimal role for the state interested in long-term development is to institutionalize rules of personal and organizational action which facilitate this process. Unleashed, it is the most powerful force on earth.

Once we accept that any specific institutional form is the *means* and not *ends* of democracy, then its existence in other parts of the world may not seem so restrictive nor so tied to socioeconomic conditions currently prevailing in Europe or the United States. Indeed, if we view "democracy" as an institutionalized way of life in which people devise rules at diverse levels to promote teamwork and teams-of-teams, its existence may already be more widespread than its diviners are willing to admit, particularly in Africa outside the "center."

Finally, there are the centralist biases of the West. Manifested perhaps most clearly in the whole colonial enterprise, Western thought since the Enlightenment has pushed ever toward centralist solutions to human problems. Lack of respect for the wisdom and ability of the common people are core assumptions of the French Revolution, the Bolshevik Revolution and even the contemporary technocratic drift of the liberal West. While leaders and followers of these movements often felt genuine sympathy and concern for the "masses," their feelings were guided by strong, paternalistic beliefs in the "center's" relative superiority over the "periphery."

We have not closed the debate on these issues in this book, although we have cited references from different parts of Africa to support the view that one of the greatest revolutions currently sweeping the African continent is an increasing recognition that the people themselves must organize to liberate themselves from the triple evils of illiteracy, disease, and unemployment. This means abandoning the messianic political expectations articulated by the center for the past three decades for more realistic and, at the same time, far more liberating objectives.

These points are suggestive of issues for further debate, just as they are also conditioned by a variety of other factors: the nature of the international economy; the amount and type of aid given to African states (social and economic aid which benefits a variety of institutions versus military aid which helps to strengthen mercantilist autocracies); the strengthening of leadership capabilities, and a host of other issues which we have not explored in this book. Still, the message of this book remains critical. Self-governance is a prerequisite for democratic organization at the national level, and is something that not only promotes the fruits of development, but is the basis for the growth of a people's very capacity to improve its own conditions. The last is the very essence of development. Discovering the rules of personal and group action that facilitate this process is the essence of institution building, and therefore the key prerequisite of development.

References

Adamolekun, L. *Politics and Administration in Nigeria.* London: Hutchinson, 1986.
_____. "Political Leadership in Sub-Saharan Africa: From Giants to Dwarfs." *International Political Science Review* 9 (2) (1988): 95–106.

Agarwala, R. *Planning in Developing Countries: Lessons of Experience.* Washington, D.C.: World Bank Staff Working Papers No. 576, 1983.

Ashford, Douglas E. *National Development and Local Reform: Political Participation in Morocco, Tunisia and Pakistan.* Berkeley: University of California Press, 1967.

Ayoade, John A. A. "The African Search for Democracy: Hopes and Reality." In *Democracy and Pluralism in Africa,* edited by Dov Ronen, 19–34. Boulder, Colo.: Lynne Reinner Publishers, 1986.

Bates, Robert. "Approaches to the Study of Ethnicity." *Cahier d'Etudes Africanies* 10 (1) (1970): 546–561.

———. *Markets and States in Tropical Africa: The Political Basis of Agricultural Policies.* Berkeley: University of California Press, 1981.

Bauer, P. T. *Nigerian Development Experience: Aspects and Implications.* Ile-Ife: University of Ife Press, Institute of Administration Monograph Series No. 1, 1974.

Blomquist, William. "Getting Out of the Trap: Changing an Endangered Commons to a Managed Commons." Ph.D. Dissertation, Bloomington, Ind.: Indiana University, 1987.

Brett, E. A. "State Power and Economic Inefficiency: Explaining Political Failure in Africa." *IDS Bulletin* 17 (1), Institute of Development Studies, Sussex (1986): 22–29.

Briand, Michael, ed. *A Way Out: Federalist Options for South Africa.* San Francisco: California Institute for Contemporary Studies, 1987.

Brown, L.R., and E.C. Wolf. *Reversing Africa's Decline.* World Watch Paper. Washington, D.C.: Worldwatch Institute, 1985.

Decalo, Samuel. "African Personal Dictatorships." *Journal of Modern African Studies* 23 (2) (1985): 209–237.

Deutsch, Karl. "Nation-Building and National Development: Some Issues of Political Research." In *Nation-Building,* edited by K. Deutsch and W. Foltz. New York: Atherton Press, 1963.

Dudley, Billy. *An Introduction to Nigerian Government and Politics.* Bloomington, Ind.: Indiana University Press, 1982.

Ekeh, P. "Colonialism and the two Publics in Africa: A Theoretical Statement." *Comparative Studies in History and Society* 19 (1) (1975): 91–112.

Emerson, Rupert. "The Prospects for Democracy in Africa." In *The State of the Nations: Constraints on Development in Independent Africa,* edited by M. F. Lofchie, 239–257. Berkeley: University of California Press, 1971.

Esman, M.J., and Norman T. Uphoff. *Local Organizations: Intermediaries in Rural Development.* Ithaca: Cornell University Press, 1984.

Gluckman, Max. "Tribalism in Modern British Central Africa." In *Social Change: The Colonial Situation,* edited by I. Wallerstein, 251–264. New York: John Wiley, 1966.

Grimm, Dieter. "The Modern State: Continental Traditions." In *Guidance, Control, and Evaluation in the Public Sector,* edited by F.X. Kaufmann, G. Majone, and V. Ostrom, 89–109. Berlin and New York: Walter de Guyter, 1986.

Huntington, S.P. *Political Order in Changing Societies.* New Haven, Conn.: Yale University Press, 1968.

Hyden, Goran. *No Shortcuts to Progress: African Development Management in Perspective.* Berkeley: University of California Press, 1983.

Joseph, Richard A. "Class, State and Prebendal Politics in Nigeria." *Journal of Commonwealth and Comparative Politics* 21 (3) (1983): 21–38.

Kabongo, Ilunga. "Democracy in Africa: Hopes and Prospects." In *Democracy and Pluralism in Africa,* edited by Dov Ronen, 35–40. Boulder, CO: Lynne Reinner Publishers, 1986.

Kasfir, N. "Prismatic Theory and African Administration." *World Politics* 21 (2) (1969): 295–314.

Kaufmann, Franz-Xaver, Giandomenico Majone, and Vincent Ostrom, eds. *Guidance, Control, and Evaluation in the Public Sector.* Berlin and New York: Walter de Gruyter, 1986.

Kilby, P. *Industrialization In an Open Economy: Nigeria 1945–1966.* Cambridge: Cambridge University Press, 1969.

Krane, Dale. "The Effects on the Public of Centre-Local Relations: A Cross-National Study." *International Political Science Review* 7 (1) (1986): 39–53.

Lewis, A. *The Theory of Economic Growth.* Homewood, Ill.: Irwin, 1955.

Leys, Colins. *Underdevelopment in Kenya.* Berkeley: University of California Press, 1975.

Lindblom, Charles E. *Politics and Markets.* New York: Basic Books, 1977.

Lipset, S. M. "Some Social Prerequisites of Democracy: Economic Development and Political Legitimacy." *American Political Science Review* 53 (1) (1959): 69–105.

Lofchie, Michael F. "The Roots of Economic Crisis in Tanzania." *Current History* 85 (501) (1985): 159–184.

———. "Kenya's Agricultural Success." *Current History* 86 (511) (1986): 221–231.

Lonsdale, R.E., and G. Enyedi, eds. *Rural Public Services: International Comparisons.* Boulder, Colo.: Westview Press, 1984.

Maas, Arthur. *Area and Power.* Glencoe: Free Press, 1959.

Mabogunje, Akin L. *The Development Process: A Spatial Perspective.* London: Hutchinson, 1980.

Marsden, R., and T. Belot. "Private Enterprise in Africa: Creating a Better Environment." World Bank Discussion Papers, No. 17, Washington, D.C., 1987.

Martin, Fenton. *Common Pool Resources: A Preliminary Bibliography.* Bloomington, Ind.: Indiana University, Workshop in Political Theory, 1985.

Mazrui, Ali. "Francophone Nations and English-Speaking States: Imperial Ethnicity and African Political Formations." In *State Versus Ethnic Claims: African Policy Dilemmas,* edited by D. Rothchild and V. Olrunsola, 25–43. Boulder, Colo.: Westview Press, 1983.

Mensing, A. "The Barefoot Revolution." *Cooperation and Development* 29 (1987): 20–28.

Moris, J. "The Transferability of the Western Management Tradition into the Public Service Sectors: An East African Perspective." *Philippine Journal of Public Administration* 20 (4) (1976): 401–427.

Moris, J. *Managing Induced Rural Development.* Bloomington, IN: Indiana University, 1981.

Mughan, Anthony. "Modernization and Relative Deprivation: Towards a Theory of Ethnic Conflict." In *Decentralist Trends in Western Democracies,* edited by L.J. Sharp, 279–312. London: Sage, 1979.

Murray, D. J. "Nigerian Field Administration: A Comparative Analysis." In *Studies in Nigerian Administration,* edited by D.J. Murray, 90–139. London: Hutchinson, 1978.

Nnoli, Okwudiba. *Ethnic Politics in Nigeria.* Enugu: Fourth Dimension Publishers, 1978.

Okoli, F.C. "The Dilemma of Premature Bureaucratization in the New States of Africa: The Case of Nigeria." *African Studies Review* 23 (2) (1980): 1–16.

Olowu, Dele. "Bureaucratic Morality in Africa." *International Political Science Review* 9 (3) (1988): 215–230.

Ostrom, Elinor. "Micro-Constitutional Change in a Multi-Constitutional Poiltical System." Working Paper. Bloomington, Ind.: Indiana University, Workshop in Political Theory and Policy Analysis, 1987.

———. "Institutional Arrangements and the Commons Dilemma." In *Rethinking Institutional Analysis and Development: Some Issues, Alternatives, and Choices,* edited by Vincent Ostrom, David Feeny, and Hartmut Picht. San Francisco: Institute for Contemporary Studies Press, 1988.

Ostrom, Vincent. "Can Federalism Make a Difference?" *Publius* 3, Fall (1973): 197–238.

———. "Nigeria: Impressions, Puzzles, Reflections." Bloomington, Ind.: Indiana University, Workshop in Political Theory and Policy Analysis, 1987. Mimeo.

Owens, E., and R. Shaw. *Development Reconsidered: Bridging the Gap Between Government and the People.* Lexington, Mass.: Lexington Books, 1972.

Owusu, Maxwell. *Uses and Abuses of Political Power: A Case Study of Continuity and Change in the Politics of Ghana.* Chicago: University of Chicago Press, 1970.

Oyovbaire, Egite. "The Context of Democracy in Nigeria." In *Democracy in Nigeria: Past, Present and Future,* 7–27. Zaria: Ahmadu Bello University, Nigerian Political Science Association, 1978.

Ralston, R., J. Anderson, and E. Colson. *Voluntary Efforts and Decentralized Management: Opportunities and Constraints in Rural Development.* Berkeley: Institute of International Studies, 1983.

Richards, Paul. *Indigenous Agricultural Revolution.* London: Hutchinson, 1985.

Ridler, N. "Comparative Advantage as a Development Model: The Ivory Coast." *Journal of Modern African Studies* 23 (3) (1985): 407–417.

Riggs, Fred W. *Administration in Developing Countries.* Boston: Houghton Mifflin, 1964.

Rivkin, Arnold, ed. *Nations by Design: Institution Building in Africa.* New York: Anchor Books, 1968.

Rondinelli, D. *Development Projects as Policy Experiments.* London: Methuen, 1983.

Rostow, W.W. *Politics and the Stages of Growth.* London: Cambridge University Press, 1961.

Rothchild, D., and V. Olorunsola, ed. *State Versus Ethnic Claims: African Policy Dilemmas.* Boulder, Colo.: Westview Press, 1983.

Rubin, L., and B. Weinstein. *Introduction to African Politics: A Continental Approach.* New York: Praeger, 1974.

Rweyemamu, A.H., and Goran Hyden, eds. *A Decade of Public Administration in Africa.* Nairobi: East African Publishing House, 1975.

Sellasie, B.H. *The Executive in African Government.* London: Heinemann, 1974.

Siebel, H.D. "Rural Finance in Africa." *Development and Cooperation* 6 (1986): 12–14.

Sklar, R.L. "Democracy in Africa." *African Studies Review* 26 (3 and 4) (1983): 11–24.

Smith, Brian. *Field Administration.* London: Kegan and Paul, 1967.

Smock, Audrey. *Ibo Politics: The Role of Ethnic Unions in Eastern Nigeria.* Cambridge, Mass.: Harvard University Press, 1971.

Subramaniam, V. "Politicized Administration in African and Elsewhere: A Socio-Political Analysis." *International Review of Administrative Sciences* 43 (4) (1977): 297–303.

Time Magazine. New York, December 2, 1985.

Todaro, M.P. *Economic Development in the Third World.* 2d ed. New York: Longman, 1981.

Tordoff, W. *Government and Politics in Africa.* Bloomington, Ind.: Indiana University Press, 1984.

Waterston, Albert. *Development Planning: Lessons of Experience.* Baltimore: Johns Hopkins Press, 1965.

West Africa. "Culture of Silence." April 6, 1987.

Young, Crawford. *Ideology and Development in Africa.* New Haven, Conn.: Yale University Press, 1982.

World Bank. *Accelerated Development in Sub-Saharan Africa.* Washington, D.C.: World Bank, 1981.

———. *World Development Report.* Washington, D.C.: World Bank, 1987.

Wunsch, James. "Administering Rural Development: Have Goals Outreached Organizational Capacity?" *Public Administration and Development* 6 (1986): 287–308.

About the Contributors

Sheldon Gellar is a private consultant on rural development and food policy and resides in East Lansing, Michigan.

John W. Harbeson is professor of political science and director of the International Affairs Program at the City University of New York.

Goran Hyden is professor of political science at the University of Florida.

Dele Olowu is professor of political science and head of the Department of Public Administration at Obafemi Awolowo University, Ile Ife, Nigeria.

Vincent Ostrom is Arthur F. Bently Professor of Political Science and co-director of the Workshop on Political Theory and Policy Analysis at Indiana University.

Amos Sawyer is the former dean of the University of Liberia and is currently a senior research fellow of the Workshop on Political Theory and Policy Analysis at Indiana University.

James S. Wunsch is professor of political science and international relations and department chair at Creighton University in Omaha, Nebraska.

Index

Abolitionists, 165(n11)
Absolutism, 23, 29, 232–236, 238, 272
  European, 234, 235, 239, 240
  See also Authoritarianism
Abuja, 212
Accelerated Development in Sub-Saharan Africa: An Agenda for Action (World Bank), 107, 109
Accountability, 95, 117, 131, 135, 159, 163, 175, 179, 258, 259, 270, 274, 276, 279, 298, 308
Achebe, Chinua, 7
ACS. *See* American Colonization Society
Actor/structure dichotomy. *See* Structural issues
Administration in Developing Countries (Riggs), 85
Africa
  agriculture in. *See* Agriculture
  -Asia comparison, 245, 257
  conditions of governance in, 246–253
  crisis in, 100–102, 246, 252, 298
  cultivated land in, 298
  dependency relationships, 2, 33, 34
  development capital, 66
  diversity in, 47, 50, 274, 283
  economies, 33, 36, 103, 189
  endogenous phenomena in, 246–250
  environmental problems, 100
  food production, 2
  and foreign trade, 34
  gross domestic product (GDP), 100, 101(table), 301(table)
  gross national product (GNP) in, 2, 4, 101, 184
  at independence, 30, 34, 45, 46, 61, 204, 245, 293
  industrial sector, 85, 101, 104, 295, 301–302, 301(table), 302–304
  instability in, 2–3, 276, 309

judiciaries in, 56, 208, 218, 279, 280, 283, 293
land tenure in, 252, 257. *See also* Nigeria, land ownership in
local governments in. *See* Local governments
market system in, 112, 113
military regimes in, 56, 57, 69, 156, 162, 195, 279, 296, 306. *See also* Nigeria, military rule in
mineral wealth, 34. *See also* Minerals/mining
modern sector, 4, 213, 215, 303
nations in, 34. *See also* Ethnicity
non-socialist states, 106
pattern of change in, 164(n4)
pre-colonial, 200–201, 258
public/private sector boundaries, 102
public/private sector transfers, 124
public sector employment, 116
rural development in, 13–14, 53
rural income, 2, 118
self-governing institutions in, 5
services sector, 92, 301, 301(table), 304, 308. *See also* Public services
small producers in, 189, 248
social problems, 100
soft states, 115, 120, 131, 260, 297
sources of problems in, 7, 18, 18(n1)
tyrannies in, 56
values in, 283–284, 285
Agriculture, 2, 13, 38, 45, 53, 103, 184–185
  and development, 299–302
  employment, 299, 301, 301(table)
  exports and development, 104, 300
  in France, 138
  and gross domestic product (GDP), 33, 301(table)
  and industry, 295, 301–302
  research, 120